Happy Lives and the Highest Good

Happy Lives and the Highest Good

AN ESSAY ON ARISTOTLE'S
NICOMACHEAN ETHICS

Gabriel Richardson Lear

PRINCETON UNIVERSITY
PRINCETON AND OXFORD

Copyright © 2004 by Princeton University Press
Published by Princeton University Press, 41 William Street,
Princeton, New Jersey 08540
In the United Kingdom: Princeton University Press,
3 Market Place, Woodstock, Oxfordshire OX20 1SY

All Rights Reserved

Library of Congress Cataloging-in-Publication Data

Richardson Lear, Gabriel, 1971–
Happy lives and the highest good : an essay on Aristotle's Nicomachean ethics / Gabriel Richardson Lear.
p. cm.
Includes bibliographical references and index.
ISBN 0-691-11466-8 (alk. paper)
1. Aristole, Nicomachean ethics. 2. Ethics, Ancient. I. Title.
B430.L43 2004
171'.3—dc21   2003042899

British Library Cataloging-in-Publication Data is available

This book has been composed in Sabon and American Gothic

Printed on acid-free paper. ∞

www.pupress.princeton.edu

Printed in the United States of America

10 9 8 7 6 5 4 3 2 1

FOR MY PARENTS

Dale and Leslie Richardson

Acknowledgments

MANY PEOPLE HAVE HELPED ME think and write about the material in this book, though whether I have made good use of their advice is for them to say. My former colleagues in the Yale philosophy department have been generous both in general support and in commenting on drafts of chapters 4 and 5. In particular, I thank Robert Adams, Tad Brennan, and Michael Della Rocca. Stephen Menn offered helpful guidance at an early stage. David Sedley offered useful comments on a draft of chapter 3. David Charles and two other anonymous readers for Princeton University Press wrote especially thorough reports on my submitted manuscript. I have learned from them and hope I have managed to go some way toward answering the problems they raised for my argument.

This book began as my Ph.D. dissertation at Princeton University. I am grateful for my time spent there. The intense conversations in seminars that spilled out afterward to the Annex made it a happy initiation into the life of philosophical leisure. In particular, I thank the members of the Philosophy Department Dissertation Seminar 1999–2000 and the members of the University Center for Human Values Mellon Graduate Seminar 1999–2000 who read and commented energetically on earlier versions of chapters 2 through 4. I also thank my fellow graduate students working in classical philosophy, in particular Jonathan Beere, Ursula Coope, and Zena Hitz. Alexander Nehamas is a teacher to whom I owe much. And I thank Christian Wildberg for his helpful comments as a reader of my dissertation.

But above all, I thank my former advisers, John Cooper and Sarah Broadie. The countless hours they spent talking me through my ideas and writing meticulous comments on drafts have made this a better piece of work than it would otherwise have been. But more than that, they have been models of scholarship and philosophical insight to which I aspire.

I wish also to thank my husband, Jonathan, who has encouraged me every step of the way; Sophia Lear for being full of poise and warmth in the midst of frenzy; my sisters, Leslie and Dana; and my parents, who encouraged me from the beginning to be a philosopher.

Happy Lives and the Highest Good

CHAPTER ONE

Introduction

ARISTOTLE INVITES US to conceive of the human good as a special kind of end (*telos*). In the very first line of the *Nicomachean Ethics* (*NE*) he says, "Every craft and every inquiry, and likewise every action and every choice, seem to aim at some good; for which reason people have rightly (*kalôs*) concluded that *the* good is that at which all things aim" (1094a1–3, my emphasis).[1] He calls this ultimate goal of the successful life *eudaimonia*, or happiness (1097a28–34). Just as an archer aims at a target, so Aristotle thinks, the happy person aims at the human good in everything he does (1094a22–24). In effect, he proposes that we think of happiness not as the property of being happy—a certain feeling of contentment or satisfaction— but as the goal or end for the sake of which the happy person acts. Aristotle's investigation into happiness is thus decidedly practical. Not only does he want to arrive at a theory of happiness that will actually help us to live well, his investigation is guided by the thought that happiness is the ultimate object of rational desire and action. If we know what a good must be like in order to serve as the end of all of our rational pursuits, then we can use those criteria to evaluate goods, such as pleasure, wealth, honor, moral virtue, and philosophical contemplation, which people have at one time or other taken to be keys to happiness.

Notice that for Aristotle the happy life needs to focus on a *single* kind of good. Throughout the *Nicomachean Ethics* he envisions the happy life as a life of devotion to a single supremely valuable thing (or kind of thing). This is the natural way to read the first book of the *Nicomachean Ethics*. In *NE* I.4–5 Aristotle considers whether lives characterized by the pursuit of pleasure or wealth are happy, and he criticizes the idea that honor or moral virtue is the good at which the political life aims, apparently as a preliminary to supplying his own account. Then in *NE* I.7 he argues that the highest good must be activity in accordance with virtue, "and if there are several, in accordance with the best and most final" (1098a16–18). It is natural (although certainly not necessary) to interpret Aristotle as saying here that happiness, the ultimate goal of the happy life, is a single kind of virtuous activity, that is, it is a monistic good. When we reach the final book of the *Nicomachean Ethics*, the impression that happiness is a single kind of good for the sake of

---

[1] All translations are mine unless noted otherwise. However, my translations of the *NE* have often been influenced by the excellent translations of Ross (in Barnes 1984) and Crisp 2000.

which the happy person makes all his choices is even more pronounced. In *NE* X.7 Aristotle argues that the happiest life is one in which the agent "does everything" for the sake of philosophical contemplation (1177b33–34). And in *NE* X.8 Aristotle allows that a life lived for the sake of morally virtuous activity (another monistic good) is also happy, though in a lesser sense (1178a9–22). Most readers are surprised, of course, when they discover that Aristotle thinks the happiest life is lived for the sake of contemplation. The lengthy discussions of moral virtue and friendship and Aristotle's evident admiration for the morally virtuous person lead most people to assume that, according to Aristotle, the human good is the exercise of practical, and not theoretical, virtue. What is not surprising (or at least ought not to be) is that, according to Aristotle's considered opinion, the happy life aims at a monistic good.

But although there is ample evidence, I believe, that Aristotle thinks of happiness as a monistic end in the *Nicomachean Ethics*, many, if not most, recent interpreters deny that this is what he has in mind. Instead, many scholars believe Aristotle's *eudaimonia* is (or ought to be) a set that includes some or all intrinsically valuable goods.[2] As I understand it, the motivation behind these various *inclusivist* interpretations is not so much that various particular passages require it, as that—despite the evidence that Aristotle *does* conceive of *eudaimonia* as a monistic end—the overall theory of the *Nicomachean Ethics* looks incoherent on a monistic interpretation of *eudaimonia*. Here is why.

There are two problems for a monistic interpretation, both of which spring from Aristotle's central claim that happiness is an ultimate end. First, Aristotle claims that the happy philosophical life includes morally virtuous activity (*NE* X.8 1178b5–6). But morally virtuous actions, in Aristotle's account, are not just *worth* choosing for their own sakes; they must be *chosen* for their own sakes (*NE* II.4 1105a32). What, in a monistic interpretation, prevents the happy philosopher from having divided allegiances—to contemplative *eudaimonia* on the one hand and to morally virtuous action on the other? Or does Aristotle imagine, quite implausibly and with no argument, that morally virtuous activity with all its social concerns always promotes contemplation? Unless Aristotle does think something like this, however, it seems that the happy person does not aim at *eudaimonia* as an end in everything he does, despite what Aristotle has claimed.

The second problem goes even deeper. In conceiving of happiness as the practical goal of the happy life, Aristotle implies that things contribute to

[2] For example, Ackrill [1974] 1980; Crisp 1994; Cooper [1987] 1999; Devereaux 1981; Irwin 1985b, Keyt 1983; Keyt 1989; Roche 1988b; White 1990, Whiting 1986. Broadie (1991) might be considered one of this number, although she thinks that Aristotle equivocates on the meaning of *eudaimonia*, which sometimes refers to a monistic good. Hardie ([1965] 1967) thinks that Aristotle usually conceives of happiness as a monistic end but sometimes has the insight that it is inclusive. Heinaman (1988), Kenny (1992), and Kraut (1989) are notable exceptions in interpreting *eudaimonia* as a monistic good.

the flourishing of a life in virtue of their teleological relationship to happiness. All goods other than the highest are relevant to our well-being and find a place in the happy life *because* they are worth choosing for the sake of *eudaimonia*. But that means that, if *eudaimonia* is a monistic end, such as contemplation, all other goods, including the intrinsically valuable goods and in particular morally virtuous action, are parts of the happy life because they contribute to contemplation. This looks implausible, however. Surely intrinsically valuable goods are parts of the choiceworthy life because they are the good things they are, regardless of what they lead to. In fact, that seems to be what we mean by saying that they are choiceworthy for their own sakes (*NE* I.7 1097b2–4). Unless intrinsically valuable goods are actually parts of the highest good, Aristotle's conception of happiness as a most final end seems utterly wrongheaded.

The inclusivist interpretation is, for these reasons, apparently attractive. But I will argue that it misunderstands Aristotle's technical concept of a *telos*, or end, so it cannot really solve the problems it addresses. (I will make this argument in chapter 2.) Furthermore, nothing in the first book of the *Nicomachean Ethics* suggests that the happy life converges on a set of good things as its ultimate goal. In particular, a close study of Aristotle's claim that happiness is a self-sufficient good will show that this criterion does not require, or even suggest, an inclusivist interpretation of *eudaimonia* as many scholars have thought (chapter 3). So we need to try a new approach.

Problems for the relationship between intrinsically valuable goods and a monistic final end arise when we assume that X is choiceworthy for the sake of Y only when X is either an instrumental means to Y or a constituent of Y. That is to say, we have trouble understanding how, in Aristotle's account, morally virtuous action could be choiceworthy for the sake of contemplation because that would seem to imply (since morally virtuous action is not a constituent of contemplation) that morally virtuous action is always an instrumental means to contemplation. Aristotle's conception of teleological relations was not so narrow, however. According to Aristotle, X may also be choiceworthy for the sake of Y when it approximates or imitates Y (chapter 4). Now, teleological approximations have an interesting feature: If the paradigm is worth choosing for its own sake, then insofar as the approximation succeeds in imitating the paradigm's nature, it too will be worth choosing for itself. Under appropriate conditions teleological approximations are worth choosing *both* for their own sakes *and* for the sake of the paradigm.

I will argue that morally virtuous action is, in Aristotle's account, a teleological approximation of contemplation (chapter 5). The excellent exercise of practical reason accompanied as it must be by the agreement of emotion and desire, grasps truth about the good in action as exactly as possible. In fact, grasping of truth is the practically wise person's aim. (The idea that the target of practical wisdom, and by extension the moral virtues, is truth may strike us as counterintuitive. Consider, however, the common opinion that whereas self-indulgent and otherwise foolish people see what they want to see, wise and good people want to see the truth. This intuition is not conclusive, of course, but it may help make Aristotle's position seem less odd). However, Aristotle believes that the project of grasping truth is more perfectly realized in the exercise of theoretical wisdom. Practical wisdom (*phronêsis*) embodies only to a degree an ideal of rational activity perfectly achieved by theoretical wisdom (*sophia*). In this way, excellent theoretical truthfulness sets the standard for the excellent practical truthfulness of morally virtuous action. So even if making the virtuous choice does not maximize contemplation, it will still be worth choosing for the sake of contemplation because it approximates theoretical truthfulness. It is a sort of contemplation in action. But precisely because morally virtuous action succeeds in approximating the more perfect exercise of theoretical reason, it is also choiceworthy for its own sake. After all, the morally virtuous agent possesses, by approximation, the most valuable human good. Thus moral virtue finds a place in the life devoted to philosophy while still being valued for itself.

Thinking of morally virtuous activity as an approximation of contemplation can seem remote from Aristotle's discussions of particular moral virtues in NE II–V. Aristotle's virtuous agent is caught up in the details of his social circumstances. He fights battles, drinks (moderately) at dinner parties, puts on dramatic festivals, and receives with grace the honors bestowed by his community. There is very little indication that he cares, above all else, for contemplation. Nevertheless, I will argue that when we attend carefully to the ways in which Aristotelian virtue is fine (*kalon*), we see that virtuous actions are chosen by the agent because they are appropriate to him as a lover of reason and truthfulness (chapters 6 and 7). When the courageous person goes shield-to-shield with his compatriots against the enemy in just the way that he does, or when the temperate person eats moderately and with attention to the flavors of his meal, he shows that happiness for him is the most excellent use of reason in leisure. (Since war is not leisure, this means that the paradigmatically courageous person pursues as happiness an excellent exercise of reason that is not itself specifically courageous.) This orientation to the most excellent and leisurely use of reason is what makes these virtuous actions fine. (It is also what it is to grasp the truth in action and, thereby, to approximate theoretical truthfulness). But since the most excellent use of reason possible for human beings is in leisurely contemplation, the morally virtuous person's sense of the fine, as Aristotle describes it, is guided by the value of contemplation, whether the agent understands this or not. I believe that if we read Aristotle's *Nicomachean Ethics* with a broader understanding of the ways in which one thing may be worth choosing for the sake of another, his conclusion in NE X.7 that the most perfect happiness is the monistic good of contemplation will not strike us as so problematic (chapter 8).

Before I begin, I should make clear this is an interpretation of the *Nicomachean Ethics*. Although I suspect that, in the end, the happy life as Aristotle describes it in the *Eudemian Ethics* will look, from the ground, so to speak, very much like the happy life as he describes it in the *Nicomachean Ethics*, Aristotle's philosophical analysis of what makes that happy life happy is, I believe, quite different in the two works. (In particular, in the *Eudemian Ethics*, even though theoretical virtue holds a special place in the good life, Aristotle thinks that happiness includes moral as well as theoretical virtuous activity.) Thus, although I will from time to time make reference to the *Eudemian Ethics*, I will not attempt any systematic treatment of the relationship between those treatises, nor will I assume that what Aristotle says in the *Eudemian Ethics* applies to his argument in the *Nicomachean Ethics*.

I will, however, frequently refer to works by Plato. This may come as a bit of a surprise. It is, of course, widely recognized that Aristotle's theory of moral education is influenced by the *Republic* and that the finality and self-sufficiency criteria for an account of the good derive from the *Philebus*, even though Aristotle does not always acknowledge his debts to Plato by name. But scholars of the theory of happiness in the *Nicomachean Ethics* have not made as much of the Platonic corpus as I believe they might. This may be because Aristotle explicitly rejects (*NE* I.6) Plato's claim that the goodness of human beings and of their lives is to be explained by their participation in the transcendent Form of the Good. He thereby presents himself as offering a new account of what makes some human lives worth living. But although Aristotle rejects Plato's claim that the goodness of *all* good things is to be explained by their being in relation to the same thing (viz., the Good), he does believe that the goodness of all *human* goods is explained by their being appropriately related to the single highest *human* good. It is true that, in Aristotle's account, this source of human good is achievable within human life. Furthermore, he believes that humanly good things can be related to this highest human good in different ways. Clearly these differences from Plato are important. But they do not constitute so radical a departure from a Platonic framework that our understanding of the *Nicomachean Ethics* cannot be greatly enhanced by an appreciation of where Aristotle may be drawing implicitly on his Platonic heritage. (Of particular importance for my project, Aristotle agrees with Plato that (1) finality and self-sufficiency are marks of the good; (2) certain activities are related to each other as paradigm to approximation [I discuss the *Symposium* and *Phaedrus* in this regard in the appendix]; and (3) human beings are motivated by "spirited" desires that are gratified by the fine or beautiful.) The lesson we should draw from Aristotle's rejection of the Form of the Good as the subject of ethics is not that we should read the *Nicomachean Ethics* in isolation from Plato's remarks about happiness and goodness but that we should read Aristotle in light of Plato with care.

Another reference that appears frequently in the chapters that follow is to Richard Kraut's *Aristotle on the Human Good*. I will leave the details of my agreements and disagreements for the footnotes. But since his is the most important recent monistic (and intellectualist) interpretation of Aristotelian *eudaimonia*, it will perhaps be helpful to say where in general I see my interpretation as coinciding with his and where there are fairly significant differences.

Kraut argues that perfect happiness, the single aim of the happiest life, is philosophical contemplation and that every other good has a place in the happy life *qua* happy because it is worth choosing for contemplation's sake. Here I am in complete agreement with Kraut and for many of the same reasons. Now since Kraut and I think Aristotle's ideal contemplative life includes moral virtue, we must both explain the nature of the teleological relationship between morally virtuous action and contemplation. Kraut believes that the causal means-end relation is the only "for the sake of" relation that Aristotle recognizes (1989, 200–203, 211–213). Thus, for Kraut this project amounts to showing how the moral virtues are instrumentally valuable in the pursuit of philosophy (1989, chap. 3). Now, I accept that morally virtuous actions may sometimes causally promote contemplation. However, I do not think that the instrumental relation is the only "for the sake of" relation Aristotle recognizes. Indeed, since I will argue that approximation is a "for the sake of" relation, I do not think a good needs to causally promote another in order to be worth choosing for its sake. (Kraut claims that approximation may be a way of acting for the sake of contemplation, but only when contemplation is not ever possible for the agent in question [1989, 87–88].) Thus, unlike Kraut, I do not argue that moral virtue finds its place in the happy life only to the extent that it maximizes the philosopher's contemplation. According to my interpretation, the philosopher has reason to choose moral virtue even when it does not directly promote theoretical reflection.

Of course, Kraut also thinks the philosopher has reason to act virtuously at the expense of spending more time contemplating. A major claim of his book is that there are some goods—in particular, the well-being of friends and fellow citizens—whose value for the agent is independent of his own happiness (1989, chap. 2). Thus, even when the agent has no reason from the point of view of his happiness to act on the basis of moral virtue, he may well have other, unrelated reasons. We should notice that Kraut's thesis is not only an interesting claim about the kinds of value Aristotle recognizes; it is a solution to what I will call the problem of middle-level ends. That is to say, it is an explanation of how in Aristotle's account some ends may be worth choosing for their own sakes *and* for the sake of happiness.[3] Friends,

---

[3] This is not Kraut's solution, however (1989, chap. 5.14). His interpretation takes the general approach of describing these goods as worth choosing for two different reasons, though. See chapter 2, section 4, below.

honor, pleasure, and moral virtue itself may be worth choosing for two reasons: for their intrinsic value and for their contribution to happiness (1989, 228–230; 300–305). Now, as opposed to Kraut, I do think that Aristotle's ethics is eudaimonistic—that every action is ultimately to be justified by reference to the agent's own happiness.[4] Thus I do not adopt this solution to the problem of middle-level ends. But I am motivated not merely by the sense that Aristotle does not recognize non-eudaimonistic value, but also by the thought that a solution of the sort Kraut proposes will not work in principle. That is to say, I will argue in the next chapter that the intrinsic value of middle-level ends is not independent of the value they have by being for the sake of the agent's happiness. Thus, while I am in sympathy with Kraut's claim that the happiest life is, insofar as it is happy, aimed at contemplation alone, our interpretation of how goods other than contemplation find a place in that life is not the same. And this is because we develop such different accounts of what, according to Aristotle, it means to act for the sake of an end. So let us turn to that question at once.

[4] I prefer to use *eudaimonistic* in the traditional sense in order not to obscure a distinction Aristotle himself is keen to draw between the virtuous person's love of self and selfishness. I take Kraut's point, however, that we ought to distinguish the question whether actions are justified by reference to the happiness of someone or other from the question whether actions are justified by reference to the *agent's* happiness (1989, chap. 2).

CHAPTER TWO

The Finality Criterion

1. INTRODUCTION

I begin by raising a problem about Aristotle's practical teleology. In *NE* I.7 Aristotle lays out some criteria that any account of the human good must meet. Perhaps the most important is that it be the most final or endlike (*teleiotaton*) of all the human goods.[1] The human good, in virtue of being most final, is choiceworthy for its own sake alone and never for the sake of any other good (1097a28–34). *Eudaimonia*, or happiness, meets this criterion, which means that whatever happiness turns out to be—whether it be the activity of moral virtue or contemplation—it will be worth pursuing for its own sake and never for the sake of anything else that might be gained through it (1097a34–b5). Aristotle's ethical theory is meant to be a practical guide in the sense that he believes that the point of examining the nature of happiness is to aid our own pursuit of it (1094a22–24).[2] So in describing *eudaimonia* as the most final end of a flourishing life, Aristotle must suppose that it is possible consciously to live our lives for the sake of whatever good turns out to be the highest. But what would it be to make a good (and in particular, contemplation, the good Aristotle argues is the highest) our most final end?[3] It would mean that *all* the goods and activities we pursue would be worth pursuing for the sake of *eudaimonia*, and that we would choose them for that reason. In particular, we would choose the goods we already value for themselves—like friends, moral virtue, and honor—for the sake of the separate good that is *eudaimonia*. This is the attraction of Aristotle's emphasizing the "endiness" of the highest good: Our devotion to the highest good gives order to our pursuit of goods that we already value for their own sakes.

---

[1] The second major criterion is self-sufficiency. I discuss this criterion in chapter 3.

[2] The human good, happiness, is an end for the statesman as well, but it is not his end alone. Indeed, when at 1094a24 Aristotle conceives of the good as a target (*skopos*), he has not even mentioned the standpoint of the *politikos* yet. It is only after Aristotle claims the good is the target of human life that he declares that the political art aims to produce it for all citizens. Thus, while I agree with Bodéüs (1993) that the *NE* is addressed to future statesmen whose job will be to create happiness for others, I believe Aristotle also intends to address his audience as individuals seeking their own happiness. See Pangle (2003, 8–16) for a good discussion of this issue.

[3] Although the problem I will raise is particularly clear when we interpret *eudaimonia* as a monistic end, it arises in an inclusivist interpretation as well.

But this very attraction of Aristotle's ethical theory ushers in serious complications. It presupposes that there are goods that are choiceworthy both for their own sakes and for the sake of some independent good, namely *eudaimonia*. (I take it to be implausible to think that only the eudaimonic good is choiceworthy for its own sake.) Or, to put it another way, it presupposes that there are goods whose ends are in themselves and also beyond themselves, in *eudaimonia*. I will call these goods *middle-level ends*.

The problem I want to raise in this chapter is that it is not at all clear that, in Aristotle's conception of a *telos* (end) there could be ends of this middle-level sort. The problem will take some time to explain, but let me give a brief outline here. In general, when something happens or exists for the sake of an end, that end sets the standards of success for the process leading to it. It is because that process happened, or that thing came into being for the sake of the end, that the process or thing is the way it is. And we can determine whether the process was successful by discovering the extent to which it achieved its end well. So an end guides the appropriate pursuit of the things leading to it and is their source of value. The problem arises, though, when we consider ends that are choiceworthy both for their own sakes *and* for the sake of *eudaimonia*. How could anything be worth choosing both for itself and for the sake of a higher goal?

Note that the problem is not merely that there are things with both an immediate and an ulterior *telos*. Instruments or tools can be ends like this; immediately, making a tool is for the sake of making the product of the relevant craft. But if the craft product is itself made for the sake of something further, it is right to say that this further goal of the craft is also the ulterior goal of the making of the tool. Notice that in this case of making instruments, the ulterior *telos* is a fulfillment of the immediate *telos*. The immediate goal of a computer hardware designer, a computer chip, is created to meet the demands of the ulterior goal of hardware design, computer processing. The ulterior *telos* is what the immediate *telos* is for. Since this is so, the interest in the ulterior *telos* determines what counts as a successful attempt at making the immediate *telos*. But notice that, according to this model, the way in which the immediate *telos* depends on the ulterior *telos* means that the former is not choiceworthy for its own sake. No one would want a computer chip as such unless he cared about using a computer.

By contrast, middle-level ends are genuinely choiceworthy for their own sakes, even though they are also worth choosing for the sake of *eudaimonia*. Aristotle says we would want them even if they did not lead to anything further (1097b3–4). The problem is to understand how this is possible.

Being choiceworthy for the sake of another end does not always imply that a thing is not also choiceworthy for its own sake. Take, for example, the connection between the disposition to be brave and acts of bravery. The disposition is clearly choiceworthy for the sake of the actions it tends to produce. But Aristotle thinks that it is also choiceworthy in itself (1097b2–

3, re all virtues). It makes sense, after all, to desire a courageous character even if, due to peaceful times, one is not called upon for a prominent display of courage. Bravery and the other virtues of character are goods choiceworthy for their own sakes that find their fulfillment in an end beyond themselves. Upon closer examination, however, it is clear that the relationship between a disposition and its actualization cannot be a model for the connection between the middle-level ends (at least not all of them) and *eudaimonia*. For, in Aristotle's theory, the middle-level ends are meant to be independent of the good that is *eudaimonia*. Although friends, moral virtue, and pleasure are choiceworthy for the sake of *eudaimonia*, they are all conceivable independently of *eudaimonia*, and they can be rationally pursued outside the context of a life lived for the sake of the highest good. Dispositions, on the other hand, are not independent of their actualizations in this way. Courage, although it is different from courageous action, is not conceivable in isolation from its actualization. That is because the disposition to be courageous is what it is—it has the form it has—in reference to actual acts of courage. Indeed, insofar as we find the disposition to be courageous worth choosing for its own sake, it is because we value its character as the sort of thing that tends to lead to courageous actions. It is hard to see how all the middle-level ends could depend on *eudaimonia* for their form. This difficulty arises no matter whether we interpret Aristotle's *eudaimonia* as a monistic end, as I think we should, or as an inclusive end.

In the relationship between a disposition and its actualization, the two goods are not sufficiently independent of each other to be a model for all middle-level ends. In the relationship between an instrument and its ulterior *telos*, the two goods may be sufficiently independent, but the instrument is not choiceworthy for its own sake. What, then, could the relationship between the middle-level ends and *eudaimonia* be? If the very idea is incoherent, as it begins to seem to be, it is hard to see how it can be of any help in planning our lives to focus on the status of *eudaimonia* as an end. We already value a variety of goods as choiceworthy for their own sakes and need to find some way to coordinate their pursuit. What good will it do me to be told that, in some mysterious way, these intrinsically valuable goods are also choiceworthy for the sake of *eudaimonia*?

In the remainder of this chapter I will try to make the nature of this problem clearer and to explain why some apparently promising solutions do not succeed. First, I will examine what it is to be a *telos* in Aristotle's sense, as described in his biological and metaphysical works. Next I will examine his concept of a *telos*, or a "that for the sake of which," as developed in the *Nicomachean Ethics*. My purpose here is twofold: I want to show that Aristotle's conception of a *telos* in the *Nicomachean Ethics* is the same one he uses in his biological works and, at the same time, to show the process of reasoning leading him to the introduction of the finality criterion, that is, to claim that the highest good (happiness) must be choiceworthy for its own sake and not for the sake of anything else. It is in this section that I will offer reasons for interpreting *eudaimonia* as a monistic end. Then, once I have clarified the problem with middle-level ends, I will examine and criticize several possible solutions.

2. WHAT IT IS TO BE AN ARISTOTELIAN *TELOS*

We are trying to understand the nature of goods that are choiceworthy for their own sakes and for the sake of *eudaimonia*. So we need to get straight at a more basic level what it is to act or find something choiceworthy for the sake of an end. There is much to be said about Aristotle's teleology, but for my purposes I want to make clear that the concept of a *telos* at work in the *Nicomachean Ethics* is broader than any merely psychological conception. That is to say, a *telos* is not defined as an object of desire or an appropriate object of desire, where that is understood as one that would allow for the greatest overall amount of desire satisfaction.

In the most concrete and literal sense, a *telos* is a result and connotes that something has been finished.[4] Aristotle appeals to this literal sense of *telos* when he identifies the end of a change (*kinêsis*) with its stopping point: "When there is some *telos* of a change, provided that the change is continuous, this last thing is also that for the sake of which (*to hou heneka*)" (*Phys.* II.2 194a29–30). However, it is not right to think of a *telos*, in the sense of an Aristotelian final cause, as being literally the "last thing" to which a change leads. For, as this passage suggests, if the change were interrupted (i.e., not continuous), according to Aristotle, its literal *telos* or stopping point would not be its *telos* as final cause. The distinction between the two senses of *telos* Aristotle points to in this passage is an intuitive one. We often talk about the interruption of natural processes. In order to do so, we must be able to distinguish ends that are mere stopping points from ends that are natural conclusions or fulfillments. It is the latter sort of *telos* that Aristotle identifies with the final cause, or "that for the sake of which."[5] Since the *Physics* is an inquiry into the causes of natural change, we can infer that a mere stopping point is not in itself a *telos* in the sense that interests Aristotle in the *Physics*.

A *telos* need not be a result separable from a process that naturally leads to it, either. Aristotle applies his framework of teleological explanation to goings-on that are never, in principle, over. These are activities that achieve

---

[4] One verb for dying is *teleô*, literally "come to one's end."
[5] Throughout I will use *telos* and "that for the sake of which" interchangeably. The two terms are not exactly coextensive. All ends in Aristotle are thats for the sake of which, but it would be odd to call certain thats for the sake of which *ends*. For instance, a beneficiary is a that for the sake of which but not a *telos*. (Aristotle himself notices this difference in thats for the sake of which; see chapter 4, below.) I believe, however, that everything I say about thats for the sake of which in this chapter applies to those that are *ends*.

their *telos* at every moment they are engaged in. Aristotle's paradigm is the activity of seeing. At each moment that I see, my capacity to see is fully realized and achieves its natural fulfillment (*Meta.* Θ.6 1048b22–25).[6] (This is an example of an *energeia* [activity] as opposed to a *kinêsis* [process]. Unlike an *energeia*, when a *kinêsis* reaches its *telos* it is over and goes out of existence.)

What, then, is a *telos* or end if it need not be a "last thing" at all? An example from the *Physics* can help:

> And further [there can be a cause] in the sense of the *telos* and this is that for the sake of which. For example, health is the cause of walking. For why does he walk around? We say, "in order that he may be healthy," and saying this we think we have pointed out the cause. (*Phys.* II.3 194b32–35)

Aristotle says that the end of walking is health, but it is clear that health is not a *telos* in virtue of its being the point at which walking comes to an end—or the result upon the achievement of which the walking ceases. Health does not bear such a direct chronological relationship to walking. When Phaedrus's doctor told him to walk in the countryside for the sake of his health he did not mean that Phaedrus should keep walking until he had achieved health. Nor did he intend for Phaedrus to quit walking simply when he became healthy. Rather, he meant that Phaedrus ought to walk for the reason that it would make him or keep him healthy.[7] In other words, health is a *telos* because it is the benefit to be achieved by walking. Furthermore, because health is the benefit aimed at in walking, it will affect the manner in which Phaedrus walks—how quickly, for how long, and over what terrain he walks. This is a feature that walking for the sake of health shares with all natural changes and activities. The nature of the goal determines the features of the process leading to it or the activity expressing it. If a certain manner of walking is especially productive of health, then it is, to that extent, a good way of walking. Thus, in Aristotle's *Physics*, a *telos* is a normative standard for a process or activity. It is the point at which a change achieves its good.[8]

Aristotle makes this point explicit at *Physics* II.2 194a30–33, immediately following the passage with which we began. It is ridiculous, Aristotle says,

---

[6] *Energeiai* (activities) have their ends in themselves and therefore, unlike *kinêseis* (processes) whose ends are outside themselves, they continue going on even though their end is already achieved (Waterlow 1982, 186). See Charles (1986, 132–139) and Reeve (1995, 101–106) for further discussion of the different ways in which activities and processes are related to their ends.

[7] At least this would be right on our own understanding of why one ought to walk. There is evidence in the *Physics*, though, that walking was believed to produce health by loosening the bowels (*Phys.* II.6 197b22–28). In that case, health might be the *telos* of walking *qua* stopping point.

[8] We may wonder how an activity can contain its own normative standard, i.e., its own end. It may help to think of the end that determines an activity as the instantiation of a certain *type* of activity. So, for example, it is because I want to dance a waltz that I move my feet in a certain

for poets to write that a person who dies (*teleutên*) has "achieved that end for whose sake he was born." "For '*telos*' does not mean any last point, but the best." The fact that a change stops at a certain point does not mean that the change is complete. It is only when the good of the process—that is, the result that sets the standard for the success of each stage and of the whole—is achieved that the process is complete.[9] A little later in the *Physics*, when he is enumerating the different kinds of causes, Aristotle says, "and then there is the end and the good of the other things; for the that for the sake of which will be the best and the end of the other things" (*Phys.* II.3 195a23–25). And, to take one last example, Aristotle says in the *Metaphysics* that wisdom is "the science of the end and [i.e.,] the good" (*Meta.* B.2 996b12).

It might be thought that, although Aristotle intends his conception of a *telos* to be normative for all cases of natural process or activity, he is only entitled to that result if he assumes that the ends of these changes are desired or intended.[10] Aristotle's example of walking for the sake of health might seem to provide a case in point. It is only because Phaedrus wants to be healthy that health is the end of his walking and so determines what counts as success in that activity. Thus, even in the *Physics*, where Aristotle tries to explain the natural changes of rocks and plants as well as of animals, a *telos* ought to be an object of desire. Questions then arise about what sense it makes to attribute desired ends to rocks and plants.

This objection misses the point, however. True, we noticed before that the character or manner of an instance of walking depends on what its end is. If the end is health, the walking will be quite different than if its end is transportation. But this does not show that the end of one and the same type of activity, in this case walking, varies with the agent's desire. From an Aristotelian perspective, the fact that walking for the sake of health and walking to the bank have different ends and thus different standards for success just shows that they are two different kinds of activity. This conclusion does no outrage to our intuitions. Walking for exercise (particularly speedwalking) does in fact seem like quite a different affair from walking to the bank. The fact that both activities involve putting one foot in front of the other is a superficial similarity.[11] (Their dissimilarity is reflected in our

---

way, but this process of dancing is itself the waltz. The end is in the activity and sets its standards for success (Reeve 1995, 104–105).

[9] See *Meta.* Δ.16 1021b23–25: "We call complete (*teleion*) ... (3) The things which have attained a good end are called complete (*teleion*); for things are complete in virtue of having attained their end" (Ross translation from Barnes 1984).

[10] See Broadie (1990) and Cooper (1982), who argue against this interpretation. I leave aside for the moment whether there is a useful distinction to be made between good *qua telos* and good *simpliciter*.

[11] Of course, there is a reason speedwalking is called a type of walking: It was derived from normal walking. Its inventors took the ordinary activity of walking and transformed it, almost beyond recognition, into an exercise activity.

language: There is a difference between going for a walk and walking to the bank.) Desire, of course, plays a role in establishing health as a *telos* for a particular person at a particular time.[12] But this is only to say that desire for the *telos* is the means by which the *telos* guides the agent's action; it has no bearing on the fact that health is the correct normative standard for exercise walking, and that all instances of that activity are to be deemed successful to the extent that they achieve this *telos*. (I will return to the connection between desire and ends in human action in section 4.)

This discussion leads us to another feature of Aristotelian ends important for my purposes. In general, Aristotle thinks that a thing's natural end is intimately associated with its essence or form. Indeed, he says that if you want to study a thing's *telos*, you will study its form (*Phys.* II.2 194a27–b15).[13] This is particularly clear in the case of growing things. Aristotle says that the nature or principle of change in something that is born and develops is the form of the mature being toward which it is developing (*Phys.* II.1 193b12–18). So, the nature of a baby is a human being; the nature of an acorn is an oak tree. And this form that is the *telos* of growth is also its (not fully actualized) form now. A growing thing develops in a particular direction because that is what it is. The connection between form and *telos* also holds for things that do not undergo processes of growth. It is part of the nature of fire, for example, that it moves up (*DC* I.2–3). We can tell that upward movement is the end of fire by its natural tendency, when unimpeded, to move in this direction. Because the natural motion of a thing aims to realize its nature or essence, Aristotle virtually equates form and *telos* on several occasions (*Phys.* II.2 194a27–b15, II.7 198a25 ff., 198b1–4, II.8 199a30–32, II.9 200a14–15). I mention the connection between *telos* and form now because it will become quite important for our discussion of the hierarchy of ends in the *Nicomachean Ethics*. A chain of teleological dependence ought, from what we see in Aristotle's physical works, to imply some sort of chain of formal or essential dependence.

According to Aristotle's technical understanding of a *telos* as presented in the *Physics*, an end is a normative standard for the activity undertaken for its sake. The end determines what counts as success in the activity. For this reason, it is closely associated with the nature of that thing whose end it is. As Aristotle says, "What a thing is, and what it is for, are one and the same" (*Phys.* II.7 198a25–26). Furthermore, the end lends its value to the process leading to it; insofar as the end is good, the things leading to it are good.

---

[12] It may be that we need to posit desire in order for a *telos* ever to be a genuine cause of human action on a particular occasion. Desire is not necessary for all human teleological behavior, however. For example, digestion is for the sake of the perpetuation of the human form (*DA* II.4), but we do not achieve this end by desiring it. There is a further question how final causes can be genuine *causes* and not merely explanations. See Furley (1996) for discussion and bibliography.

[13] Charlton 1970, 97 not. ad 194a21-b9. See also his introduction, p. xvii.

These are the features of ends as they figure in Aristotle's biology and metaphysics, and, as the close association between an end and a good suggests, it is this very same technical concept of an end that Aristotle uses in the *Nicomachean Ethics*.

3. Teleology in the *Nicomachean Ethics*

3a. NE I.1: Ultimate Ends and Hierarchies

When we turn to the *Nicomachean Ethics* we see that human ends, like ends in the rest of nature, are goods determining the form and conditions for success of the things leading to them. Furthermore, like ends in the rest of nature, human ends are sources of value for the things leading to them.[14] This close connection between goods and ends is familiar to readers of the *Nicomachean Ethics*, for Aristotle appeals to it in the very first line: "Every craft and every inquiry, and likewise every action and every choice, seem to aim at some good, for which reason people have rightly concluded that *the good is that at which all things aim*" (*NE* I.1 1094a1–3, my emphasis). Carpentry aims at houses, and houses are what make carpentry a good skill to employ. My decision to run three miles a day aims at making me healthy, and health is also the benefit that comes from running. This is what Aristotle has in mind by saying that an action's end is also its good. An end is the source of value for the process leading to it.[15] From this it follows that since there is such a thing as *the* good, it too will be an end of a special variety. It will be the end at which all actions and crafts and so forth aim.[16] From this point of view, such a good would most of all be an end.

---

[14] I take this way of phrasing Aristotle's point from Korsgaard 1996b. Richardson denies that ends, at least in the *NE* (he acknowledges that the Prime Mover may be a special case), are sources of value. Instead, he argues, they play an action-guiding role. What I have argued is that Aristotelian ends are sources of value *because* they play a regulative role. Richardson himself admits that his separation of these two ways of conceiving an end depends on thinking of ends of action as essentially objects of desire (1992, 329 n. 4). This is the view of Aristotelian human ends against which I will argue in the remainder of this chapter.

[15] "And [happiness] seems to be this way [i.e., one of the honorable and final (*teleiôn*) things] also because it is a first principle (*archê*); for it's for the sake of this that we all do everything else, and we suppose that the principle and cause (*aition*) of goods is something honorable and divine" (*NE* I.12 1102a2–4). Here *eudaimonia* is both the goal of all other activity and the source of the goodness of all human goods.

[16] Aristotle is not innovating here; Plato and Eudoxus also thought of the good as an end. The *emphasis* on the fact that the human good, or happiness, is an end is peculiarly Aristotelian, however, and was enormously influential. Think, for instance, how natural it is for Cicero in *De Finibus* to expound the different Greek moral philosophies in terms of a dispute about the nature of the human end.

Note also that I do not think that the first line of the *NE* offers an argument for the existence of the highest good. This is something Aristotle takes for granted. What he argues here is that we should conceive of the good as a special kind of end.

Immediately afterward Aristotle draws our attention to a distinction among ends with which we are familiar from our examination of Aristotle's scientific works. Some ends, he says, are in the activities—goings-on that attain their end at every moment—while other ends are results (*erga*) beyond the actions that produce them (1094a4–6). In the latter case, the ends are better than the activity. This will become an important claim, and it is one with which we might disagree. For instance, we tend to recommend productive activity for its therapeutic value. From this perspective, it doesn't matter if your clay pots are a bit wobbly or your mosaic made of broken dishes is rather hideous. The value of undertaking handicrafts is in doing something—anything—with your hands. Similarly, we think it is an open question whether the excellent exercise of carpentry is less valuable than the house it produces. After all, such activities can constitute a valuable life. There is no doubt that for Aristotle, however, crafts' production of useful results—results that are for the sake of something else—detracts from their intrinsic value. For the moment, let us notice only that according to Aristotle, in every case the good is in the end, whether that end is the activity or something beyond the activity. So to this extent, at least, Aristotle's talk of ends in the *Nicomachean Ethics* is consistent with his treatment in the scientific works.

Now what particularly impresses Aristotle about the ends of human activity is that they tend to fall into hierarchies. Bridles are the end and good of bridle making, but saying that tells only an incomplete story about why bridle making is good. For bridles—along with stirrups and saddles—are in turn good for the sake of cavalry riding. And the end of cavalry riding, even though it is one of those ends immanent in the action, is itself for the sake of the general's craft, whose end is victory.[17] Just as an ulterior *telos* is better than the

---

[17] As Kraut has pointed out, Ackrill is wrong to argue that those ends found in the activity that "produces" them cannot be for the sake of something else (Kraut 1989, 213–217; Ackrill [1974] 1980, 18–19). For such activities can have results that can be used by superior crafts. Or as I would put it, such activities in action can be used by a superior craft (see note 20, below). (Aquinas [I.i.18] suggests gymnastics as an activity subordinated to another end, viz., health.) I think, however, that Kraut is wrong to agree with Ackrill that these activities are always choiceworthy for their own sakes, if by that he means that they are ceteris paribus worth pursuing regardless of any relation they may have to a higher end. It is true that in *Meta.* Θ.6, the locus classicus for the distinction between activity and process, all of Aristotle's examples of activities are choiceworthy for themselves. But the activities described by Aristotle in *NE* I.1 suggest a different picture. Though the end that governs the performance of the activities mentioned in *NE* I.1 is the activity itself, these activities (at least in I.1, where ends choiceworthy for their *own* sakes are not mentioned or explicitly envisaged) are only means for the production of some further end. That is to say, they cannot be properly understood or sensibly aimed for outside the context of the higher crafts whose ends they serve. Ends choiceworthy for their own sakes, on the other hand, are precisely those ends that need not be for the sake of something further. For, as Aristotle says in I.7, they would be choiceworthy even if they led to nothing else. Perhaps there is additional support for my claim that activities are not all choiceworthy for themselves in *Phys.* II.3 (and *Meta.* Δ.2): "The same is true of all the means that intervene before the end, when something else has put the process in motion (as e.g. thinning or purging

activity that produces it, so too Aristotle notices that whenever ends fall into hierarchies, the higher ends are better (more choiceworthy) than the subordinate ones. In particular, the highest end is the most choiceworthy of the ends in the hierarchy, for it is for the sake of the highest end—the end of the architectonic craft—that the lower ends are pursued in the first place. The value of the highest end makes the subordinate ends worth pursuing (1094a9–16).

What is it for an end to be for the sake of another end? Unless Aristotle has relaxed his definition of a *telos*, he must mean at the least that the higher ends provide the criteria of success for the subordinate ones.[18] This is confirmed by *Physics* II.2 194a36–94b7. Aristotle distinguishes between the craft of making a tool and the craft of using a tool. The craft that uses a tool determines the tool's form for the craft that makes it.[19] The job of the craft that makes the tool is to know about the materials required—what material can best realize that form. In other words, the *telos* of the higher craft, what the craft knows how to make and do, determines the form of the *telos* of the subordinate craft (i.e., the tool it produces). The purpose of riding, for example, determines the form of the end of bridle making; because riding aims at a certain kind of activity, bridles must be constructed in a certain, appropriate way. This means that, in general, the higher end is not just any chance (or even regular) result of a subordinate end, or of our using a subordinate end; it must be that for which the subordinate end was, so to speak, naturally directed all along and by reference to which it was, all along, to be evaluated.[20] Of course, this does not mean necessarily that the lower end

---

or drugs or instruments intervene before health is reached); for all these are for the sake of the end, though they differ from one another in that some are things the doctor does (*erga*) while others are instruments (*organa*)" (194b35–195a3). If some of the things a doctor does are activities, then Aristotle describes activities here as for the sake of an ulterior end. Since a doctor's activities are unpleasant, they would hardly be choiceworthy for their own sakes.

It is a trick of language that all activities, because they have their ends in themselves, seem to be choiceworthy for their own sakes in the strict sense. Activities have their ends in themselves in the sense that the correct engagement in that activity is guided by the end of producing that activity itself. In the same way, a craft product guides its proper production. Therefore, in the first instance at least, just as the craft product makes its production valuable, the activity *qua* end makes the engagement in that activity worthwhile. But notice that this does not commit us to the thought that the activity is necessarily valuable regardless of what it leads to. That would be as unfounded as saying that the craft product, because it functions as an end for the craftsman, must be intrinsically valuable.

[18] Kraut (1989, 200–201) also partially analyzes the "for the sake of" relation as having "a normative component: when A is pursued for the sake of B, then B provides a norm that guides A." In addition Kraut believes that a causal connection between A and B is essential if A is to be chosen for the sake of B. Although, of course, I believe that there is a causal connection when the "for the sake of" relation is instrumental, not all "for the sake of" relations are (efficiently) causal in Aristotle's teleology. (See chapter 4, below.) Kraut (1989, 13) believes that all "for the sake of" relations in Aristotle are instrumental.

[19] Aristotle is following Plato's *Cratylus* 388a–390d.

[20] Thus we cannot explain the fact that activities (whose ends are in themselves) are subordinated to other ends as Kraut (1989, 213–217) does in his response to Ackrill (see note 17,

(the tool) was made with the conscious intention of achieving the higher end (though in the human case this is often true). All that's necessary is that the lower end's standards for success are determined by the contribution it makes to the higher end. To take one of Aristotle's examples (*Phys.* II.2 194b5–7), a rudder that does not allow the pilot to steer accurately (perhaps because it is warped) is a bad rudder. Thus the process of making a warped rudder is an example of bad rudder making.[21]

Now higher ends do not set limits for subordinate ones (such as tools) only by determining their form or nature. Higher ends also determine the extent to which subordinate ends are worth pursuing. So, for example, if I want to make a dinner, that end not only determines *that* I should have a dessert; it also determines *how much* dessert to have. Thus, we might say that in chains of ends, higher ends limit lower ones in terms of (1) the form of the lower end and (2) the appropriate extent of pursuit. (Again, this is not limited to the human case. Leaves are for the sake of photosynthesis, which is for the sake of the existence of the tree. This higher end determines not only that the tree should have leaves of a certain sort but how much of it ought to consist of leaves [since all leaves and no roots make a hungry tree].)

It seems clear that Aristotle intends the higher ends he discusses in *NE* I.1 to limit their subordinates in both these ways. The general's craft determines not only that there should be a cavalry (and hence bridles) and what counts as a good cavalry (and so a good bridle); it also determines how many riders, and hence how many bridles, there need to be. And though Aristotle must be aware that bridle making can have more than one result, he identifies as the highest end that result of bridle making that plays both normative functions.

A lower end in a hierarchy is a genuine end, then, because it provides the normative standard or criteria for success for the process that leads to it. But its value, in turn, is given to it by the higher end toward which it aims. In the first chapter of the *Nicomachean Ethics* Aristotle suggests that the human good is the end of all choiceworthy human activity in just this way. Because the human good is our ultimate object of pursuit, all the things we

---

above). Kraut says that, although activities are choiceworthy for their own sakes, they have results that can be used by other crafts, so they are also choiceworthy for the sake of those ulterior craft products. But now we see that an activity, Φ, cannot be subordinated to Y simply in virtue of Y's being a result of Φ.

[21] The craft example might cause us to worry that subordinate ends are not really bad or good in themselves depending on their usefulness; it might be that they are only bad or good relative to a purpose. After all, I can use a stone as a hammer, and it might be good or bad *for that purpose*. But that is hardly relevant to whether or not it is good *as a rock*. It is to avoid this worry that we should remember the role crafts play in giving a new form to matter. The usefulness of found objects is not the product of craft since their forms are not changed simply by our using them. Craft can fashion a stone (and wood) so that it has a new form. When it has a new form—of a hammer or of a stone wall, for example—it also has a new *telos*, dictated ultimately by our well-being.

make and do are as they are. And to the extent that these lower pursuits succeed in achieving the human good, they are good themselves.

3b. NE I.2: Two Kinds of End

Actually, Aristotle has not quite said everything in *NE* I.1 about what the good *qua* ultimate end must be like. For there may be some good upon which all our chains of ends converge but which is itself for the sake of something further. A good like this would certainly be the source of value for our subordinate ends, but it would play this role in the way that cavalry riding is a source of value for bridle and saddle making: It would be incomplete. That is to say, the choiceworthiness of such a convergent end could not be fully explained without reference to the further end for whose sake it was worth choosing. In *NE* I.2 Aristotle argues that given that ends derive their value from that for whose sake they are worth choosing, hierarchies of ends cannot go on ad infinitum. Or, as Aristotle puts it, "we do not choose everything for the sake of something else" (1094a19–20). Thus, there is a difference between ends choiceworthy for the sake of something further and terminal ends at the apex of the hierarchy. The highest good will be an end of the terminal sort.[22]

We should pause a moment to examine why Aristotle thinks there must be terminal ends. The reason he gives in the *Nicomachean Ethics* is that without a final resting point, "our desire (*orexis*) would be empty and vain" (1094a20–21). Aristotle uses the same sort of argument in *Metaphysics* α.2. There he says that an infinite series of ends would undermine final causation altogether, and that this is equivalent to saying that an infinite hierarchy would destroy the very notion of the good. For "no one would try to do anything if he were not going to come to a limit (*peras*)" (*Meta.* α.2 994b13–14). I take it what Aristotle means is that purposeful endeavor aims at success that is unconditional. But when a chain of ends continues indefinitely, each success is always conditional on the success of the next end down the line. Under these circumstances, all the work seems to lead one nowhere. We need an end that is sufficient of itself to give purpose to the subordinate ends, whose value is not itself dependent on a higher end.[23] In a similar vein Aristotle continues that without an ultimate end, "there would be no reason

---

[22] Notice, I think Aristotle is assuming that there is a good, and that it is a convergent end. See section 3c for further discussion.

[23] See Frankfurt (1992), who uses this premise from Aristotle in an interesting argument that final ends have instrumental value. For the record, Aristotle might agree that treating certain (correct) ends as final produces valuable results and so is instrumentally valuable in that sense. What he could not agree with is the implied further claim that the final ends themselves are, in a technical sense, choiceworthy for the sake of their instrumental value. That is to say, these goods do not take their form and standards of success from the nature of the good they do us when treated as final.

in the world; the reasonable man, at least, always acts for the sake of something; and this is a limit, for the end is a limit" (994b14–16).[24] The very possibility of practical reason depends on there being limiting ends, conceivable outside the context of a further purpose to be achieved by them, which can serve to justify the lower aims.

I must confess that as a point about practical reason as related to desire, I do not think Aristotle's arguments succeed. All we need for desire is an end that is desirable for its own sake, an end we need not desire for some further purpose in order to lend value to the means for and ends subordinate to it. As far as desire is concerned, I see no reason why it matters whether this end is in turn desirable for the sake of further ends. What is important is that it be genuinely desirable for its own sake. If it is, my desire and action will not be in vain.[25] In other words, what would be objectionable about an infinite chain of middle-level ends? Aristotle does have a point, however, when we think of ends outside the context of the psychology of human desire. If lower goods (even goods in themselves) derive their value from higher goods, then there must be some unconditional good that is an ultimate source of value. Otherwise it would be indeterminate whether the subordinate goods really are good.[26] If X is a means to Y, then we can only know if X is good of its kind by seeing how well it contributes to Y. And if Y, in turn, is by nature a means, then its value will be indeterminate until we see how well it contributes to *its* further end. Until we do this, we will not know whether Y is good of its kind. And so long as that is in question, we will be unable to judge the value of X. (This is one of the many places where I think Aristotle's tendency to discuss ends in terms of desire can be misleading.)

Nicomachean Ethics I.2 shows us, then, that there are two kinds of ends: those choiceworthy for the sake of something further and those choiceworthy for their own sakes alone. The good must be of the latter sort. If it exists, it will be the final resting point for all chains of ends; the end that everything aims at but does not look beyond itself for a source of value.

---

[24] Translation of these lines modified from Ross (in Barnes 1984).

[25] Thus, while I agree with Broadie (1991, 13) that "[m]y desire must settle at some point because until it does I do not actually desire anything for the sake of which I then desire the things through which I can accomplish it," this does not settle the question of why there needs to be some absolutely ultimate end.

[26] This suggests another solution, proposed to me by John Cooper. The sort of *orexis* (desire) that Aristotle has in mind in *NE* I.2, where he says that it cannot go on forever without being empty, is *boulêsis*, or rational desire (1094a19). (Note the connection between reason and the existence of terminal ends in *Meta.* α.2, cited above.) Whereas other kinds of desire might be readily satisfied by achieving any good choiceworthy for its own sake, rational desire might not be satisfied by goods of that kind if they are also choiceworthy for the sake of something further. For so long as a good derives its value from some other, higher, good, it will be rational not to be satisfied until we can, in some way or other, possess that higher good. Our wanting the lower final end will give us reason to aspire to the higher end, which is its source of value. This seems to me a promising suggestion.

3c. NE I.4: Happiness as a Convergent End

I have been talking about the human good as if it were obvious that Aristotle intends it to be the goal of *all* chains of ends. This is an assumption that appears to be supported by the very first line of the *Nicomachean Ethics*: "[I]t has been rightly concluded that the good is that at which *all* things aim" (1094a2–3, my emphasis). Admittedly, however, Aristotle is here reporting a respected opinion, which he may modify before endorsing. Furthermore, the argument of *NE* I.2 requires only that for each chain of ends there be an ultimate end. Nothing Aristotle has said in the first two chapters *requires* that all chains of ends terminate at the same point.[27] Of course, Aristotle does compare knowledge of the good to having a target at which to aim; but the metaphor does not *force* us to think of the good as a bull's-eye toward which *all* our actions shoot.

I do believe that Aristotle thinks of the good as a convergent end from the beginning of the *Nicomachean Ethics*, and certainly before he formulates the finality criterion in *NE* I.7. For instance, he claims it is the business of the political craft to study the nature of and the means for producing the human good because it is the most architectonic craft. All of the most honored crafts—strategy, rhetoric, household management—are subordinate to it, meaning that their products are choiceworthy for the sake of the good that politics produces (1094b2–3). Furthermore, according to Aristotle, it is the job of political craft to determine the shape of childhood education (1094a28–b2) and indeed of our entire lives, telling citizens what to do and not do (1094b5–6). We may wonder whether it is literally true that the end of the political craft encompasses *all* other ends (1094b6), but Aristotle certainly intends to say in chapter 2 that it orders the ends of all other crafts. This is sufficient to establish the political *telos* as the human good (1094b6–7). As described at the beginning of the *Nicomachean Ethics*, then, the good, as the end of *politikê* (political craft), is the unique goal of at least a significant portion of human striving. As far as I can see, this is an opinion Aristotle never withdraws. For example, later in book I he says that "we all do everything else for the sake of happiness" (1102a2–3), and in the last book, when he argues that contemplation is the human good, he urges us to do *everything* for it (*NE* X.7 1177b33–34).

According to *NE* I.2, then, there is an architectonic craft, and when someone acts as the architectonic craftsman, he arranges all human rational activity toward the production of a single end. Aristotle's point is deeper than this, however. In *NE* I.4 he suggests that people typically organize their own

---

[27] Richardson 1992, 344–349. Richardson is particularly concerned to show that convergence is not assumed before the *NE* I.7 discussion of degrees of finality. In other words, "convergence is [not] built into Aristotle's *notion* of the highest good." He admits that *eudaimonia*, as a matter of contingent fact, may be a convergent end (349 n. 51).

lives with respect to a single goal. Everyone can agree to call this goal happiness, though naturally people cannot agree among themselves about what happiness is (1095a14–22). This may seem implausible. But Aristotle does not mean that each person pursues a unique goal throughout his entire life. He says that a single person may change his mind about the nature of happiness depending on his circumstances. When he is poor, he will think that happiness is wealth; when he is sick, he will think it is health (1095a23–25). How can we tell that a sick person thinks happiness is good health? Presumably it is because sick people make regaining health the focus of their lives. They think and talk about it; they endure painful treatments for it; they decide how much and what to eat with an eye to it. In other words, we can determine a person's conception of happiness by discovering the single end where all, or at least the most important, of his activities converge. So Aristotle is not making the obviously implausible claim that everyone's life aims at the same goal throughout. Rather, he is making the more likely (though still controversial) suggestion that at each point, everyone's life aims at some one good thing or other. At least it does *if* the person has a substantive conception of happiness. (If he has no idea what happiness is, his choices may lead him in a number of different directions and nowhere in particular.) In *NE* I.4, then, happiness is being treated as the name for whatever end is the terminus of *all* a person's choices (or all the important ones). And it's for *that* reason, Aristotle suggests, that everyone can agree that it is the good. The good just is the convergent end of a life worth living.

Aristotle never explicitly justifies this assumption, but it should not surprise us if we consider it against the background of Aristotelian natural teleology. *All* living things have a single *telos*, according to Aristotle. This is the thought at work in the famous function argument (*NE* I.7), where Aristotle draws implications from his claim that the ultimate end of a living thing (or its parts) is its *ergon*, or characteristic work. The *ergon* of a flautist, for example, is flute playing (1097b25), while the *ergon* of an eye is seeing (1097b30). Everything that a flautist (*qua* flautist) or an eye does is for the sake of realizing this end. Now when something has an *ergon*, there is another way of describing it. We can say that a flautist is a person who plays the flute, and that an eye is the part of the body which sees. In other words, naming a thing's characteristic work is a way of naming its essence. This is a point we saw earlier in the discussion of ends in Aristotle's biology. A thing's *telos* determines its essence and form. If this is so, then we can see why Aristotle might have assumed that there is only one ultimate end toward which a flourishing human life aims. For if a thing has only one essence, it is not possible for it to have more than one *ergon* and ultimate end.[28] (What we may think of Aristotle's claim that human beings as such

---

[28] Aquinas (I.ix.106) makes a similar point. (I thank Chris Shields for bringing this passage to my attention.) See pp. 43–45 for further discussion of the function argument.

are the kind of thing to have an *ergon* is another question. But it is not outlandish to think that the unity of a person's identity hinges on his valuing a certain activity as ultimately good and essential to his self, and that happiness is the expression of one's identity by successfully acting for the sake of that good.)

I want to leave open for the moment whether or not Aristotle's teleology requires that the human function be a monistic end. For all I have said so far, the human function might be an appropriately organized set of activities through which human nature is expressed.[29] My point for now is that whatever the human good is like, Aristotle's teleology gives him reason to think it must be a convergent end. Any activity not leading to that end would be, in an important sense, outside the life of the human being. Thus, despite Aristotle's failure to argue that the good is a convergent end, there is every reason to expect that this is what he believes.[30]

3d. NE I.5: Using the Concept of an End to Specify Happiness

We have seen that Aristotle's approach to ethics emphasizes the endiness, or finality, of the human good, or happiness. Given what Aristotle thinks an end is, this approach is promising. An end provides the standards for success for the processes and goods subordinate to it. If happiness is the end of a flourishing human life, then understanding its form should provide insight into what subordinate goods we ought to pursue and how we ought to pursue them. There is reason to think there is such an ultimate end, according to Aristotle, both because all chains of ends must terminate somewhere and because the unity of our essence depends on there being a characteristic activity through which it is expressed. The only task left for Aristotle seems to be figuring out which good activity plays this role.

In *NE* I.5 Aristotle considers three conceptions of happiness closely tied to three prominent visions of the good life: pleasure (the end of the voluptuary's life), honor or virtue (possible ends of the statesman's life), and contemplation (the end of the theoretical life).[31] Pleasure is dismissed more by slander than by argument: Aristotle says that the life of pleasure is slavish and

---

[29] However, I do think that what I have said shows how unlikely it is that Aristotle would think of the human good or function as an inclusive end. What would it be to have a set of activities as one's function? Since the realization of one's function expresses a single form or self, the members of an inclusive end would have to be connected closely enough for a unified conception of the self to be expressed through them. This would be possible if, for instance, the activities making up the set were species of the same genus. (Notice that the function argument is sometimes read as saying that the human function is all the various activities of reason.) But in that case the pursuit of the various species would be choiceworthy for the sake of the genus; there would in fact be a single good, not several, for the sake of which everything is to be done.

[30] See note 42, below, on convergence in *NE* I.7.

[31] See Joly (1956) for a fascinating account of how the lives were a trope in philosophical and poetic discussion of happiness.

fit for cattle (1095b19–20). And he defers discussion of the end of the theoretical life (1096a4–5). But in his discussion of the political life, Aristotle uses the concept he has been developing of the human good as an end to argue that neither honor nor virtue can be the human good. Neither of these goods has the degree of finality that *the* good must have.

Refined men of action (some of whom would have been in Aristotle's audience), those who believe the political life is best, are inclined to equate honor with happiness, so perhaps it is the *telos* of the happy life (1095b22–23). However, "they seem to pursue honor for the sake of believing themselves to be good" (1095b26–28). Since even honor-lovers choose honor for the sake of something else, it cannot be an adequate account of happiness. For happiness, the human good, must be an ultimate end, choiceworthy only for its own sake. Thus, the admirers of the political life show by their actions that they, at least, consider virtue to be better than honor (1095b29–30).[32] But not even virtue is sufficiently final to be the ultimate end of the political life. Aristotle says that virtue seems *atelestera*, not fully completed or finished (1095b32). Presumably this is because the value of virtue points to the value of virtuous activity. The refined men of action do not want to be good simply in the sense of having a capacity, as if one could be happy even if one slept through life; they want to be good in action. The statesman pursues honor for the sake of virtue, but there is reason to think he also pursues virtue for the sake of performing virtuous deeds.[33] Thus, another potential candidate for happiness is shown not to be final enough to be the ultimate end of a life worth living.

We see Aristotle employ the same strategy in his criticism of the money-making life. Aristotle says it would make more sense to suppose that any of the ends he has already discussed—pleasure, honor, virtue—is the human good than it would to propose wealth. At least those former goods are loved for their own sakes (1096a7–9). Wealth, on the other hand, is for the sake of something else (1096a6–7). As such, it does not meet the requirement that

---

[32] If the refined men of action choose honor for the sake of *thinking* themselves to be good, why does Aristotle say they think *being* good is better than honor? The fact that they seek approval from those who are practically wise and who know them (1095b28–29) shows that they care about the truth of the matter and not simply about having high self-esteem. We need not argue that justified self-esteem is instrumental to being virtuous in order to claim that virtue is functioning as a *telos* here. The goal of actually being virtuous is functioning as a normative standard when it determines the conditions under which the refined person thinks it appropriate to approve of himself.

[33] Aristotle does not go so far as to say that virtuous activity is the end of the political life until he returns to the topic of the prominent happy lives in *NE* X.6–8. It is interesting to speculate about why Aristotle is so coy in *NE* I.5 about the true end of the political life. Aristotle is rehearsing the common opinions in this chapter, so perhaps he thinks of the emphasis on the *activity* of virtue as his own innovation. See Kraut (1989, 17–18) for a discussion of Aristotle's inconclusive attempts to locate the proper end of the political life in *NE* I.5.

the human good be an ultimate end, not worth choosing for anything beyond itself.[34]

By the end of *NE* I.5 Aristotle has shown that his approach to the human good as an end bears fruit. By keeping in mind that the good is an ultimate end, we can reject many very common accounts of happiness on the grounds that the goods prized in them are worth choosing for the sake of some further end. But the discussion has also revealed an incompleteness in Aristotle's account. Notice that the problem with pleasure, honor, and virtue is not that they are not genuinely final ends. He says (and seems throughout the *Nicomachean Ethics* to agree) they are all loved for themselves. The problem is that they are not final *enough*. Choiceworthy as they are in themselves, they are *also* worth choosing for the sake of a further end. In other words, *NE* I.5 points the way to Aristotle's articulation of middle-level ends in *NE* I.7. (In fact, pleasure, honor, and virtue are his very examples of what I call middle-level ends [1097b2–5].)

3e. Inclusivism and the Approach to the Finality Criterion

Aristotle's discussion of the finality criterion is the most sophisticated treatment in the *Nicomachean Ethics* of the concept of an end and its connection to the good. It also depends on a significant innovation in Aristotle's understanding of how ends fall into hierarchies. Whereas previously (*NE* I.2) Aristotle divided ends into those choiceworthy for the sake of something further and those choiceworthy for themselves, he now explicitly distinguishes a third, middle group: ends choiceworthy both for their own sakes and for the sake of something further. These are the perplexing middle-level ends. We have seen why Aristotle should mark out this third category of ends. These are the goods that due to their relatively high degree of finality, are likely to be mistaken for *the* good. The finality criterion is intended to help us make the distinction. But as I suggested earlier, it is not clear how these goods that have their ends both in and beyond themselves can fit into Aristotle's theoretical framework. How can a good both determine its own standards for success and have them determined from the outside by a higher good?

In recent decades many scholars have thought that the relationship between middle-level ends and the highest, most final good—at least in *NE* I.7—ought to be interpreted as the relationship between part and whole.[35] At the end of this chapter I argue that this is an ingenious, though ultimately flawed, solution to the problem. Mistaken as I believe them to be, however, inclusivist interpretations of *eudaimonia* (which say that happiness *includes* middle-level ends as parts) have become so commonplace among contempo-

---

[34] Notice that Aristotle is here dismissing an account of happiness suggested at *NE* I.4 1095a22–23.

[35] See, e.g., Ackrill 1974; Irwin 1991.

rary readers of the *Nicomachean Ethics* that even those of us who do not accept them tend to give them more credence as interpretive possibilities than I think the text warrants. Thus, before I discuss the finality criterion itself, I want to argue that if Aristotle does intend the finality criterion to specify happiness as an inclusive end, this ought to *surprise* Aristotle's readers, given everything he has already said.

Consider the passage immediately preceding the discussion of the finality criterion:

> But let us return again to the good we are seeking and see what it might be. For it seems to be different in different actions and crafts since it is one thing in medicine, another in military science, and so on for the rest. What then is the good in each case? Surely it is that for the sake of which the rest [of the actions comprising the craft] are done? This in medicine is health, in military science, victory, in housebuilding, a house, and in other cases something else. And in every action and choice the end is the good, since it is for the sake of the end that everyone does everything else. So if there is some end of all the things done, this would be the practicable good,[36] and if there are several ends, these would be. Coming around from a different angle, the argument has arrived at the same point. And yet we must try to clarify this further. (I.7 1097a15–25)

Aristotle's discussion here flows directly from considerations he raised in *NE* I.1–2.[37] Indeed, the passage seems to be a summary of the argument of these first two chapters. Although he says nothing explicit about whether the good is a monistic or an inclusive end in I.1–2, the ends of the crafts upon which Aristotle's conception of the good is modeled are all monistic goods—health, ships, victory, wealth, cavalry riding, bridles. Furthermore, nowhere between *NE* I.2 and the passage quoted above does Aristotle suggest that the good might be an inclusive end. On the contrary, while we learn in *NE* I.4–5 that everyone disagrees about what happiness is, all the prominent accounts of the good specify monistic ends—health, wealth, pleasure, honor, virtue. Inclusive ends simply are not on the table in the chapters preceding the finality criterion.[38] In other words, the implication of the entire discussion prior to the introduction of the finality criterion is that *eudaimonia* is a monistic end.

---

[36] The practicable good versus the good *simpliciter*: The contrast Aristotle has in mind is with the good of the whole ordered world (e.g., Plato's Form of the Good, criticized in *NE* I.6), which presumably no human being can rationally pursue.

[37] The list of crafts and their ends in the *NE* I.7 passage is virtually identical to the one in *NE* I.1, except that whereas I.1 says that wealth is the end of household management (*oikonomikē*: 1094a9), I.7 says that houses are the end of housebuilding (*oikodomikē*: 1097a20).

[38] Kraut (1989, 225–227) also argues that *NE* I.5 fails to support an inclusivist interpretation of *eudaimonia*. However, he thinks that this passage, and in particular 1097a22–24, shows that Aristotle still keeps the inclusivist possibility open.

Of course, Aristotle may think that an inclusive good would avoid problems faced by the monistic goods proposed in NE I.4–5. Since he himself argues in the *Eudemian Ethics* that the highest good includes all the moral and intellectual virtues, the possibility of an inclusive end was at least available to him.[39] And in fact, many scholars think he refers to this possibility in the penultimate line of the passage from NE I.7 quoted above: "If there is some end of all the things done, this would be the practicable good, and if there are several ends, these would be" (1097a22–24). The implication seems to be that several ends might together compose *the* practicable good.

We should hesitate to accept this reading, however. First, Aristotle makes it clear that he is still summarizing the results of his previous investigation during the sentence in question. Immediately afterward, he says, "Coming from a different angle, we have arrived at the same point." But as we have seen, there is no hint of an inclusivist conception of happiness in the previous discussion. We should, if possible, avoid interpreting Aristotle as including a novel idea in what is intended to be a summary of well-established facts. Second, the Greek leaves us free to read the sentence as saying that if there are several ends of everything we do, these would be the practicable *goods*. In fact, the only other time Aristotle has used the term "practicable good" it was in the plural (NE I.4 1095a16–17).[40] It is not obvious there which goods are the practicable goods, but it is likely they are final ends that have a serious claim to being happiness. Thus, more likely than an inclusivist interpretation of 1097a22–24 is one that reads it as saying that if only one good is an end—that is, is worth choosing for itself—then it will be the practicable good, but if several goods are ends, these will be the practicable goods. The discussion from NE I.4–5 has shown that the first option is not a realistic possibility, however. We already know there are, in fact, many goods worth choosing for themselves.

My interpretation is supported from another direction. Remember I said that the only previous use of the phrase "practicable good" comes in NE I.4. It occurs at the very beginning of NE I.4 in a passage where Aristotle says he is taking up the argument he left off in NE I.2. But as we have seen,

---

[39] *EE* II.1 passim, and in particular 1220a3–4. We should notice that in this chapter Aristotle compares the parts of the human good to the parts of physical health. This suggests that the parts of human goodness form an organic whole. If so, we can ask what is the principle of their unity. The last chapter of the *EE* suggests that this principle is the contemplation of god. Thus, even if Aristotle's conception of the good in the *EE* is inclusive of several goods, I doubt it provides a precedent for the sort of inclusivism commentators claim to find in the *NE*, according to which *eudaimonia* is a set of independent goods, structured (perhaps) by moral virtue.

[40] At NE I.6 1097a1 Aristotle speaks of the "attainable and practicable goods (*ta ktêta kai prakta tôn agathôn*)." See also NE VI.7 1141b9–14, where Aristotle says all deliberation aims at a practicable good (*prakton agathon*) and that the practically wise person aims at the best of these. This best of the practicable goods is, of course, happiness.

28 • Chapter Two

our passage from *NE* I.7 also takes up the argument left off in *NE* I.2. In other words, both references to practicable good, in chapters 4 and 7, occur at the same logical moment. But notice how Aristotle characterizes that stage of the argument in *NE* I.4:

> Since all knowledge and choice seeks some good, what is the good at which we say the political art aims, that is (*kai*) what is the highest (*akrotaton*) of the practicable goods? (1095a14–17)

According to Aristotle in *NE* I.4, the project after *NE* I.1–2 is to discover which one of the practicable goods is *the* good. It is likely, then, that this is the same project he points to in *NE* I.7 when he says, "Coming from a different angle, we have arrived at the same point." In other words, the point at which we have arrived is the stage of determining which of the practicable goods is the highest. But if this is correct, we should interpret Aristotle as saying in the previous sentence that if there are many ends, these would be the practicable *goods*, not that all together they would constitute the practicable *good*. Figuring out which of a plurality of goods is *the* good is a task that still faces us. (As I said, after *NE* I.4–5, the possibility that there is only one practicable good is no longer viable.)

Finally, an inclusivist reading of 1097a22–24 must make sense of Aristotle's apparent dissatisfaction with the state of the argument in the last sentence of our passage: "And yet we must try to clarify this further." He goes on to argue that of genuinely final ends—ends worth choosing for their own sakes—some are more final than others. The highest good will be the one that is most final (*teleiotaton*). In other words, Aristotle gives a more precise account than he has so far of which of the practicable goods is the best. In the inclusivist reading of 1097a22–24, according to which Aristotle says that if there are multiple ends they will together comprise the practicable good, it is less certain why Aristotle thinks he hasn't been sufficiently clear about the nature of the highest good already. For in this reading he has already told us that the highest good is all the practicable goods, however many of them there happen to be.

Nothing I have said disproves that only an inclusive end satisfies the finality criterion. All I want to show is that nothing in the discussion leading up to the finality criterion suggests an inclusivist conception of *eudaimonia*.[41] Thus, when we learn in *NE* I.7 about the middle-level ends, it is not at all obvious that we should understand these goods to be constituents of happiness.

---

[41] See *DC* II.12 292b3–10, where Aristotle seems to take it for granted that the human good is a monistic end: "For man is capable of attaining many goods and so is capable of doing many things, and for the sake of still other things. . . . But the other animals have less [variety of action than man]; . . . For either there is but one attainable good, as indeed man has, or, if several, each contributes directly to the best."

3f. NE I.7: The Finality Criterion

So we should expect Aristotle to try to find a way to narrow down the multitude of practicable goods to the single good we are seeking. And this is precisely what the finality criterion does.[42] If there are many final (*teleia*) ends, the highest good will be the most final (*teleiotaton*) among them (1097a30).[43] As we should expect, the relationship between more and less final ends is one of subordination.

---

[42] As I argued in section 3c, Aristotle always assumes that the good is a convergent end. As several people have rightly pointed out, all that is necessary for a good to be most final is that it be *haplôs teleion* (final without qualification). And as Aristotle describes it, a *haplôs teleion* end is merely one that is not subordinated to any other end; he does not say it must be at the top of a hierarchy of ends, much less that it must be at the top of *all* chains of ends. Thus, there might be several most final ends of an individual life, each one most final relative to its own hierarchy of ends. (Kraut 1989, 204–205; although ultimately he argues that Aristotle's most final end is meant to be convergent.) Now, it is certainly true that Aristotle does not provide a definition of the most final end that guarantees there will be only one, convergent end. Be that as it may, it is clear from the way Aristotle argues that *eudaimonia* is the most final end that this is what he has in mind. First of all, he says that *eudaimonia* is especially a most final end not simply because it meets the *haplôs teleion* requirement but also because pleasure, intellectual wisdom, and the moral virtues are choiceworthy for its sake. That is, its claim to be the good is determined not only by the fact that it is not subordinated to some other good but also by the fact that other important final goods are subordinated to it. Apparently, then, Aristotle assumes that the most final end tops a chain of ends. Second, the goods that Aristotle claims to be subordinated to happiness even while loved for their own sakes—pleasure, honor, virtue, and intellectual wisdom—are the very goods mentioned in *NE* I.5. He does not argue there or anywhere that these are the only goods loved for their own sakes. But they are at least the most important ones. And in *NE* I.7 he claims that they are all choiceworthy for the sake of *eudaimonia*. This suggests that for Aristotle, happiness is meant to be an end upon which *all* chains of ends—or at least the most important ones—converge. Finally, there seems to be only one most final end (1097a29–30). Since Aristotle has ruled out the possibility that there are chains of ends that continue ad infinitum, that means all chains of ends must come to a stop in the one, most final good.

Although Aristotle does not justify his assumption that the most final end is unique, this is not as grave an omission as it might at first seem. It would be a problem if Aristotle thought that, under the aegis of the finality criterion, he could prove a good was uniquely *eudaimonia* simply by showing that it is not choiceworthy for the sake of something else—that it is merely *haplôs teleion*. For, as I have said, there might conceivably be several goods fitting this description, given all Aristotle has shown us. Happily, however Aristotle does not use the finality criterion in this way. In *NE* X.7 he tries to argue not only that contemplation is not choiceworthy for the sake of anything further but also that it is the *only* candidate good in this position, since pleasure and moral virtue are choiceworthy for its sake.

[43] The translation of this word is highly disputed. Those who espouse an inclusivist interpretation of *NE* I often translate it as 'complete', while those who favor a monistic-end reading often prefer 'perfect' or 'final'. These are all legitimate translations of the Greek. I prefer to translate *teleia* here as 'final'. This is meant to leave open which of the two interpretations of *eudaimonia* is appropriate. It also calls our attention to the fact that Aristotle is here talking about the endiness of the good (*finis* = end). It is impossible, however, to translate *teleion* as

And we say that [an end] which is worth pursuing (*diôkton*) for its own sake is more final (*teleioteron*) than one which is worth pursuing for the sake of something else; and [an end] that is never choiceworthy for the sake of another is more final than those which are choiceworthy for their own sakes and for the sake of that other; and [*dê*] [an end] which is always choiceworthy for its own sake and never for the sake of another is final without qualification (*haplôs teleion*). (NE I.7 1097a30–34)

Some ends are worth choosing merely for the sake of some further end, which they serve. These are the subordinate craft products, like bridles and ships, that Aristotle discussed in the first chapter. A feature of their being instruments is that one cannot give an adequate account of them without reference to their higher end. Other ends, as we know from *NE* I.2, are chosen always and only for their own sakes, being that for the sake of which the instrumental goods are worth choosing. These ends, Aristotle says here, are unqualifiedly and most final. In achieving them, our goal-directedness is entirely successful. Clearly, a most final end is more final than a mere instrument. But there are other ends more final than instruments but less final than *eudaimonia*. These are the middle-level goods, goods choiceworthy both for their own sakes and for the sake of the most final good. The examples Aristotle gives make his meaning clearer:

> And *eudaimonia* most of all seems to be this sort of thing [i.e. a final end without qualification]. For we always choose this because of itself and never because of another, but honor and pleasure and intelligence (*noûs*) and all the virtues we choose both because of themselves (for even if nothing resulted from them, we would still choose each of them), and we choose them for the sake of happiness, supposing that through them we will live happily. But no one chooses happiness for the sake of these things, nor in general because of anything else. (*NE* I.7 1097a34–b6)[44]

(Notice that Aristotle uses the finality criterion to rule out goods like honor and moral virtue, which, as we already saw in *NE* I.5, seem to be but are not the highest goal of the happy life.) The middle-level ends are genuinely final or terminal. That is to say, they are ends that can bring a chain of activity to a close in the sense that (unlike most craft products) on their

---

'final' in all contexts in the *NE*. In particular, we must translate it as 'complete' in the phrase *en biôi teleiôi* (1098a18). Still, this should not encourage us to translate *teleion* as 'complete' elsewhere. I believe that the emphasis in this line (1098a18) is on having happiness through to the conclusion (or *telos*) of a natural length of time, not, primarily, on having all the different parts of a whole. (So we might translate *en biôi teleiôi* as 'in a finished life'.)

[44] Contra Broadie (1991, 30–34), Aristotle is not, strictly speaking, proving in this passage that happiness is the good. We can take that for granted because (1) it is the goal of the architectonic craft, politics, and (2) everyone agrees on calling the highest good *happiness* (*NE* I.4 1095a14–22). What Aristotle is doing in this passage is demonstrating that the finality criterion can serve to distinguish *the* good and happiness from other practicable goods.

own they provide a sufficient normative context for justifying the pursuit-worthiness of the goods subordinated to them. This is the point of Aristotle's counterfactual: If nothing further resulted from these goods, we would still choose them.[45] And yet middle-level goods do not top the hierarchy of ends. Though they are intrinsically valuable, they are also choiceworthy for the sake of the most final end: happiness.

4. Teleology, Desire, and Middle-Level Ends

4a. What Kind of Goods are Middle-Level Ends?

If goods like honor, friends, and, moral virtue are worth choosing for their own sakes, how can they also be worth choosing for the sake of something else—that is, something quite separate from these, in the way that basking in honor, enjoying our friends, and acting virtuously could not be independent of them?

It might seem that the answer to this question is obvious. Goods choiceworthy for their own sakes and for the sake of something else are valuable for two independent reasons: They are intrinsically valuable, and they are also (broadly speaking) instrumentally valuable. We might say that their value for us is overdetermined.[46] So, for example, I desire moral virtue and pleasure each for its own sake. Even if happiness is impossible for me to achieve, I would still want each of them (1097b2–4). But, as a matter of fact, moral virtue and pleasure also tend to lead to happiness, either because they are parts of happiness (an inclusive conception of *eudaimonia*) or because they contribute to or are instruments to some further good that is identified with happiness (a monistic-end conception of *eudaimonia*). Under these circumstances, it is an additional reason why I value and pursue moral virtue and pleasure that they have this result.

In effect this interpretation draws a parallel between this passage of the *Nicomachean Ethics* and the threefold division of goods in book II of the *Republic*, and it might be thought that the precedent provides some reason to interpret the *Nicomachean Ethics* along the same lines. There, Glaucon asks Socrates to distinguish (1) the kind of good, such as the harmless pleasures, "that we welcome not because we desire what comes from it, but because we welcome it for its own sake";[47] (2) the kind of good, like knowledge and health, that "we like for its own sake and also for the sake of what comes from it"; and (3) the kind of good that is valuable only instrumentally,

---

[45] Since Aristotle says we would choose these middle-level ends even if we did not think they resulted in happiness, I do not agree with Weller (2001) that pursuing an end as choiceworthy for its own sake is just to pursue it as a way of realizing *eudaimonia*.

[46] Richardson (1992, 327–351) is perhaps the clearest exponent of this position. See also Kraut 1989, passim; and Reeve 1995, 114–117.

[47] *Republic* translations are from Grube and Reeve 1992.

while being in itself unsavory. Glaucon's examples are medicine and money-making (*Rep.* 357b–c). In the interpretation we are now considering, Aristotle's middle-level goods, choiceworthy for their own sakes and for the sake of *eudaimonia*, correspond to Glaucon's second class of good desired for their inherent benefits and for their results.[48]

But if this interpretation is correct, why would Socrates and Aristotle disagree about which group of goods is best? If happiness belongs in Glaucon's first category, as it would if the division were equivalent to the one in the *Nicomachean Ethics*, then Socrates would be preferring the (constitutive?) means to happiness to happiness itself. This is most unlikely.[49] In fact the threefold division of goods in *Republic* II is not equivalent to the threefold division of goods in *NE* I.7.[50] Notice that Socrates says that the second group is the finest because it provides its possessor with happiness by two routes: The good thing will itself make him happy, and it will lead him to other sources of happiness (*Rep.* 358a). This suggests that Glaucon's groups are distinguished by the different ways they supply us with happiness.[51] Since Glaucon's middle group is more useful in causing happiness, it is the best according to the terms of his division. Aristotle's groups, on the other hand, are distinguished by different levels of teleological subordination. From Aristotle's point of view, insofar as the goods in all three of Glaucon's groups are valuable because they provide us with happiness, they are choiceworthy for the sake of happiness. That is, none of them is valuable as something *haplôs teleion*.[52] Thus, despite superficial similarities, Plato's threefold division of goods as objects of desire gives us no reason to think that middle-level ends in the *Nicomachean Ethics* are essentially ends desired for themselves and for their results.

Nevertheless, as I have said, it is attractive to interpret Aristotle's middle-level ends as ends desired for two reasons. It is clear from *NE* I.1 that Aris-

---

[48] Korsgaard (1996a, 230) connects this attractive reading with Glaucon's challenge, although she notices that the fit is not good, and takes this fact as demanding a different interpretation of Aristotle's classification.

[49] See *Symp.* 205a1–3, where Socrates suggests that happiness is the most desirable practicable good. Notice here that happiness seems to be the best *as an end* (or at least it is the end in a line of justification for action).

[50] Both Plato and Aristotle classify goods in more than one way. For instance, both distinguish goods of the soul from goods of the body; and Aristotle further distinguishes goods of the body from external goods (*NE* 1098b12–16). These classifications are not meant to be the only way to divide the pie.

[51] Irwin 1999, 165.

[52] There is a further oddity about thinking of Glaucon's kinds of goods as tracking a hierarchy of ends. His example of the kind choiceworthy for its own sake is "harmless pleasures." But Plato, unlike Aristotle, thinks that pleasures are processes. That is to say, he believes that pleasures have ends beyond themselves (*Gorg.* 492e7–493d3; *Phil.* 54c6–d2, 32a6–b4; *Rep.* IX 583e9–10; Frede 1993, xlii–xliii). If Plato meant Glaucon to be distinguishing levels in a teleological hierarchy, he ought not have provided as the sole example of a good choiceworthy for

totle thinks that human practical reasoning is shaped by the perception of hierarchies of ends. Our perception of the desirability of victory, for example, sets in motion a process of discovering the means to that end which, due to their instrumental value, we also find choiceworthy. And it is a feature of our practical reasoning that we can desire an end for itself and for some separate result it produces. Nevertheless this very feature of this interpretation—that it ties the hierarchy of ends very closely to our habits of practical reasoning and desire—makes it an inadequate reading of the *Nicomachean Ethics*. It is a presupposition of this interpretation that what it is to be an end is to be an actual object of desire, or at least an appropriate object of desire, where appropriateness is judged in terms of general or overall desire satisfaction.[53] Thus it presupposes that to understand Aristotle's talk of hierarchies of ends all we need do is to study the ways in which our actual desires may be subordinated to one another. But the concept of an end in Aristotle is much broader than any such psychological conception. As we saw, this is particularly evident in Aristotle's natural philosophy, where he is quite willing to talk about the ends of plants, material elements, and a host of other things to which he clearly does not attribute desire or any kind of conscious intentions (e.g., *Phys.* II.8 199a20 ff.). Even in the animal and human cases, where desire psychology is integral to the workings of natural teleology, an end is not by definition an object of desire or even an appropriate one. It is rather what some creature is naturally *for* and what *therefore* it ought naturally to desire.[54] Aristotle must believe, therefore, that he can explicate the finality relation in terms that do not make reference to desire or conscious intention. Our interpretation of the various levels of ends must be sensitive to this fact.

We can press the point further. Although it may seem that middle-level goods are those goods desired for themselves and for their results, our examination of Aristotelian ends showed that this apparent solution is not in the spirit of Aristotelian teleology. For we can desire to perform an action to get any of its results. But as we now know, an end is not any chance result. Rather, an end is the good of an activity that determines its form and what it is to be a successful instance of that activity. So, for example, a doctor may treat patients not because he wants to make them healthy but simply because he wants to make a buck. Nevertheless, we judge the quality of his care not by whether it causes the patient to give him money—a horrible quack may be quite adept at satisfying his desire for money—but by whether the patient is cured. To use Aristotelian terminology, desire aims at the apparent good,

---

its own sake a good that, in Plato's philosophy, is notorious for not having its end in itself. Of course, Glaucon is not Plato's mouthpiece, so this point is not decisive in my favor.

[53] Richardson (1992, 335), who adopts this interpretation of middle-level ends, is quite clear about this: "something is an end of action, for Aristotle, just in case it is pursued."

[54] Indeed, as Sarah Broadie has pointed out to me, if it is part of an animal's end to have desires at all, then an animal cannot achieve its end by first desiring it.

but the apparent good can come apart from what truly is good (*NE* III.4; *DA* III.10). Thus, the set of all objects of desire is wider than the set of genuine ends. The genuine ends are those results in terms of which the action in question, as such, truly is subject to evaluation.

So Aristotle's scientific conception of an end is not consistent with thinking of middle-level ends as goods desired for two independent reasons. It is conceivable, I suppose, that Aristotle relaxes his conception of an end in his ethical works. It might be that, so far as the *Nicomachean Ethics* is concerned, a *telos* is simply an object of desire, or an appropriate or correct such object (as that might be judged relative to satisfaction of desire in general). (Of course, as we saw in section 3a, Aristotle does seem to employ that concept at the beginning of the *Nicomachean Ethics* in the same way as he does in the *Physics*.) But this is not a move those of us who are sympathetic to Aristotelian ethics should be happy to see him make. After all, as Aristotle is himself aware, different people can desire different things for all kinds of reasons. Indeed, people can even desire for their own sakes things that are quite clearly instruments. (Misers and those who emulate the money-making life do this, for example.)[55] The whole point of examining teleology in an ethical work, however, is that discovering what our ends really are will reveal to us what we *ought* to desire. If Aristotle relaxes his definition of *telos* now to include any object of desire or objects of desire authorized by the overall satisfaction of desire, we have no reason to think that the structure of our ends (i.e., objects of desire) can tell us anything about how we ought to guide our lives. In particular, Aristotle will not be able to argue from the (quite implausible) fact that people do aim at a unified conception of the good throughout their lives to the conclusion that it would be a great folly not to do so (*EE* I.2 1214b10–11).[56] Any realist framework that uses teleology as a means of discovering the good should resist collapsing the distinction between an end and an object of desire.

4b. Human Desires and Human Ends

It is important to realize that Aristotle's vocabulary in the *Nicomachean Ethics* is often normative. He often talks about ends as being *diôkta* and *haireta*, and often he does intend to point to our actual patterns of desire to support his claim. But although *diôkta* and *haireta* can mean 'pursued' and 'chosen', respectively, they can also mean 'worth pursuing' and 'choiceworthy'. It is the normative claim that is primarily important to Aristotle. He draws our attention to the fact that, by nature, we tend to desire in certain

---

[55] I take it that the point of claiming that relaxation is for the sake of work in X.6 is to prove that hedonists have been choosing the pleasures of relaxation for the wrong reason.

[56] Indeed, the *phainomena* collected by Aristotle suggest that people do not organize their projects for the sake of a single goal. See *NE* 1095a20–25, discussed in section 3c, above.

ways as a piece of his argument that we ought to desire in these ways, that is, that these really are our ends. But the ends exist independently of desire, whether or not we happen to want our true end on a given occasion.

More needs to be said, however, about the connection between human ends and desires. For in some sense the apparent good can play the role of a *telos*, as Aristotle is well aware (*MA* 6 700b28–29).[57] After all, the fact that a person wants X will shape his behavior in pursuit of X. And to some extent the nature of what he wants will determine what counts as a successful attempt to get it. But only to some extent, for even though a particular representation of the apparent good may aim at what is not in our interests, the apparent good as such does aim at our true interests. Our capacity for desire (which as such aims at our apparent good) is the natural means by which we fulfill our nature, that is, our *telos*. This capacity would not fulfill its function if it pointed us to the genuine good only by chance. (Indeed, in Aristotle's understanding, this could not *be* desire's function if the connection were only a chance one.) Thus, there is a perfectly good teleological sense in which our actions may not be successful even though they achieve the particular end the agent intended. If a person has an incorrect image of his *telos* and thus of what actions are appropriate under the current circumstances—think, for example, of Don Quixote—what he does can be successful so far as his conscious intentions go, but strictly speaking it is not successful at all. But even when people are wrong about what particular thing they ought to pursue, it is still true in a general sense that they are pursuing their human *telos*; they are exercising a capacity that, by nature, is *for* that.

This is all quite abstract. The crafts provide a concrete manifestation of the way in which normative goals can come apart from individual desires. The different elements of, for example, medicine—cutting and burning, alterations in diet—were developed to achieve particular results, which the practitioners took to be good. And because the results *were* in fact good, a pattern of activity emerged as the craft of medicine. The *telos* of medicine and the standards for right medical practice are now cut loose from the desires of the individuals who practice it. A particular doctor may effect a cure for any number of reasons; indeed, he may not care about the health of the patient at all. Nevertheless, so long as his actions are guided by the medical craft, they are for the sake of health. If the doctor makes a mess of cauterizing a patient, it will be no good for him to say, "Look, I don't really care about whether this person lives or dies. I only wanted money and my "cure" certainly got me that." It is still appropriate for us to judge his practice of medicine by whether it produces health, because medicine *is* for the sake of health.[58] An activity that is not correctly judged by its conduciveness to

---

[57] Nussbaum 1978, 338 not. ad 700b28.
[58] Broadie 1991, 8–12.

health, whether or not a doctor happens to perform it, is simply not the exercise of medicine.

The independence of a craft's ends from the desires of the individual craftsman is even more starkly displayed in hierarchies that span over several crafts. To return once again to an example from *NE* I.1, the craftsman whose actions are directed toward the production of bridles may have no knowledge of the cavalry. Indeed, if the bridle maker is a slave, the freedom that good horsemanship will achieve under the direction of a good general may not even be open to the craftsman to enjoy; and we do not deliberate about how to produce impossibilities. Thus it simply is untrue that every craftsman makes bridles because he wants the peace that follows in the wake of victory and which victory itself is for. Nevertheless, Aristotle says that the bridle maker acts for the sake of the general's end (1094a15–16). That is because the norms by which he knowingly guides his bridle making depend ultimately on the victory that is the general's end. What these considerations reveal is that the norms established by the ends that guide our actions may not be determined by the results *we* hope to achieve by them.

Nevertheless the results we hope to achieve by our actions, and with reference to which we consciously make our decisions, are in some sense their ends. And the standards for the agent's actions will *appear* to the agent to be set by their contribution to this apparent good. (The craftsman may judge his performance as a craftsman by the number of bridles he sells rather than by whether expert riders approve and buy them.) The point is just that his actions would in truth be better judged by another standard.

Aristotle seems to assume we can see true ends behind the actual objects of desire throughout the *Nicomachean Ethics*. For instance, in *NE* I.5 he says that the refined men of action take honor to be their *telos*. As a matter of fact, however, the end of their actions is moral virtue, since the honor they knowingly want depends on that. Aristotle's idea is not that these gentlemen unconsciously desire virtue as their most final end.[59] (To my knowledge, Aristotle never discusses unconscious desire.) Rather, they desire honor as their most final end and lead their lives in its pursuit. But since they desire honor only when given as a reward for virtue, Aristotle believes that virtue is their true *telos*; virtue is what sets the standard for their actions. (And, as I mentioned before, even this may turn out not to be their true end.) Again, at *NE* X.6, Aristotle says that many people act for the sake of relaxation as their final end, but relaxation is for the sake of work (1176b32–1177a1). So these people have misjudged their end and thus the norms for their behavior. (We can easily see here what the bad consequences would be. If I think that life is for the sake of relaxation, I may be proud to have reduced myself to a

---

[59] Although I am not certain, this seems to be the way Kraut (1989, 234) interprets this passage in *NE* I.5.

state of such lassitude that I can hardly lift a pinky. But since relaxation is for the sake of work, in reality I will be an utter failure.)

We should not be misled, then, by the connection between desire and natural goal-directedness. While our desires can provide important evidence about the nature of the human good, they do not in themselves determine what the human *telos* and good are. An end, or "that for the sake of which," is not, strictly speaking, an object of desire. Thus, the fact that a good can be desired for two reasons does not explain how it can have an end in itself and an end in some other, independent good.

5. The Puzzle in *NE* I.7 and Two Possible Solutions

The upshot of the examination of Aristotle's notion of an end, or "that for the sake of which," is this: It's not at all clear how there *could* be goods that are worth choosing both for their own sakes and for the sake of *eudaimonia*, if *eudaimonia* is something other than just another name for particular middle-level ends. For goods like these would be goods that, in being of value for some further end, have a normative limit outside themselves on whose value their own value depends, and at the same time, in being of value just in themselves, need no such external source of value but set for themselves the norms of their own goodness. They are goods that somehow or other contain within themselves the standards for what it is to be a good of that kind and, at the same time, have normative standards imposed from the outside. But how could this be? It seems as if any intrinsic value a good might allegedly have would be denied by its being for the sake of something further;[60] and conversely, any instrumental value a good choiceworthy for its own sake might have would seem to be a mere happy coincidence and irrelevant to the natural, intrinsic value of the good as determined by its *telos*.

We have seen that we cannot analyze middle-level goods as goods that are desired for two independent reasons—for themselves and for some separate thing that they serve as instruments for achieving. There are two other possible solutions that do not make the mistake of confusing a *telos* and an object of desire.

First, perhaps the two ends coincide by chance. That is to say, it might be that middle-level goods have their ends in themselves but, in addition, regularly promote some further goal. As it so happens, what it takes to be a good instrument to that further goal is exactly coincident with what it takes to be a good thing of that kind for its own sake. In this case, we might call the chance result a further end of the intrinsically valuable activity. This account of middle-level goods is unpromising as an interpretation of the *Nicoma-*

---

[60] With the exception, of course, of potentialities, which are conceptually inseparable from their actualization.

chean Ethics because it posits a regular but *chance* connection between their two ends. In the *Physics* Aristotle denies regular chance connections (II.8 198b35). But at a deeper level, this interpretation is questionable because it supposes that a good may have two separate, teleologically unconnected ends. Although I have not yet found evidence to this effect, I doubt very much that Aristotle would admit that the proper pursuit of or natural coming to be of a thing could have two entirely independent ends. For if we say that a thing has two ends, we are saying that it has two separate natures or forms. (That's because, as we saw above (pp. 22–23), a natural *telos* is closely tied to the form or essence of the thing.)[61]

Another and more interesting interpretation of middle-level goods is to say that, for these goods, the two normative functions of the *telos* come apart into the function of determining the form and success conditions for activities in pursuit of it and the function of determining how many such pursuits there should be or how frequent they are (p. 18 above). Intrinsic goods might determine their own natures but have the limits of their appropriate pursuit set by a further end. In other words, the most final good might function as a side constraint on the pursuit of other intrinsically valuable goods—the middle-level goods.[62] So, for example, a good dinner party is choiceworthy for its own sake; what it is to be a good dinner party makes no reference to some external result it might have. Nevertheless, how often we ought to have dinner parties is not a question we can decide without looking to some further goal. In particular, different conceptions of happiness will endorse the joys of fine dining to different degrees. In this way, a middle-level end could be choiceworthy for its own sake, in the sense of not depending on some further end for its form, while yet being choiceworthy for a separate further end that imposes the limits for when and how much it is to be pursued.

For two reasons, however, this interpretation of middle-level ends is unsatisfactory. First, in this reading, *eudaimonia* no longer seems to be a convergent end. The highest good is a special kind of intrinsic good, but it is no longer the ultimate object of all the happy person's activity. But as I have

---

[61] Cooper (1975, 168–178) and Whiting (1986) have argued that Aristotle's position in *NE* X.7–8 is that human beings do have a dual nature. My interpretation of these chapters will show that there is no need to read Aristotle as making this metaphysically suspect assumption. See chapter 8, below.

[62] Broadie (1991, 31–32) adopts this sort of strategy. This kind of solution seems to be suggested at *EE* VIII.3 1249b16–19 (where Aristotle says that contemplation of god is the limit [*horos*] of the right pursuit of other goods). I would not be certain of this, however, since (1) contemplation of god is not equivalent to happiness in the *EE*, (2) Aristotle does not stress the sense in which happiness is an end in the *EE*, and (3) the *EE* does not contain the discussion of the hierarchy of ends/goods so central to the *NE*. Kullman (1985, 172–173) thinks there is evidence at *Pol*. I.8 1256b15–22 for an end that limits only the extent of pursuit of a lower good, but this example of a limiting end is not a *telos* or "that for the sake of which," in the sense of an end we have been describing, but is rather a *hou heneka tini*, i.e., a beneficiary. See chapter 4, section 2, below.

argued, in the *Nicomachean Ethics* a good is to be conceived of as an end or "that for the sake of which," and the highest good is to be conceived of as the super end on which all chains of ends converge.[63] In the example above, the person does not aim at the highest good when having a dinner party. Rather, the highest good trumps all others in a conflict—including the good of having a dinner party. And that raises the second problem with this interpretation. In what acceptable sense do I pursue X for the sake of or for the end of Y just because the way I pursue X on this occasion does not obstruct my pursuit of Y? Treating a more final good as a trumping good stretches the meaning of "acting for the sake of an end" beyond recognition. It is not, at least, what Aristotle usually means by "acting for the sake of an end" in his technical sense. Thus, middle-level ends cannot be related to *eudaimonia* as to a side constraint, or at least this does not capture the sense in which middle-level ends are choiceworthy for the sake of *eudaimonia*. In this interpretation, *eudaimonia* is not a convergent end for all the happy person's choices; indeed, it hardly seems to be a *telos* at all for his choice of middle-level goods.

There may be some confusion on this point. The supreme finality of *eudaimonia* is not to be understood as its carrying more weight than other, subordinate goods in our deliberations. A craft product, insofar as it is an end, does not carry more weight in our deliberations than the means leading to it do. There is no conflict between means and end that is resolved in favor of the end because, as an end, it is more important than the means (in the way that a conflict between health and tasting something sweet might be resolved by an appeal to the superior value of the former). Rather, its being an end specifies what those means should be and is the source of their value. A means does not simply have less value than the end (1094a5–6); it has *no* value outside the context of aiming at its end. If someone were to pursue a means beyond the point that was conducive to achieving the end, we would urge him to stop on the grounds that what he was pursuing was a means to something else. But the force of this advice would not be that the end is more important than the means. Rather, we would tell him that in pursuing the means excessively, he would be defeating the good of having those means in the first place. So we should not imagine that the supreme finality of *eudaimonia* can be grasped in terms of its weightiness. The highest good is more important and more valuable than other goods, but that is not the significance of its being most final. To call *eudaimonia* most final is to specify the way in which it is more important than the other goods: It is what our pursuit

---

[63] We do not have to think of the highest good as a convergent, most final end. My point is just that in the *NE* Aristotle does, and that this interpretation of middle ends, according to which *eudaimonia* functions only as a side constraint on their pursuit, does not do justice to this fact.

of the other goods ultimately aims at realizing. This sort of weightiness is more profound than being a side constraint.

6. Ackrill's Inclusivist Solution

It seems, then, that we must find some other way of interpreting the relationship between middle-level ends and the highest good. It was just our problem of figuring out how ends that are choiceworthy for their own sakes could also be for the sake of *eudaimonia* that John Ackrill addressed in his famous article, "Aristotle on *Eudaimonia*." Ackrill thinks it is mysterious how, in *NE* I.1, "one action or activity [can be] for the sake of another, in cases where the first does not terminate in a product or outcome which the second can then use or exploit" (1974, 18).[64] And in general Ackrill wonders how "some things may be done for their own sake and may yet be done for the sake of something else."

Ackrill suggests that if *eudaimonia* is an inclusive end—in this case including all intrinsic goods—then a middle-level end will be choiceworthy for *eudaimonia*'s sake, as a constituent is for the sake of the relevant whole. Now, although I disagree with Ackrill's particular solution to this problem, I believe there is something importantly right in the motivation that underlies it. For, in essence, Ackrill says that Aristotle's position about the relation between final and most final goods is coherent so long as the relation holds precisely because middle-level goods are intrinsically valuable.[65]

... [O]ne can answer such a question as "Why do you seek pleasure?" by saying that you see it and seek it as an element in the most desirable sort of life. ...

---

[64] Although Ackrill ([1974] 1980) believes that he finds the problem cropping up already in *NE* I.1 (Gauthier and Jolif [1970, 6–7] make a similar point about this distinction in *NE* I.1, although unlike Ackrill they do not mention the problem again at *NE* I.7), I believe it emerges only in *NE* I.7. Therefore he explains the problem differently and, I believe, somewhat misleadingly. (See notes 17 and 20, above, for an explanation of why I do not think the problem Ackrill finds in *NE* I.1 is genuine. See also Richardson 1992.) I will make Ackrill's case only for *NE* I.7 here.

[65] Weller (2001, 96–98) makes an interesting point that Ackrill's examples of an inclusive end—putting as a part of golf and golf as a part of a good vacation—suggest different interpretations of the relationship between part and whole. Putting is intrinsically valuable precisely because it is a part of a whole that is independently valuable. The value of golf makes its constituents valuable. Conversely, a vacation is good because golf and the other parts of the vacation are intrinsically valuable. As Weller rightly says, Ackrill's considered analysis of the relationship between *eudaimonia* and its parts is analogous to the relationship between a good vacation and golf. Weller favors the golf/putting model. In other words, he thinks *eudaimonia* has an independent value that alone makes its constituents choiceworthy for their own sakes. I do not think this can be correct, however, since the model implies that middle-level ends have no intrinsic value except via their connection to happiness. I take Aristotle to deny this at 1097b3–4: We would choose the middle-level ends even if nothing followed from them. (See note 66 on similar issues.)

The answer to the question about pleasure does not imply that pleasure is not intrinsically worth while but only a means to an end. It implies rather that pleasure *is* intrinsically worth while, being an element of *eudaimonia*. *Eudaimonia* is the most desirable sort of life, the life that contains all intrinsically worthwhile activities. (1974, 21)

Ackrill has discovered a very natural way of explaining the idea that we can seek intrinsic goods for the sake of the highest good without downgrading their status as intrinsically valuable. Their instrumental value *depends* on their being intrinsically valuable.[66] From this point of view, some form of inclusivism is quite attractive.

I see no problem with supposing that X can be for the sake of Y in virtue of being one of Y's constituents.[67] This seems to me a perfectly legitimate

---

[66] Although Korsgaard (1996a, 231–32) intends her interpretation of middle-level ends to differ from the inclusivist interpretation, it has a similar strategy. Middle-level ends or, in her terminology, conditional ends are "valued for their own sake, given that we are human beings living in human conditions.... The unconditional end plays a different role: it is what makes it worth it to be a human being and to live in human conditions.... It will be a mark of a conditional end that it is also a means. But this "also" is not merely conjunctive; rather, its being a "means" or constituent of a worthwhile life will be what makes it possible to choose it as an end." So whereas Ackrill proposes that middle-level ends are choiceworthy for the sake of *eudaimonia* because they are choiceworthy for their own sakes, Korsgaard proposes that middle-level ends are choiceworthy for their own sakes because they are choiceworthy for the sake of *eudaimonia*. Unfortunately, Korsgaard does not explain how it is that conditional ends are genuinely final and not mere instruments. According to her interpretation of Aristotle, the constituents of a human life are valuable only on the condition of contemplation. But since Korsgaard analyzes all conditionality as instrumental (if Y is a condition of X's value, then X is, broadly speaking, an instrument to the production of Y), that means human life is valuable because it is instrumentally valuable. But then where is the *intrinsic* value of the constituents of a good human life? (No doubt, Korsgaard would think I am illegitimately conflating finality and intrinsic value [1996b]. But if I am, then so is Aristotle. A successful interpretation of the *NE* cannot act as if he kept these concepts distinct.)

There is a deeper problem with Korsgaard's interpretation worth mentioning here. She interprets Aristotle as saying that human life, with all its needs, is only conditionally valuable. The philosophical search for happiness is the search for this condition. But it's not clear to me that Aristotle would agree. The fulfillment of needs—for sex, food, friends—is the expression of our animal and political nature; that is to say, it is the fulfillment of our *human* nature. As such, these fulfillments are ends, for Aristotle, standing in no need of further justification. They are final even if they are not most final. Of course, Aristotle *does* think that these soul activities are choiceworthy for the sake of something further. But the concept of these activities as ends does not require that he think so, and that's part of the mystery of middle-level ends.

[67] Cooper [1975] 1986, 19–22. Kraut (1989, 212 n. 10) is quite right that this is not possible on a simple or weak inclusivism, i.e., one that says that Y is an unorganized set of goods. Kraut emphasizes that there is no causal connection between part and whole in this model. Although I do not think the "for the sake of" relation need always be causal, I do agree that it must always be normative. An unorganized set of goods does not play a normative role in the pursuit of its constituents. However, Aristotle does seem to maintain in his biological works that the part-whole relation can be teleological. E.g., the liver is for the sake of the life of the body by being a part that plays a certain role in the functions of the body as a whole. Thus, on a strong

application of the "for the sake of" relation. Nevertheless, as I have argued, a careful reading of *NE* I.1–7 makes it most unlikely that Aristotle intends all intrinsic goods to be constituents of *eudaimonia*, as Ackrill suggests.[68] It is a further strike against an inclusivist interpretation of *NE* I that it is hard, if not impossible, to reconcile with *NE* X, in which Aristotle says that contemplation is true *eudaimonia*.[69] But there is also a philosophical reason for denying that a set of goods can perform the function of a higher end of giving the form to its subordinate goods. That is because the set in question is conceptually dependent on its members. Suppose happiness is the set of all intrinsic goods. There cannot be a set (with members) of goods choiceworthy for their own sakes unless there are already various determinate (or determinable) goods to fill it. Thus, the idea of the set in no way shapes the essence of its members. But in that case, an inclusive end cannot function as an end, in Aristotle's sense. This is a rather crude version of inclusivism. But even more-sophisticated versions run into trouble. Terence Irwin (1991, 389), for example, has argued that *eudaimonia* is the set of all intrinsic goods structured by the demands of moral virtue. Moral virtue limits the amount of the other intrinsic goods the happy person should pursue. Even here, though, what goods we ought to pursue are not determined by the nature of *eudaimonia*. We can know what things are intrinsically valuable only independently of *eudaimonia* (since *eudaimonia* just is the appropriately structured set of intrinsic goods). Thus happiness, even in a more sophisticated version of inclusivism, does not play the value- and form-conferring role I have argued is essential to its being the most final end.[70] In fact, insofar as morally

---

form of inclusivism, X could be for the sake of Y by partially constituting Y. Kraut seems to recognize the theoretical possibility of strong inclusivism, but he does not believe (for some reason) that this sort of inclusivism is possible in the ethical case. (See also Kullmann [1985, 169–175] for his discussion of how organs are for the sake of the whole.)

[68] See section 3e, above. Of course, Ackrill has a response. Aristotle says that "if there are several virtues, [the human good] will be activity in accordance with the best and most *teleion*" [*teleiotatên*] (1098a17–18). Ackrill says that since, for reasons I have just outlined, the only way to interpret *teleiotaton* earlier in I.7 is as the set of all *teleion* goods, the *teleiotatê aretê* must be the set of all the virtues. Ackrill's reading is bolstered to some extent by the fact that this is precisely the way Aristotle uses *teleiotatê aretê* in *EE* 1219a35–39. However, Cooper ([1987] 1999, 222–224) has argued persuasively that there is no reason to read *teleiotatê* inclusively in the context of 1098a17. (See Purinton [1998, 287–291] for an argument that Cooper's translation of *teleiotatê aretê* cannot be supported by appeal to *teleiotaton* in lines 1097a25–b6. Of course, if Purinton is correct, this does not help Ackrill's case, as he admits.) Cooper's argument is strengthened, I think, by looking at Aristotle's attempts to define the different kinds of soul in *DA* II. There, Aristotle notices that animals do all kinds of things—perceive, desire, move, etc.—but seems to want to define the function of the animal soul as, strictly speaking, the capacity only to do one of these things (*DA* II.3).

[69] Of course, there have been inclusivist interpretations of *NE* X as well. I will argue against some of them in chapter 8.

[70] Barney (1999) argues that inclusivism is anachronistic insofar as it assumes that, according to Plato and Aristotle, there could be, or we could (philosophically) identify, goods choiceworthy for their own sakes absent the highest good.

virtuous action determines how much of the other goods the happy person ought to pursue, *it* (and not happiness as a whole) is playing something like the role of a most final end. As we saw, a *telos* determines (1) the form of subordinate goods and (2) the appropriate extent of their pursuit (p. 18). Thus a structured inclusivist end, such as Irwin proposes, does not fulfill (1) at all and fulfills (2) only in virtue of one of the members of the set: morally virtuous activity.

Still, although Ackrill's interpretation of NE I.7 is, I think, incorrect, we can learn something from his argument. What is needed is an interpretation of the relationship between the middle-level goods and the highest good that makes the intrinsic value of the lower goods a necessary part of their being for the sake of the highest good. That way, when the happy person pursues *eudaimonia* through honor and pleasure and the like, he must do so by recognizing their final value.

In this chapter I have argued that, although the human good or happiness is understood by Aristotle as a most final end for the sake of which ultimately all other goods are worth choosing, it is unclear exactly how middle-level ends—those goods choiceworthy for their own sakes and for the sake of something else—are related to happiness. But this problem is particularly acute if it turns out that morally virtuous activity is a middle-level end, choiceworthy for the sake of something beyond itself. For not only is morally virtuous action *worth* choosing for its own sake, it is part of the definition of such action that it be *chosen* for its own sake (NE II.4 1105a31–32). An action just is not fully virtuous unless the agent desires it for its intrinsic value. Thus, not only is it unclear how morally virtuous action could be subordinated to an independent end, such as contemplation, it seems as if no life could be morally virtuous unless it made the exercise of moral virtue and not some independent good its ultimate goal.

Let me be clear. Nothing that Aristotle says in the opening book of the *Nicomachean Ethics* suggests that morally virtuous action is a middle-level end. (He says that moral virtue is a middle-level end, and that is presumably in part because it is worth choosing for the sake of its actualization.) And yet it is important for us to see that there are suggestions in NE I that some virtuous activity or other may turn out to be teleologically subordinated to the highest good.

First, there is the function argument of NE I.7. Aristotle argues that whenever something has a function or characteristic work, performing that function well is its good (1097b25–27). This is not really a new approach to the subject of the human good. The function of a thing just is the end to which it is naturally suited.[71] Playing the flute just is the activity for the sake of which the flautist *qua* flautist does all that he does. Seeing is the end for the

---

[71] Cf. Aquinas, I.x.119.

sake of which the eye is directed. Aristotle's point is not that a thing's function is the *only* activity it has a capacity to perform. A carpenter is capable *qua* carpenter of doing many things in addition to building a house—selecting screws and wood, building sawhorses, reading architectural plans. Rather the point is that where there is a function, all the other typical capacities and activities are worth choosing for its sake. In fact, it is more correct to say that *excellent* functioning is the end, since it is the excellent activity that serves as a normative standard for that kind of activity in general. This is why, although Aristotle does not say so explicitly, if a thing has a function, excellent or virtuous functioning will be its good. Virtuous functioning is a thing's ultimate end.

Now, Aristotle claims that activity in accordance with reason is the human function (1097b34–1098a5); thus, activity in accordance with rational virtue or excellence is the highest human good (1098a16–17). But after this he adds a phrase that has been the object of much scholarly debate. Punctuating in accordance with Bywater's text, it reads: "If it is thus, the human good is activity of the soul in accordance with virtue, and if there are many virtues, in accordance with the best and most final (*teleiotatên*)" (1098a16–18). What sort of activity is activity in accordance with the most final virtue? In thinking about this question, it is important to bear in mind the connection between functioning and ultimate ends. Since Aristotle has so recently been defining *most final* as "choiceworthy for its own sake alone and never for the sake of another," there is a strong presumption that we should understand "most final" here in the same, teleological sense.[72] Of course, in the function argument, Aristotle is talking about the most final virtue, whereas in discussing the finality criterion he was talking about the most final end. But it is likely that the most final virtue is the virtue whose activity is a most final end. At least it is unlikely that there is any virtue that is worth choosing only for its own sake and never for the sake of the activity it makes possible. Thus it is unlikely that any virtue (as opposed to virtuous activity) could be most final, strictly speaking, in the sense specified by 1097a30–34. And, as I said before, excellent functioning *is* a thing's ultimate end. It is probable then that the most final virtue is the virtue whose actualization is the most final activity and end. If I am right, we can rephrase the conclusion of the function argument this way: The human good is virtuous rational activity or, if there are several virtues, the virtuous activity that is a *most* final end.[73]

---

[72] Cooper [1987] 1999, 221–224. Ackrill ([1974] 1980, 28) also believes that *teleiotaton* must mean the same thing in the finality criterion and in the function argument, although of course he interprets it to mean "most inclusive." My interpretation is closer to Kraut's (1989, 178–179).

[73] I believe the clause at the end of the function argument—"if there are many virtues, in accordance with the best and most final"—is a legitimate conclusion of the preceding argument (contra Roche 1988a, 182–184). If it is part of the implicit understanding of *the* function of something that excellence in that activity is its ultimate end, then where there are several func-

We should notice that this qualification at the end of the function argument is reminiscent of the finality criterion: "So that if there is only one [end] that is final, this would be the [good] we are seeking, but if there are several, the most final (*teleiotaton*) of them [would be]" (1097a28–30). As we have seen, Aristotle goes on to explain that one end will be more final than other final ends if it is choiceworthy for itself alone while the other ends are choiceworthy for its sake. Thus, if one form of virtuous human functioning is most final, that ought to mean that the other forms of virtuous activity are teleologically subordinated to it. Aristotle does not emphasize the subordination of the other forms of virtuous activity, but it is entirely appropriate to infer that this is what he has in mind.[74] Excellent functioning is an ultimate or final end; thus if one such kind of activity turns out to be more final than another, that means that the latter is worth choosing for the sake of the former. That is just what it means for one end to be more final than another. Thus we see Aristotle leave room in *NE* I.7 for the possibility that some virtuous activities are middle-level ends.

The possibility seems to be suggested again at *NE* I.8 1099a29–31: "And these [best activities], or one of them—the best—we say is happiness." If only one of the excellent activities is happiness and the best, then only one of them will be the most final end. The others ought to be subordinated to it. Of course we do not know yet which one exercise of virtue is best. I do not mean to suggest that in *NE* I.7–8 Aristotle is already saying that there is certainly a teleological hierarchy of rational virtuous activities, much less that the exercise of some other virtue is more final than the exercise of those moral virtues with which Aristotle's well-bred audience is familiar. That argument does not come until *NE* X.[75] But in retrospect we can see that he is laying the groundwork for his argument that this one highest virtuous activity is contemplative. And that means that morally virtuous action is choiceworthy for its own sake *and* for the sake of something higher.

---

tions, we should expect that the most final among them will constitute *the* function and most final end. (See Lawrence [1993, 26–28] for a different view.) I will not insist on this point here, however. What is important, as I argue below, is that the meaning of *most final virtue* requires that if there is a most final virtue, its activity will be the teleological focus of other, less final virtues. Thus, the activity in accordance with the most final virtue is not merely a particularly important aspect of the human good (Cooper [1987] 1999, Broadie 1991); as the highest end, it *is* the human good.

[74] Purinton (1998, 265) suggests that Aristotle is referring to the subordination of our nutritive and perceptive functions to our rational function. (See also Roche 1988a, 187.) I think this is an entirely plausible interpretation of the text. But if it is plausible, then in my reading the door is open for someone to show that if contemplation is more final than morally virtuous activity, then it is the highest human good.

[75] Or rather it is not explicitly tied to conclusions about happiness until *NE* X. As Lawrence (2001, 447) correctly points out, Aristotle argues in *NE* VI that theoretical virtue is more final than practical virtue. See also Lawrence (2001, 447–451) for an argument that we ought to read the conclusion of the function argument formally, i.e., as referring to the best and most final virtue, *whatever it is*.

In the last book of the *Nicomachean Ethics*, Aristotle denies that morally virtuous action is the ultimate aim of the happiest life. Instead, the best life aims at theoretical contemplation as perfect, most final (*teleia*) happiness (1177a17, 1177b24). Since Aristotle clearly believes that the philosophical life will be morally virtuous (1178b5–6), and since he also thinks that all choices ought to be made for the sake of contemplative activity (1177b33–34), it is likely he thinks that in the best life, morally virtuous activity is chosen for the sake of contemplation.

So, if we cannot come to terms with middle-level ends, we cannot understand—despite eight books of the *Nicomachean Ethics* devoted to the subject—how, in Aristotle's account, moral virtue figures into the happiest human life. I suspect there will be a variety of ways in which middle-level ends are choiceworthy for the sake of happiness. The account of how the happy person seeks honor for the sake of happiness may not be the same as the account of how he chooses his friends for the sake of happiness. But since there is a special problem about the status of moral virtue, I will devote the rest of this discussion to understanding how it is that the activity of moral virtue can be choiceworthy for the sake of an independent good, such as theoretical contemplation, without undermining its own intrinsic desirability.

CHAPTER THREE

The Self-Sufficiency of Happiness

BEFORE I GO ON, I must confront a lingering doubt. So far I have focused on the finality, or endiness, of happiness. This can make Aristotle's conception of *eudaimonia* seem quite remote from our ordinary use of the word *happiness*. *Eudaimonia* is an end—probably a monistic good—that makes a life achieving it admirable and godlike. But Aristotle's happiness is not really so alien as that. For in addition to being the most final end of action, Aristotle claims that the human good, *eudaimonia*, is self-sufficient (*autarkes*; 1097b20), where this means that happiness is sufficient of itself to make a life desirable and lacking nothing (*NE* 1097b14–16). I take it that the self-sufficiency criterion is an intuitively plausible constraint on any account of happiness. At least, it answers to a common image of the happy and flourishing person as satisfied. The happy person may suffer occasional misfortune, but he is essentially untroubled, and certainly does not lament his lot in life. And this is so because he has happiness.

But what sort of thing must happiness be if it is to satisfy Aristotle's self-sufficiency criterion? Commentators often argue that it must be a set that embraces several, if not all, goods.[1] Indeed, even those who otherwise think Aristotle's *eudaimonia* is a monistic good have been inclined to think the self-sufficiency criterion could not be satisfied by a monistic conception of happiness.[2] After all, if happiness ensures that a life lacks nothing, then surely it must include everything worth desiring. So it might seem that my project of showing how a monistic good could be the ultimate goal of a happy life is misguided from the start. Self-sufficiency requires that happiness be an inclusive end. Thus, whether or not it is philosophically satisfying, Aristotle must believe that middle-level ends are worth choosing as constituents of an inclusive happiness.

---

[1] Ackrill [1974] 1980; Crisp 1994; Devereaux 1981; Irwin 1985b; Irwin, trans. 1985; Whiting 1986. On the other hand, Heinaman (1988), Kenny (1992), Kraut (1989, 294–300), and White (1990, 115–126) have challenged the inclusivist interpretation of self-sufficiency (though White ends up endorsing a version of inclusivism).

[2] For instance, Hardie ([1965] 1967)—who introduced the vocabulary of dominant and inclusive ends—thought that although Aristotle's official view is that happiness is a dominant (i.e., monistic) end, in the self-sufficiency criterion Aristotle has the rare insight that happiness is an inclusive end. Cooper ([1975] 1986) argues that contemplation fulfills the self-sufficiency requirement only because, in *NE* X, Aristotle identifies human nature with *noûs*. For purely noetic souls, contemplation does include all intrinsically desirable things. See Scott (1999) for a similar view about the sufficiency of contemplation in *NE* X.

This is the claim, however initially plausible it may be, that I wish to dispute. The sufficiency of *eudaimonia* does not imply inclusiveness to any degree or in any manner at all. This is because, for Aristotle, the sufficiency of happiness is the sufficiency peculiar to the most final end of a life worth choosing. In other words, happiness is sufficient by itself to make a life worth choosing *insofar* as it is an ultimate *telos* or goal of all the actions, projects, and decisions that together constitute the happy person's life. The eudaimonic good, whatever it turns out to be, is enough on its own to direct—by being the ultimate goal of practical reasoning—a life that is attractive and worthwhile. Thus, anything that could play the role of a most final end could, in principle, be self-sufficient as well. Once we see that a monistic good can play the role of the most final end, it will become clear that such a good could also be self-sufficient in Aristotle's sense. And it is, furthermore, a kind of self-sufficiency we can recognize as important for any account of happiness.

1. Self-Sufficiency: Three Problems for a Monistic Reading of *Eudaimonia*

Let me begin by quoting the relevant passage in full:

> The same result [viz., that happiness is the unqualifiedly final human good][3] seems to follow from self-sufficiency also. For the final good is thought to be self-sufficient (*autarkes*). Now, by *self-sufficient* we do not mean self-sufficient for a person on his own, for a person leading a solitary life, but also for his parents, children, wife, and in general for his friends and fellow citizens, since man is political by nature. But some limit must be set to these, since if we extend the requirement to ancestors and descendants and friends of friends, there will be an infinite series. But we must look into this later. We define the self-sufficient as that which on its own makes life worth choosing and lacking nothing; and we think happiness is a thing of this sort. (*NE* I.7 1097b6–16)

How much must an end include in order to make a life that succeeds in reaching it "lack nothing"? Clearly it need not include *everything* good. A life that succeeds in achieving fame, for example, will include whatever means are necessary for obtaining that end. So if there are instrumental means to happiness, it would be reasonable to suppose that a life with happiness also has those instrumental goods. And in fact later we find Aristotle saying that happiness needs external goods as tools (*NE* I.8 1099a29–33). Since this passage comes after his discussion of the self-sufficiency criterion, we can assume that happiness needs external goods even though it is self-

---

[3] The result for which Aristotle has just argued is that *eudaimonia* is the most final or unqualifiedly final end of human action. Since the most final end is the human good, this is as much as to say that *eudaimonia* is the human good.

sufficient.[4] So the self-sufficiency of happiness does not require that it contain the most important goods plus whatever is necessary for their existence. Rather, when judging the sufficiency of a good, we can assume that all the necessities are in place.[5]

But even though a good need not include everything valuable in order to make a life lack nothing, there are at least three reasons to think Aristotle must have thought it would have to include an awful lot more than a monistic end, such as morally virtuous activity or contemplation. First, let us suppose, for the sake of argument, that happiness is some single good or type of good among the good things of life. Even if we recall that what Aristotle is saying is that the final good *plus everything required to support its existence* must be enough to make a life happy, it is preposterous to think that Aristotle would find so spare a life most worth choosing for human beings. (God's life, of course, is composed only of contemplative activity, Meta Λ.7.) After all, Aristotle is the one who claims that good looks matter to the goodness of a life (ugly people are just barely happy), not to mention the fortunes of one's friends after one's own death, honor, children, and good family background (1099b2–4, 1101a22–b9). Are we to imagine that all these goods are *necessary* for contemplation or morally virtuous action? If not, then neither of these monistic goods is sufficient to guarantee everything the happy person ought to want. So that is one reason it appears we must read Aristotle's self-sufficiency criterion as requiring an inclusive conception of *eudaimonia*.

Here, then, we have a broadly *philosophical* reason for thinking that any theory that attributes self-sufficiency to happiness thereby commits itself to an inclusive conception. The second and third reasons are more peculiar to the interpretation of Aristotle. What are we to make of Aristotle's remarks in the self-sufficiency passage quoted above about the connection between one's happiness and one's family and friends? Is Aristotle claiming that our

---

[4] Thus while I agree with Nussbaum (1986) (and Kenny [1992, chap. 3], who follows her in this) that there is a link between the self-sufficiency of happiness and the happy person's invulnerability to changes in fortune, I do not agree that it implies that happiness can only rarely be taken away. (Aristotle believes this [NE I.10 1101a8–11] but notice that his insistence on the permanence of happiness [1100b12–13] arises in the context of his claim that the happy person needs happiness for a complete life [1100a4 ff.]; it does not arise immediately from consideration of the self-sufficiency criterion.) Rather, the implication of self-sufficiency is that once we have happiness, we will be able to fashion a life worth choosing regardless of reversals of fortune, so long as the bad luck is not too severe.

[5] The application of the self-sufficiency criterion in NE X.7 confirms this point. There, when Aristotle compares contemplation and the activity of moral virtue in terms of their self-sufficiency, he asks us to presuppose that both the person devoted to contemplation and the one devoted to moral virtue have the necessities of life. Given that they have these necessities, we should ask which end is sufficient by itself to make a life worth choosing (1177a27–b1). It is clear that in NE X.7, at least, Aristotle does not think the self-sufficient good includes everything necessary for its self-maintenance.

own possession of happiness must ensure the happiness, or at least the non-wretchedness, of those whom we care about? Or is he saying that somehow our happiness must ensure that we live in a political context, that is, with family, friends, and fellow citizens? There are problems with both of these interpretations, but if either one is correct there seems to be no way of avoiding the assumption that Aristotelian happiness actually includes all the things necessary for a social existence. Once again, it seems that happiness must be inclusive in order to meet the self-sufficiency criterion.

Finally, a third problem arises for a monistic interpretation when we situate the *Nicomachean Ethics* in its intellectual context. Aristotle's requirement that the highest good be self-sufficient is clearly inherited from Socrates' demand in the *Philebus* that it be *hikanon*, or sufficient.[6] Readers of the *Philebus* may recall, however, that Plato thought that *none* of the good things achievable by human action could play the role of the highest good precisely because no such good could be sufficient for a happy, choiceworthy life.[7] Instead, Plato claims, the good is outside the realm of particular good things; it is right or beautiful proportion. The good life, in this view, is one that partakes of goodness or right proportion by having good things distributed according to suitable ratios. This is Plato's solution, but it will not do for Aristotle. Aristotle insists that the good that *ethics* (as opposed to theology or metaphysics) seeks to understand must be something of this world, which is peculiarly the *human* good and which we can actually attain through our action (I.6 1096b31–35). The highest human good must be among the good things present in human life, and it must also be sufficient of itself to make a life choiceworthy and lacking nothing. Given that Aristotle will not permit the human good to be transcendent, and if he has learned from the *Philebus* that no single practicable good thing meets the sufficiency criterion, it may seem as if he has no choice but to suppose that the final end is inclusive of all the good things in appropriate proportion. Otherwise, how could he maintain that the self-sufficiency criterion is a legitimate one? Of course, Aristotle may have ignored the arguments of the *Philebus*. But it is not charitable to interpret the *Nicomachean Ethics* in a

---

[6] Gauthier and Jolif (1970, 49) agree. In the *Philebus* Socrates proposes that goods be tested by their ability to fulfill the same three criteria that Aristotle discusses in *NE* I.7: perfection or finality (*to teleon*), sufficiency, and choiceworthiness (20d1–10). Plato's word for sufficiency is *to hikanon* rather than Aristotle's *to autarkes*. Nevertheless, it is clear that the requirement is the same. In the *Philebus* a good is sufficient if it lacks nothing or if it makes a life that contains it lack nothing (20e5–6; 21a11, 21a14-b1). This latter is precisely the way in which Aristotle formulates the self-sufficiency criterion in the *NE*. *NE* X.2 1172b23–34, where Aristotle describes an argument that appears in the *Philebus*, provides further support for the idea that Aristotle had the *Philebus* in mind when composing the *NE*.

[7] Socrates only considers the sufficiency of pleasure and intellectual accomplishment, but the point holds for other contenders, since if a life of pleasure cannot be worth choosing, devoid as it is of reason, no other sort of life without reason could be worth choosing either.

way that reads him as adopting Plato's criterion but ignoring the lessons of the arguments in which it figures.

So there are at least three reasons for thinking that Aristotle's self-sufficient good must contain many distinct goods (or kinds of good). Nevertheless, there is something odd about arguing from the self-sufficiency of happiness to its inclusiveness. The intuition behind an inclusivist reading—that a life of only one good thing would lack so much that we value—tends in the direction of saying that *eudaimonia* is the happy life itself.[8] For if, on the basis of the self-sufficiency criterion, a monistic good is barred from being *eudaimonia* because a life containing it alone lacks so much that we value, so too a set containing many, but not all, goods would be barred because a life containing just those things would lack goods we might reasonably desire. In other words, the inclusivist intuition leads us to suppose that only the happy life is sufficient of itself for a happy life. But this answer does not respond to the question we asked in the first place. Aristotle assumes that the choiceworthy life is constituted by the pursuit of the human good. This final end or target is the organizing principle of a life worth choosing. Thus, we want to know what this principle is, not what all the elements are of the life that it shapes. We want to know what the good is that characterizes the best human life. The self-sufficiency criterion is meant to help us determine which of all the elements of a good life is the target at which we should be aiming, not to reiterate that the happy life contains many good things.

2. Self-Sufficiency as a Mark of Finality

Before we decide that a monistic good could not be self-sufficient, we should think more generally about what, in this context, self-sufficiency is. When we look again at Aristotle's formulation of the self-sufficiency criterion, we notice that the self-sufficient good is a sufficient *cause*. It "on its own *makes* (*poiei*) life worth choosing" (1097b14–15, my emphasis). But how does Aristotle imagine that happiness *makes* a life worth choosing? One model comes quickly to mind. If I have Rit dye, a white T-shirt and some rubber bands, then what I have is sufficient of itself to make a tie-dyed T-shirt. In a similar way, we might think that happiness is sufficient of itself to make life worth choosing by being (roughly) an efficient cause acting on appropriate matter. Since happiness is exceedingly valuable, any life containing it is infected by or infused with its value. But there is another possibility, suggested by Aristotle's conception of *eudaimonia* as an end. In general, the realization of a final good makes the steps leading to it successful; the subordinate steps are good because the end is good. Thus, like all final ends, the highest good

---

[8] What it says is that a certain organized package of goods suffices for a happy life. Assuming that this package will include good actions, this package is the life, but not extended in time. See Wilkes 1978, 342.

should make the chains of ends leading to it good and worth choosing by being their final cause. Since these chains of pursuit together constitute the happy life, it ought to be true, whether or not Aristotle has this in mind in the self-sufficiency passage of NE I.7, that happiness makes the happy life good by being its organizing principle.

There is some reason to think that this is in fact what Aristotle means when he says the good is self-sufficient. For instance, when he introduces the self-sufficiency criterion he treats it as a mark of the ultimate goal of action: "The same conclusion seems to follow from self-sufficiency also. For the final good is thought to be self-sufficient" (1097b7–8). This idea that self-sufficiency is linked to the endiness of the good is clearly important to Aristotle, since he concludes his discussion by saying that happiness is final *and* self-sufficient because it is the end of actions (*teleion dê ti phainetai kai autarkes hê eudaimonia tôn praktôn ousa telos*; 1097b20–21). If we see that a good is self-sufficient, that is evidence that it is most final. This fact ought to influence our understanding of what Aristotle means by the self-sufficiency of happiness.

It is not particularly surprising to discover that Aristotle thinks final ends are self-sufficient. An ultimately final end is a goal that terminates (or ought to terminate) a chain of desire. If you achieve it, there is nothing more of that chain of ends to strive for. Less final ends, on the other hand, are ones that, when wanted, logically imply that something beyond them is wanted. So, while Rit dye, white T-shirts, and rubber bands are sufficient as *tools*, as *ends* they are not sufficient at all. Once we succeed in gathering them together, we are still left wanting a tie-dyed T-shirt. Satisfaction of a desire for a less final end by its nature leaves one with more to want. Now, Aristotle believes that the human good is a final end on which *all* (or all important) chains of ends converge. Thus, we can assume that in possessing it there is nothing from *any* chain of ends left to want.

I suggest that when Aristotle says the human good is self-sufficient, he means that when a person treats that good as his most final end he develops a network of decisions, actions, and projects undertaken for its sake which, taken as a whole, is worth choosing. The realization of all (genuine) final causes makes the networks leading to them desirable. A self-sufficient final cause makes the network lack nothing *further* for its desirability. There will be nothing outside the life lived for its sake (i.e., not part of the chain of ends it determines) that the happy person would reasonably pursue. All on its own (*monoumenon*), the highest good is sufficient to be the organizing principle of a life worth choosing.[9] But if my hypothesis about how the self-

---

[9] There is evidence in NE I.6 (the only previous reference to a good's being "on its own") that *monoumenon* has this teleological sense, and does not mean 'when isolated'. "What sort of thing would we say are goods in themselves? Or would it be whatever things are pursued even on their own (*monoumena*), for example thinking and seeing and certain pleasures and

sufficient good makes a life worth choosing is correct, we can begin to understand why Aristotle ties the self-sufficiency of the good so closely to its finality. *Eudaimonia* is sufficient to cause the value of the choiceworthy life as a *final* cause. The question whether a monistic good such as contemplation is self-sufficient, therefore, is the question whether a person who does everything for the sake of that good would have a life worth choosing. Such a good would not itself need to satisfy every particular desire we may have. It will need only to make sense of—as an end—everything (including middle-level ends) we reasonably pursue. If a monistic good is suited to play this role, it will also be self-sufficient.

3. SELF-SUFFICIENCY IN THE *PHILEBUS*

Of course, as I said before, it might be thought that Plato has already shown in the *Philebus* that no monistic good is suited to play this role, for there Socrates argues that neither intellectual virtue nor pleasure is perfect (*teleon*) or sufficient (*hikanon*). However, unlike Aristotle, Plato does not suggest that the sufficiency of the good is the sufficiency it has in virtue of being an ultimate end. (In fact, it is not clear what the connection between perfection [or, in Aristotle, finality] and sufficiency is supposed to be in his account. Because Plato does not seem to have in mind the technical notion of endiness when he uses *teleon* that Aristotle implies with his *teleion*, I will translate Plato's *teleon* as 'perfect' rather than 'final'.) I suggest that if we read the *Philebus* while keeping in mind Aristotle's idea that happiness is sufficient *as a final end*, we will see why he is free to maintain (with Plato) that self-sufficiency is a criterion of the good and yet also maintain (against Plato) that *the* good is one of the humanly achievable monistic goods. In the next section I will suggest how, in fact, a monistic end might be sufficient of itself to be the ultimate end of a life worth choosing, including even the happiness of our family and friends.

The passage that concerns us (*Philebus* 20b ff.) shows Socrates and his interlocutor, Protarchus, debating the relative merits of wisdom and pleasure to be the highest good.[10] Whatever the good turns out to be, it must be sufficient.[11] Socrates suggests they test the sufficiency of their candidates by

---

honors? For even if we pursue these things on account of something else, one would consider them to be goods in themselves" (1096b16–19). Here, being pursued *monoumenon* does not simply mean being pursued in isolation. It means being pursued in isolation from some further goal, i.e., as a final end.

[10] I will refer to Socrates' candidate as either wisdom, reason, or *noûs*, though he calls it by a variety of names—usually wisdom (*phronêsis*) and intellectual virtue (*noûs*), but also knowledge (*epistêmê*), opinion (*doxa*), reasoning (*logismos*), and memory (*mnêmê*). In other words, Socrates proposes (though he later rejects) that intellectual virtue is the good.

[11] I read the trial passage as measuring most directly the sufficiency and desirability of these goods. Protarchus understands the trial to reveal most immediately that pleasure and wisdom

attending to their choiceworthiness or, rather, by attending to the choiceworthiness of the lives devoted to them alone (20e4–21a2).[12] (Socrates does not propose to consider a life that might, possibly, lack the necessities. As with Aristotle, sufficiency is tested under the assumption that the necessities of life are supplied.) Socrates' rationale must be that if we have the good, then we will also have all that we desire. If, on the other hand, we desire something more than our life provides, that shows there is something missing from the goods we possess and, thus, that they are not sufficient. So the sufficiency of the good and its choiceworthiness go hand in hand.

It is surprising how readily Protarchus, the defender of hedonism, capitulates to Socrates' argument that pleasure fails the test of sufficiency. Initially Protarchus says he would welcome the life of the greatest pleasures alone since in "taking pleasure I would have everything" (21b2). But when Socrates rejoins that without wisdom, knowledge, and right judgment, such a life would essentially be the life of a mollusk, Protarchus concedes: "Socrates, this argument has left me utterly speechless" (21d4–5).

We should begin by noticing that Socrates does not ask Protarchus what he would desire if, as it turns out *per impossibile*, he lived a life devoid of reason.[13] Protarchus cannot know what a mollusk desires, and chances are that mollusks are content, or at least not *dis*content, with their lot. Rather, Socrates asks whether Protarchus now finds the life of pleasure worth choosing. Is it a life he longs for and envies in others? Is it a life he would choose to live now if he could? Protarchus uses a conditional mood to explain his preferences—"if I lived such a life, I would have everything"—but the preferences in question are ones he has in this life. He knows what his preferences are because he already knows what sort of life he, as a hedonist, finds worth living. Thus, Protarchus must capitulate because he recognizes that the life of pleasure alone does not, in fact, correspond to the ordinary hedonist's picture of the good life.[14] Presumably, Socrates brings to his attention that

---

are not sufficient (22a9-b2). See also 60c11-d1, where Socrates reminds Protarchus that the trial showed that neither the life of pleasure nor the life of wisdom is sufficient. Irwin (1995, 333–335) interprets the trial as a test of completeness, but this depends on an inclusivist reading of *teleon* that is not, I believe, warranted by the text.

[12] Plato appears to treat these formulations interchangeably. (Indeed, he very readily switches between attributing all three marks of the good—perfection, sufficiency, and choiceworthiness—to the good and attributing them to the good life.) This shift in object of the sufficiency and choiceworthiness requirements is problematic, as we shall soon see.

[13] Gosling 1975, 182; Irwin 1995, 333. Though I agree with Gosling and Irwin that Socrates cannot be asking what a person living, e.g., the life of pleasure alone would desire, I disagree with their reading—that Socrates asks what a person taking full account of his rational nature would desire—insofar as it suggests that he asks Protarchus to suspend the hedonist point of view. There is no prima facie reason the hedonist should be particularly concerned about the fulfillment of his rational nature. If the suspension of hedonism is required for Socrates' argument, it will not be a convincing refutation of that position.

[14] Irwin (1995, 334) thinks on the basis of 21b3–4 that Socrates stipulates from the outset that the life of pleasure alone is the life that would appeal to a hedonist. It is not clear, however,

the ideal life as he has been picturing it includes not just any pleasure whatsoever but in particular the pleasures connected with our rational nature. Thus, on the hedonist's own terms, pleasure is not sufficient for a desirable life.

It is important to see that Socrates' argument against hedonism cannot be successful unless it is ad hominem in the way I have described. Let us go through Plato's argument more slowly to see why this is so. First, Socrates points out that pleasure *simpliciter* is not limited to rational creatures. Thus, since the life of pleasure alone does not specify a human life, a fortiori it does not specify the best human life. What the life of pleasure is missing, Socrates claims, is truthful intellectual activity. But *this* prize—that is, the best peculiarly *human* life—may not be one for which the hedonist cares to compete.[15] We can easily imagine a hedonist finding our rationality an unfortunate, if unavoidable, obstacle to the good that other animals more readily achieve. Thus, the first step of Socrates' argument, that intelligence is an inescapable part of human nature, and thus must be a part of the good human life, is not enough on its own to persuade the committed hedonist of the insufficiency of pleasure. We need a second step.

Protarchus will be convinced to abandon his defense of pleasure, however, once he recognizes that the life of pleasure *he* has been imagining includes as an essential ingredient the satisfaction of our rational nature. Socrates does not prove to him that he *must* think of his well-being this way; the only charitable interpretation is that Socrates shows Protarchus that he *does*. This, I take it, is Socrates' point in asking Protarchus to reconsider whether he really would enjoy the greatest pleasures in a life without reason (21b3–9). We should not think Plato has depicted a straw man in Protarchus. His capitulation is quite plausible for at least two reasons. First, it just does seem to be true that the hedonist's ideal of insatiable indulgence involves intellectual pleasures of remembering past pleasures and the consequent delight of self-congratulation, not to mention the pleasures of poetry, politics, and rhetorical display. (Mick Jagger is after all a maker of *logoi*.) A life without these pleasures of the mind is bound to seem boring to a human being. Notice that self-congratulation requires more than mere consciousness of past pleasure. One must also recognize it *as good*, indeed as *the* good, and see it as characterizing what Aristotle would call "a complete life." This understanding is the excellent activity of reason (or would be if hedonism were true). On the other hand, we feel pain in using reason poorly. People do not enjoy being wrong or stupid. Given that human nature is unavoidably rational, the hedonist must be concerned to pursue rational achievement and

---

whether Socrates is stipulating in 21b3–4 that the life of pleasure alone contains the greatest pleasures, or whether he is instead asking Protarchus to think again about whether such a life really does contain the greatest pleasures. Thus, this line is inadequate evidence for denying that Socrates makes an ad hominem argument. Furthermore, as I hope to show below, the argument can only be satisfactory if we read it as ad hominem.

[15] Notice that Philebus's position is that pleasure is the good for *all* animals (11b4–5).

avoid rational failure. These intellectual pleasures are central to the hedonist's conception of a choiceworthy life.

But second, even if the hedonist does not particularly prize the pleasure of self-congratulation, he must care about knowing that he has the good. Otherwise he will be unaware that he possesses that in virtue of which his life is satisfactory. He will, of course, be conscious in feeling pleasure, but without *noûs* he will not know that he possesses the good that makes a life fully successful. And this will be, for a human being, a significant source of dissatisfaction. In order genuinely to possess the good (conceived as pleasure), the happy person must *know* that in having pleasure he has "his all in all." But if this is so, then on purely hedonistic grounds Protarchus must admit that the life of pleasure, without *noûs*, is not the most desirable life.[16]

As I read Socrates' argument, he succeeds in showing that *noûs*, unlike many other goods, occupies a special place in the good life as the hedonist conceives it. Its value is still dependent on the value of pleasure, but it is also more than merely instrumental. Things that are valuable merely instrumentally occupy roles in the good life that could, in principle (though not necessarily in fact), be played by other things. We value them because they help us to achieve a certain end. But if that end can be achieved by other means, then the presence of the instrumental good in question will not be missed. The special value of reason, however, though derivative, is irreplaceable.[17] Thus, Protarchus must reconsider the value of reason. Pleasure alone without the aid of *noûs* is not sufficient for the life Protarchus found choiceworthy when he took up the cause of pleasure in the first place. For this reason, Protarchus concedes that pleasure is not the good.

Plato uses the same strategy for proving the insufficiency of wisdom. No one, not even Socrates, the lover of wisdom, would choose "to live in possession of *phronêsis* and *noûs* and knowledge and memory all about everything, but possessing no pleasure, neither great nor small, nor again any pain, but to be totally insensible to that sort of thing" (21d9–e2). Why not? After all, a life devoted to reason alone, absent any pleasure or pain, is the life of the gods (33b2–11). I believe we must pay special attention to Socrates' qualification that this argument has shown only that *human* reason is not the good

---

[16] Plato may think he has made an even stronger argument against the hedonist. He may think he has shown that the good hedonistic life contains as an essential element something—*noûs*—whose value is not dependent on the value of pleasure. This would not be an outrageous claim for Plato to make, but, as I said, it is not a charitable reading. Nor is it necessary, for on quite plausible and purely hedonistic grounds Socrates can show Protarchus that he must care about awareness of pleasure as good, and so about *noûs*.

[17] Thus, while I agree with Gosling (1975, 183) that "the admission that intelligence is needed ... is extracted on straight hedonistic grounds," I thank John Cooper for helping me to appreciate that the value of reason has been shown to be more than purely instrumental. Showing the mere usefulness of *noûs* would not be adequate for the goal of proving the insufficiency of pleasure, since sufficiency is tested on the assumption that the mere necessities are present.

(22c5–6). Socrates does not explain what he means, but his discussion of pleasure supplies the rationale. Pleasure and pain, according to Socrates, are essentially attendant upon processes. In particular, pain is the perceived dissolution of our harmonious state, while pleasure is the perceived restoration of the harmony (35e2–5). The gods do not experience processes, particularly not processes that imply the loss of perfection. Thus they can avoid the passions. We human beings, however, inhabit a state of flux, and so our lives are interwoven with pleasure and, unless we are lucky, with pain as well. We can infer, then, that Socrates so readily capitulates in the competition between lives because he realizes that the life of human wisdom alone is not a happy human life. The point is not merely that pleasure is an unavoidable feature of any person's life. Rather the philosopher will embrace pleasure as a genuine, though derivative, good. The philosopher loves truth and perfection, the proper objects of *noûs*, but the imperfection of human wisdom makes uninterrupted contemplation appear tedious—perhaps even painful—to a human being (as well as being impossible). Thus the human philosopher cannot maintain his perfection, or internal harmony. Under these circumstances a truly wise person will seek restorative pleasures because they attend the return to perfection. (At 30e6–7 Socrates says that play provides a rest from seriousness, recalling, perhaps, the saying of Anacharsis quoted at *NE* X.6 1176b33–77a1 that play is desirable in order that we may be serious.) Once again, it turns out that a good is disqualified from being *the* good because it is not sufficient to create the sort of life that those who pursue it admire as the best human life.

But let's be clear about what Protarchus and Socrates ought to believe at the end of the trial argument. Protarchus has not abandoned his belief that the highest single value is pleasure. Instead, he has realized that certain pleasures—intellectual pleasures—are indispensable to a life worth choosing for a human hedonist. Furthermore, without intellect the person living the life of pleasure could not know he had the good. So Protarchus must reevaluate the importance of reason. Nevertheless, the value of reason at this stage of the argument is still derivative. Protarchus need not forgo his hedonism in any practical sense because the trial has left unchallenged the claim that the value of other goods is explained and limited by the value of pleasure. Indeed, I have argued that Socrates' argument is persuasive precisely because it leaves untouched the hedonist's claim that pleasure is the principle for choosing all other goods. Likewise, there is reason to think that Socrates admits pleasure as only instrumentally valuable for the human philosopher. Thus, at the conclusion of the trial, Socrates and Protarchus still disagree about the relative value of pleasure and wisdom. "For one of us may want to give credit (*aitiômetha*) for the combined life to reason, making it responsible, the other to pleasure" (22d1–2; Frede's [1993] trans.). This motivates the next portion of the dialogue in which pleasure and wisdom contest for second prize as the cause (*aition*) of the good mixture.

It is important to see that from an Aristotelian perspective, Socrates' argument so far does not settle the issue of whether a monistic, humanly achievable good could be *the* good. Socrates has shown that a life worth choosing must contain more than a monistic good. Aristotle would agree. But we Aristotelians want to know whether either pleasure or wisdom is sufficient to make a full life of this sort worth choosing by being its organizing principle. This is the question Socrates addresses when he considers which good wins second prize as cause of the good life. But an interesting thing happens in this passage (27c–31b). As I have described the argument so far, Protarchus believes that pleasure deserves second prize (over *noûs*) because he continues to think it is responsible for the goodness of the life and every valuable thing in it. It is the organizing principle of a happy life in this particular sense: It is that good by pursuing which we guide the pursuit and use of all other goods. According to Protarchus, pleasure—although not everything we need to satisfy our desires—is more important than the others because it determines their inclusion and place in the good life. In other words, to use Aristotelian terminology, Socrates and Protarchus ought to be prepared to give second prize to the final cause of the good life.[18] However, Socrates goes on to talk about the organizing principle as if it were in effect an *efficient* cause. (Plato does not distinguish the four kinds of causation as Aristotle later does.) Indeed, he even goes so far as to call it a demiurge (27b1) and declares that wisdom is a cause of this sort (30d10–e1). But from an Aristotelian point of view one can not help but notice that when *noûs* sets about determining the mixture of goods in the good life, it does so as what Aristotle would call a final cause. For example, reason rejects all the intense pleasures dear to a hedonist because they are an impediment to thought (63d5).[19]

As I have already pointed out, Aristotle is careful to link the self-sufficiency of *eudaimonia* to its finality and to say that they are both features of the good as an end in practical reasoning. It is not necessary that a most final end contain everything that is desirable. What is required is that it explain the desirability of everything else we (correctly) pursue and not lead us to desire something beyond it. But Plato's trial of lives and his subsequent discussion of the competition for second prize leave untouched the sufficiency of pleasure and wisdom to do that. It is worth noting in this regard that Plato himself seems uncertain what the sufficient good is supposed to be sufficient for. Sometimes he suggests that pleasure or wisdom must themselves satisfy all our desires, while on other occasions he says it is the life of

---

[18] Notice that Aristotle says the good makes (*poiei*) a life worth choosing (*NE* 1097b15), suggesting his willingness to think of it as a sort of making cause. Plato awards second prize to the agent (*to poioun*) of the mixed life that alone is worth choosing (26e6–9).

[19] Reason also admits the pure pleasures (e.g., the pleasure of looking at a patch of pure white) because they are akin (*oikeias*) to reason (63e3–4). Plato may mean that these pleasures and reason share a similar form, but my discussion in the next chapter will show that Aristotle might be willing to think of this as an instance of final causation by approximation.

pleasure or wisdom that must be fully satisfactory (20d4, 22a9–b2). No doubt this is because Plato thinks a life is fully satisfactory on account of its containing a good that is fully satisfactory (22b3–6). But according to Aristotle, the eudaimonic good makes a life happy not simply by being contained in it but by being the target at which the life successfully aims. Thus he never says the self-sufficient good itself lacks nothing desirable. Rather he says the self-sufficient good makes *life* worth choosing and lacking nothing.

If we read the *Philebus* with Aristotle's conception of the good as a final end in mind, Socrates' trial of lives does not show that neither *noûs* nor pleasure could be the good. For it does not test the sufficiency of pleasure and *noûs* to be final ends of lives worth choosing. Aristotle would agree with Plato that such lives have the right proportion of the various goods. But the idea of right proportion itself, which all good things share, will be of very little practical benefit to someone who is trying to figure out how to realize that proportion in his life (cf. 1097a8–11, where Aristotle argues that the Form of the Good is practically useless). Instead he will determine the appropriate balance of goods by looking to the supremely valuable good that he treats as his final end. For instance, if the agent's final end is *noûs*, he may, like the personified *noûs* of the *Philebus* (63c5–e7), pursue pure pleasures as an aid to contemplation but avoid those sensual pleasures that tend to distract him from the business of life. Thus the peculiar way in which Aristotle conceives of *eudaimonia* as causing the goodness of the happy life frees him to accept Plato's sufficiency criterion without giving up his assumption that there is a monistic good achievable by human action that will satisfy it.

4. THE SELF-SUFFICIENCY OF MONISTIC GOODS

For Aristotle, then, *eudaimonia* causes the goodness of the happy life as a final cause. Thus, when we deliberate about whether one of the contenders for the title of happiness is sufficient by itself for a good life, a lot will hang on what ways the final good can operate as final. For a good will be self-sufficient only if all of or most of the things we are already committed to as desirable are choiceworthy for the sake of that good in one way or another. In the next chapter I will argue that, according to Aristotle, goods may be teleologically subordinated to happiness in more ways than recent scholarship has tended to emphasize, but let me summarize what I have in mind. First of all, anything that is a means to the final end (the highest good) is worth choosing for its sake; thus all instrumental goods will appear in the network of ends that constitutes a happy life.[20] A good can also be chosen for the sake of happiness when it instantiates or partially constitutes it. These

---

[20] Or at least they *may* appear in the happy life. If two goods are instruments to the same goal, only one will be necessary.

ways of choosing one good for the sake of another are familiar. But I will argue that Aristotle also recognizes *approximation* as a teleological relation. If our circumstances do not allow us to achieve our highest end directly, we may act for its sake by approximating it. Thus any good that is an approximation of the highest will find a place in the network of ends chosen for the sake of happiness. (Some approximations are middle-level ends—choiceworthy for the sake of the end they approximate and choiceworthy for their own sakes in virtue of capturing by approximation the intrinsic value of the highest good.) So we could add approximations to instruments and constituents in the list of things choiceworthy for the sake of a higher end. Furthermore, it may be that one good is choiceworthy for the sake of another when it is the proper ornament to it.[21] Thus, if physical beauty is a proper ornament to philosophy, then a beauty regimen (or at least *some* attention to appearance) will be a part of the contemplative life (*NE* I.8 1099b2–3). In any form of teleological dependence the final good explains in some sense why a person does what he does in the way that he does it; because the happy person treats the highest good as most final, these subordinate goods find a place in his life. What I hope these considerations suggest is that a monistic human good may actually be sufficient to produce (as a final cause) a life containing a much richer variety of pursuits than Plato's depiction of such monistically oriented lives in the *Philebus* suggested. It may be more plausible, then, to suppose that a monistic conception of happiness could succeed in shaping a genuinely happy life, one that lacks nothing essential to a life's desirability. Once again we can refine further what the self-sufficiency requirement in the *Nicomachean Ethics* demands: If there are features of the good life—the life that is choiceworthy for the happy agent—that cannot be explained either as instruments to, ornaments for, or instantiations of, or instantiations-by-approximation of a candidate for the final good, then that candidate is not sufficient of itself for the happy life, so that good is not *eudaimonia*.

We may still wonder, however, whether a monistic conception of the good could really be self-sufficient. For Aristotle says that a self-sufficient end is enough by itself to make a life choiceworthy and *lacking in nothing*. The fact that *eudaimonia* functions as a final end may show that a wide variety of goods *could* be properly introduced into the happy life (i.e., with appropriate reference to their being for the sake of the final good), but it does not guarantee that they *will* be. Final causes do not carry this kind of security. For instance, the final good may direct us to seize honor when the opportunity arises, but it cannot ensure that such a chance ever will arise. If, however,

---

[21] The idea of ornamentation was inspired by my reading of Broadie (1991, 412–419), though I use it in precisely the opposite way. In her reading, the complete good—i.e., the most central activity of the good life, viz., contemplation—*celebrates* the rest of the happy life. As such it is a use of leisure. My idea here is that other activities may celebrate or ornament the most central one and thus be choiceworthy for its sake.

the final good can direct us to take it, that must be because honor is valuable from the point of view of the final good. Thus the fact that the final good cannot ensure the presence of honor shows that it is not sufficient of itself to provide everything someone who aspires to the happy life would want. It appears then that a life devoted to a single good might well be lacking in something. Or so the objection would go.

Insofar as this objection describes the Aristotelian happy person, as I understand him, as possibly having more to wish for, it describes my position correctly. But this is no criticism of the position. For it seems clear that Aristotle imagines happy lives as varying in quality. A happy life may contain many small misfortunes (and perhaps a few big ones, too). These misfortunes will not make a person's life less happy, Aristotle claims, but they will still be genuine misfortunes, and it is reasonable to suppose that the happy person would have preferred to avoid them. Thus, insofar as he misses out on good fortune, the happy person's life may be said to lack something.[22] Conversely many great strokes of good fortune will make a happy life more blessed (1100b25–26, and really all of I.10). Furthermore, in book X when Aristotle applies the self-sufficiency criterion to contemplation, he specifically says that though the happy contemplator does not need fellow workers, it would be better for him to have them. It is no wonder that Aristotle believes that happy lives are improvable. For if we are to make sense of the happy person's deliberating and making decisions and indeed acting at all, we must assume there are things that he values but does not yet possess. There is no guarantee, however, that anyone will achieve the intermediate goals of action, for deliberation operates in the sphere of uncertainty where we are to a certain extent at the mercy of fortune. Thus the very nature of the human practical situation entails that the happy person will not at a particular moment, and may never, have everything he could wish for.

[22] In *NE* I.10 Aristotle allows the possibility that someone has the highest good—activity of virtue—but is so unfortunate that he is not happy. This might be taken to suggest that activity of virtue is not by itself *eudaimonia*, since it is not by itself sufficient to make a life choiceworthy and lacking nothing. Instead, in this reading, activity of virtue is the most important element of a set of goods which together constitute happiness; that is the point of Aristotle's saying that *eudaimonia* is activity of virtue "in a complete life" (*NE* I.7 1098a18). I have two responses to this objection, which I will make in brief: (1) Aristotle's claim that we must possess happiness "in a complete life" in order to be happy stipulates that the happy life must last a certain length of time, not that it needs a complete set of the goods of fortune. This is clear when Aristotle draws out the implications of this requirement at *NE* I.9 1100a2–9. A child cannot be happy, strictly speaking, because he has not engaged in virtuous activity for a complete span of time, which happiness requires. (2) We are not required to suppose that misfortune destroys happiness by directly removing constituents of happiness. Misfortune may destroy happiness by making it impossible to exercise the virtues as the happy person would. In other words, misfortune may prevent the philosopher from exercising *sophia* or the *politikos* from exercising moral virtue on a grand scale (see chapter 8, below). (Of course, the morally virtuous person can never have virtuous action entirely taken from him; 1100b34–1101a3.) Thus, we are not required by anything Aristotle says on this score to suppose that the goods of fortune are constituents of *eudaimonia*.

When Aristotle says self-sufficiency makes a life lacking in nothing, he means it lacks nothing for being happy (as opposed to lacking nothing that the person could desire). And, as we saw, that means it will seem worth living to a person who values above all others the final good characterizing that life. So if, for example, contemplation is *eudaimonia*, it will ensure that all lives in which contemplation is present and is the final good will be choiceworthy philosophical lives. Or if honor is self-sufficient *eudaimonia*, it will justify as a final end the pursuit of everything essential to a desirable honor-loving life. (Of course, the pursuit of honor cannot explain the desire to *be* just and courageous instead of merely seeming to be. It is precisely because the political ideal lionizes *deserved* honor that Aristotle decides that honor is not really the highest good of the political life [I.5 1095b22–30].) Happiness is sufficient of itself to make a life worth living, but it does not follow from this that happiness, or *eudaimonia*, is also sufficient to make a life the best we could hope for. Happiness in the sublunary world cannot achieve the degree of perfection found in the lives of the gods. Thus, Aristotle's self-sufficiency criterion does not require that *eudaimonia* include everything a person might reasonably desire. We can see, then, that the proper interpretation of the self-sufficiency criterion does not support an inclusivist interpretation of *eudaimonia*.

There is one final problem I mentioned earlier that perhaps we are now in a position to answer. I noted that if *eudaimonia* is a monistic end, it is hard to make sense of this claim: "By self-sufficient we do not mean self-sufficient for a person on his own, for a person leading a solitary life, but also for his parents, children, wife, and in general for his friends and fellow citizens, since man is political by nature" (1097b8–11). We would like to say that what Aristotle means is that *eudaimonia* must be sufficient for someone living in a political context, but what Aristotle says is that it must be sufficient for the members of our political context.[23] This cannot simply be a slip-up or a poetic way of speaking, for Aristotle goes on to say that we must limit at some point the friends and loved ones who will be included, since otherwise we would include an infinity into happiness.

I suggest that Aristotle is saying that the good that is happiness must be sufficient to yield a life that expresses our human, political nature.[24] But this does not mean simply that the life must be compatible with our living in communities; nor does it mean only that the instrumental means to our final end will be provided by our communities. For in addition to these things, a good life for a political creature includes appropriate concern for one's fam-

---

[23] Thus Irwin sometimes says, on the basis of this passage, that happiness must include friendship and the virtues "expressed in relations with other people and in political community" (1981, 215), and at other times that "it must include the happiness of family, friends, and fellow citizens" (1985b, 93).

[24] In a similar way Socrates showed Protarchus that any analysis of the human good must take into account our rational nature. The hedonist does not want the life of a mollusk.

ily, friends, and neighbors. Thus, the highest good must make sense of and appropriately order our concern for the happiness of our loved ones and our desire to seek happiness in common with them. The final good must also make sense of our caring about the lives of our ancestors and doing what is necessary to honor them (or to live them down, as the case may be). It must also make sense of our wanting to have children and grandchildren. (It is relatively easy to see how valuing moral virtue as the highest good could direct this sort of behavior. After all, friendship is a kind of virtue itself. It is a challenge for anyone who wants to argue that contemplation is the human good to explain how it is sufficient for a *political* life. I take this question up in the final chapter.)

I have argued that Aristotle's criterion of self-sufficiency is compatible with conceiving of happiness as a monistic good. That is because the self-sufficiency appropriate to happiness is the sufficiency it has of itself to be the ultimate end of a network of pursuits that is worth choosing. The self-sufficient good causes the happy life to lack nothing, in the sense that the successful pursuit of it leaves nothing beyond it (teleologically) that the happy person might reasonably desire. If we broaden our understanding of the ways in which we may choose one thing for the sake of an end, we see that it is at least possible that a monistic good could play the role of a self-sufficient final end. Nothing I have said so far *prevents* an inclusive conception of *eudaimonia* from meeting the self-sufficiency criterion. But it does show that the self-sufficiency criterion does not support, much less require, an inclusive interpretation of Aristotle's concept of *eudaimonia*.

5. Choiceworthiness and Self-Sufficiency

So far I have argued that, if we understand the self-sufficiency of the good to be its self-sufficiency as the final end of a life worth choosing, the three problems that seem to face a monistic interpretation of *eudaimonia* can be resolved. We can understand (1) how Aristotle could borrow the self-sufficiency criterion from the *Philebus* without drawing Plato's conclusion that no practicable good could be *the* good; (2) how a monistic good could be sufficient to make a life "lack nothing"; and (3) what Aristotle means by saying that the good is sufficient for family and friends. But the lines immediately following the self-sufficiency criterion (1097b16–20) might seem to pose a problem for my interpretation. There Aristotle claims that happiness is most choiceworthy of all things "not being counted together (*mê sunarithmoumenê*)."[25] This gloss is obscure, but it is frequently believed to require

---

[25] Superlative choiceworthiness is probably not a third criterion, contra Hardie ([1965] 1967), since Aristotle does not mention it again at the summing up of the formal criteria (1097b20). But though choiceworthiness is not introduced as a third criterion, neither is it reducible to or merely an elaboration of the self-sufficiency criterion, contra Whiting 1986, 74.

an inclusivist conception of happiness. In this interpretation the reason happiness cannot be "counted together" with other goods—and so the reason it is most choiceworthy—is also the same reason it is self-sufficient. What is this reason? It is, allegedly, that happiness includes all intrinsically good things. But this interpretation of the superlative choiceworthiness of happiness is incorrect. Whatever we decide happiness is, there is no reason in principle why we cannot count it together with other goods. Rather, what Aristotle is saying, I will argue, is that *eudaimonia* is most choiceworthy in a special sense of most choiceworthy that is not discovered by counting goods together. Namely (and not surprisingly at this point), *eudaimonia* is most choiceworthy as being the ultimate or final object of desire.[26] Since *eudaimonia* has this property, that is reason to think it is sufficient by itself to be the final end of a life worth choosing.

Let me begin by giving a literal rendering of the choiceworthiness passage:

> Moreover, happiness is the most choiceworthy [good], not being counted together (*sunarithmoumenên*)—and it's clear that if it were/is counted together[27] it would be/is more choiceworthy with the least of goods; for the thing added is an excess of goods, and the greater amount of goods is always more choiceworthy. (1097b16–20)

Notice that I leave the precise interpretation of the participle *sunarithmoumenên* ambiguous between the causal and conditional senses. The Greek sentence in question could mean either of the following:

1. Moreover, we think that happiness is the most choiceworthy of all goods *since* it is not counted together.
2. Moreover, we think happiness is the most choiceworthy of all goods, *provided that/when/assuming that* it is not counted together.

On reading (1) Aristotle is saying the reason happiness turns out to be the most choiceworthy good is that it cannot, for some reason, be counted together with other goods. As I mentioned before, (1) raises the question why happiness cannot be so counted. The need to discover an answer inspires an inclusivist response: It is something about the all-encompassing nature of happiness that bars this possibility.[28]

Self-sufficiency says that happiness makes a life choiceworthy, not that *it* is most choiceworthy. Furthermore, the entire discussion of self-sufficiency is directed toward showing that happiness is unqualifiedly final. In my interpretation, choiceworthiness is linked both to self-sufficiency and to finality.

[26] See Lawrence (1997) for a somewhat different argument to the same conclusion.

[27] I agree with Heinaman (1988, 42 n. 29) that, *pace* Cooper (1981) and Whiting (1986), a monistic-end reading of this passage does not require us to translate this instance of *sunarithmoumenên* as an indicative. An indicative translation does make the monistic end's interpretation more evident, however.

[28] And notice that *eudaimonia* on this account really does need to encompass *all* goods worth choosing for their own sakes, such as honor and pleasure, as well as moral and intellectual

A lot hinges, then, on the meaning of the rather obscure technical term *counting together*. How does one count things together? And what is it about counting together that makes goods so counted amenable to improvement?

Rhetoric I.7 1363b18–21 might suggest that *sunarithmoumenê* means 'aggregated'.[29] Here Aristotle wants to argue that a larger set of goods is better than a smaller set, provided the smaller set is included in the larger set. "It's necessary that the more is a greater good than the one and the fewer, the one and the fewer being counted together (*sunarithmoumenou*), for [the more] surpasses and [the fewer] being contained is surpassed." It seems clear that, in this passage, "counting together" means, or at least implies, aggregation.

But I do not think 'aggregated' can be what this word means in our passage in the *Nicomachean Ethics*. There, Aristotle asks us to weigh the desirability of happiness *after* it has been *sunarithmoumenê* (counted together). His argument seems to be that once a good is counted together, it can be improved by the aggregation of other goods. The consequence is that *sunarithmoumenê eudaimonia* is not the best thing. But for this argument to make sense, *sunarithmoumenê eudaimonia* cannot be happiness plus other things. It must be happiness considered as aggregatable, not aggregated.

I suggest that *sunarithmoumenê* means 'treated as a member of a set of goods.'[30] (Thus in the passage from the *Rhetoric* above, Aristotle says a larger set is better than a smaller set, provided the smaller set is counted together with, i.e., treated as a member of, the larger set.) Nevertheless, we should notice that being counted together with other goods implies that a good can be aggregated with them. It also implies that we can rank or compare it with the other goods in terms of its desirability.

Is there any reason that *eudaimonia* as an inclusive end could not be aggregated or ranked with, and thus not counted together with, other goods? If *eudaimonia* is an all-inclusive end, it could not be aggregated with other goods, for there would be no difference between the all-inclusive set and that set plus something further. But it is unlikely that Aristotle thinks *eudaimonia* cannot be "counted together" for this reason; Aristotle does not think of happiness as *all*-inclusive. A little later in the *Nicomachean Ethics* he is happy to talk about adding external prosperity to happiness. "And these [virtuous activities], or the one of them that is the best, we say is happiness. But nevertheless it will need external goods in addition" (*prosdeomenê*; I.8 1099a29–32). So the impossibility of counting together happiness does not appear to follow from its being impossible to add anything to an all-inclusive set.

---

virtue. A smaller set will not do since, in an inclusivist interpretation, Aristotle is saying that *eudaimonia* cannot be counted together because it cannot be improved. Unless *eudaimonia* contains *all* intrinsically valuable goods, it could surely be improved (Heinaman 1988, 47–49). See Whiting (1986, 74 n. 12) for a response to this problem.

[29] Lawrence (1997, 32 n. 1) translates in this way, depending in part on this passage.

[30] This is, I take it, the sense Ross's "counted as one good thing among others" is meant to convey.

Another possibility is that we cannot count an inclusive happiness together with other goods because we cannot rank it in comparison to those goods. If we rank a composite good with its constituents we end up counting the constituents twice when we rank the composite good as number one. Thus the composite good ends up being better than itself, since it is better than all the goods below it in the ranking.[31] This interpretation claims support from the *Magna Moralia*. Aristotle is quite clear in MM 1184a14–25 that *eudaimonia* is a set containing many goods.[32] When discussing the choiceworthiness of happiness he says, "if, in looking for the best, you count it together also, it will be better than itself, because it is the best thing"—a result he finds absurd. We will return to the *Magna Moralia* in a moment, but notice that if this is the correct explanation of what is happening in the *Nicomachean Ethics*, the choiceworthiness passage begins to look quite mysterious. Aristotle tells us, in this interpretation, that we cannot rank *eudaimonia* or compare its desirability to that of other goods because it is a set. But why should Aristotle think it is impossible to rank an inclusive set as more desirable than its members on their own, particularly when elsewhere he says that sets of goods are more choiceworthy than each of the constituents on its own (*NE* X.2 1172b26–28)? I suggest that even when Aristotle conceives of happiness as a set of goods, as he does in the *Magna Moralia*, the absurdity of ranking happiness along with other goods has nothing to do with its inclusivity.

When we rank goods in terms of choiceworthiness, we rank them in terms of their importance for achieving some goal. So, for example, if someone asked me to rank the elements of a good breakfast, I would put coffee at the top (since a breakfast without coffee cannot possibly satisfy), and after that eggs, and then perhaps juice, close behind which would be sausage, bacon, and biscuits. What foods are on the list and what ranking they receive depends on my understanding of what a good breakfast is like. I rank with an eye not only to the constituents of a breakfast but also to my understanding of what a breakfast is in essence, so to speak. (A breakfast is supposed to get you going, thus it's not breakfast without coffee.) In other words, the *telos* effects the ranking. Or consider the relationship between health and "healthy" things (i.e., producers and instances of health), as Aristotle does in

---

[31] White (1990, 119–120) suggests this possibility, although he rejects it as a problem for counting an inclusive happiness together with other goods since, in any plausible interpretation, *eudaimonia* does not include *all* good things. Thus, he thinks, there is no reason a plausible inclusive happiness could not be counted together, improved, and found less desirable than the new, larger set.

[32] The authorship of the *MM* is disputed (see Cooper [(1973) 1999] and Rowe [1975] for discussion), however I will write as if Aristotle wrote it. If he did not, then we can ignore the problems it seems to pose for my argument. If he did, then I must explain why the inclusivity of the good in the *MM* does not account for its not being proper to seek it by counting it together.

the *Magna Moralia* in order to explain the absurdity of ranking *eudaimonia*. Surely it *is* absurd to consider health as one good among many when ranking healthy things. To do so is to make a category mistake. For how will you rank health along with other healthy things? Surely by appealing to the standard of health itself.[33] My suggestion, then, is that in the *Nicomachean Ethics* and the *Magna Moralia* the highest good is not ranked with other goods chosen for its sake precisely because it is the final good. Final goods are criteria for ranking other goods. As such they cannot be ranked along with the subordinate goods. Consequently, final goods cannot be better than the goods subordinate to them in the ranking sense. Their superiority is of a different order.[34] Thus the eudaimonic good considered as a final end cannot be counted together with other goods because it cannot be ranked alongside them.

This does not mean, however, that there is no other perspective from which we *could* rank the highest good, so long as we are not considering it *qua* final end. What Aristotle says in the *Nicomachean Ethics* is that the good that turns out to be *eudaimonia* is not most choiceworthy *in the sense of* being number one in a ranking. Again I repeat, what Aristotle says is silent about whether we could rank whatever turns out to be the final good. His point in the *Nicomachean Ethics* is simply that it is not most choiceworthy *in this way*.

Why is that so? Let us return to my example above. I said that coffee is the most important ingredient in a good breakfast. In virtue of that, coffee is the most choiceworthy of all breakfast foods. But its superiority is not absolute, for coffee plus scrambled eggs would be better than coffee alone. This would be true for the same reason that coffee is most choiceworthy when we rank goods singly: Coffee plus eggs achieves the final end of an energizing breakfast more perfectly than does coffee alone. So, as Aristotle says, in any rank ordering of goods, the highest can always be improved by the addition of even the least important of goods in the ranking. "It's clear that, if [*eudaimonia*] were 'counted together,' it would be more choiceworthy with the least of goods; for the thing added is a surplus of goods, and of goods, the greater is always more choiceworthy" (1097b17–20). So if there

---

[33] The lesson the *MM* asks us to glean from this, I believe, is that we should not look for the best good by ranking all goods to see which is the most desirable. For if the good is the standard, it is better than all the goods it ranks. If you put the good itself as the topmost item on the ranked list, you will imply that it (as standard) is better than itself (as top item on the list).

Topics 117a18–21 suggests a similar point about the aggregation of goods. In opposition to those who argue that two goods are better than one, Aristotle says that one may argue that this principle does not hold when one of the goods is choiceworthy for the sake of the other, as for example becoming healthy and health itself.

[34] Lawrence (1997) makes a similar point, although he takes it to be an indication that *eudaimonia* cannot be aggregated with other goods. I agree with him if we take *eudaimonia* to be the name of the good as it plays its role as standard for ranking. But I do not agree if Lawrence means that instances of the eudaimonic good can never be ranked.

is a ranking in which the eudaimonic good came first, it can still be improved by the addition of some other good in the ranking. This fact would not show that the eudaimonic good was not, in fact, *eudaimonia*. Instead it shows that *eudaimonia* is not most choiceworthy in this way.[35] If *eudaimonia* is most choiceworthy, it is so in some other way. But we already know what that way is. *Eudaimonia* is most choiceworthy because it is the final end and organizing principle of the good life. And in that sense it is impossible for anything to be more choiceworthy, for it is impossible for something to be a more final object of choice than the final good itself.

Failure to distinguish the two kinds of choiceworthiness—the ranking sense and the final or absolute sense—and their connection to the self-sufficiency criterion is what causes Plato in the *Philebus* to deny that any single human good could be the good. Socrates thinks that because neither a life

---

[35] Some commentators (Crisp 1994; Devereaux 1981; Kraut 1989; Scott 1999) think that, according to Aristotle, whatever the eudaimonic good turns out to be, it is not the kind of thing that could be improved in any way. They cite as their evidence *NE* X.2, where Aristotle says "the good does not become more choiceworthy by the addition of anything. And it is clear that no other thing which becomes more choiceworthy by the addition of some other good thing could be the good" (1172b31–34). They claim that Aristotle rules out the possibility that anything improvable in any way could be the good. There are reasons to doubt this interpretation, however. Let us begin at 1172b23. Aristotle is trying to show that one of the arguments Eudoxus gives in favor of hedonism is invalid. Eudoxus claims that since pleasure improves everything, pleasure is the good. But, Aristotle says, this consideration only shows that pleasure is *one* of the goods (1172b26–27); it does not show that it is *the* good, "for *everything* is more choiceworthy with another good than on its own" (1172b27–28, my emphasis). Notice that Aristotle says here that there is no good thing that cannot be improved. Then, from 1172b28–34, Aristotle shows that the same sort of consideration that Eudoxus brings to bear in favor of hedonism is used by Plato to argue against hedonism. In the *Philebus*, as we have seen, Socrates argues that since pleasure can be improved by intellectual virtue, pleasure is not the good. Plato's reason is that "*the* good does not become more choiceworthy by the addition of anything else" (1172b31–32). Now, in a sense Aristotle accepts this principle of the nonimprovability of the good. (*Pace* Heinaman [1988, 43], the principle does not contradict 1172b27–28, where Aristotle says that all goods can be improved. A good—including an instance of the eudaimonic good—can always be improved, but *the* good cannot.) But it is important to see that he does not accept the use Plato makes of it in the *Philebus*. The tenor of X.2–5 makes it clear that Aristotle does not think that anyone (and in particular, Plato) has adequately refuted hedonism. (We do not get Aristotle's argument against hedonism until *NE* X.6.) Although this is certainly debatable, I believe that at 1172b34–35 Aristotle expresses his frustration with Plato's use of the nonimprovability principle. Plato concludes from the principle (I believe Aristotle is still reporting here) that "no other good that becomes more choiceworthy with one of the intrinsically valuable things could be *the* good" (1172b32–34). Then Aristotle asks *in propria persona*, "So what is something of this sort, in which we also can participate? For this is the sort of thing we are seeking" (1172b34–35). In other words, Aristotle is rejecting Plato's conclusion on grounds familiar from *NE* I.6: The human good must be something human beings can achieve by human action (Heinaman 1988, 44). As I have argued above, Aristotle accepts that the good cannot be improved so long as we consider it as a standard for ranking goods and not as a member of a ranking. See pp. 202–203 for further discussion of this passage.

of *noûs* alone nor a life of pleasure alone is the most choiceworthy life—in the ranking sense—neither of these goods is itself the most choiceworthy good. Aristotle, on the other hand, can think that a good is sufficient to make a life worth choosing and still think that that it can be improved when considered as ranked number one. Indeed a person's valuing the final end as supreme (i.e., most choiceworthy in the absolute sense) explains his wanting other goods in his happy life in addition to instances of the eudaimonic good.[36] The improvability of the final good when considered as one good among many does not imply that it is not most choiceworthy; it only shows that it is not most choiceworthy rankwise. Happiness is self-sufficient because it is a final good, and as a final good it provides for (by making it rational to pursue) the presence of many goods that make a life more choiceworthy (rankwise) than it would be with the final good alone. It is because *eudaimonia* plays this special role that it is most choiceworthy absolutely, not merely comparatively.

6. Self-Sufficient Happiness

I have argued that the self-sufficient good is sufficient of itself to be the final end of a life that lacks nothing essential to its desirability. I have intended to emphasize that the self-sufficiency of the highest good depends on its being the end of the happy life, but we must still leave room for a genuine distinction between the self-sufficiency criterion and the finality criterion. The finality criterion describes where the human good fits in the chain of ends whose pursuit constitutes the happy life. We could say that the finality criterion specifies how happiness figures in excellent practical reasoning. The self-sufficiency criterion, on the other hand, describes the relationship between the highest good and the satisfaction the happy person finds in the network of ends organized for its sake. In other words, the self-sufficiency criterion treats the desirability of the happy life as a whole when *eudaimonia* is successfully pursued as a most final end.

But what does it really mean to think of happiness as self-sufficient in this way? Scholarly disputes about Aristotle's self-sufficiency criterion can sometimes seem ingenious but remote from any legitimate, intuitive constraint on a theory of happiness. As I mentioned at the beginning of this chapter, however, it is important to see that something we might want to call self-sufficiency is integral to an ordinary ideal of happiness. The state of being happy is closely associated for us with being deeply satisfied. (No doubt this is why, these days, happiness is virtually synonymous with a certain feeling of contentment and pleasure.) Furthermore, though perhaps this

---

[36] Zena Hitz has reminded me that Plato would agree with Aristotle that the highest good should be the measure of other goods.

intuition is less widespread, there is a sense that the happy person is untroubled by fears that chance could destroy his well-being. The happy person is self-sufficient, not necessarily in the sense of being free of the need for the help of others, but in the sense that he is aware of and confident in his grasp of the things that make his life worth choosing (rather than merely worth enduring). This confidence is part of the happy person's satisfaction. Now even if we accept that, for Aristotle, *eudaimonia* is the *telos* of the happy life and not the property that qualifies a life when it is successful in reaching this *telos*, it still seems that if Aristotle is talking about *happiness* at all, *eudaimonia* ought to give the person who has it this confidence and contentment that we might choose to call self-sufficiency. Is there any reason to think that, by having a monistic good sufficient of itself to be the final end of a good life, a person will be confident and contented in the right way? In other words, does Aristotle's self-sufficiency criterion in my interpretation correspond to our intuitive one?

In one way of thinking about our intuitive notion of self-sufficiency, it seems to me that Aristotle's criterion does not correspond. We might have in mind that the happy person is confident that his life does and always will contain a sufficiency of desirable experiences. For happiness to be self-sufficient in this way, it would have to be an inclusive end,[37] and I have argued that Aristotle's conception of self-sufficiency does not require this. But notice that if we think happiness is sufficient to ensure the choiceworthiness of a life by containing everything a person might reasonably desire, then, although happiness will certainly be worth pursuing, it is unlikely that it will ever be achieved. Or even if it is achieved, it is unlikely that a person could be confident that he possessed it. What mortal person, subject to bad luck, could be sure that he had firmly in his grasp everything that he would want, or even the means to get it? The inclusivist interpretation of the self-sufficiency criterion makes Aristotelian happiness something beyond human reach and a rather foolish thing to spend much time seeking.

But our intuitive sense that the happy person is self-sufficient might refer not to his sufficiency as a subject of experience but to his sufficiency as an agent. In other words, we might think that what the happy person has is not the assurance that he will always have what he desires but the confidence that, no matter what life may bring, he will be able to make something of it that is worth choosing. If this is an intuitive picture of happiness, then I believe Aristotle's self-sufficiency criterion answers to it. For his criterion says the good must be sufficient to fashion a life that is worth choosing for someone who is successful in pursuing it as his ultimate end. In this interpretation, the happy person is confident because he knows that no mat-

---

[37] Unless, of course, we limit our desires to a single object. The reduction of desires as a route to happy sufficiency was a theme in antiquity (Plato, *Gorgias* 492d5–494a5; Epicurus, *Letter to Menoeceus* 130–131; Epictetus, *Encheiridion* 2), but it is absent from the *NE*.

ter what turns fortune may bring, he will be able to react in a way that is worth choosing. As the happy person navigates life's ups and downs, he keeps his eye firmly on the target of happiness. And because happiness is sufficient to be the most final end of a life worth living, the happy person can rest assured that no matter what he does, so long as he does it (well) for the sake of happiness and so long as his misfortunes are not so grave as to deprive him of the ability to realize the eudaimonic good at all, his life will be good.[38] In my interpretation, the self-sufficiency of happiness gives the happy person practical confidence. And although that is a more modest benefit than the inclusivist's self-sufficient good would bring, it is a benefit that ought to be precious to the practically rational creatures we are. Furthermore, it seems reasonable to think we may achieve it.

[38] Note that I am not suggesting that a life is happy if it is *merely* oriented to the highest good without ever achieving it. Aristotle's comparison of the happy, practically wise person to a skilled cobbler who is able to make the finest shoes possible from the leather given him is relevant here (*NE* I.10 1100b33–1101a8). The skilled cobbler is able to turn any leather into good shoes becasue he understands clearly what shoes are. Of course, if the leather is too poor and full of holes, he will not be able to achieve his goal. In this case, the cobbler will not do anything to be ashamed of from the point of view of his craft, but neither will he be in any way successful. Likewise, the practically wise person will never make something shameful out of his fate and is almost always capable of making something fine.

CHAPTER FOUR

Acting for the Sake of an Object of Love

So THE TASK is to show that a single kind of good could be the ultimate end of a life worth choosing, and in particular that middle-level ends, such as morally virtuous action, could be worth pursuing for the sake of this highest good while also being worth choosing for their own sakes. It is usually assumed that, according to Aristotle, a good can be choiceworthy for the sake of another end only by being, broadly speaking, an instrument to that further end. Aristotle encourages this assumption when he describes teleological subordination in the first chapter of the *Nicomachean Ethics* by means of instrumental examples. Bridles are choiceworthy for the sake of cavalry riding, and riding is choiceworthy for the sake of military victory, and this is evidently because these lower goods are instruments for achieving the higher ends. As we saw in the second chapter, this theory of the way goods may be choiceworthy for the sake of an end leads to problems for Aristotle's ethical theory. But is it true, in Aristotle's account, that all goods choiceworthy for the sake of another end are choiceworthy as instruments to or as constituents of that further end? In this chapter I will argue that it is not. Central to Aristotle's cosmology and biology is the teleological relationship of approximation or imitation. It is this relationship of imitation that Aristotle refers to in *Metaphysics* Λ when he makes the obscure remark that the heavenly spheres act for the sake of the Prime Mover as for an object of love. When we love something, in the sense relevant to the *Metaphysics*, I will argue, we strive to approximate it insofar as that is possible for us. This may seem an odd claim to make about love, and it is not one that Aristotle himself endorses as a description of friendship.[1] But Plato called the urge to approximate a superior mode of being "love" (*Symp.* 206e2–207a4), and Aristotle follows Plato in finding that this kind of teleological relationship is ubiquitous in the natural world (including among human beings), starting at the very top.[2] It would not be surprising to find that it has a place in human ethical life as well.

---

[1] Although, according to Aristotle, even perfect *philia* depends on likeness (*NE* 1156b7–8) and a friend is "another self" (*NE* 1170b6–7). Furthermore, Aristotle says that character friends improve each other because each friend's character is molded by the pleasant (i.e., virtuous) aspects of the other's character (*NE* 1172a11–14). This might mean that, in competing with each other in virtue, friends emulate the best qualities of each other. But I do not want to press this interpretation here.

[2] I discuss this interpretation of Plato in the appendix.

Now, I am not the first to suggest that approximation is one of the ways of acting for an end that Aristotle has in mind when he describes people as doing everything for the sake of *eudaimonia*.[3] But it has not played any significant role in the interpretation of how the happy person could act for the sake of contemplative *eudaimonia*. Perhaps this is because readers of the *Nicomachean Ethics* have not sufficiently recognized how important this way of acting for an end is for Aristotle in other areas of his philosophy. In the next chapter I will argue that it is in this sense that morally virtuous action is choiceworthy for the sake of contemplation. But before we get there, we need to examine Aristotle's more explicit discussions of this finality relation in the *Metaphysics* and *De Anima*, among other texts. I will argue that paradigms for approximation meet the conditions of determining the form and standards for success for their subordinate "imitations," so approximation is a genuine teleological relationship in the sense described in the *Physics* and *Nicomachean Ethics*. Furthermore, I believe that, far from being a bar to the intrinsic value of the subordinate good, acting for the sake of an object of love in this rather technical sense grounds its choiceworthiness for its own sake. Thus, recognizing that approximation is a possible way of acting for the sake of an end can help resolve the difficulties raised in the second chapter for middle-level ends. If morally virtuous activity is an approximation of excellent theoretical contemplation, then choosing virtuous action for the sake of philosophy is not inconsistent with recognizing and acting for the sake of the intrinsic value of the moral virtues.

1. Love and Final Causation in Aristotle's Scientific Works

1a. Metaphysics Λ

First, let us see how approximation emerges as a way of acting for the sake of an end in the *Metaphysics*. According to Aristotle, the eternity of the changing world, and indeed of time, depends on there being a substance that is continuously moved in a circle (*Meta.* 1071b5–11).[4] And if there must

---

[3] Kraut (1989, 87–88) argues that Aristotle accepts approximation as one way of acting for the sake of an end, but I do not find his argument convincing. Kraut claims that since Aristotle says all people act for the sake of *eudaimonia*, even though he does not think all people are happy, Aristotle must mean that people act for the sake of *eudaimonia*, by approximating it. A more likely alternative is that all people aim at *eudaimonia* but many fail to achieve their end.

[4] It is not clear why in *Meta.* Λ.6 Aristotle thinks change must be eternal. He says simply "it must always have existed" (1071b7). But perhaps it depends on the necessary eternity of time. Time must always exist, for there can be no before or after time without presupposing time itself (1071b8–9). But time either is change or depends on it (*Meta.* 1071b10). Therefore, change must always be, and in particular there must be one eternal change—the circular motion of the first heaven. We may wonder, of course, why the eternity of time could not be guaranteed by an eternal succession of changes. Aristotle thinks such a succession would not have the continuity requisite for the continuity of time (*Phys.* VIII.6). See Berti (2000, 182–185) for discussion of these difficulties.

be something continuously moved, there must be something continuously moving it. Aristotle's task in *Metaphysics* Λ.6-7 is to show that there is an eternal substance, separate from sensible things, which is the Prime Mover of the sensible world (*Meta.* 1069b1-2, 1070b34-35, 1073a3-5).[5] He must also explain how such a substance sets things in motion. But it is not at all clear how the Prime Mover could move anything at all.

This is because, in the first place, if there is going to be a *first* moving cause, it must itself be unmoved. Otherwise it would have to be moved by something prior to it (*Meta.* 1072a24-26). But, of course, it is not so easy to find something that has the power to move something else—in this case, the first heaven—without transferring its own motion to it, and so itself moving or changing. That is, it is not easy to see what could be an *unmoved* cause of motion and, in particular, of the first heavenly motion. As a first answer to this question, Aristotle argues that something that moves other things "as an object of desire or thought [*to orekton kai to noêton*]" would be such an unmoved mover (*Meta.* 1072a26-27). For when we desire something, the attractive (apparently *kalon*; 1072a27-28) object first moves our faculty of desire, which then moves us to action, without itself changing in any way. If there is some supremely beautiful or noble[6] object that the first heaven (so to speak) desires, this could be an absolutely unchanging first efficient cause of the motion of the heavens. In other words, the first efficient cause is a final cause.[7]

---

[5] This Prime Mover is the appropriate object of theological inquiry (*Meta.* 1074a38-74b14) and is superior to all other substances. Thus a person knowledgeable in this subject would be, above all others, *sophos* (wise) (*Meta.* A.2); and if he devoted his life to its contemplation in the sense specified by the *NE*, he would be the happiest (X.7 1178a6-8).

[6] Notice how throughout this chapter Aristotle talks about the beauty or nobility or fineness of unmoved movers in general and of the first unmoved mover in particular. This seems to me an important fact, which ought to be expressed in translations. However Ross (in Barnes 1984) translates *kalon* throughout this chapter as *good*.

[7] Although it is traditional to interpret the Prime Mover as a final cause (e.g., Elders 1972; Ross 1924, cxxx-cxli; not. ad 1072a26), the view has recently come under criticism (Berti 2000; Broadie 1993). The principle objection, as I understand it, is that Aristotle seems clearly to describe the Prime Mover as an efficient cause, and it is not at all clear how an efficient cause could be the same as a final cause. Of course, it is often the case for Aristotle that final, formal, and efficient causes coincide. But that is not quite what is going on here, since here the final cause acts as an efficient cause *insofar as* it is a final cause. (For a discussion of how this might be possible, see Caston 1999; Judson 1994, 164 ff.)

I cannot do full justice to the details of the debate in this note, but three remarks seem worth making at this point: (1) There is precedent in *Phys.* II.7 198b1-4 and *DA* III.10 433b13-16 for identifying unmoved causes with final causes. Furthermore, the context of that passage suggests that these causes may be efficient. See Judson 1994, 166. (2) At *Meta.* 1072a24-27 Aristotle says (a) we need a mover that is unmoved, and (b) the desirable and the knowable are movers of this sort. Berti (2000, 203) suggests that Aristotle's reference to objects of thought and desire is merely metaphorical. But if so, the remark gives only a spurious sense of advancing the argument. What good does it do us to be told that *some* things cause motion without moving if the Prime Mover, in its role as efficient cause, could not in principle be an unmoved cause in a similar way? It is more likely that Aristotle wants us to see that final causes are, in a sense, origins of motion; they move other things. (3) The passage following this one, in which Aristotle explains in greater

Still, it is not enough for Aristotle to show that the Prime Mover is in fact immobile when it causes motion. For Aristotle thinks that a Prime Mover must not be movable even in principle, not even in the loose sense of being capable of greater or lesser actualization. That is to say, the Prime Mover cannot contain any potentiality. If the Prime Mover was changeable, there would be no necessity to its always having been and continuing to be a mover of the *kosmos* (*Meta.* 1071b12–19).[8] Of course, it must still be active if it is going to cause change (1071b20). Thus, Aristotle needs a Prime Mover that is completely unchanging and unchangeable, yet still purely active. And this is where Aristotle's theory that the Prime Mover initiates change as a final cause or a "that for the sake of which" might seem open to criticism. Even if we grant Aristotle that objects of desire generate motion in us without first being moved, we might nevertheless think that they could not move us in the way that they do—to act for their sakes—if they were not *in principle* movable.

This criticism might take two forms, one of which Aristotle addresses explicitly. First, consider, for example, that craft products are for the sake of human beings under the assumption that human beings can be benefited. When a person desires for his own sake to acquire shoes or a house, for example, he assumes that he can be brought into a better condition by possessing them. Or, when a mother takes care of her baby for its sake, she acts under the condition or principle that she can change her baby's condition for the better. (This need not be a conscious assumption on her part. Mother animals also would not do things for the sake of their offspring if it were not the case that their behavior could affect them.) In general, when we act for the sake of objects to be benefited, our actions are guided by what will most efficiently change them (in the right way). Thus, it is central to their being "thats for the sake of which" that they are changeable.

Aristotle forestalls this criticism by reminding the reader of what was apparently a common philosophical distinction between two kinds of "for the sake of which":[9]

---

detail how unmovable things can be "thats for the sake of which," reinforces the impression that it is as a final cause that the Prime Mover is an unmoved cause. For these reasons, then, the traditional interpretation seems a more persuasive reading of the text.

However, Broadie (1993, 381) points out a serious problem for Aristotle's view in the standard interpretation. If the Prime Mover is purely "self-absorbed" contemplative activity which the first heaven desires, then the fact of the first heaven's desire and its subsequent motion looks accidental, at least from the Prime Mover's point of view. That is, the Prime Mover's activity does not have the motion of the first heaven as its *telos*. But could this really be Aristotelian efficient causation? I am not sure, however, that this problem is one for the interpretation rather than for Aristotle himself.

[8] Aristotle also probably does not think it makes sense to talk about something's being potentially F unless it has been or will at some point be F.

[9] Ross 1924, not. ad 1072b2. Aristotle mentions this distinction in several places (*DA* II.4 415b2–3, b20–21; *EE* VIII.3 1249b15; *Phys.* II.2 194a35–36). It is apparently a Platonic distinction (*Euthyphro* 13b–e). See also Laks 2000, 227.

> And that the 'for the sake of which' is present among the group of unmovable things is made clear by the distinction. For there is the 'for the sake of which' as an object of benefit (*tini to hou heneka*) and the 'for the sake of which' as an object to be attained or realized (*to hou heneka tinos*), and of these the one is [moveable] and the other is not. (*Meta*. 1072b1–3)

When something is a "for the sake of which" because it is a beneficiary, then it is true that it must be in principle movable. A baby's being the end of a mother's activity depends on the baby's condition being changeable. But not all "thats for the sake of which" are ends as objects of benefit. There are also, Aristotle says, "thats for the sake of which" *qua* goods to be attained or realized. These are the ends we discussed in chapter 2. It is no part of this sort of finality that the end must be movable. Thus, among ends as objects to be attained or realized may be ends that are not movable in principle. It is possible, then, to act for the sake of an end that is not ever in fact moved.

Now, it is clear that objects of desire will be among ends as objects to be attained (*hou heneka tinos*). We pursue them to improve our own condition, not to affect theirs. But there is another problem, which Aristotle does not explicitly address, though implicitly he makes allowances for it. It is not obvious that even among ends *hou heneka tinos*—that is, ends in the sense of goals to be attained or realized—there could be thoroughly unmovable ends. And in particular, it does not seem that an object of desire could be unmovable. Let us consider a normal case of desire. It is true that an apple can stimulate my appetitive desire and, in this way, move me to action without itself suffering any change. But would an apple have this effect on my appetite if it were not the sort of thing that *could* be changed? It seems that it would not. It is, after all, part of the goal of my action that I bring the desired object under my power: I will eat the apple; I will acquire money for my own use, and so on. How can something be an end in the sense of a goal to be attained unless it can be brought under my power? And if it can be brought under my power, must it not be movable?

It is clear, however, that Aristotle thinks that ends *hou heneka tinos* (as goals to be realized) need not be, in principle, movable (*Meta*. 1072b1–2). After all, the first cause of the celestial rotations is supposed to be an unmovable end in this sense. And as Aristotle describes the being that plays the role of the Prime Mover, it is unmovable. For Aristotle says that the Prime Mover is a pure actuality which never alters from its characteristic intellectual activity or changes in any way (*Meta*. 1072b7–8, b15 ff., 1075a7–10). Aristotle calls this being "god," or the divine, and from this point of view it is perhaps easier to see that, if the Prime Mover is indeed an end, it could not be so *qua* movable. For god's perfection implies that his condition cannot be improved. (God is not an end *hou heneka tini*; *EE* 1249b13–16; *Euthyphro* 13b–c.) Nor could the action of any subordinate being bring the divine under its power.[10] We need to consider more carefully, then, how Aristotle thinks something can act for the sake of an unmovable end.[11]

One way a thing can act for the sake of an end without bringing it under its power is to become it. In other words, when a living thing realizes its own form, it acts for the sake of an unmovable end (*Phys.* II.7 198b1–4).[12] Forms are, after all, final causes. When a living thing grows, for example, its development is limited by the nature of the mature thing that it is becoming. The form itself does not change—what it is to be an oak tree or a lion is always the same. (After all, continuity of form assures the continuity of the identity of the changing thing through change.) Rather, the growing thing that potentially or incompletely possesses the form alters so that the form becomes actual. So Aristotelian forms seem to be unmovable final causes *hou heneka tinos*.

But although Aristotelian forms are a kind of unmovable final cause, it does not look as if this is the kind of final end that the Prime Mover is (at least in *Meta.* Λ).[13] That is, it does not seem as if the first heaven is meant to pursue its form or soul as an object of desire or thought. This is not simply because the metaphor of an object of desire or thought suggests that the end is metaphysically distinct from the pursuer. In addition, the Prime Mover—or at least the divine—is related to so many things as their final cause that it is hard to see how it could be the form of them all.[14] For instance, plants and animals act for the sake of the divine, or god (*DA* II.4 415a25–b7; *GA* II.1 731b22 ff.), and so do the earth and *all* the heavenly bodies (*DC* II.12

---

[10] This would not be because Aristotle's god, or any Greek god, is omnipotent, but because his power is greater than that of a subordinate being.

[11] This suggests, then, that 'that to obtain which' is not the best translation for ends *hou heneka tinos* in general. I am not sure that there is a single English translation that captures all the ways one thing can be for the sake of another that Aristotle gathers here under one heading. (Ross's 'that towards which' [in Barnes 1984] is correct but unilluminating. Kullman's [1985] 'that *tending* towards which' is much better.)

[12] Souls are "thats for the sake of which" in both senses, *to hou heneka tinos* and *to hou heneka tini*. As forms of the living body, they are unmoving ends which the creature constantly seeks to realize. But Aristotle's comparison of the living body to a tool of the psychic craftsman suggests that the soul is also its benficiary (Menn, 2002, 113). The pereceptive soul, for example, uses the body and in particular the sense organs to actualize its capacity for perception. Notice this is a reason not to think of the Prime Mover as literally the soul of the first heavenly sphere. Since souls of embodied creatures need their bodies to keep them actualized, this suggest that these souls are not in essence perfect actualities. But the Prime Mover is pure actuality and could not possibly become less actual through a defect in any body associated with it. Although Kosman acknowledges for similar reasons that the Prime Mover can only be *like* a soul (1994, 145), this disanalogy between the relationship of plant and animal souls to their bodies and the relationship of the Prime Mover to the first heaven seems so significant as to cast serious doubt on the usefulness of the soul/body relationship as a model for the efficacy of the Prime Mover.

[13] Kosman (1994) argues that, in the *Physics*, the Prime Mover is something like a soul or form. See Judson's (1994) reply.

[14] Bodéüs (2000, chaps. 1–2) has argued that the Prime Mover is not Aristotle's god.

292b15–25).¹⁵ If the unmoved mover is the form of all these things, then how could we distinguish them into different kinds? Furthermore, it is usually thought that Aristotle's first unmoved mover is a transcendent being. After all, Aristotle makes a point of the Prime Mover's separability from the sensible world (1073a3–5, 1075b24–28). So it is not clear how acting for the sake of one's own form could provide a model for the final causation of the Prime Mover. A living thing can realize its own form, but it cannot become god. So although forms are unmovable ends *hou heneka tinos*, we need to find some other way to understand the ultimate unmovable end.

After Aristotle distinguishes "thats for the sake of which" as objects of benefit and as objects of attainment, he makes the somewhat odd claim that the Prime Mover moves the heavenly bodies as something loved (*hôs erômenon*; 1072b3). This might be just another way of stating his previous claim that the Prime Mover moves as an object of desire. But talk of *erôs* is rare in Aristotle generally, and it is new for this discussion in the *Metaphysics*.¹⁶ Previously Aristotle had talked about unmoved movers in general as objects of desire (*epithumia, boulêsis,* and *orexis* more generally; 1072a26–29) now he says the Prime Mover in particular is (or is like) an object of love. Is there something special about objects of love that would solve the problem of finding an end that is not in principle movable?

Let us speculate for a moment. Love (ideally) does not seek to bring its object under its power. And though it is typical of lovers to give gifts and to help each other, it is equally true that a lover—at least of an idealistic stripe—does not think his object needs to be changed or improved in any way. Insofar as he loves it, the lover finds his object perfect. It has been traditional to interpret the first heaven's desire for the Prime Mover as a sort of emulation, the effect of which is not a (vain) attempt to change the Prime Mover, but an activity that imitates it in the closest way possible for a thing of the kind that it is—the outermost sphere of the heavens.¹⁷ This is recognizable to us

---

¹⁵ Here the first heaven is, itself, the divine and its perfectly circular motion the best movement (*DC* II.3). The stars are able to achieve the *telos* (i.e., the best state), but only with a multitude of movements, while the earth cannot achieve the *telos* at all but can only approximate it. It is for this reason that the earth is at rest; presumably rest is as close to the perfect movement of the first heaven as the earth can come.

¹⁶ Usually for Aristotle *erôs* refers specifically to sexual relationships (except for *Rhet.* 1391a5, where wealth is an object of *erôs* for the money lover) and does not seem to bear any similarity to attraction to a cosmic first principle! On the other hand, Aristotle often brings up Empedocles' view that Love is among the *archai*. Perhaps Aristotle has this in mind when he describes the Prime Mover as an object of love. After all, he has just mentioned Empedocles with some approval in Λ.6 1072a4–6. If so, however, Aristotle must be modifying Empedocles' view: (1) Empedocles thought that Love itself is the first principle of motion, while Aristotle says that the Prime Mover is effective by being loved and (2) Aristotle complains that Love as Empedocles understands it is too vague to explain particular movements (*GC* II.6 333b12 ff.).

¹⁷ Broadie (1993, 380) objects to the traditional view that if the first heaven can contemplate the Prime Mover (which there is some reason in the traditional view to think it can), surely that

as (a rather idealistic) form of love. But furthermore, Aristotle would have a historical precedent for this theory, since it is the way Plato conceives of love in the *Symposium* and *Phaedrus*.[18] For Plato, love is a special kind of desire, or series of desires, embracing a range of natural behavior in which each stage more perfectly approximates the unmovable Form of the Beautiful. If the traditional interpretation of *Metaphysics* Λ.6–7, which I have been describing, is correct, then perhaps Aristotle wants to indicate with his use of the word *erômenon* that the first heavenly bodies are related to the unmoved mover as lovers are related to the Forms of the Good or the Beautiful in Plato's *Symposium* and *Phaedrus*. (Notice that Aristotle describes the Prime Mover as *kalon* at *Meta.* 1072a28, 1072a34, 1072b11.)[19] The first heaven loves the Prime Mover so much it tries to be just like it.[20] The first heaven does not first desire the Prime Mover and then desire to imitate it. Rather, imitation of the Prime Mover is the means by which the first heaven possesses it, insofar as that is possible. Since continuous circular motion is the closest approximation to the perfect activity of god possible for an eternal but enmattered being, the first heaven expresses its love by moving in a circle. (When something travels in a circle each moment of the journey is as much the end as any other. Thus, circular motion is as much like an *energeia*—whose end is in itself—as it is possible for a *kinêsis* to be.)[21] In this interpretation, Aristotle's Prime Mover is an object of desire of a special sort: It is an object of Platonic love. As such, it is a final cause as an object of aspiration, imitation, or approximation. Such an end may be, in principle, unchangeable as well as separable from the physical world.

In effect, I am suggesting that Aristotle introduces a new (or at least new to us), mode of acting for the sake of an end (*hou heneka tinos*) in order to solve a particular problem he faces in the *Metaphysics*. It makes no sense to think of the first heaven as acting for the Prime Mover by doing something

---

activity is a closer approximation than circular motion. This is true, but it does not take into account the *whole life* of the first heaven. Given that the first heaven *is* a sphere, it must either stand still, twist back and forth, or move in a continuous circular motion. The first heaven would make its *whole life* more like the Prime Mover's by choosing the last option.

[18] Elders also connects finality causality as imitation to Plato's *Symposium* (1972, 35–36).

[19] The first two references are, in the first instance, to any object of desire or thought. See Menn (1992) for the argument that the Prime Mover is Aristotle's version of Plato's Good-in-Itself.

[20] There is another reason it makes sense to call this desire "love," for whereas an ordinary object of desire need only change one's life temporarily and superficially, acting on love (in Plato's account) involves a shift in one's whole life. The first heaven does not desire the Prime Mover for only a moment; if his love of the Prime Mover is to ensure the eternity of change, it must be everlasting. Love is the name of the desire to devote one's life to the object of desire. Perhaps this is what Elders (1972, 174 not. ad 1072b3) has in mind when he says that, unlike an object of love, an object of desire need not *actually* desired. This fact, he believes, explains Aristotle's preference for *erômenon* instead of *orekton* at 1072b3.

[21] *Phys.* VIII. 9; Kosman 1994, 149 n. 16. Elders (1972, not. ad 1072b9) argues that perpetual circular motion imitates the continuousness of pure thought.

to produce it, nor can we think of the first heaven as constituting (or being) it. It does make sense, however, to think of the first heaven as being moved by desire to become as much like the Prime Mover as it is possible for it to be. Admitting that one thing can act for the sake of an end by imitating it solves a real problem facing Aristotle about the mobility of ends *hou heneka tinos*. If unmovables can be among this group of ends, what sort of thing are they? One plausible answer is that they are objects of love in the Platonic sense, that is, they are objects of approximation. Thus teleological approximation is at the very heart of Aristotle's cosmology.

1b. Imitation in Aristotle's Natural Philosophy

It must be granted, however, that in *Metaphysics* Λ Aristotle never explicitly says that the first heaven imitates the Prime Mover, or even that it is the first heaven doing the loving. Fortunately, though, other passages make it clear that Aristotle does recognize this imitative form of final causation modeled on Platonic love.[22] When Aristotle explains some animals' behavior as for the sake of the divine in *De Anima* and *On the Generation of Animals*, he lifts an example straight from the *Symposium*.[23] Notice that Aristotle classifies the purpose of reproduction as an end *hou heneka tinos*:

> The acts in which [the nutritive soul] manifests itself are reproduction and the use of food, because for any living thing which has reached its normal development

---

[22] Broadie (1993, 382) suggests that the traditional interpretation describes the Prime Mover as an *exemplary* cause and not as a *final* cause. Even though I believe I can show that paradigms are final causes (pp. 82–83), I will not use the term *exemplary cause* lest it suggest that this is not a genuine form of final causation.

[23] The *GA* passage is slightly more complicated, tying animals' approximation of the divine not to the divine's immortality but to its more perfect way of being. (In this respect it is similar to the passage from *Meta*. Θ.8 (quoted on p. 82, below) that explains the eternal coming-to-be of elemental change as an imitation of the stable actuality belonging to imperishable things. (See also GC II.10, quoted on p. 82 below.) "Now some existing things are eternal and divine while others admit of both existence and non-existence. But that which is noble and divine is always, in virtue of its own nature, the cause of the better in such things as admit of being better or worse, and what is not eternal does admit of existence and non-existence, and can partake in the better and the worse. And soul is better than body, and the living, having soul, is thereby better than the lifeless which has none, and being is better than not being, living than not living. These, then, are the reasons of the generation of animals. For since it is impossible that such a class of things as animals should be of an eternal nature, therefore that which comes into being is eternal in the only way possible. Now it is impossible for it to be eternal as an individual—for the substance of the things that are is in the particular; and if it were such it would be eternal—but it is possible for it as a species. This is why there is always a class of men and animals and plants." (*GA* II.1; 731b24–732a1; Platt, trans., in Barnes 1984)

There is, of course, no mention of love or desire in this passage. This is not a problem for my account, however, since I am interested primarily in the teleological structure that is inherited from Plato's account of love. However, in the appendix I argue that there is a close connection between love and the desire for happiness in the *Symposium*. Perhaps Aristotle's reluctance to say that animals love the divine is an indication of his thought that animals cannot even aspire to happiness.

and which is unmutilated ... the most natural act is the production of another like itself, an animal producing an animal, a plant a plant, in order that, as far as its nature allows, it may partake in [*metechôsin*] the eternal and divine. For all things desire this, and do whatever they do in accordance with their natures for the sake of [*heneka*] this. The phrase 'for the sake of which' is ambiguous; it may mean either the end to achieve which or the being in whose interest the act is done. Since then no living thing is able to partake in what is eternal and divine by uninterrupted continuance (for nothing perishable can ever remain one and the same), it tries to achieve that end in the only way possible to it, and success is possible in varying degrees; so it remains not indeed as the self-same individual but continues its existence in something like itself—not numerically but specifically one. (*De Anima* II.4 415a25–b7)[24]

Here Aristotle says that whatever a living thing does in accordance with its nature, and in particular that most natural activity of reproduction, is done for the sake of partaking in the divine. But this is the same account we find in the *Symposium*, when Diotima tells Socrates that natural reproduction is an expression of love, which is a desire for immortality:

For among animals the principle is the same as with us, and mortal nature seeks so far as possible to live forever and be immortal. And this is possible in one way only: by reproduction, because it always leaves behind a new young one in place of the old. . . . And in that way everything mortal is preserved, not, like the divine, by always being the same in every way, but because what is departing and aging leaves behind something new, something such as it had been. By this device, Socrates, what is mortal shares [*metechei*] in immortality, whether it is a body or anything else, while the immortal has another way. So don't be surprised if everything naturally values its own offspring, because it is for the sake of immortality that everything shows this zeal, which is Love. (*Symp.* 207c9–208b6)[25]

For both Aristotle and Plato, familial love or, less romantically, mating, reproduction, and the rearing of offspring are the means by which mortal creatures have a share of or partake of (*metechein*) the immortal and divine. (In the *Symposium* the desire for immortality is not simply a desire to live forever; it is the desire to possess the good forever, which is to say that it is a desire to be godlike, eternally *eudaimôn* [*Symp.* 202c, 204e–205a].) The desire to partake of or to have a share of the divine and immortal is a desire to *be* immortal, just as the desire to partake of beauty or happiness is the desire to *be* beautiful or happy. Thus, in Plato and Aristotle's account of reproduction, the immortality of the particular creature is its *telos*. But since this end cannot be achieved literally, mortal creatures act for its sake by

[24] J. A. Smith, trans., in Barnes 1984, modified.
[25] Nehamas and Woodruff, trans. 1989.

means of approximation. We all have a desire to be like god, insofar as that is possible for us and, as Aristotle says, we try "to achieve that end in the only way possible to us" (*DA* 415b5). When we do, we act for the sake of the divine as a *hou heneka tinos*—an end to be realized.

We should not suppose that Aristotle limits this mode of final causation to the relationship of god to lower beings. In *On Generation and Corruption*, after affirming the principle that all things desire or strive for (*oregetai*) the better, which is to say that they act for the sake of an end, Aristotle says:

> That, too, is why all the other things—the things, I mean, which are reciprocally transformed in virtue of their qualities and their powers, e.g. the simple bodies—imitate (*mimeitai*) circular motion. For when water is transformed into air, air into fire, and fire back into water, we say the coming-to-be has completed the circle, because it reverts again to the beginning. Hence it is by imitating (*mimoumenê*) circular motion that rectilinear motion too is continuous. (GC II.10 337a1–7)[26]

We should notice that whereas in *Metaphysics* Λ.7 and *De Anima* II.4 Aristotle only implies that things act for their end by approximating it, here he is explicit that a thing may act for its end—the better—by imitating it. Circular motion is the best form of locomotion, so the simple bodies aim at that sort of motion in their own changes. But they cannot achieve it directly; rather, they aim at it by imitating circular motion insofar as that is possible, by undergoing cyclical transformations. Why is circular motion better? In the passage immediately preceding this one Aristotle says circular motion is better because it in turn is the closest approximation to eternal being (336b32–34). Aristotle does not say so explicitly, but the implication seems to be that the cyclical transformations of the elements imitate circular motion, which in turn imitates eternal being. (Notice that Aristotle does not say the simple bodies imitate eternal being directly. Rather they imitate eternal being by imitating circular motion. Less perfect levels of imitation approximate the best condition via approximating more perfect imitations.) When we turn to another passage, this time at *Metaphysics* Θ.8 1050b28–29, Aristotle makes plain that ultimately fire and earth aim at immortality: "Imperishable things are imitated (*mimeitai*) by those that are involved in change, e.g. earth and fire." There is good reason, therefore, to find in Aristotle a relationship of finality founded on imitation or approximation. When a subordinate object behaves in this way, we may say that in some, admittedly technical, sense, it is a lover of its end.[27]

All these passages suggest, then, that in addition to instrumental and constitutive relations, Aristotle recognizes imitation or approximation as a way

[26] H. H. Joachim, trans., in Barnes 1984.

[27] In other words, there may not be the pathos normally associated with love. I do not mean to deny that the emotion is there. The first heaven, for example, may well experience the emotion of love for the Prime Mover. But I am not interested in the emotion of love so much as the teleological structure underlying that emotion *as it is described by Plato* in the *Symposium*.

of acting for the sake of an end (*hou heneka tinos*). Indeed, this teleological relation is behind some of the most significant natural events: the movement of the first heaven, the cyclical transformation of the elements, and reproduction. Notice that an object of love in this Platonic sense is a genuine *telos* as we have seen that concept developed in the *Physics*. A *telos*, we said, determines what counts as a successful instance of the subordinate end or activity. But if a good is an object of imitation or approximation, then it is the paradigm by which the subordinate good is to be judged.[28] To the extent that the subordinate good manages to express the nature of its final end, it fulfills its aspirations and is good of its kind. (We can see now why Aristotle need not have felt obliged to single out approximation, alongside instrumentalism and constitution, as a third way of realizing an end. Because approximation is a second best way of realizing a form, it is quite similar to constitution. It is a matter of becoming, rather than being.) Furthermore the value of the approximation depends on the value of the object it approximates. In other words, the paradigm is a source of value for the things approximating it. According to Aristotle, reproduction is good for animals because it is the closest they can come to being eternal, which is divine and better. Thus objects of approximation are guiding ends and sources of value. Aristotle rejected Plato's theory of Forms as an account of how sensible things are related to their own natures. Corporeal things are able to possess their forms fully; they do not just approximate them. But he did not reject the imitation or approximation at the heart of that theory as a possible mode of final causation. It appears, then, that we have found a third way for one thing to be choiceworthy for the sake of another.

This conception of the source of value may strike us as odd. If one thing is good because it manages to instantiate properties that make some other thing good, we might be inclined to think that what makes both things valuable is the properties they possess. The approximation is not valuable because it is an approximation of something else. Rather, it is valuable because, in successfully approximating something valuable, it manages itself to realize those valuable characteristics. Thus there is no relation of dependence between the two objects, at least not as pertains to their value.[29] There is a question, then, whether approximation really meets Aristotle's criteria for a teleological relation.

First of all, we should see that Aristotle's point of view is not entirely alien to ordinary experience. Charismatic people often make certain tastes and interests valuable in the eyes of their admirers. For instance, in *The Prime*

---

[28] Scott (1999) also sees that this relationship of approximation meets the conditions for finality, though he does not say so explicitly.

[29] I thank Kieran Setiya for raising this problem, and the other participants of the 1999–2000 Mellon Graduate Seminar, including guests Rachel Barney, Sarah Broadie, John Cooper, and John Doris, for discussion.

of Miss Jean Brodie, Jean Brodie isn't marvelous because she holds her head high, speaks with rounded vowel sounds, and prefers the Classics; rather, holding one's head high, speaking with rounded vowel sounds, and preferring the Classics seem marvelous to her students because that's what Jean Brodie does. But though this phenomenon is recognizable to us, we tend (perhaps wrongly) to think of it as a typically adolescent phenomenon. It is the way ignorant and impressionable people come to see the value in things whose value is in fact independent of the approval of the charismatic leader.

I am not sure that there are any arguments to show that we ought (or ought not) to see things as Aristotle does, at least not any I can rehearse in the scope of this book. There has been a paradigm shift: Aristotle believed that imitation—and teleology in general—is a fundamental feature of the cosmos. Many of us do not. If you accept that some substances are just better than others, and if you think that lower substances imitate higher ones, it will be natural to think that what makes the lower substances good is that certain of their characteristics are images of the more perfect reality. But it is not clear what you could say in defense of your view. Imagine a religious person confronted by someone who says, "The reason God is better than we are is that knowledge is good, and He has more of it than we do." The skeptic has got it the wrong way around; *God* is perfectly good, and the reason human knowledge is worth pursuing is that it is an approximation of this most perfect being. So while it is intelligible enough to suggest that an imitation is good to the extent that it instantiates properties whose value is independent of the paradigm, it seems to me that this is not so much an objection to Aristotle's view as it is the statement of a worldview that precludes the possibility of the one Aristotle has in mind. Aristotle believes we can act for the sake of an end by approximating it. If the paradigm is genuinely to be an end, it must confer value as well as form on the approximation.

Furthermore, notice that to someone who believes, as Aristotle does, that there is an especially valuable substance which other things approximate, our alternative account of value is inadequate to describe the nature of lower creatures. Where the relationship of approximation or imitation does hold, Aristotle thinks we are only able fully to recognize the less perfect case for what it is by understanding it *as* an approximation of the paradigm. Thus, according to Aristotle, the perpetuation of a species from one generation to the next is the mortal form of the individual immortality of the Prime Mover. Unless we know this, however, the animal desire to reproduce might seem to be a brute instinct demanding satisfaction but the source of no particular benefit, and perhaps of suffering, to the individual animal. On the other hand, once we see that reproduction is an imitation of something more perfect, we can (according to Aristotle) see that it is the apex of animal experience because it is most godlike. Or, to take another example, philosophy is often accused of being useless and debilitating (*Gorgias* 485a–e; *Pol.* VII.3).

But this can only be the accusation of people ignorant that (according to Aristotle) the dialectical and fitful intelligence of human beings is a spark of the divine. Thus, if there is a relationship of approximation between two things, the paradigm will function as an end in the sense of determining form and standards of success.

2. How Teleological Approximation Could Solve the Problem of Middle-Level Ends

Let us remind ourselves of where we now are. I have tried to show that, in addition to taking an instrumental means to an end and constituting an end, Aristotle recognizes in his scientific treatises a third way of acting for the sake of an end. Indeed it is central to his account of the first heaven's relationship to the Prime Mover. In the *Metaphysics* Aristotle calls this acting for an end as an object of love. Less poetically, we can call it approximating, imitating, or emulating an end. The *telos* is not just similar to its subordinate goods, it sets the standards of success for them. An excellent example of the subordinate good is as much like its *telos* as it is possible for a thing of that kind to be. Essentially perishable creatures, for example, cannot be immortal, but they can approach immortality to some extent by procreating.

Now, if morally virtuous activity approximates contemplation, this would help solve the problem we faced, in the previous chapter, in our interpretation of the *Nicomachean Ethics*. We wondered how middle-level ends, choiceworthy for their own sakes, could also be worth choosing for the sake of *eudaimonia*. And in particular we wondered how, if *eudaimonia* is contemplation, morally virtuous action might be worth choosing for its sake. When one thing approximates another it inherits the kind of value possessed by the paradigm. That is to say, the approximation of a good choiceworthy only for the sake of another will itself be choiceworthy for the sake of another. Alternatively, the approximation of a good choiceworthy for its own sake will itself be choiceworthy for its own sake. So if morally virtuous activity is choiceworthy for the sake of contemplation as an approximation or imitation of that activity, it will not be merely instrumentally valuable. Rather, to the extent it succeeds in realizing the form of contemplation in action, it will itself be worth choosing for its own sake.

This claim—that approximations are valuable in the same way as their paradigms—needs defending. I take it to be uncontroversial in the case of the approximation of ends that are only instrumentally valuable. For instance, if I need a hammer but have none available, I may try to create a makeshift hammer that manifests the (functionally) essential properties of a hammer in the materials I have at hand. So, for instance, I may turn a book into a hammer. Notice that the standards of success for my approximation are determined by the nature of the paradigm: A hammer is for driving nails into wood; therefore, I should choose a heavy book rather than a light one, and a hardcover will be better than a paperback. In other words, I need to choose materials for my approximation in light of the end in terms of which my original is defined. Since the original in this case is essentially a tool, my makeshift hammer will also be a tool, worth choosing for the sake of something else.

It is more controversial to say that something that approximates an intrinsically valuable end must be itself worth choosing for its own sake. But recall that, for Aristotle, whether a thing is for the sake of another or for its own sake follows immediately from its form. Tools are for the sake of another because their forms are suited to the production of something beyond themselves. Likewise, it is an inseparable aspect of certain other forms that their embodiments are good in themselves. Thus, to the extent that something succeeds in approximating an intrinsically valuable paradigm, it too will be worth pursuing for itself.

At any rate, we should notice that in the passage from *De Anima* II.4 discussed above, Aristotle seems to think that activities chosen for an end by approximating it can be intrinsically valuable *for the creatures doing the approximating*. That is because there appears to be a special connection between a thing's form and the activity it undertakes for the sake of the divine as an object of love. The activity of lower beings that approximates the Prime Mover or god is the very activity that expresses or actualizes their forms. Generation, for example, is not just an approximation of the divine; it is the characteristic activity of the nutritive soul (*DA* 415a25–28, quoted above). That is to say, generation is the function of the nutritive soul. But when this soul performs its function, that is just the actualization of the soul as form and first actuality of the body (*DA* 414a14–28). Thus to act for the sake of the divine is in this case the same as to act for the sake of one's form. The same is true for the other kinds of soul. Aristotle says *everything* living things do in accordance with their natures (which I take to mean "that realizes their nature as form") is undertaken for the sake of the divine (*DA* 415b1–2). And indeed, to take an example relevant to our study of Aristotle's ethical theory, when we contemplate we become godlike. But *noûs*, the faculty of contemplation, is most of all what we are (*NE* 1178a2–7). Furthermore, as we saw, the first heavenly body moves in a perfect circle as a way of approximating the divine, but it is also the nature of the first sphere to move in this way. Its circular imitation of the divine *is* the expression of its nature. To the extent that something acts for the sake of the divine as an object of love, then, it acts for the sake of its form. Or, to put it another way, when we approximate the divine to the extent possible for us, we realize our own nature. But according to Aristotle, the forms of living things are valuable in themselves. They are not instruments of a cosmic soul.

So Aristotle seems to think that approximations can be worth choosing for their own sakes. This might strike us as surprising, given that, as I believe,

Aristotle takes the notion of approximation from Plato. For in *Republic* X, Plato is explicit that imitations are not worth choosing for their own sakes and indeed are scarcely worth choosing at all. But a closer look at that passage shows that Plato's criticisms of dramatic imitation are not relevant to the sort of imitation Aristotle has in mind (or that Plato has in mind in the *Symposium*). According to Socrates, whereas a true craftsman tries to realize the form or nature of a thing in the physical product he creates, the artist aims only to make an image of the appearance of craft products (*Rep.* 598b1–5). In other words, the imitation that Plato criticizes in the *Republic* is an imitation of the way things seem rather than the way things are. The imitation of divine immortality in animal reproduction, on the other hand, is not (allegedly) an imitation of the *appearance* of immortality. It is an imitation of its nature. This explains why teleological approximation transmits the kind of value from the paradigm to the subordinate end. When one thing approximates another in the sense relevant to Aristotle, it approximates the higher good's essence or form. Since intrinsic value will be intrinsic to the essence of the higher good, the subordinate good, insofar as it manages to realize that higher form in new matter, will capture whatever it is about the higher good that makes it worth choosing for its own sake.

If an approximation really has captured the nature of an intrinsically valuable paradigm, it ought to be self-sufficient in its goodness when approaching it from the bottom, so to speak. That is to say, we do not have to recognize the approximation as an approximation in order to value it and have our actions guided by it. After all, if it approximates the paradigm successfully, it is a final end, worth pursuing for itself. Nevertheless, it will still be the case that more can be said about the approximation's value: It is also for the sake of the higher good that it approximates under imperfect conditions. It has the intrinsically valuable nature that it does because it is approximating a more perfect nature.

This is an important point to bear in mind when we return to the *Nicomachean Ethics*. If morally virtuous action is an approximation of contemplative happiness, it ought to be choiceworthy for its own sake, for an approximation is worth choosing in the same way as its paradigm. Thus, even though we can attain a deeper understanding of the value of morally virtuous activity by seeing it as an approximation of contemplation, the virtuous agent will not have to recognize his actions as approximations in order to see them as worth pursuing in themselves.

One last point: Even though Aristotle himself sometimes uses the verb *mimeisthai* (*GC* 337a1–7; *Meta.* 1050b28–29; both quoted above), I am somewhat leery of describing the third kind of finality relation as imitation. Talk of imitation as a phenomenon in the natural world is subject to the same sort of misinterpretation as talk of teleology in general is. Just as some think a thing must desire its end in order to act for its sake, I suspect that some will think a thing must consciously try to copy its end in order to imitate it.[30] Certainly we do not want to attribute to Aristotle the claim that rabbits intend to be as much like the divine as they can be when they fill the garden with bunnies. But conscious intention is not necessary for the relation I have in mind, as the *Symposium* shows us. Someone or something acting for the sake of a Platonic object of love does not need to have any idea of the ultimate *telos* of his actions in order to be imitating it. It is enough to say that its actions or behavior will be good to the extent it is like something better. For those in a position to comprehend the better, however, valuing the subordinate end will point them to a proper appreciation of the higher end.

So teleological approximation could solve the problem of middle-level goods because it is a relation of noninstrumental dependence and if I approximate something of intrinsic value, the approximation—to the extent it is successful—also ought to be intrinsically valuable. Furthermore, the agent need not be aware that the middle-level good he chooses for its own sake is also choiceworthy for the sake of something beyond it.

3. Approximation in the *Nicomachean Ethics*?

So is there reason to think that middle-level goods, and in particular morally virtuous actions, are worth choosing for the sake of contemplation because they approximate contemplation? At NE I.6 1096b27–28 Aristotle briefly entertains the idea that all good things are called 'good' either because they are all focally related to one thing (*pros hen*) or by analogy (*kat' analogian*).[31] He defers discussion of this question to a different, presumably metaphysical, sort of philosophical inquiry (1096b30–31), but it is natural to wonder whether we might explain the relation between all *human* goods, and in particular the relation between morally virtuous action and contemplation, in one of these two ways. Now, it might be thought that they are human goods by analogy.[32] Moral virtue, in Aristotle's account, is inextricable from

---

[30] Although in modern biology could we not say that a praying mantis imitates the leaf or the bark on which it sits? Another problem: Imitation is often understood as facsimile. But as I said, telelogical imitation captures the paradigm's form in *new* matter.

[31] See Owen ([1960] 1979) for the explanation of *pros hen* predication as a focal relation between terms.

[32] Charles (1999) claims they are related by analogy and argues on this basis that while contemplation is *eudaimonia* in a primary sense (*teleia eudaimonia*), morally virtuous activity is also *eudaimonia*, though in a derivative way. In other words, the happy life could aim at *eudaimonia* in both the primary and the analogous, though derivative, senses. Not surprisingly, I cannot accept this interpretation for precisely the reason I suspect Charles supports it. Namely, it allows that the happy life has a dual (or multiple) focus. As I argued in chapter 2, however, the point of Aristotle's search for *eudaimonia* is to discover the one good that can serve as the principle of our pursuit of all the other goods that constitute a happy life. (Charles's interpretation could also imply that a life may aim either at paradigm *eudaimonia* or at derivative *eudaimonia*. But if so, there will be the problem of explaining how morally virtuous activity fits into

the intellectual virtue of practical wisdom. Thus it is not a stretch to say that morally virtuous activity is rational activity. And presumably, as contemplation is related to its end (grasping scientific truth), so virtuous practical reasoning is related to its end (grasping ethical truth). We should notice, however, that if contemplation and the exercise of practical wisdom are good merely by analogy, there is no reason to think that one is worth choosing for the sake of the other or is indeed inferior to it in any way at all. In an ordinary analogy, where A:B::C:D, there need be no priority of one relation over the other. Since Aristotle believes that contemplation *is* superior to the exercise of practical wisdom (*NE* VI.7) and is indeed its end (as I hope eventually to show), mere analogy does not sufficiently describe the connection between contemplation and morally virtuous action.[33] However, a focal relation—in which the essence of one thing is defined by reference to the other—would capture this asymmetry in value. And if practical wisdom is an approximation of theoretical wisdom, this will be a focal relation.[34] For as I have just shown, as an imitation of theoretical wisdom, its form or essence would be determined by the form of the paradigm.[35]

---

the contemplative life in which everything—including, presumably, morally virtuous action—is chosen for the sake of contemplation.)

Although I do not believe Charles's interpretation of the relationship between perfect and secondary happiness can be sustained, thinking about his article and Scott's (1999) has been enormously fruitful for me.

[33] As Charles himself admits (1999, 212 n. 4). This poses a problem for Charles's interpretation. If contemplation and morally virtuous action are analogous but neither is superior to the other, there seems to be no reason to call the former *teleia* or perfect *eudaimonia*, as Aristotle does (1177b24).

[34] Aristotle often uses instruments to illustrate *pros hen* predication (*Meta.* K.3; *NE* I.6), suggesting that if something is, in general, choiceworthy for the sake of some independent, good thing, then it will be called good *pros hen*. Furthermore, there is evidence that Aristotle would have recognized the relationship of approximation as calling for *pros hen* predication, for there is evidence that members of the Academy may have appealed to focal meaning as a way of explaining the relationship between Forms and sensibles that avoids the problem of the Third Man (Owen [1960] 1979, 27–29). Lawrence (1997, 74–76) argues that there is a focal relation between practical and theoretical excellence and he bases it on the instrumental relation between the two.

[35] Owen ([1960] 1979, 30–31) argues that insofar as the Platonists use depiction as their model for the connection between sensibles and Forms, Aristotle refuses to call the connection *pros hen*. For instance, in *Cat.* 1a1–6 the fact that we call both the animal and the painting "man" is a case of ambiguity, not focality. That's because, Owen says, essences are defined in terms of function, and the function of a painting is not focally related to the function of a living person. This is certainly true, but it should not lead us to think that, according to Aristotle, approximation or imitation can never be *pros hen*. If a thing's function is the approximation of the function of some other thing, then they will be related in the way necessary for *pros hen* predication. In my analysis I have been careful to point out that the imitations in question are imitations of function or form. In the next chapter I will show how morally virtuous activity—the function of the practically rational soul—is an approximation in particular of the function of the theoretically rational soul.

Fortenbaugh (1975, 58–59) claims that when two goods are focally related, we cannot pursue

Admittedly, Aristotle never explicitly says that excellent practical reasoning is good because its essence is defined with reference to wise contemplation. However, at *NE* X.7 1178a7 he claims that human beings are *malista noûs* or, loosely, most of all *noûs* (which in context clearly refers to a theoretical rational capacity). We are by nature practical in some other way. Dominic Scott has argued that when Aristotle wants to say that something is paradigmatically or strictly speaking X, he says it is *malista* X. That is to say, it "fully exemplifies the requirements for [an X], and so acts as the central case from which we may assess the claims of other [things] to count as [an X]" (1999, 228). So, for example, those who are friends in the primary way are *malista* friends; other kinds of friendship are only qualified cases of friendship (*NE* VIII.3 1156b9–10). But character friends are not *malista* friends because their relationship instantiates *all* the features of friendship, only some of which are present in the qualified cases. Rather, character friends are *malista* friends because they are paradigms of friendship by which the other varieties are measured and understood. Thus Scott believes that, according to Aristotle, we are theoretical *noûs* strictly speaking, but the part (or parts) of our soul expressed in moral activity in some looser sense (1999, 230–233).[36]

Now if the *malista* qualification of our human nature as *noûs* is working in the same way as it does in the discussion of friendship, Aristotle must mean that excellent practical reason is a qualified case of or approximation to *noûs*. And since practical reason and *noûs* are the names of dispositions, themselves defined in terms of the activities through which they are expressed, he must mean that morally virtuous action is by nature an approximation of philosophical contemplation. And, as I have argued, such a relationship would be teleological and *pros hen*. (Notice that in this interpretation Aristotle must think that choosing to express our practical virtue is choosing to express an approximation of ourselves as purely noetic.)

---

the derivative case without recognizing it as derivative and without understanding the paradigm case itself. This cannot be an adequate reason to deny focality between primary and secondary *eudaimonia*, however, since Aristotle thinks we can pursue all kinds of things effectively without having a philosophical understanding of them. All that must be true is that, if we are to have an adequate philosophical grasp of a derivative good, we must understand its relationship to the paradigm.

[36] If something has two natures must it not be two separate things? Scott's way of conceiving our dual nature avoids this problem since our noetic and practical selves are not two radically different natures but more and less perfect instances of the same thing. Given that we have reason to understand ourselves in the looser as well as the stricter sense, Scott concludes that we have reason to choose the activity of moral virtue as well as contemplation. Both will be the excellent expression of our nature in a looser and stricter way, and thus both will be *eudaimonia*, though contemplation will be perfect (*teleia*) *eudaimonia* and morally virtuous action will be *eudaimonia* only *deuterôs* (secondarily) (*NE* 1177b24; 1178a9). I do not accept this as an interpretation of *NE* X.7–8 for the same reason I do not accept Charles's solution (see note 32, above): It allows the happy person to aim at two nonteleologically related ends.

Finally, we should consider Aristotle's somewhat enigmatic response to an objection raised in *NE* X.7. Since contemplation is a divine activity, might it not be better to keep our place and not overreach our human condition by seeking it? Aristotle responds, "[W]e must become immortals insofar as possible ([*chrê*] *eph' hoson endechetai athanatizein*)" (1177b33). This is a meticulous paraphrase of the Platonic "likeness to god insofar as possible (*homoiôsis theôi kata ton dunaton*)" (*Theaetetus* 176b1; I call the paraphrase meticulous because Aristotle carefully avoids using any of the words used by Plato),[37] and in the context of Aristotle's biology and cosmology we can see that this is, according to Aristotle, precisely what all living things do.[38] All plants, animals, and living heavenly bodies, in realizing their own natures, are striving to partake of the divine life by imitation. So, far from being impious, we ought to assimilate ourselves to the gods as much as we can. Such people will, in fact, be dearest to the gods (1179a22–30).[39]

So how do we take on immortality?[40] In the context, it is clear that Aristotle means that we should devote ourselves to contemplation, since human contemplation is (an imperfect form of) the divine activity (*Meta.* 1072b14–26). But it would be surprising if this exhausted the implications of Aristotle's advice. The first heavenly sphere is presumably also capable of thought, but as we have seen its natural desire to immortalize leads it to rotate in a continuous circular motion. This too is a way for the first heaven to become as godlike as possible. Given that contemplation is necessarily a relatively small part of any human life in quantitative terms, the person who would follow Aristotle's advice ought to consider whether there are other ways for him to approximate divine activity so that his whole life may be as godlike as possible. (Presumably it won't do for us to tear around town in circles, since we would become exhausted in no time. As we will see, there are better ways to assimilate our physical movements to perfect contemplation.)

Aristotle tells us that insofar as the philosopher is human, he acts in accordance with moral virtue (1178b5–6). As will become clear (in chapters 5 and 8), morally virtuous activity is itself a way of extending contemplation of a sort (*theôria tis*) into human life (1178b28–32). (If morally virtuous activity is not a *theôria tis*, I will argue, then it is mysterious why Aristotle

---

[37] Sedley (1999, 325), though Plato himself uses different formulations, e.g., *Phaedrus* 253a4–5: *kath' hoson dunaton theou anthrôpôi metaschein*.

[38] Notice that in the *Metaphysics* Aristotle describes the divine activity (*diagôgê*) as similar to the best human activity (1072b14–15). Although Aristotle uses something better known to us to explain the nature of god, it is certainly more correct to say that our life at its best resembles the life of the divine. Indeed, there is no reason to think that our life could show us anything about the divine nature unless we presupposed that our life, at its best, was an approximation of the divine life.

[39] Sedley (1999, 314) shows that this closing passage of Aristotle's discussion of the contemplative life is yet another Platonic inheritance.

[40] This is Crisp's (2000) translation of *athanatizein*.

thinks the political life devoted to this kind of activity is happy in any way at all. For Aristotle says that lives are happy only insofar as they participate [*koinônei*] in some kind of contemplation [pp. 194–196].) When a person exercises *phronêsis* while dealing with distinctly human concerns springing from our animal and political nature, he engages in something like (*homoiôma ti*) divine contemplative activity (1178b27). (Animals, on the other hand, do not have a share of [*metechein*; 1178b24] happiness because they do not participate [*koinônei*; 1178b28] in *theôria*.) Thus, in Aristotle's account, the happy philosopher lives like a god not only by directly engaging in the divine activity but also and necessarily by pursuing an approximation of contemplation in his practical life. I suggest that in passages such as these in *NE* X.7–8, Aristotle is reiterating that the most happy person makes himself like a god *to the extent possible for a human being*. In other words, Aristotle thinks that the happiest person's devotion to contemplation must sometimes take a distinctively human form. *Eph' hoson endechetai athanatizein*, or 'make oneself immortal insofar as possible', invokes not only the optimism at the heart of Platonic ethics (and this is its function at *NE* 1177b33) but also the humility of that hope as it is expressed in the *Symposium*. We mortal, political creatures cannot engage continuously in divine activity. When we cannot, we should do the next best thing, approximating contemplation insofar as possible. This activity is morally virtuous action.[41]

These passages from *NE* X.7–8 that I have been discussing justify the superiority of contemplation by reference to a goal outside human life. The bulk of the *Nicomachean Ethics*, however, asks us to conceive of the standard of human goods as itself a good achievable within human life. Nevertheless, I believe these meta-ethical passages suggest an ethical description of the relationship between contemplation and moral virtue. If morally virtuous action is an imitation of divine contemplation, then possibly it is worth choosing for the sake of human contemplation as an approximation of it. In the remaining chapters I will argue that this is what Aristotle believes.

---

[41] Elders (1972, 38) suggests that all animals' pursuit of their proper pleasures is an imitation of divine pleasure. *NE* VII.13 1153b29–32: "But since neither the same nature nor the same state is or is thought to be the best [for all animals and people], they do not all pursue the same pleasure, but all pursue pleasure. But perhaps they do not actually pursue the pleasure they think [they pursue] nor that which they would say [they pursue], but the same pleasure; for all things by nature have something divine in them." Notice that, if Elders is right, (1) we have an additional case of animals pursuing ends that are rightly thought of as imitations of a divine paradigm, (2) Aristotle does not think we need to recognize something as an imitation in order for it to be an imitation, and (3) we have another case of something choiceworthy for its own sake (viz., our animal pleasures) being an imitation of a distinct thing (the pleasure of contemplation).

CHAPTER FIVE

Theoretical and Practical Reason

IS IT TRUE that the morally virtuous approximate contemplative excellence? If so, then, as I argued in the last chapter, morally virtuous activity would be choiceworthy for the sake of contemplation as for an object of love. Aristotle's happy person could make all his choices with an eye to contemplation without rendering irrelevant the intrinsic value of courage, justice, temperance, and the other moral virtues.[1] In this chapter, I will try to show that, in Aristotle's account of the intellectual virtues in NE VI, there is a structural similarity between practical wisdom and theoretical wisdom that would give us partial grounds for saying that the one is an approximation of the other. Of course, as I said earlier, which of these virtues is the paradigm and which the approximation cannot be determined solely by noticing that there is an analogy between them. Nevertheless, it is important to notice the similarity, for in NE VI Aristotle himself seems to emphasize it. It is interesting for two reasons. First, since Aristotle also believes that contemplative virtue is the most perfect exercise of our rational capacity, the analogy between the two kinds of reason suggests that practical wisdom is not just an*other* kind of reason, but a derivative kind, deserving of the title reason in virtue of its similarity to contemplation.[2] Of course, at the beginning of NE VI, when Aristotle presents the two kinds of reason as analogous, he does not present practical reason as derivative from theoretical reason, and that leads me to the second reason his emphasis on the structural similarity is important. For if one already values practical excellence very highly, as Aristotle's well-bred audience does, then coming to understand its similarity to theoretical excellence will be a step toward recognizing that *theôria* has a nobility that one might not have attributed to it before. Aristotle has already shown in books II–V that morally virtuous actions are praiseworthy because they are in accordance with right reason. When he turns to NE VI, Aristotle argues that the sense in which right reason is right is analogous to the sense in which excellent theoretical reasoning is right. So, if we admire right practical reasoning, we should also admire right theoretical reasoning. In other words, I believe the

---

[1] I mean that the happy person *could* choose the moral virtues for this reason. As will become clear, he will not *have* to choose virtuous actions for the sake of contemplation in order to be genuinely virtuous and happy (in a secondary way).

[2] Aristotle claims that *sophia* is the superior rational virtue and, in particular, that it is superior over *phronêsis* in the last two chapters of NE VI (1143b33–34, 1145a6–11). I will discuss the superiority of theoretically rational virtue at the end of this chapter.

structure of NE VI is protreptic, leading the audience raised in fine moral habits to an appreciation of theoretical wisdom. Indeed, I will argue that by the end of NE VI Aristotle takes the reader a step further: to appreciate that in some sense theoretical wisdom is a standard for practical wisdom.

1. THE SEPARATENESS AND SIMILARITY OF THEORETICAL AND PRACTICAL REASON

We encounter the analogy between practical wisdom and theoretical virtue almost immediately upon beginning NE VI. Indeed, it is the first discussion to which Aristotle turns after his introductory demand for a clearer account of the standard of right reason.[3] At VI.1 1139a3–5 Aristotle reminds us of a claim he made in I.13 that practical virtue is actually the good condition of two parts of the soul: the rational part and the irrational part attentive to some degree or other to reason. In other words, the activity of practical virtue is acting and feeling in accordance with reason's understanding of what ought to be done.[4] This account of moral virtue might lead to two mistakes about the picture of human psychology underlying it. In the first place, it might lead us to suppose that (1) while the irrational part cannot be in a good condition unless the reason it obeys is in a good condition, the good condition of the rational part itself is independent of the irrational part it directs. We might think a person can be quite correct in his opinions about what ought to be done regardless of whether his desires and emotions correspond to his considered judgments. If he does not desire as he believes—if, for instance, he is akratic—well, that is a problem with his desire, not with his reason. Furthermore, if the virtue of practical reason is independent of the good condition of desire, we might suppose, bearing in mind Aristotle's realism about ethics, that (2) the virtue of theoretical reason is not in any interesting way different from the virtue of practical reason. In both cases, rational virtue is a matter of judging truly about facts of biology, cosmology, and mathematics on the one hand, and about facts concerning human action on the other. In the first two chapters of NE VI, Aristotle denies both (1) and (2). Theoretical and practical rational virtue *are* interestingly different, and they are so because the virtue of practical reason is not independent of the virtue of nonrational desire. This allows Aristotle to develop an account of the relationship between moral and theoretical virtue according to which they are structurally analogous but genuinely different types of rational virtuous activity.

[3] Commentators often find it to be a rough transition from the demand for a clear account of right reason in the first half of NE VI.1 to the discussion of the two rational parts of the soul in the second half of VI.1. This may well be due to Aristotle's having added, for the NE, a new introduction to EE material (Gauthier and Jolif 1970, not. ad VI.1). I hope that, by the end of my discussion of NE VI, however, the transition will not seem a non sequitur.

[4] That is, virtue requires not only correct rational wishes but appropriate feelings and nonrational (non-good-oriented) desires.

Let me begin with a sketch of Aristotle's argument for the distinction between theoretical and practical rational virtue. In *NE* VI.1 Aristotle notices that theoretical reasoning concerns objects that differ in kind (*ta tôi genei hetera*, 1139a9) from the objects of practical reasoning. Whereas scientific or theoretical reason examines things whose principles cannot be otherwise, calculative or practical reasoning examines things that can vary (*ta endechomena*; 1139a6–8). Now, because the objects of theoretical and practical reasoning differ in kind, Aristotle believes we must attribute our ability to study these two kinds of thing to two different parts of the soul. This is because, according to Aristotle, the soul must be similar to that which it thinks if knowledge is to be possible (1139a8–11). If things whose principles cannot be otherwise are genuinely different from things that can be otherwise, then the parts of the soul by which we know them must be different as well, and in corresponding ways: Theoretical reason must be fixed and unchanging, while practical reason must be able to change to suit the variability of the circumstances it addresses. Thus, Aristotle concludes that the strictly speaking rational capacity[5] has two parts (*merê*), distinguished by the two kinds of object they reason about: The scientific part (*to epistêmonikon*) is set over things with unchangeable principles; and the calculative part (*to logistikon*) is set over the rest (1139a5–8).[6]

We are now in a position to begin to see how excellent theoretical activity is analogous to excellent practical reasoning. For in some sense, the work or function [*ergon*] of both parts of the rational soul is the same: truth (1139b12). Thus, since virtue is defined in terms of function (I.7 1098a8–15), there is also a sense in which the virtues of practical and theoretical reason are the same.[7] On the other hand, since the two rational parts seek truth about fundamentally different kinds of thing, there is also a sense in which they have their peculiar (*oikeia*) work to do, and thus a sense in which their virtues and virtuous activities differ as well (1139a15–17). Virtuous practical reasoning is truthfulness about things to be done, by oneself and others, while virtuous theoretical reasoning is truthfulness about the unchangeable aspects of nature and the world more generally.

Now, Aristotle will want eventually to argue not only that practical and theoretical reasoning are analogous but that theoretical reasoning is superior to practical reasoning. Furthermore, partly on the basis of this claim, Aristotle

---

[5] As opposed to the irrational part that shares in reason in a way.

[6] Thus, Aristotle uses a Platonic principle to argue for an un-Platonic conclusion (*Rep.* V 477c ff.). Gauthier and Jolif (1970, not. ad 1139a6–8) also notice that not only does Aristotle use a Platonic principle of soul division, he also divides objects of thinking along Platonic lines. The result is that, in *NE* VI.1 at least, Aristotle's *logistikon* looks to be the same as Plato's *doxastikon*, although now endowed with genuine knowledge. (See *NE* VI.5 1140b25–30, where Aristotle actually calls the practically rational soul the *doxastikon*.) This will cause problems, as we shall see in note 9.

[7] Greenwood (1909, 74) notices the connection between VI.2 and the function argument. Kraut (1989, 58–59) also notices the similarity in function of practical and theoretical reason.

will argue that the philosophical life, devoted as it is to theoretical contemplation, is the happiest, and in particular that it is happier than the political life devoted to excellence in practical reasoning. We should pause a moment, then, to see what sense we can make of Aristotle's claim that practical and theoretical reasoning are genuinely different activities, legitimately requiring different parts of the soul and different soul capacities to be their ground. I suspect readers have been content to accept Aristotle's separation of theoretical and practical reason because humility requires us to admit that excellence in the one does not guarantee excellence in the other. Philosophers would probably not make good kings. But this piece of conventional wisdom is not grounds for accepting Aristotle's claim that these two kinds of reasoning are fundamentally different activities springing from different "parts" of the soul. After all, not every distinction in subject matter calls for a new part of the soul with which to contemplate it. What I ought to do and what the city, through its officials, ought to do are different, but both are the objects of practical reasoning (1141b23–24). And this is so despite the fact that we think people can be good at managing public affairs while making a mess of their personal lives. Furthermore, as Aristotle himself takes pains to point out, there is an important difference between *praxis* (action) and *poiêsis* (production), but despite this difference both are objects of kinds of practical knowledge (1140a1–5).[8] The situation is the same on the side of theoretical reason as well. Both mathematics and theology are theoretical sciences. Why, then, is the distinction between things whose principles cannot be otherwise and things that are changeable not an arbitrary basis for dividing the rational soul?

In fact, matters seem to be worse, for it is not at all clear that these objects really do distinguish theoretical from practical reasoning. Aristotle thinks that things happen in the natural world "for the most part" (*Phys.* II.5 196b10–13). For example, the form of an oak tree is the final and formal cause of the acorn. It is genuinely explanatory, Aristotle thinks, to appeal to form when describing why the acorn sprouts and grows as it typically does. But not every acorn becomes an oak. Things realize their forms, their forms act as causes, only "for the most part." So, as Aristotle has described the range of theoretically knowable objects in NE VI.1, biology and physics—the study of changing things—are not theoretical knowledge. The study of physics certainly isn't practical, though.[9] Aristotle must, in fact, mean to include the physical sci-

---

[8] Obviously I mean practical in the broad sense, i.e., pertaining to things we can change or bring about. I do not mean practical in the sense of pertaining to *praxis*.

[9] Gauthier and Jolif (1970) think this problem arises from Aristotle's adopting Plato's way of distinguishing the *logistikon* (reasoning) from the *doxastikon* (opining) as his way of distinguishing the *epistêmonikon* (scientific knowing) from the *logistikon* (calculative or deliberative knowing). They point out that in *De Anima* Aristotle drops this way of dividing the rational soul and opts instead to identify the parts on the basis of what they do, i.e., as the speculative and practical intellects (not. ad 1139a14–15). It is clear from what follows in NE VI that Aristotle intends these two rational faculties to cover theoretical speculation and practical reasoning, respectively. It may be that he is simply being careless in VI.1. But we should also note that very many things that are changeable are, insofar as they are changeable, of particular concern to us *as agents*.

ences among the types of theoretical knowledge (*Meta.* E.1).[10] The point is that even when the theoretical sciences study things that change, they study the unchanging aspects of the phenomena. The objects of practical reasoning, on the other hand, are *ta endechomena* (whatever can be otherwise than it is) *as such*. That is, practical reason knows whatever concerns us as agents insofar as it concerns us as agents.[11] *Ta endechomena* in the sense relevant to Aristotle's distinction between theoretical and practical reason are whatever can be changed by us or what can, by changing, affect our fortunes. Theoretical and practical reason do not necessarily think about different objects, though; they think about the world under different guises.

But if theoretical reasoning can at some level study things that happen for the most part, then good chunks of practical reasoning look to be theoretical. After all, much practical deliberation—particularly artisanal reasoning—is about means to our ends; but this is just a matter of figuring out what can be relied upon, for the most part, to cause what. And insofar as practical reasoning considers what constitutes our ends, it examines the forms of our ends and their parts. No doubt, Aristotle is more impressed than we are by the difference between the products of craft and of nature. In the case of craft, Aristotle thinks we impose form on matter; natural objects, on the other hand, come to be and change on account of the form they have in themselves. Thus, for Aristotle there is a real difference between things that change through our own efforts and those that change themselves: The latter are natural and the former are not. But this distinction is bound to seem less significant to us, and probably not significant enough to warrant thinking of practical and theoretical reasoning as two distinct kinds of reasoning. Aristotelian scholars are accustomed to wondering whether science, as we now understand it, vitiates the function argument. Does it also threaten Aristotelian ethics by failing to support the ontological categories necessary for an interesting distinction between practical and theoretical reasoning?[12]

---

[10] Aristotle can cause confusion on this point himself when he explains the nature of physical science by analogy to *technê* (craft) (*Phys.* II.2). But this is not because he thinks there is anything practical about physics. Rather, he thinks the objects of natural science are related to their own changes in the way that craftsmen are related to changes in the materials with which they work, namely, natural substances move themselves toward their own ends (Broadie 1990, 392–396). Thus, Aristotle thinks the science of craft changes can provide a model for the structure of physics; in particular, the fact that *technê* must know about the matter as well as the form is reason to think that even though physics is primarily concerned with form, it must study matter to a certain extent as well (*Phys.* 194a12 ff.).

[11] This is presupposed in Aristotle's argument in *Meta.* E.1 that physics is a branch of theoretical science, along with mathematics and theology (which he assimilates with knowledge of separable and unmovable substance). His argument is that whereas practical and productive knowledge studies things that are changed by independent agents (i.e., people) and not by themselves, physics studies things whose principle of change is internal (1025b18–24). The idea must be that physics is genuinely a theoretical science because it does not view the world from the point of view of human agency.

[12] There are, of course, different ways of distinguishing practical and theoretical reasoning, e.g., Kant believes that practical reason is able to discover the necessity of our freedom, whereas

Finally, though the different objects of knowledge will sometimes require different methods of inquiry,[13] methodological difference is not the basis for distinguishing theoretical and practical reason, according to Aristotle in *NE* VI, and it is not particularly promising anyway. Sometimes their methods will in fact look quite similar. At least, Aristotle encourages us to think so when he puts some bits of practical reasoning in syllogistic form (*NE* VII.3).[14] At any rate, both kinds of reason draw conclusions on the basis of premises of one sort or another; presumably the same logical rules of inference apply in both cases. And eventually both kinds of reason ultimately need to appeal to premises that are established not by demonstration or deliberation but by dialectic and experience.[15] Now, these observations about method support the thought that theoretical and practical reasoning are analogous. Indeed, at this point they look virtually identical, distinguished merely by an ontological prejudice and an accident of Aristotle's theory of knowledge. Practical reason does not seem to be a different *kind* of reasoning, much less a kind subordinate to philosophical contemplation and choiceworthy for its sake as an object of approximation.

Despite these reasons to doubt the coherence of Aristotle's distinction between practical and theoretical reasoning, I believe it is a valuable and a legitimate one for him to make. The difference lies not so much in the methods employed by the practical and scientific faculties or in the difference per se

---

speculative reason can discover only its possibility ([1785] 1977, 4:461). As I understand Kant, however, practical and speculative reason are not distinguished as faculties, nor are the two sets of reasoning two kinds of activity. Rather, we distinguish practical from speculative reason depending on the use to which reason itself is being put.

[13] In particular, things with unchanging, necessary principles are amenable to strictly scientific demonstration (*Post. An.* I.4), whereas particular events are not. Thus, while it would be inappropriate to attempt a scientific demonstration of what ought to be done on a particular occasion, genuine knowledge of mathematics (for example) requires such rigor (*NE* 1094b23–27).

[14] The practical syllogism may not be part of deliberation proper (Cooper [1975] 1986, 51), but it is certainly an expression of intellectual activity. Aristotle says that, in *akrasia*, the failure of the premises of reason's syllogism to be synthesized into a conclusion (action) is a failure of knowledge to be fully realized (see note 18, below).

[15] Cooper ([1975] 1986, 65–70) and Reeve (1995, 56–61). We might also notice that the argument structures discussed in the *Rhetoric* are meant to be pieces of practical reasoning, but they are often the same as those discussed in the *Topics*, a handbook of argumentation in general. Even if such debates do not yet rise to the level of philosophical wisdom, they are exercises of theoretical rational capacity. See Kraut (1989, 58–59) for discussion of methodological similarity.

When Frede suggests that genuine knowledge that, e.g., poultry is good to eat requires scientific knowledge of human physiology in Aristotle's very rigorous sense (1996, 168), he implies that genuine practical knowledge is almost identical to true theoretical knowledge. For reasons I give below, I believe there are important dissimilarities. This should not cause us to think that practical wisdom does not rise to the level of genuine rationality, however. Even though Aristotle believes that practical reason fails to achieve the epistomological ideal set by theoretical wisdom, it is important for the interpretation of his moral theory to see that nevertheless practical reason and its virtue, *phronêsis*, express genuine rationality. Practical reason, like theoretical reason, essentially aims at and grasps truth. See pp. 114–115, 117–119 below.

between the particular kinds of fact they consider as they engage in a course of reasoning. Rather, the difference is in what it takes to be living *truthfully* with respect to the objects of theoretical and practical knowledge. Reason, like our capacity for nutrition, is a part of the soul; it is, in other words, a life capacity, according to Aristotle. Thus its activation is a way of living. Since the function of the whole rational soul is truth, we can call this way of living "grasping the truth" or, as I will tend to say, "living truthfully."[16] Aristotle believes that the manifestation of truthfulness (i.e., of reason's performing its function) with respect to theoretical and practical objects is quite different. And so, though a person might be quite capable of living theoretically truthfully, this will not guarantee any capacity to live practically truthfully. In particular, Aristotle believes that without the agreement of the irrational part of the soul, a person will not be able to manifest a grasp of practical truth, and so will not be able, properly speaking, to *have* that grasp. "For theoretical thought (*dianoia*), which is neither practical nor productive, the virtuous and bad states (*to eû kai kakôs*) are truth and falsehood (for this is the function [*ergon*] of the whole *dianoetic* part of the soul); but for the practical and *dianoetic* part [the virtuous state] is truth agreeing with right desire" (1139a27–31).[17] The good condition of a person's practical reason is not enough, as it turns out, for him to live truthfully with respect to objects of practical concern.[18]

---

[16] By "living truthfully" I mean to indicate a wide variety of ways in which a person may grasp the truth, only one of which is entertaining a true proposition. The verb *alêtheuô*, which can mean 'be right about', indicates that *alêtheia* (truth) can be attributed to the knower himself as well as to what he knows. See 1139b12–13, where Aristotle says that the parts of the rational soul *alêtheusei* when they possess their proper virtues. Also see 1127a24, where Aristotle talks about the virtue of being prone to truthfulness (*ôn alêtheutikos*) in words and in life.

[17] Some may object that this passage does not commit Aristotle to saying that practical reason needs the cooperation of *nonrational* desire, since Aristotle distinguishes rational desire (*boulêsis*) from various nonrational desires. It does not particularly matter for my argument whether we think of the right desire here referred to as *boulêsis* (rational wish), on the one hand, or *epithumia* (appetite) or *thumos* (spirit), on the other. (Although, since *boulêsis* is *rational* desire and so cannot ever disagree with reason, it would be odd, if Aristotle is referring to *boulêsis* here, for him to insist that the right desire must agree with reason.) I would point out, though, that the highest form of practical truthfulness is practical wisdom and it *does* require the cooperation of nonrational desire.

[18] Cooper ([1975] 1986, 61–62) offers a similar rationale for the difference between theoretical and practical knowledge. Unlike theoretical knowledge, "[p]ractical knowledge must make, or tend to make, a practical difference in what a person prefers on the whole to do and does do in his life." Cooper's caveat leads me to suspect, however, that we do not interpret the difference in exactly the same way. In a footnote he writes, "[t]he qualification is necessary to take account of sufferers of *akrasia*, who know what to do, but fail to do it." Now, while it is true in some sense that the akratic agent knows what to do, it is also true that he does not *fully* know what to do. For what the akratic's desires prevent him from doing is fully actualizing his knowledge (1146b31–1147a24). Thus, in interpreting Aristotle we must resist the temptation to say that the akratic perfectly well knows what to do. He does not know it perfectly well, for perfect practical knowing, according to Aristotle, is chosen action. (The akratic knows what to do in the much same sense

Let us take a case of deliberation, a paradigmatic expression of practical reasoning, to see how this is so. The objects of deliberation about my own life are not just anything that could be otherwise; they are the things I could bring about (1112a28–31). That is to say, I reason about them under the description "things I could bring about." Thus, unlike idle reasoning about things that could happen, practical reasoning, as Aristotle understands it, carries with it an interest in changing things.[19] The point of practical reasoning is to figure out which of these possibilities is good for me to bring about. This is not idle speculation. As Aristotle repeatedly claims, we deliberate not in order that we might know the variety of ways of obtaining the good but in order that we might actually have it (e.g., 1095a5–6, 1179a35–b2). In other words, the specific function of practical reason, the way in which it expresses or aims to express truthfulness, is choice.[20] Practical reason aims

---

as I know the elevation of Sewanee, Tennessee, I just can't think of it right now. The difference in these two cases is the role nonrational desire plays in preventing actualization of knowledge.)

[19] This is why for Aristotle reason is desiderative; not just any reason, of course, but reasoning with a view to an end we can bring about (1139a35–36).

[20] I infer this from the flow of argument in VI.2: Aristotle begins by saying he will look for the virtue, and thus the function, of the theoretic and practical parts of reason. Then Aristotle discusses choice and the way in which it involves both desire and reason. I take it his point is to show that, just as moral virtue—the virtue of the nonrational soul—is a prohairetic state (1139a22–24), so too practical rational virtue, coming from a different angle, is a prohairetic state (i.e., a state concerned with *prohairesis*, or choice). Then, once Aristotle has established the function of practical reason as deliberation issuing in choice, he can define practical rational virtue in terms of its contribution to good choice. Gauthier and Jolif (1970, not. ad 1139a15–b13) agree that the discussion of choice in VI.2 is an elucidation of the species of truthfulness that is practical.

Notice that in my interpretation, Aristotle thinks *all* kinds of practical reason are expressed in choice, and so *all* practical reasoning—*phronêsis* and *technê* alike—requires the cooperation of desire. But is this correct? Sarah Broadie has argued (1991, 78–82) that moral virtue is distinguished from craft knowledge precisely insofar as the former but not the latter is a prohairetic state, a state involving a settled disposition to choose and so involving a settled disposition to desire certain things. It is indeed true that in *NE* II.4 Aristotle says that while virtue requires (1) knowledge, (2) choosing the actions and choosing them for their own sakes, and (3) a firm and unchangeable character, craft requires only knowledge (1105a26–b2). That seems proof against my claim that the exercise of craft knowledge requires a certain state of desire. We should note, however, that in the next line Aristotle goes on to say that knowledge is of almost no account in the possession of virtue (1105b2–3). This clearly is an opinion he will revise (in *NE* VI.13) when he argues for the inseparability of moral virtue and *phronêsis*. So even though in *NE* II.4 Aristotle does want to distinguish craft knowledge and virtue on the basis of their relationship to *prohairesis* it is not immediately clear what the distinction is supposed to be. (Perhaps Aristotle only means that moral virtue, unlike craft, chooses its actions for their own sakes? If so, this would correspond to Aristotle's distinction between *praxis* and *poiêsis* ([Gauthier and Jolif 1970, not. ad 1105a29; Irwin, trans. 1985, not. ad 1105a28].) Aristotle's explanation of choice in *NE* III.2 only exacerbates the obscurity of his point in II.2 about the connection between moral virtue, *technê*, and choice. The only positive characterization Aristotle gives of choice there is that it is the natural outcome of prior deliberation (1112a15). But when we turn to Aristotle's discussion of deliberation in the next chapter, he always uses examples of craft deliberation to explain his meaning. The implication, although admittedly Aristotle never says so, is that craft knowledge, when used, issues in choice. At least, Aristotle says that we choose to do what deliberation leads us to (1113a2–5).

at a determination *to do* such and such.[21] Action and choice (in normal cases the former follows unproblematically upon the latter)[22] is the *telos* of practical reasoning; it shapes my considerations, for example, by getting me to look for the most expedient route to my practical goal (1112b16–17). But choice is a mixture of reasoning (a proper choice, according to Aristotle, is

---

When we turn to *NE* VI, where Aristotle addresses the difference between craft and *phronêsis* directly, we see that Aristotle does *not* appeal to desire and choice as a way to make this distinction. On the contrary, it is assumed that both are deliberative activities and that they differ in their objects of deliberation: Craft deliberates about a part of life; *phronêsis* deliberates about the whole thing (1140a25–28). Now as I said, *NE* III.2–3 suggest that deliberation naturally ends in choice. We also know, from *NE* III and again from *NE* VI (1113a9–12, 1139b4–5), that choice is deliberative desire. So, if craft is a deliberative activity, it seems we ought to conclude that craft per se is realized in choice and requires the cooperation of desire just as much as *phronêsis* does. And since craft is a state of the soul, it ought also to be some sort of prohairetic state.

Still, I confess that the evidence of VI.2 is unclear. Aristotle claims to be talking about the function of practical reason as a whole, but he slips into talking about the *virtue* of practical reason, whose desiderative counterpart is moral virtue (1139a22). Presumably Aristotle slips back and forth in book VI because the virtue of practical reason, and not craft, is his real interest there. This can cause difficulties for interpretation, however. Aristotle is quite clear that craft, although a rational accomplishment, is not a practical rational virtue (1140b21–25), so not everything true of the desiderative counterpart of *phronêsis* will necessarily hold for the desiderative counterpart of craft.

Perhaps we could say that *technê* is an ancillary prohairetic state. After all, a person may possess craft knowledge as a first actuality without ever having an actual desire to exercise it. Unless producing that particular product is desirable from the point of view of his life as a whole, the craftsman will never engage in craft deliberation. (This is why choice is particularly indicative ([*oikeiotaton*] of moral character [*NE* III.2 1111b5–6].) Thus, for the virtuous person, craft will depend on *phronêsis*. The ancillary status of craft does not imply, however, that the craftsman's desires *qua* craftsman can be in any old state when he uses his special knowledge. In other words, the regulation of his nonrational soul is not entirely the work of his moral character. For it is part of having a craft that, while it is being exercised, at least some of the craftsman's desires conform to whatever it is his craft reasoning tells him to do. These desires are not external to the craft. Broadie gives an example meant to show that emotional disturbance does not make us deny craft knowledge to a person. If a person makes a mess of building something from fear of the enemy at the gate, we do not say that he doesn't *know* how to build; we say, rather, that his cowardice prevented him from using his knowledge. I agree that this sort of emotional disturbance does not impugn artistic knowledge. But not all emotional disturbance is external to craft in this way. For example, think of a builder who is easily satisfied with mediocre products, whose laziness leads to sloppy execution. Or think of a person whose love of excess leads him to unsuitable ornamentation of the things he makes. Such people are bad *as craftsmen*. It seems to me, then, that craft, like *phronêsis*, requires something like a prohairetic state.

However we solve these difficulties, though, this much is clear: full possession of craft knowledge requires that in the appropriate conditions the craftsman has the right desires and performs the right actions. Craft knowledge does not, on its own, issue in all-things-considered judgments; it needs the exercise of *phronêsis* to decide what craft product is needed. But once *phronêsis* gives the go-ahead, the craftsman needs the cooperation of desire in order to possess craft truth, since the craftsman must decide to proceed in such and such a way.

[21] I am persuaded by Cooper ([1975] 1986, 24–46) that choice is a decision to perform an action of a certain *type*. That decision is realized in a specific action. I do not think anything in what I say depends on this interpretation, however.

[22] Mele [1985] 1999, 184–188.

the consequence of rational deliberation toward an end) and desire" (1139a23). "Choice is desiderative thought (*noûs*) or intellectual desire (1139b4–5). Notice that choice needs more than mere rational wish (*boulêsis*); it needs nonrational desire as well. For Aristotle, choice is not a mere desire; it is a desire that *moves* the agent, barring outside interference.[23] The akratic agent shows that without some degree of cooperation from appetite, a person's judgments of practical goodness will not express themselves in chosen action. In Aristotle's analysis, the akratic makes a choice in the sense of determining the particular sort of action he ought to perform but fails to actualize this knowledge because of the interference of independent, nonrational desires.[24] The akratic's knowledge exists only as a capacity; it is not active knowing. Thus, practical reason cannot express truthfulness without the cooperation of desire. Or, to put it more perspicuously, *we* cannot live truthfully concerning what we ought to do unless we choose well. But given what choice is, "the reason (*logon*) must be true and the desire right if the choice is to be good, and the one must assert and the other pursue the same things" (1139a23–26) Our ordinary, even nonakratic, experience confirms Aristotle's point. It may be true that you really do know Serbo-Croatian, but if right now you cannot speak it or read it or understand a word, then in the most important sense you *don't* know it. Grasping practical truth—really possessing it and not just being capable of having it—just is the activity of choosing and desiring and acting well.

This point about the exercise of practical reason holds not only in cases of deliberation, where we are trying to decide what *we* should do. It holds for all cases of thinking about the world insofar as it interests us as practical beings, including cases where we direct our attention to thinking about other people's affairs. For correct thinking about the affairs of other people is expressed in appropriate feelings of pity and indignation (*Rhet.* II.8–9). And although the desire to act does not necessarily accompany pity and indignation, these emotions are inclined to make a practical difference (*Rhet.* II.1 1378a19–22).[25] But even when they do not lead us to act, it is nevertheless true that we do not fully grasp the practical truth on these occasions without the accompanying appropriate emotional reaction.

---

[23] On the other hand, because choice is the result of rational deliberation, choice is not necessary for voluntary action. Children and animals, for example, act voluntarily but not from choice (*NE* III.2 1111b8–9). So desire is necessary for choice, but choice is not necessary for voluntary action.

[24] I will not take a position here about precisely how the akratic's epistemic faculties break down. All that's necessary for my argument here is that *akrasia*—the failure to be moved by one's deliberations—is an epistemic as well as a conative deficiency.

[25] Aristotle defines the emotions as things that cause people to change their judgments (*Rhet.* 1378a19–20). Since this definition is given in the context of a study of rhetoric, the judgments that emotions can incline us to change are, at least in part, judicial judgments. Thus, Greenwood (1909, 67) is wrong to infer from 1143a9–10 ("understanding is only critical" and not directive, as *phronêsis* is) that "*sunesis* is quite detached from *orexis* and so from *prohairesis*."

So, as it turns out, the proper objects of practical reasoning—*ta endechomena*, the things possible for us to bring about—do demand a kind of truthfulness peculiar to them and not shared with the objects of theoretical reasoning. Practical reason examines the possible actions available to a person with an eye to doing the one it would be good for him to do. It would be incorrect to say that practical reasoning is complete once it formulates the true proposition, "Φ-ing would be best." The interest of practical reason in the particular aspects of a scene relevant to action, the search for the most direct means to an end, the abandoning of a train of thought when reason finds out that, in this situation, action by *me* is not possible, all suggest that the proper *ergon* and final cause of practical reasoning is not idle knowledge but action. Whereas theoretical knowledge is manifested most fully in understanding scientific demonstrations and the first principles from which they are derived, practical knowledge is manifested in choice. Anything less is incomplete knowing.

Theoretical and practical reasoning are analogous, then, because, when done well, both are ways of being truthful. They are genuinely distinct, however, because the objects of the two kinds of reason demand different activities if they are to be grasped successfully. *Ta endechomena*, the things that can be changed by us, are grasped in action and choice. Thus, practical truthfulness requires the activity of desire. The unchangeable objects of theoretical reason, on the other hand, can be achieved by reason alone. Theoretical truthfulness, then, is the activity of pure thinking.

So far I have been emphasizing the ways in which theoretical and practical reasoning are genuinely different, taking it for granted that the common aim of truthfulness, combined with similar methods of reasoning, will be sufficient to establish their similarity. But if grasping truth in the practical case is a matter of making good choices while grasping truth in the scientific case is a matter of contemplating demonstrations of truths from known principles, we may begin to doubt how similar these two modes of truthful living really are.[26] Why should we think we have not stretched the meaning of *truth* beyond recognition when we apply it to choices and actions as well as to propositions? If we cannot establish a robust enough similarity between the two kinds of truthful living, how likely will it be that love of practical truthfulness will ever develop, in the course of reading the *Nicomachean Ethics*, to love of theoretical contemplation?[27]

We can begin by noticing the connection between *akribeia* and truthfulness. There is not an English translation of *akribeia* that does it justice in all contexts. Usually it is translated as 'precision' or 'exactitude', though in *NE*

---

[26] This is why, although I agree with Charles (1999, 216–217) that Aristotle does describe practical and theoretical reason as being analogous, I believe he is too blithe in grounding the analogy in the fact that both kinds of virtue consist in "grasping truths."

[27] I thank Tad Brennan for helping me to see the seriousness of this problem.

VI.7 Ross translates the adjective as 'finished.'[28] The word does have both the sense of perfection and of precision.[29] Something is *akribês* when it is rendered to absolute perfection, with neither too much nor too little.[30] And "in general, being *akribês* seems to amount (vaguely enough) to being of good epistemic quality."[31] Now, Aristotle says that, for each part of the rational soul, the virtue of each part is the state by which one is most of all truthful (*malista alêtheusei*; 1139b12–13). But how do we determine which state this is? Aristotle says that of all the good states of theoretical reason, philosophical wisdom (*sophia*) turns out to be its proper virtue because it is *akribestatê* (most *akribês*) (1141a16). This suggests, then, that *akribeia* is a mark of truthfulness. It is a sign that the truth has been perfectly grasped. Practical reasoning can also be *akribês*, or precise. For instance, Aristotle says that craft reasoning may be more or less *akribês* (1141a9–10), although it is always less *akribês* than moral virtue (1106b14).[32] This suggests that even though Aristotle tells us not to look for *akribeia* in ethical philosophy (1094b19–27, 1103b34–1104a10), he does not mean that practical knowledge is lacking in *akribeia* altogether.[33] Rather, his point seems to be that we should not look for as much precision as we would in theoretical sciences. So one reason it is appropriate to talk about practical and theoretical reason as modes of truthfulness seems to be that it is appropriate to measure their

---

[28] Irwin (trans., 1985) translates in VI.7 as 'exact expertise' or 'exact knowledge' depending on whether Aristotle is discussing craft or science.

[29] Thucydides, the *akribeia* of the ship (LSJ). To the ideas of perfection and precision (completeness and accuracy), Greenwood (1909, 35) adds stability: Scientific knowledge would be stable, then, because in grasping the truth of the demonstrations and their premises, a person would not be vulnerable to changing his mind. Though this sounds plausible, I'm not sure what basis, if any, Greenwood has for saying this.

[30] *Akribês* can also mean frugal or stingy (LSJ).

[31] Barnes 1994, 189, not. ad *Post. An.* I.27.

[32] Why does Aristotle think that moral virtue is more *akribês* than craft? Aristotle may mean that moral virtue is more *akribês* because it grasps the first principle of practical activity (i.e., happiness, the human good), while the goodness of crafts can be understood only with reference to this first principle. See my discussion (pp. 111–112) of Aristotle's claim that one science is more precise than another when "it is at the same time of the fact and of the reason why" (*Post. An.* 87a31–32). Another possibility, suggested by Broadie (Broadie and Rowe 2002, not. ad 1106b14–16), is that, unlike the craftsman, the morally virtuous person must be utterly uncompromising about his goals. Whatever Aristotle's rationale for calling moral virtue more *akribês*, *akribeia* is a sign of greater truthfulness. For *phronêsis* combined with moral virtue is the perfection of the part of the soul that seeks practical truth.

[33] Though I agree with Reeve (1995) that there is some reason to think there can be a proper science of human life (*Pol.* 1279b11–15), I doubt that the *NE* is meant to be such an exercise. Aristotle repeatedly says that his object is action, educational reform, and happiness, and not only knowledge. Furthermore, Aristotle dismisses theoretical speculation of matters to do with the human good that are not practical, for instance, an intensive examination of the human soul (I.13 1102a23–26) or the way in which good things are good (I.6 1096b26–31). In other words, he emphasizes that the *NE* is reasoning with a view to an end in action. That's what practical reasoning is.

success in reaching their goal in terms of precision. I'll discuss *akribeia* in more detail in the next section.

It is also likely that Aristotle considers both practical deliberation and theoretical speculation to be forms of reasoning because in a sense they are both precise in grasping the same kind of thing. Like Plato, Aristotle thinks of the good as the characteristic concern of reason. It is perhaps no surprise to find that, according to Aristotle, *practical* reason knows the good. *Phronêsis*, in particular, is concerned with the human good on the most general level (1140b4–6), but even technical reason aims at the good in its particular sphere (1140a25–30). Insofar as an artisan lets the intended product guide his actions, he accepts it as a source of value for his actions.[34] What may be more surprising is that theoretical reason, like its practical cousin, also contemplates the good. Of course, in the theoretical case reason will not consider the good as an end to be achieved. But according to Aristotle the good is not only a practical first principle; it is a metaphysical and physical first principle as well. For example, in the *Metaphysics* Aristotle says that *sophia*—the most authoritative kind of knowledge—is the science of that for the sake of which, and this is the good at the most general or universal level (*Meta.* A.2 982a19–82b10). And in *NE* VI Aristotle says *sophia* is directed toward the most honorable things (*timiôtatôn*; 1141a18–20, 1141b2–3). Even when Aristotle has a more modest conception of theoretical inquiry, for instance, in his biological and physical writings, we see that the good is never far from the surface. For instance, Aristotle argues that we cannot give an adequate account of the parts of animals without explaining their final cause or relationship to the good of the whole animal (*PA* I.1). In *De Anima* Aristotle differentiates the kinds of soul with reference to their ends and defines soul itself as the final cause of the body (415b9–17). Scientific explanation, then, seems to be very much a matter of getting it right about what the good of each physical thing is. In that way it is analogous to practical reasoning. In both cases, reasoning is more truthful to the extent that it is precise about the good in its sphere of inquiry.[35]

---

[34] It strikes me that in the passage at 1140a25–30 Aristotle is explaining how *phronêsis* aims at the good in a way that is different from the way *technê* aims at goods. That suggests that *all* practical reason aims at the good in some way or other.

[35] There are, of course, some passages that militate against this view. I mentioned above that Aristotle says *sophia* contemplates the most honorable things. But it is not obvious that the most honorable things are good. For instance, at *Meta.* M.3 1078a30–b6, Aristotle seems to say that the good is not found among unmovable things (although the beautiful is). If wisdom is concerned with unmovables, that ought to mean that it is not concerned with goodness. Aristotle's meaning here is ambiguous, however. Immediately after saying this, he contradicts "those who say that the mathematical sciences say nothing of the beautiful or of the good"; on the contrary "these sciences say and prove a very great deal about *them* [presumably]" (1078a33–35, my emphasis). Why does Aristotle say that mathematics can teach us about the beautiful *and* the good if only the former is found among the unmovables? Perhaps all Aristotle means by his first remark is that good does not exist *for* the unmovables. They might themselves

We may still feel, however, that Aristotle is equivocating in some way when he says that the desires as well as the formulation of the appropriate reasons for those desires are true. So let me explain in greater detail what I think Aristotle has in mind. Aristotle thinks we grasp the practical truth not by entertaining correct propositions about what would be good for us but by desiring the right things for the right reasons. The affective element of morally virtuous action is partially constitutive of our fully knowing the human good. This seems to us an odd way to think about truth since for us truth is usually taken to be a feature of propositions that we can schematize in a truth table. But we should bear in mind that Aristotle's picture of knowing the truth is never that of a person entertaining (with appropriate justification) a proposition that corresponds to reality. Aristotle's knower *himself* corresponds to the object known. However we are to interpret the obscure discussion of the active intellect in *De Anima* III, it is clear that, according to Aristotle, *noûs* in some way *becomes* the form of the object it knows. From this point of view it is not a gross equivocation on the notion of truth to say that the virtuous agent knows the truth by choosing and acting. In realizing the human good in his actions, he corresponds to the object of knowledge in the appropriate way.[36] We might say that for Aristotle, all rational excellence is a matter of being in a truthful relationship to the object of knowledge. We will, of course, want to know why choice is the appropriate way to grasp practical truth, while all other truth can be grasped by reason alone. I leave that question, however, for a fuller study of Aristotle's moral epistemology.[37]

---

still be good, however. At any rate, Aristotle describes the first mover as thinking the good and "the most excellent of things [viz., itself]" (*Meta.* Λ.9 1074b23–34). Since the activity of the divine is the exemplar of theoretical reasoning, it seems safe to conclude that excellent theoretical reasoning, like excellent practical reasoning, is a matter of getting it right about the good.

If I am right then Aristotle's allocation of these two kinds of reasoning to two parts of the rational soul is not such a radical departure from Plato as we might have thought. For both Plato and Aristotle, the first principle of *all* reasoning is the good. Aristotle differs from Plato when he claims that the practical human good is distinct from the goods of other things. They are not the same, although they are analogous. Furthermore, Aristotle, unlike Plato, thinks that the good condition of the nonrational parts of the soul is not just a prerequisite for virtuous practical reasoning but is actually partly constitutive of virtuous practical reasoning.

[36] I thank Robert Adams for suggesting to me that Aristotle's theory of practical truthfulness might be an instance of a correspondence theory of truth. See Adams (1993) for a discussion of this topic with respect to Kierkegaard.

[37] For example, Thomas Nagel ([1974] 1979) has argued that we can know what a subjective point of view is like only by inhabiting it or something analogous to it. Rudolf Otto ([1917] 1923) has argued that the holy can be known only via a feeling of "mysterium tremendum."

A suggestion by Reeve (1995, 56–66) is worth mentioning in this context. (This following point is limited to moral reasoning and does not include the other modes of practical reasoning.) Aristotle claims throughout his discussions of individual moral virtues that the virtuous person performs fine (*kalon*) actions for the sake of the fine. Thus, the person of practical wisdom must be adept at knowing or in some sense seeing which actions are fine and good. But, as I will

So practical reason and theoretical reason are truthful when, in their different ways, they grasp precisely and fully the nature of the relevant good. Of course, desire on its own also aims at good things; and desire, like reason, is right when it aims at what really is good. There is an important difference, however, in the way reason and desire are directed at the good. While reason treats the good *as* the good, nonrational desire does not. Nevertheless, although the proper object of appetite is pleasure, its natural purpose (i.e., its tendency in a healthy person) is to lead people to the food they need. Appetite, then, aims at the good though not *as* the good. Here, then, is a way that desire itself is analogous to the activity of theoretical and practical reasoning. In this light it is striking to note the way in which Aristotle draws an analogy between the movement of desire and the actualization of reason. Aristotle says that what affirmation and denial are in thinking (*dianoia*), pursuit and avoidance are in desire (1139a21–22). In other words, pursuit is desire's way of saying "yes." Thus, the activity of the desiderative aspect of practical virtue is analogous both to the thinking aspect of that same virtue and to the activity of purely scientific virtue.[38] And when desire is shaped by reason, as it is in choice, that rational desire becomes a grasping of the truth of the human good.

In summary, then, the activity of practical reasoning is structurally analogous to the activity of theoretical reasoning. Both kinds aim at being truthful and *akribês*. And, at least in part, the truth at which reason aims is inextricable from the good of the object of rational consideration. Furthermore, insofar as practical reasoning has a desiderative element, it aims at the analogue of truth—right avoidance and pursuit. Thus, the person of practical excellence and the philosopher engage in activities that bear a close structural similarity. Despite initial impressions, the politician's activity is closely akin to the philosopher's.

---

discuss in greater detail in the next chapter, though the virtuous person is rationally drawn to the good, the fine attracts him at a nonrational level as well. Indeed, it is an identifying mark of the fine that it produces a particular kind of pleasure in those who have been raised well. It is hard to imagine, then, how a person could see a potential course of action as fine without desiring it and feeling a nonrational pleasure in its anticipation. I'm not suggesting that the feeling of desire is itself the knowing. Children may be attracted to the fine without realizing that it is the fineness of the action that is appealing. But if one does not take pleasure in, say, the prospect of giving a fine gift to one's community, it's not clear that one can be sure such an action is, in fact, fine on this occasion. One may triangulate to the fine as best one can, but the opinion that this action is indeed fine will be to some extent a piece of guesswork. The fine, as the special object of moral reasoning, may not be the sort of thing that can be known without the appropriate emotional response.

[38] Gauthier and Jolif (1970, not. ad 1139a30–31) suggest that the analogy between practical reasoning and desire is also presupposed at 1139a29–31 when Aristotle says that the function of practical reason is truth *homologôs echousa têi orexei têi orthê* (being in agreement with—having the same *logos* as—right desire). The question, then, is what prevents theoretical reason from having truth in agreement with right desire? Gauthier and Jolif correctly answer that there can be an agreement only when reason and desire are for the same objects.

But there is more to be said than this. For according to Aristotle, theoretical contemplation is not only akin to practical reasoning; it is superior (1143b33–34, 1145a6–11). Is it also the case that practical excellence is derivative from theoretical excellence, so that it is right to say that its exercise is a teleological approximation of *theôria*? We have taken the first step by showing that, according to Aristotle, the two kinds of reasoning are analogous. In the remainder of this chapter I will argue that, according to *NE* VI, practical wisdom is theoretical wisdom in practice.

2. Theoretical *Sophia* versus Practical Wisdom

After distinguishing theoretical and practical wisdom in the first two chapters of book VI and arguing that in both cases, though in different ways, virtue is excellence in truthfulness, Aristotle turns to an examination of the various theoretical and practical rational states: scientific knowledge and *noûs*, or grasping of the first principles of scientific demonstration, on the one hand, and *phronêsis* and craft knowledge on the other (VI.3–6). *Phronêsis* turns out to be the excellence of practical reason (1140b24–30). In the seventh chapter Aristotle turns to a discussion of *sophia*, or wisdom.[39] Aristotle argues that a person is wise when he both knows the scientific demonstrations of theological (or quasi-theological) truths and grasps the first principles from which they are derived.[40] In other words, *sophia* is the excellence of theoretical reason. This is a tendentious claim, and Aristotle knows it. Describing the nature of wisdom is not (as it was in the case of craft, for example) a matter of refining our understanding of an activity that we all more or less recognize as wisdom. It is to argue that a particular kind of intellectual accomplishment is the highest of which we are capable.[41]

---

[39] It is true that in VI.6 Aristotle claims that *sophia* involves scientific demonstration, but the point there is to argue that the grasping of first principles (*noûs*) is not *sophia*. The discussion of what *sophia is* is undertaken in earnest in VI.7.

[40] Aristotle says that *sophia* studies the most honorable (*timiôtatoi*) objects. It is unclear whether he intends this to be the study of divine objects, or cosmology, or whether he thinks cosmology *is* theology. In any case, the objects *sophia* studies are more honorable than human affairs.

[41] Notice in his argument that *phronêsis* is not wisdom, Aristotle says it would be strange if someone thought that *politikê* or *phronêsis* was the most important (*spoudaiotatê*). He realizes that the debate over the nature of wisdom is a debate about the highest form of human knowledge. This is a point Gauthier and Jolif miss entirely in their determination to translate *sophia* as '*philosophie*' (1970, 479–480). The fact that by *sophia* Aristotle refers to philosophical contemplation is beside the point here. This is a use of the word for which he must argue. See *Meta.* A.1 for evidence that Aristotle was well aware of the variety of accomplishments one could call *sophia*. His point there, by the way, presupposes that *sophia* always refers to the highest form of knowledge.

Despite the inaccuracy on this point, Gauthier and Jolif have an interesting overview of the development of the concept of *sophia* in Greece (1970, 480–489).

Now some have interpreted this chapter as primarily an argument that theological science is the highest form of *theoretical* knowledge. After all, Aristotle frames the argument as a debate over which objects of full scientific knowledge are the most honorable and so are fitting objects of wise contemplation (1141a18–20). The point that wisdom is *some* sort of full scientific knowledge and is not practical wisdom is quickly won (or at least insisted upon).[42] This interpretation cannot be correct, however. Immediately after Aristotle declares that theology or cosmology is *sophia*, he considers the argument that politics or practical wisdom is *sophia* and rejects it on the grounds that human beings are not the best things in the cosmos (1141a20–22). In rejecting human affairs as the object of the highest form of knowledge, Aristotle is rejecting the claim of *practical* intellectual accomplishment to be the best. That's because, according to Aristotle, the most perfect knowledge of human affairs is realized in action, not in theory.

Aristotle's championing of theoretical knowledge may come as a bit of a surprise. He begins the chapter on wisdom by noticing that, in the arts, we call those artisans wise whose artistic ability is most *akribês*. Phidias, for example, the sculptor of the Parthenon, most perfectly realizes the ends of his craft, and is for that reason called a wise sculptor (strange to our ears) (1141a9–10). But, Aristotle says, excellence in craft is not what we mean when we call someone wise *simpliciter*. "We think some wise people are wise generally (*holôs*) and not with respect to a part or some other particular thing" (1141a12–14). This contrasting of intellectual accomplishment "with respect to a part of life" (*kata meros*) as opposed to "with respect to the whole of life" (*pros to eû zên holôs*) is a familiar one. It is Aristotle's way of distinguishing artistic excellence from excellence in living well generally, that is, *phronêsis* (1140a25–28). Thus, when he makes this contrast again at the beginning of the chapter on wisdom, one might expect him to argue that wisdom *simpliciter*, as opposed to wisdom with respect to a part, is *practical* wisdom.

It is not clear how Aristotle's first argument in favor of theoretical wisdom is meant to tell against the superiority of practical wisdom. He notices that Phidias and other master artisans are called *sophoi* because the craft as they possess it is most *akribês* (1141a9–11). Thus, as we saw earlier, *akribeia* is a sign of wisdom (1141a16–17). Why, though, is complete scientific knowledge more *akribês* than practical wisdom? *Posterior Analytics* I.27 gives three rules (which I will discuss in reverse order) for determining the relative *akribeia* of two sciences. One science is more precise than another when (1) "it depends on fewer items and the other on an additional posit (e.g., arithmetic and geometry)" (87a34–35).[43] It is not clear that *phronêsis* fares worse than theoretical wisdom with respect to this test and, in any case, the *Poste-*

---

[42] Gauthier and Jolif 1970, not. ad 1141b2–3; Greenwood 1909, 35.
[43] All translations of the *Posterior Analytics* are from Barnes 1994.

rior Analytics does not explain why this feature affects *akribeia* or epistemic quality. (Perhaps because, by being derived from fewer premises, it is closer to first principles and the source of truth?) I will leave it aside for now.

The second rule does seem relevant to the status of theoretical and practical knowledge, however. One science is more precise than another, Aristotle says, if (2) "it is not said of an underlying subject and the other is said of an underlying subject (e.g., arithmetic and harmonics)" (87a33–34). The underlying subject is the matter of an object. What Aristotle is saying, then, is that sciences that concern form alone are more precise than those that concern embodied form. Since *phronêsis* not only concerns the embodied human good but is realized in action, it will, by this measure, be less precise than scientific knowledge of god, a pure, eternally actualized form.

Although Aristotle's greater respect for knowledge of the disembodied is, perhaps, at bottom the result of a Platonic disdain for matter, it is not a piece of mere prejudice. As I mentioned earlier, Aristotle accepts the common Greek belief that like can be known only by like.[44] The result is that he believes only form is truly knowable. Our minds can receive the perceptual and intelligible forms of things in the world, but (obviously) cannot accept their matter. (Otherwise our minds would literally become the things they sensed and knew!) Matter can be known only to the extent that it has form. Thus, when the mind turns itself to the examination of things that are, by nature, embodied, there will always be something in the object of inquiry slightly beyond the reach of the mind. But the situation is actually worse than this, for even when our minds do grasp the form of a material object, we do not grasp something that is necessarily, though only partially true. The matter of objects not only eludes our knowledge, it resists the form that shapes it. As Aristotle says, "matter cannot be easily brought under rule" (*GA* 778a4–9).[45] So, knowledge of the physical and human world is less precise, less complete, less *akribês* than the knowledge whose object is pure form. In the latter case, on the other hand, the mind in some (albeit mysterious) sense *becomes* the object of knowledge. Thus it grasps it completely.

There is evidence in *NE* VI.7 that Aristotle is thinking of *akribeia* as a matter of grasping form. The master craftsmen at the beginning of the chapter are most *akribeis* in their fields because they most of all are able to realize the form of a statue in marble.[46] The matter is too intractable for a lesser

---

[44] For evidence of this belief prior to Aristotle, see Empedocles (Kirk, Raven and Schofield 1983, fr. 392–394) and Plato and *Phaedo* 79c–d. For Aristotle's theory, see *DA* III.4. Aristotle does not think that before the soul actually knows (or perceives) it possesses the qualities of its object; but it takes on those qualities, in a way, when it is actually knowing.

[45] For this reason Barnes (1994, 190) links the second rule of *akribeia* in *Post. An* I.27 to *NE* 1094b11–27, where Aristotle says ethics is less precise than mathematics because it holds only for the most part.

[46] I am not confident in this interpretation. At *Meta.* 981b5–6 Aristotle says, "master craftsmen are wiser [than ordinary manual craftsman] not because they are capable of acting but

craftsman to express his knowledge of form. The virtuous person is *akribês* is a similar way. When he chooses the intermediate action, doing and feeling neither too much nor too little, he manifests his knowledge of the fine and good. Nevertheless, because excellent practical reasoning is knowledge of embodied things, it can only imperfectly do what theoretical reasoning can do perfectly.

Finally, let us turn to the third criterion of *akribeia*: "One science is more precise than another and prior to it if [3] it is at the same time of the fact and of the reason why and not of the fact separately from the science of the reason why" (87a31–33). *Akribeia* in this sense is surely a mark of intellectual accomplishment. As Aristotle often remarks, people are wise not in virtue of knowing facts but in virtue of understanding their cause (e.g., *Meta.* A1 981b27–29). Furthermore, he seems to have this rule in mind in *NE* VI.7 when he writes, "Then it's necessary that the wise person not only know the things from the first principles [i.e., the demonstrations], but grasp the truth of the principles also. So that *sophia* would be *noûs* and *epistêmê*" (1141a17–19). This is an argument, though, about what sort of *theoretical* knowledge is *sophia*. It is not at all obvious that *practical* wisdom fails this test, for the wise person also knows both *what* he should do and *why*.

But perhaps Aristotle thinks that theoretical wisdom grasps "the why" more securely than practical wisdom does for the same reason practical wisdom is more *akribês* than craft. From the point of view of excellence in grasping truth, practical wisdom's broader scope (it knows about all of life, whereas craft knows only a part) is important not simply because it incorporates a greater quantity of facts. What matters is that practical wisdom grasps a first principle—happiness or the human good—that explains the value of each part of life, including the crafts.[47] (Remember craft products are good because the ends they lead to are good.) It can provide a deeper, more systematic explanation of what craft knows in a more limited way. If this makes practical wisdom more *akribês* than craft, we can expect theoretical knowledge of the Prime Mover (if this is, indeed the object of *sophia*) to be more *akribês* still. The order of the entire world depends ultimately on the Prime Mover. Thus, whereas the practically wise person takes the nature and value of happiness as given, the student of cosmology understands why

---

because they have the account and understand the causes." Notice that if this is what he means here in the *NE*, then he praises Phidias not because his statues are so particularly beautiful but because he understands the principles of his craft. This would be akin to admiring Michelangelo for his extraordinary understanding of marble and the proportions of the human figure.

[47] There has been some controversy about whether the *phronimos* needs to know the nature of happiness—the first principle of ethics—in order to act well (Broadie 1991, 198–202, 232–242; McDowell 1998). I am inclined to think that he must have some kind of general grasp of happiness (i.e., he must know that the human good is the most excellent rational activity, though he may not realize that this specifies *theôria*), but I do not think anyone would deny that he must in some sense know why what he does is the right thing to do.

human happiness is ordered in the way that it is. Aristotle suggest something along these lines at *Metaphysics* A.1 981b27–982a1:

> Everyone supposes that what is called wisdom (*sophia*) concerns first causes and first principles. So that, just as we said before, the experienced person seems to be wiser than those having any perception whatsoever, and the craftsman seems wiser than experienced people, and the master-craftsman than the manual craftsman, and theoretical science more than the productive ones.[48]

I have constructed what I suspect may be Aristotle's reasons for thinking that theoretical wisdom is more precise than its practical cousin. However, this is not the front on which Aristotle makes his case against *phronêsis*. Instead, he launches an attack on the dignity of the things practical wisdom thinks about. This is fortunate since, no doubt, the supporters of practical wisdom would feel that the test of *akribeia* was rigged in favor of the theoretical sciences to begin with. The question at issue in deciding what to call *sophia* is which form of knowledge is a more worthwhile possession. Theoretical *sophia* may be more *akribês*, but it's a further question whether it is, for this reason, more desirable. As I read it, Aristotle has two criticisms of practical reasoning, each of which he formulates once with respect to *phronêsis* (1141a20–28) and once with respect to politics (1141a28–1141b8): (1) there are many things better and more divine than human beings and their affairs (1141a21–22, 1141a33–1141b8), and (2) "the wise"—that is, what one must know in order to be counted wise[49]—is a plurality in the case of practical wisdom but unitary and universal in the case of theoretical wisdom (1141a22–28; 1141a29–33).

In arguing for (1), Aristotle simply asserts that the heavenly bodies are more divine than people are and calls for his witnesses Anaxagoras, Thales, and other men reputed to be wise because they know "extraordinary, amazing, difficult, divine (but useless) things" even though they are incapable of taking care of themselves (1141a34–b8). These wise men live as much among divinities as it is possible for a human being to do. So much is to be expected from Aristotle. Nevertheless, it is a point worth Aristotle's while to make (and would have been more worth arguing for!), since Aristotle's rival, Isocrates, claimed that the deeds of heroes and great men were the proper object of *philosophia* on account of *their* great superiority.[50] Of

---

[48] See also *Meta.* 982b4–10. If this is the argument Aristotle has in mind in *NE* VI.7 it would explain the move from his remark that craft is not broad enough to be wisdom to his subsequent claim that, since wisdom must be the most *akribês* form of knowledge, full theoretical excellence is wisdom (1141a16–20). Otherwise the invocation of *akribeia* at this point is a nonsequitur; he will not have shown that theoretical wisdom passes the test of breadth that craft failed.

[49] Stewart (1892, not. ad 1141a22) suggests that *to sophon* is the subject or agent of *sophia*, that is the "wise being or faculty."

[50] *Panegyricus* 48, cited in Broadie (Broadie and Rowe) 2002, not. ad 1141a33–34. At *Antidosis* 266–269, Isocrates claims that the best that can be said for Academic philosophy is that

course, if Aristotle is correct about the superiority of the objects of theoretical study, that would be a persuasive consideration in favor of the superiority of excellent theoretical reasoning. Aristotle's point is not just that these philosophers spend time with the divine objects of their thought in the way that someone might say he spends time with Plato by reading his dialogues. If we in some way become like what we know as we are knowing it, then philosophers who study the divine heavenly bodies actually make themselves similar (in a way) to the best things in the world.

In (2) Aristotle exploits the fact that practical reason examines the world from the practical point of view, seeking to understand how its changes could affect the agent's good. Since what is practically good will depend on whom it is good for, practical knowledge is not a unitary accomplishment. There will be as many different practical knowledges as there are individuals (or groups, in the case of political science)—including animals—to be benefited.

There are two reasons this fact tells against the claim that *phronêsis* is *sophia*. First, if a person (a veterinarian, say) is practically wise with respect to dogs, he will be unable to apply that knowledge anywhere but the canine world. Thus, a person can be practically wise about the good even when there are many practical goods he does not know. But this limitation of understanding to only a part of nature was the reason we rejected the idea that craft might be wisdom (1141a12–14). Craft knows about only a part of life; practical wisdom knows about the whole thing. But now we see that *phronêsis* knows only about *human* life. Theoretical *sophia*, on the other hand, if it studies the first mover(s) of the cosmos, in some sense knows the principles of *everything*. But surely the wise person knows all. So *phronêsis* seems too limited to be wisdom. Second, we might think that the principles that knowledge grasps ought to hold true universally. But far from being universal, practical wisdom must be ready to act against whatever generalizations about the human good there may be if, in a particular circumstance, something else would be good. A good doctor, for example, will not prescribe aspirin for a headache to a patient who is allergic to aspirin. In an important sense, then, practical knowledge is not interested in grasping general principles of the good or even of the good of a particular thing. What it seeks is the ability to produce particular goods on particular occasions.[51] Theoretical science, on the other hand, meets the expectation that knowledge provides universally applicable understanding of a subject. Once a person

---

it prepares one for the "greater and more serious (*ta meizô kai ta spoudaiotera*)" subjects that Isocrates himself teaches. See also Broadie and Rowe 2002, 52–54.

[51] Aristotle's discussion of equity (*epieikeia*) is interesting in this regard: "In those matters where it is necessary to speak universally, but it is not possible to do so correctly, the law takes what is for the most part, but is not ignorant of possible mistakes. And [the law] is no less correct, for this mistake is not in the law, nor in the lawmaker, but is in the nature of the case. For the matter of practical affairs is simply of this sort" (*NE* V.10 1137b14–19). Thus, the judge does not break the law when he (correctly) makes exceptions to it.

knows about colors, for example, or straight lines, his knowledge will apply wherever colors and straight lines appear. Thus, theoretical knowledge seems to be more of the character of knowledge than practical wisdom does.

So according to Aristotle the excellence of theoretical reason is true wisdom because it elevates us by causing us to know better things, and because it is more universal in its applicability and aim and, therefore, more perfectly captures the essence of what we take to be knowledge. These strike me as genuine reasons to consider theoretical wisdom to be superior as a kind of knowledge to practical wisdom. If knowing is what you care about, then you ought to prefer theoretical knowing. Of course, it is not clear that we *do* care about practical wisdom as a kind of knowing (even though it is plausible to define the function and good of reason as grasping truth). But Aristotle has already made the case in the function argument of NE I.7—and perhaps now we wish he had said more—that human happiness is a form of rational living. Thus, if practical wisdom is to have any claim at all to ultimate concern, it must be as a form of rationality. (Does the conception of rationality against which Aristotle measures theoretical and practical reason perhaps beg the question in favor of theoretical reason? It is notable, however, that he does not play his trump card, viz., that contemplation is the activity of god [NE X.8 1178b8–22]. The main argument of the *NE* is always made from the standpoint of our interest in *human* goods.)

But let us turn our attention to the interesting, and somewhat surprising, fact that in making these arguments, Aristotle assimilates theoretical wisdom to divinity and practical wisdom to bestiality. In order to argue that the practically wise is variable while the theoretically wise is not, Aristotle claims there is a practical wisdom, at least in a loose sense, for animals as well as for human beings. This leads Aristotle to suggest that practical wisdom does not distinguish human beings from animals: "For they say that the one who looks well to the particular things concerning himself is practically wise.... For which reason they even say that some of the beasts—those which seem to be capable of having foresight with regard to their own life—are practically wise" (1141a25–28).[52] This observation is of profound importance for the project of the *Nicomachean Ethics*, for in suggesting that some animals may have practical wisdom, Aristotle plants the seed for the thought that the activity of practical wisdom cannot be our human function, and hence not our good. Ultimately, of course, Aristotle does believe that practical reasoning is a distinctively human capacity. The genuine exercise of practical reason is something more than the memory and foresight of some animals (*Meta*. A.1 980a27 ff.). (Notice how even here he presents the alternative position as something that *seems* to be true.) But he does nothing to dispel

---

[52] At *Meta*. A 980b21–24 bees are said to be *phronimoi*. See also *History of Animals* 611a15–16, 612b18–31, 623a7–8, 630b18–21, where deer, birds, spiders, and elephants are said to be *phronimoi*. Cf. *GA* 753a7–17.

this misconception in *NE* VI.7. On the contrary, he uses the similarity between practical wisdom and animal "foresight" to further denigrate *phronêsis*. If we are willing to assimilate human and animal abilities to plan ahead, then we must be thinking of practical wisdom as a capacity to get what is good for us. This is, in fact, the aspect of practical reasoning which Aristotle stresses in this chapter (1141b8–14). But if that is so, then what universal knowledge is constitutive of *phronêsis* will appear to be of secondary importance. As Aristotle says, "if a man knew that light meats were digestible and wholesome, but did not know which sorts of meat are light, he would not produce health, but the man who knows that chicken is wholesome is more likely to produce health" (1141a25–28 [cited above], 1141b18–21).[53] People with experience but little learning are often more adept at producing the good result than are the sheltered and well-read (1141b16–18). But the intellectual accomplishment *phronêsis* gives a person is practical (1141b21). *Phronêsis* now looks to be an ineffective or, at best, redundant capacity to acquire goods. In arguing that theoretical wisdom is superior to the best practical reasoning, Aristotle seems to overshoot his mark. *Sophia* is more *akribês* and divine; *phronêsis* does not make us any more *akribeis* than animal desire does. We may now be wondering whether *phronêsis* is really such a valuable possession at all.

3. The Relationship of *Phronêsis* to Theoretical Wisdom

In the wake of *NE* VI.7, it is unclear how the two kinds of truthfulness are connected to happiness. *Sophia*, on the one hand, has been celebrated as useless, while *phronêsis* has come close to being demoted to an animal accomplishment. Thus VI.7 leads directly (or almost directly)[54] to the *aporiai* of VI.12. They are: (1) What use is *sophia*, since it is not in any way concerned with human happiness (1143b18–20)? (2) What use is *phronêsis*, given that, if our desires are in a good condition, we will reliably go for the good regardless of whether we know it? Indeed, even if we don't have perfectly trained desires, all we need is to obey someone else who knows what we ought to do (1143b20–33). Finally, (3) "in addition to these problems, it would seem to be strange if [practical wisdom] were authoritative over *sophia* even though it's worse than *sophia*; but the art producing each thing rules it and issues orders about it" (1143b33–35). In order to solve these *aporiai*, particularly the second, Aristotle must rehabilitate the value of practical wisdom. *Phronêsis* is different from mere animal cunning at acquiring the goods of

---

[53] Broadie (1991, 78 ff. and chap. 4) argues that Aristotle is concerned elsewhere to show that *phronêsis* is not a craft. This is correct, and we should notice that Aristotle is to some extent responsible for the misconception!

[54] Further discussion of practical and political wisdom, as well as the related topics of understanding and judgment, intervene.

fortune, and it is essential for human happiness. Students of Aristotle expect that this reassessment of the importance of practical rationality must come at some point, but when it does we may wonder if it will weaken Aristotle's claim that excellent theoretical reasoning is superior. I will spend the last part of this chapter examining how Aristotle answers the problems raised in these *aporiai*, particularly the second and third, because I believe his discussion explains how, even in its rehabilitated form, the activity of practical wisdom is subordinate to and acts for the sake of theoretical wisdom.

The solution to the first *aporia* is fairly straightforward and I will not discuss it here. In brief, Aristotle claims that *sophia* is useful for happiness because its exercise constitutes happiness (1144a3–6).[55]

The passage in which Aristotle solves the second *aporia* includes some of the most notoriously difficult claims to interpret in the entire *Nicomachean Ethics*. In my discussion I will try as much as possible to avoid the thorny issues surrounding what role in particular Aristotle intends *phronêsis* to play in practical virtue and what its connection to cleverness (*deinotêta*) and discovering the means to an end is meant to be. Instead, I will concentrate on Aristotle's claims about what intellectual practical excellence adds to nonrational dispositions to pursue what is good. For it seems that Aristotle's primary purpose in this passage is to rehabilitate the status of practical wisdom after the beating he gave it in VI.7. *Phronêsis* perfects a distinctively human function, Aristotle argues now, and what it enables us to do is not something of which beasts are capable.

In response to the charge that we are no more able to acquire the noble by knowing it, Aristotle asks us to step back to an earlier stage of the *Nicomachean Ethics*. In book II, when he was first defining moral virtue and the actions it produces, he said that although a person does not have to be virtuous in order to do actions that *look* virtuous from an external point of view,

---

[55] There has been some disagreement over whether *sophia* produces happiness (1) as health produces happiness (Greenwood 1909), (2) as the state of health produces actualizations of health (Joachim 1951), or (3) as health formally constitutes health (Gauthier and Jolif 1970; Stewart 1892). I am inclined to accept (3) for reasons similar to those given by Gauthier and Jolif. Namely, Aristotle is here explicitly contrasting the way health causes health with the way the medical art causes health, i.e., with the efficient cause. But both (1) and (2) describe forms of efficient causation.

There is also some question whether this argument is supposed to apply to the usefulness of *phronêsis* as well. Aristotle explicitly discusses only *sophia*, but because of the plural at 1144a3 Greenwood (1909), Ross (1924), and Stewart (1892) think it must apply to both. Gauthier and Jolif (1970) concur with the opinion of Burnet (1900) and Joachim (1957), however, that Aristotle means to speak only of *sophia*. While both *sophia* and *phronêsis* produce happiness, only *sophia* produces it in this way. Their argument is supported by similarities between this passage and a passage in *EE* VIII.3, where *phronêsis* is said to produce happiness as a doctor produces health. Even if the first interpretation is correct and the activity of *phronêsis* does constitute happiness, *NE* X.8 shows us that *phronêsis* does not constitute happiness as *sophia* does, since its activity is happiness only in a secondary way (secondary, I believe, because it is an approximation to the full happiness to be found in contemplation).

a fully virtuous action is one performed in a virtuous way (1105b5–9). In other words, a fully virtuous action is not just the one that is intermediate; it is one that is chosen and chosen for itself (1144a13–20). Now, as we saw earlier, choice is a kind of desire. And no matter how clever our reason is in figuring out how to achieve the general object of desire in this situation, if the desire is not right, there will be nothing laudable in the cleverness (1144a20–28). Thus the denigrators of practical wisdom are right to the extent that they say the value of practical reasoning depends on having the right emotional dispositions. But we also learned that choice is the termination of a train of rational deliberation. This suggests that an action will not be chosen, much less fully virtuous, unless it springs from practical reasoning as well as from right desire.

Now the origin of chosen action in reason does not on its own establish that it is any particular excellence of practical reasoning that makes us better able to achieve the good. Aristotle claims here that cleverness at reaching a preestablished goal is not the same thing as *phronêsis* or practical intellectual excellence (1144a23–29). So, at this point, it looks as though if we have good habits of desire, mere cleverness should be sufficient to satisfy them. But Aristotle's purpose here at the end of VI.12 is to remind us that fully excellent human action is the product of choice. As such, excellent human action is the product of *reasoning of some sort or other*. Thus a human being's capacity to pursue and secure his good, unlike the same sort of capacity in an animal, is an expression of human rationality.

But once we see this, we are in a position to see that excellence in practical reasoning transforms our nonrational desires for our good. At the beginning of VI.13 Aristotle says we need to reexamine moral virtue in light of the discussion of the connection between reasoning and desire (1144b1). Just as there is a difference between cleverness oriented by right desire and cleverness on its own, so too there is a difference between the nonrational state of soul that we tend to call virtue—Aristotle calls it "natural virtue"—and full virtue, which implies the presence of rational excellence. Natural virtue is an innate tendency to desire the kinds of things fully virtuous people desire, but it is in no way peculiar to adult human beings. Certain animals, for instance, and children are naturally aggressive in defending their own against threats. It is common to call such people and animals brave, even though we are not at all inclined to think that they have chosen their actions as the result of deliberation. Now, although the naturally virtuous want the right sorts of things in general, they realize their desires in a scattershot fashion, often to their ultimate harm (1144b4–9, III.8 1116b23–1117a9). Excellent practical reasoning, involving understanding of which particular actions in a given situation really do have the general character sought by desire, changes this natural tendency into a disposition that always hits the mark toward which these natural dispositions direct us. In other words, practical wisdom ensures that we really do those fine actions we may naturally desire to perform. This is just practical truthfulness: accurately realizing the practical good.

Yet it seems to me that Aristotle says a bit more than this. In introducing this discussion he says that people want the characteristics of courage and justice and temperance to be present in them "in another way" (1144b7–8). And at the end of the discussion he says that true virtue is not desire in accordance with right reason but desire that is *with* right reason (1144b26–27). The presence of reason in some way or other transforms the way in which we desire. It is not enough that we want what reason would command. Otherwise what would be needed would be not be *phronêsis* but mere cleverness. Our desiring must be more intimately connected to our rationality. How could this be so?

I suspect that Aristotle must think practical wisdom transforms the target of natural moral virtue so that it is similar to the end of natural virtue, but not quite the same.[56] In fact, the end of full virtue is not the same as the end of natural virtue. Earlier, in the chapter on *phronêsis* (VI.5), Aristotle said that the end or *telos* of practical wisdom is *eupraxia*, that is, doing or faring well. The end is also the actions themselves, for true actions, as opposed to productions, have their ends in themselves (1140b6–7). Now in a colloquial sense it is natural to all human beings, and perhaps all animals with foresight as well, to aim at *eupraxia*, for everyone, virtuous and ordinary alike, aims at a sufficiency of external goods. So we cannot, in the first instance at least, claim that practical wisdom transforms the end of the naturally virtuous just by saying that it makes that end be *eupraxia*. Nevertheless, the conception of *eupraxia* at which the practically wise person aims will be different from the *eupraxia* of the naturally virtuous. Not only does *phronêsis* aim at *eupraxia*, Aristotle says it aims at the virtuous action itself. When a person chooses a virtuous action *for its own sake*, he's choosing it *as worth choosing in itself*. That is to say, in choosing a virtuous action as the chosen action it essentially is, the person chooses it as an expression of his practical rationality.[57] Whereas the naturally virtuous person chooses his actions for the sake of defending his family or being fair, the fully virtuous person chooses to defend his family or to be fair because that is what it makes most sense to do. And if this choice is excellent, it will express *excellent* rationality. So *phronêsis* added to natural virtue makes excellently chosen action or practical truthfulness the target of full virtue.

Thus the presence of *phronêsis* transforms the conception of *eupraxia* at which good nonrational desires aim. From the point of view of natural vir-

---

[56] I do not mean to claim that *phronêsis* is *of* the end. I mean only that the presence of *phronêsis* transforms the end at which moral virtue aims. In other words, by a nonrational process the presence of *phronêsis* makes something different look attractive to desire.

[57] This is how the *enkratic*, or continent, person will become fully virtuous. By repeatedly choosing virtuous actions as the products of his choice, he will habituate himself to desiring those actions *as* the products of his choice.

tue, faring well is efficacy in obtaining the external goods we desire in virtue of our sociable animal nature: sufficient food and other pleasures, protection of family and friends, fairness in social order, and so forth. As we saw in the discussion of VI.7, *eupraxia* in this sense does not require the presence of *phronêsis* or even of choice. But the fully virtuous person values his actions as excellently chosen. That must mean that he aims now, not just at external goods, but at the pursuit of those goods in a way that manifests practical reason. From the point of view of full virtue, then, the *eû* ('well' or 'good') of *eupraxia* is the product of practical reason.[58] In other words, the presence of *phronêsis* transforms the animal pursuit of the good into an expression of rationality. "This state, although it is similar [to natural virtue], will then be virtue in the strict sense" (1144b13–14). Just as excellent practical reasoning is inseparable from good desire, so too good desire in the strictest sense is inseparable from excellent practical reasoning (1144b14–17). This is why Aristotle insists on a modification to his original definition of moral virtue: "All people are likely to attest that the state in accordance with (*kata*) *phronêsis* is virtue. But we need to go a little further. For virtue is not only the state in accordance with the right reason, but it is the state *with* (*meta*) the right reason; and *phronêsis* is right reason concerning things of this sort" (1144b24–28).

Now, this is all a very handy way of solving the second *aporia* with which VI.12 began. *Eupraxia* for human beings is *rational* pursuit of external goods, and practical wisdom is indispensable for that. But this solution seems to make the third *aporia* even more intractable. After all, practical wisdom is the state of practical truthfulness regarding things that are good and bad for human beings (1140b4–6), and *sophia* is one of those good things. If *sophia* is one good among many, then according to the solution of the second *aporia* its correct pursuit will be valuable to the agent as just another occasion to express his practical rationality. This would be odd if what Aristotle argued in VI.7 about the superiority of *sophia* is correct, however. For now it looks as if *phronêsis* will be using a superior form of truthfulness as a means of manifesting its imperfect form of truthfulness. In other words, it looks as if practical wisdom will be authoritative over philosophical contemplation. But unless there is some way for *phronêsis* to express a sense of its inferiority to theoretical wisdom, it doesn't look as if it really will grasp the truth about human goods and bads.

Aristotle's solution is to claim that practical wisdom relates to *sophia* in a different way than it does to other good things. In the pursuit of other

[58] I want to be careful not to read Aristotle as a Stoic here. My point is not that practical wisdom makes people value their pursuit of food, etc., *solely* as expressions of rationality. Rather, practical wisdom makes people value their pursuit of things that really are good for them as primarily valuable because it expresses the human rational function. Aristotle would not count an action as practically wise if it did not figure out the best way to acquire or otherwise use something external (in a broad sense) that really was good.

goods, we live well and truthfully by the way in which we pursue them. Namely, when we choose them in a way that expresses excellent practical rationality—when we choose them in a way that makes sense and do so because it makes sense—we perform our human function to perfection. But in the pursuit of *sophia*, practical wisdom "does not use it, but it looks to how it may come to be; so it issues orders for its sake, but not to it" (1145a8–9). In other words, in practical wisdom's pursuit of *sophia* it aims at doing well and manifesting truthfulness not by the *way* in which it conducts its pursuit (although this will still matter), but by the fact that *this* is what it is choosing—this is the goal of the choice it issues in. We express our rational nature by making our final end be the highest form of reasoning available to us. In the pursuit of all other goods, excellent practical reason pursues practical truthfulness; but in the pursuit of philosophy, its goal is theoretical truthfulness. (Thus, actual contemplation is a practical as well as a theoretical accomplishment.)

It is often a subject of debate in interpretations of *NE* VI just what Aristotle intends his discussion in this book to show. He begins by noticing that, so far in the *Nicomachean Ethics*, he has said the virtuous person figures out the intermediate action by looking to some target (*skopos*), and there is some limit (*horos*) that determines the intermediate, virtuous states and makes them in accordance with right reason (1138b22–25). But, Aristotle complains, this isn't very informative. If we wanted to know what medicines to apply to the body of a sick person (perhaps ourselves), it would do us no good to know that we should do what the medical art prescribes or what the doctor would order (1138b25–32). So, Aristotle says, now he will tell us what right reason is and what limit (to the intermediate virtuous states) it sets (1138b32–34).[59] The problem is that it's not clear what his answer is. Absent is any rule for determining which actions are right such as we find at the end of the *Eudemian Ethics*.[60] What, according to Aristotle in the *Nicomachean Ethics*, is the target at which right reason aims? What help does *NE* VI give us?

---

[59] Some commentators read *kai toutou tis horos* in 1138b34 as 'i.e., what the boundaries of right reason are' (Joachim 1951, not. ad 1138b34; Stewart 1892, not. ad 1138b32). But 1138b23–25 suggests it is the mean states that have a *horos* in virtue of being in accordance with right reason. (Joachim considers my interpretation but rejects it without comment.) I will not discuss here Tuozzo's (1995) claims that *ho orthos logos* refers to a rule or measure and not to a capacity. It seems to me that even if we think of the *orthos logos* as a capacity, we can only know it if we know the *skopos* at which it aims. This *skopos* will function as some sort of rule or measure for the capacity of reason.

[60] "What choice and possession of the natural goods—whether bodily goods, money, friends, or other goods—will most of all produce contemplation of god, that choice or possession is best and this the finest standard (*horos*)" (*EE* 1249b16–19). But even here it is not clear that *theôria* provides the sole limit for the use of the goods of fortune. Aristotle may mean only that

I hope that the preceding discussion suggests an answer. In the remainder of *NE* VI.1 and in VI.2 Aristotle argues that the target (*skopos*) of practical reason is excellence in truthfulness. That is, reason aims at the excellent exercise of its function. Furthermore, he argues that practical reason cannot fully achieve this aim unless desire pursues the very same things that reason asserts (1139a25–26). This, then, is the way in which right reason marks off the limits of the intermediate, virtuous states. In order for a person to attain complete practical truthfulness, he must be disposed to desire and feel as reason directs. Aristotle does not deny the truth of the intuition described back in *NE* I that the happy and virtuous person aims at *eupraxia* (1094a22–24, 1098b20–22). In the second chapter of *NE* VI Aristotle says the unqualified end of action and the object of desire is *eupraxia* (1139b1–4), and in the chapter 5 discussion of *phronêsis* Aristotle says *eupraxia* itself is the end (*telos*) of practical wisdom (1140b7). But whereas in the beginning of the *Nicomachean Ethics* we were likely to think of *eupraxia* as doing brave or temperate or just deeds, now we must give *eupraxia* a slightly different interpretive spin. As the ends of practical reason, these deeds are ways of being truthful.

This already must come as a surprise to us members of Aristotle's audience who have been raised in fine habits. We might have thought that virtuous actions were fine and valuable as ways of doing good; now Aristotle tells us that they are valuable as ways of being rational and true. But as I have suggested, Aristotle goes a step further. Once we see that the primary aim of *phronêsis* is truthfulness, we are in a position to see that the good at which practical wisdom aims is but a paler version—from the point of view of truth—of the good at which theoretical wisdom aims in contemplating the most divine objects. It is not unreasonable to say that *sophia* is the implicit standard of right practical reason, even if *sophia* does not figure explicitly in the deliberations of the virtuous person. (We will look in the next two chapters at the extent to which concerns with truthfulness and contemplation *do* figure explicitly in the deliberations of the virtuous agent, according to Aristotle.) This superiority of contemplative wisdom is expressed in the fact that *sophia* is the only good achievable by action over which *phronêsis* is not authoritative (*kurios*).

When we ask what Aristotle intends to accomplish in *NE* VI, then, I think we should answer that he intends to give us a more substantive account of the goal of right practical reason than he has given so far. This will not, of course, be an algorithm for discovering the right action under any circumstances, nor will it be a description of the happy life so detailed as to function as an algorithm.[61] Instead, just as it would be of some help to tell the medical

---

theôria is the noblest of such standards, another one being morally virtuous activity itself (Broadie 1993, 384–386).

[61] In other words, Aristotle is not promising an objectionable version of the Grand End theory of practical reasoning. I should say here, though I will not attempt to argue, that I think

questioner that the right medical treatment aims to restore a balance to the elements of his bodily nature, so Aristotle promises a richer description of what the virtuous person is trying to do, in light of which we can guess the kinds of considerations the virtuous person takes into account in his deliberations. So, what is the target of the practically wise? In one sense it is practical truthfulness. Suppose, for example, that a virtuous person must decide how to respond to an injury. In the first instance he will aim at doing whatever he has most reason to do; in other words, his goal will be excellently chosen, truthful action. This already affects his deliberation, for instead of immediately being carried away by anger to seek some gruesome revenge, the practically virtuous person will determine whether revenge is good. He will ask what his relationship with his assailant is. Do they share a common good? Was the injury a purely personal affair, or was it part of broader social discord? Would revenge (or punishment) be a move toward or away from the restoration of social order? The relevant considerations may be many, but throughout his deliberations the morally virtuous agent will aim at choosing the action that most of all is true to the good in these circumstances, and he will value his action as such. We might say that in choosing and acting just as he does, the *phronimos* aims insofar as possible to realize and act appropriately to his rational nature. (It does not seem to me inaccurate of Aristotle to describe the virtuous agent as committed to the truth. Martin Luther King, Jr., for example, seemed not only just but truthful. Indeed, his justice was a way of being truthful.) So in one sense the target of practical wisdom is truthfulness in action. But in another sense it is contemplative truthfulness, not as the target of production (though it is sometimes this, too), but as a target of emulation. For in acting just as he does, the morally virtuous agent holds himself to a standard of truthfulness more perfectly realized in theoretical contemplation. And his actions aim at this standard whether he understands it fully or not.

---

my interpretation of the NE allows Aristotle to think of moral virtue as having an end distinct from virtue itself, with reference to which it deliberates without succumbing to the problems associated with the so-called Grand End interpretation of the *NE*. See Broadie 1991; Cooper [1975] 1986; McDowell 1998; and pp. 145–146 below, for further discussion.

CHAPTER SIX

Moral Virtue and *To Kalon*

IN *NE* I.7 Aristotle argued that the human good at which the happy person aims is virtuous activity of reason. And he opaquely hinted that "if there are many virtues, [the human good] is the activity of the soul in accordance with the best and most final virtue" (1098a16–18). By the time we finish *NE* VI, we understand that activity in accordance with theoretical rational virtue is superior to the excellent practical reasoning that guides the moral virtues Aristotle describes in *NE* II–V. Theoretical wisdom sets a standard of excellence that virtuous practical reason approximates in aiming to grasp the practical truth. However, approximation is a teleological relationship. Thus, as readers of the *Nicomachean Ethics* we begin to suspect what Aristotle will in fact conclude in *NE* X: The happy person aims at excellent contemplation as his highest good, choosing all other good things, including morally virtuous actions, for its sake. His morally virtuous actions will also be worth choosing for their own sakes, for insofar as they succeed in approximating theoretical truthfulness, they inherit excellent contemplation's intrinsic value.

But what are we to make of *NE* II–V, where Aristotle analyzes the nature of moral virtue in general and provides rich descriptions of many particular moral virtues? Even if he has not yet established the superiority of theoretical wisdom, surely there ought to be some hint that morally virtuous action is subordinated to theoretical knowing. In particular, if my interpretation of the nature of practical wisdom is correct, it ought to cohere in some way with Aristotle's famous theory that moral virtue is a mean or intermediate state (*NE* II.6–9). Now, the doctrine of the intermediate is important because it seems to specify the intrinsic value of morally virtuous action. At least, Aristotle's insistence that genuine morally virtuous actions are chosen for their own sakes (*NE* II.4 1105a32) immediately precedes his definition of such actions as intermediate. (Virtuous *states* are called intermediate because they are dispositions to perform intermediate *actions*, 1106b27–28.) It seems reasonable to assume, then, that when the virtuous person chooses his actions for themselves, he chooses them for their intermediacy. So if my solution to the problem of morally virtuous action as a middle-level end is correct, we might expect some indication in the description of these acts as intermediate that they are to that extent also worth choosing for the sake of contemplation.

Rather than approach the doctrine of the intermediate head-on, I want to examine what makes morally virtuous action *kalon*, that is fine, noble, or beautiful.[1] This is not really a different topic. I believe that what makes morally virtuous actions intermediate and thus worth choosing for their own sakes is, in Aristotle's account, the very same thing that makes them fine. My argument for this claim will have to come after a more general analysis of what it is for something to be fine, but for now we can at least notice that fittingness or appropriateness is a mark of beauty. (At *Topics* 135a13–14, Aristotle actually defines the fine as the fitting.) And of course intermediate virtuous actions are perfectly calibrated to suit the circumstances in which the agent finds himself. "Getting angry and giving and spending money are things anyone can do and are easy; but doing them in relation to the right person, in the right amount, at the right time, for the sake of the right thing, and in the right way—that is no longer something anyone can do, nor is it easy" (II.9 1109a26–29). Like a joiner, when the virtuous person scrupulously avoids excess and deficiency in his actions, he fits his choices to his situation. Indeed, Aristotle says the magnificent person is like a craftsman of the fitting (1122a34–35). So there is reason to hope that an examination of the beauty of virtuous action will shed light on Aristotle's claim that it is intermediate.

There is another reason to attend to moral virtue's beauty: Although in the general description of moral virtue Aristotle defines virtuous actions as ones that are chosen for their own sakes, in the discussions of the individual moral virtues he drops this part of the definition and says instead that the courageous or temperate or magnanimous action is chosen because it is *kalon*, or fine.[2] It seems safe to assume, then, that the virtuous agent's disposition to choose actions for their own sakes is interchangeable with his disposition to choose them because they are fine.[3] I do not mean that a virtuous

---

[1] Throughout this discussion I will usually translate *kalon* as 'fine' because I think it best captures the aesthetic and moral connotations present in the Greek word *kalon* as applied to action. In some contexts, however, I will translate it as 'beautiful'. The reader should be aware that in my discussion of love in *Meta.* Λ and the *Symposium*, the word I translate as 'beautiful' is also *kalon*.

[2] I will discuss specific passages in chapter 7.

[3] Tuozzo (1995, 130) is right to complain that scholars often "tacitly assum[e] that choosing something for its own sake is equivalent to choosing it for the sake of the noble," but neither is it right, I think, to suppose that these two ways of choosing virtuous actions are entirely disconnected. Aristotle often describes virtuous actions as fine, suggesting that they are fine by definition. Furthermore, whereas in *NE* II Aristotle emphasizes that virtuous actions are chosen for their own sakes, in the descriptions of the virtues in *NE* III–V he emphasizes that they are chosen for the sake of the fine. This suggests to me that drawing attention to their nobility and beauty is a more concrete way of showing what those features of the action are that make the virtuous agent choose them for their own sakes.

Tuozzo's interpretation, although fascinating, has the unfortunate consequence that insofar as virtuous actions are fine they are *not* chosen for their own sakes. According to Tuozzo, actions are noble insofar as they express (virtuous) dispositions that promote the psychic leisure

action is choiceworthy for its own sake *because* it is beautiful, as if the virtuous agent were an aesthete (although Aristotle does compare the good person's pleasure in fine actions to the delight a musical person takes in beautiful songs [1170a8–10]). For Aristotle, as for Plato, the good and the fine are related, but they are not the same.[4] Rather, the reason for a virtuous action's fineness is the same as that which explains its being choiceworthy for its own sake as the intermediate action it is. Since this is so, we can learn about the basis for the intrinsic value of morally virtuous actions by studying the way in which they are fine.

I will argue that, according to Aristotle, actions are fine when their determination by the human good makes the agent's commitment to his good visible. Since Aristotle thinks that the human good is the most perfect use of reason, this means that morally virtuous actions are fine because, in being just as they are, they express the agent's devotion to most excellent truthfulness. And in fact, an examination of three virtues will bear this hypothesis out (see chapter 7). Courage, temperance, and greatness of soul are fine because they show the agent's commitment to the most excellent *leisurely* use of reason. In the press of practical affairs, the virtuous agent orients his actions—both in terms of the states of affairs they aim to produce and, more important, in what they celebrate—toward a conception of the human good that is both leisurely and excellently rational. This emphasis on the leisurely use of reason turns out to be significant. For when we get to book X, Aristotle will argue that the most leisurely use of reason, and therefore the use of reason most suited to be an end, is philosophical contemplation. Thus, even though Aristotle does not explicitly refer to the superiority of contemplation in his description of the moral virtues, this attitude turns out to be implicit in the virtuous person's orientation. In grasping the practical truth on particular occasions, the morally virtuous person approximates and thereby acts for the sake of contemplation. But in addition, the practical truth that he grasps itself points to the superiority of theoretical wisdom.

A person need not be aware of this in order to act finely, however. I have been careful to say that the *phronimos* chooses morally virtuous actions for features that point to the value of contemplation, rather than to say that he chooses these actions because they point to contemplation. In other words, I have been careful to put the reference to contemplation outside the description of the agent's intention. Like Plato's incompletely educated lover, Aristotle's moral agent need not be fully aware of the source of the value and beauty of his actions. All that needs to be true is that the things about virtu-

---

necessary for happiness. But since their nobility is entirely instrumental, in what respect are they choiceworthy for themselves? (Presumably we are not free to choose just any instrument, direct or otherwise, for its own sake simply because we value it qua productive.)

[4] Indeed, it would be preferable to say that, for Aristotle, a thing is beautiful because it is good, rather than that it is good because it is beautiful.

ous action that the agent finds choiceworthy for their own sakes are, in fact, from a broader point of view, intrinsically choiceworthy because they reflect the value of contemplation. Thus, even if he thinks the exercise of *practical* reason is the human good, as no doubt many in Aristotle's well-bred audience do, so long as the agent chooses his actions because they are appropriate to a person who lives for the sake of excellent reasoning, his actions will be fine and choiceworthy for their own sakes. Of course, if the morally virtuous agent is also a philosopher and understands the value of contemplation as the highest human good, he will choose moral actions not only for themselves, but for the sake of excellent theoretical reasoning whose superior value they express.

After discussing what, in general, it means for an action to be fine and chosen for that reason, I will turn, in the next chapter, to Aristotle's discussions of the individual moral virtues. I hope to show that, as expected, their fineness is connected to their being oriented toward the value of the most excellent use of reason.

1. *To Kalon* Outside human Action

It is unfortunate that Aristotle never explains in the *Nicomachean Ethics* what *to kalon* is. This omission is striking, for Aristotle repeatedly describes virtuous actions as *kalon* and describes the virtuous person as one who is fixed on *to kalon*.[5] I will return, at the end of this chapter, to Aristotle's odd silence on this issue. But for Aristotle beauty is not only of concern to human beings in their actions, art, and romantic attachments. As we saw in chapter 4, it is a cosmological and biological force. Thus, Aristotle's nonpractical works yield clues about the nature of fineness. Let us begin with Aristotle's description of beauty at the most general level. In *Metaphysics* M.3 Aristotle says the chief forms of beauty, in both the changeable and the unchangeable realms, are order (*taxis*), symmetry (*summetria*), and definiteness or boundedness (*hôrismenon*) (1078a36–78b1). Now, it is not so clear what Aristotle thinks these qualities are in the unmovable realm, and in particular among mathematicals, where, he nevertheless insists they are to be found. But in the changeable world of nature Aristotle is quite explicit about what order is. Order is the arrangement of parts with reference to or for the sake of a common end. As we know, this common end or *telos* is, in some sense, the good. So, for example, the whole of nature contains the good because it is ordered with reference to the good. Indeed, the goodness of this order depends on the fact that its *telos* is good (*Meta.* Λ.10 1075a11 ff.). In the changeable world, then, order is not a mere formal property, a relation of parts *to each other*. It is an effective teleological arrangement (i.e., it does

---

[5] In saying this I echo the complaints of Cooper ([1996] 1999, 271) and Irwin (1985a, 122).

not merely aim at the good, it succeeds in so aiming). And, as we discover elsewhere, the beauty *qua* order of a thing lies precisely in its being well arranged for the sake of its end.⁶ For instance, in the *Parts of Animals* Aristotle says all living things, no matter how humble, reveal something beautiful and elicit in us the pleasure felt in the presence of the beautiful, because they are organized for the sake of an end (645a21–26).⁷ And in the *Politics* (VII.4 1326a33 ff.) Aristotle says that a beautiful city is one whose size is limited by its proper order. It is clear that the order Aristotle has in mind is the one realized in the city's fulfilling its function (i.e., the happiness of its citizens).⁸ So one way changeable things—and this includes human action—are beautiful is by being ordered with reference to their *telos* or good.⁹

We may doubt whether this can be the general description of *to kalon* that Aristotle has in mind in *Metaphysics* M.3, however. For Aristotle says that, unlike *to kalon*, the good does not exist among the unmovables. Thus, mathematicals cannot be beautiful by being arranged for the sake of their good. What I am about to say is speculative, but it does seem to me desirable that in interpreting this passage from *Metaphysics* M.3 we should not abandon the general account of beautiful order as an arrangement for the sake of the good. Unmovables do not *have* a good, of course, because they do not change (*Meta.* K.1 1059a35–38) and do not engage in action (*Meta.* M.3 1078a31). But that does not mean that their order has no principle. Numbers, for example, might be ordered with respect to the principle of unity, so that each number is analyzable into a collection of units.¹⁰ Geometrical solids

---

⁶ Halliwell (1986, 98) argues that in Aristotle's discussion of beauty at *Poet.* 7, what's beautiful about the appropriate magnitude is that it reveals the goal-directedness of the order. (For a less laudatory version of the same point, see Lucas 1968, 113 not. ad 1450b37.) I will discuss this passage from the *Poetics* in a moment. Also, at *Rhet.* 1361b7–14, Aristotle claims that physical beauty varies with time of life. In youth, it is the body of an athlete; in the prime of manhood, the body of a warrior; and in old age, a body capable of enduring the necessary toils and otherwise free from pain. The idea seems to be that, since what counts as a well-functioning body varies with what a body is expected to do at different stages of a person's life, beauty will also vary. Again, beauty is a matter, at least in part, of suitability to the end.

⁷ Actually, Aristotle seems to say that the teleological structure of living things reveals beauty not because it is itself beautiful, but because the *hou heneka*, or for the sake of which, is the province (*chôran*) of the beautiful. That is, living things reveal beauty because their teleological structure points us to the beautiful. If this is correct, then the connection between beauty and goodness is even closer than I suggest in the body of this book, for the *telos* of a thing is also its good.

⁸ Kraut (1997, not. ad 1326a5–b25) argues that the beauty and good order of a city are not means to the city's fulfilling its function. Rather, they are constituted by the city's fulfilling its function. Thus, a city is beautiful when organized in such a way that it realizes its good.

⁹ So, while I agree with Cooper's ([1996] 1999, 274) examples of order in virtuous action, I would insist that they possess order, and so beauty, not per se because the parts of a life fit with each other nicely, but because those parts are arranged for the sake of the human good.

¹⁰ I thank Jonathan Beere for suggesting this possibility. Allan (1971, 67) suggests that mathematicals are teleologically organized for the sake of the fine instead of for the sake of the good. In other words, mathematicals are arranged as they are *for the sake of* order, symmetry, and

might be ordered with respect to lines and planes. (At least, Aristotle says the arithmetician and the geometer deal with physical objects insofar as they are units and solids, respectively [*Meta.* M.3 1078a21–8].) But if there is a principle of order, then, whatever it turns out to be, that principle will be metaphysically primary and, in this sense, better. Thus, while it may not be strictly speaking true to say that unmovables as well as natural objects are beautiful when arranged with respect to the good—that is, teleologically—there will be an extended sense in which this is correct. (We will also need to extend the teleological account of beauty to explain how the first principle of the physical world—the Prime Mover—is *kalon*. There is no separate principle higher than it with respect to which it displays order, symmetry, and boundedness. In fact, the Prime Mover does not even have parts to be ordered [*Meta.* Λ.7 1073a5–11]! However, Aristotle does say it is the pure activity of thought thinking "the most divine and honorable thing" [*Meta.* Λ.9, 1074b25–26], which turns out to be itself in some way [*Meta.* Λ.9 1074b33–35]. And although Aristotle does not say so explicitly, it is possible that the perfection of divine thinking is due to the perfection of itself *qua* object.[11] If so, then the first mover *qua* contemplative activity would be fine because it is determined to be as it is by the best object of thought, namely itself. In other words, the cause of its beauty would be its teleological—in a nonhierarchical sense—order.)

Once we see that *to kalon* as order is effective teleological structure, at least in the physical and changing realm, we can see that the *kalon* as symmetry and as definiteness also consists in an object's orientation to its good. According to *Politics* 1284b8–22, something displays symmetry or proportion (*summetria*) when the size of its parts conduces to its benefit. A sculptor may create a foot that taken by itself, is beautiful. He may model it perfectly, with instep neither too high nor too low, to be the image of a foot that could be stood upon. But if it is proportionally larger than all the other parts of the body he has sculpted, he will reject it on the grounds that it has no place in this particular sculpture. Likewise, if certain citizens acquire too much

---

definiteness themselves. Thus, their order makes them beautiful, and it is on account of this beauty that they are arranged that way. There is no principle or good of their order other than order itself. This may be what Aristotle has in mind, but if so, there would be a question of whether order in the moveable realm is at all like order in the unmovable realm.

[11] Aristotle leaves the source of the value of divine thought as an *aporia* (1074b36–38); to use Ross's (1924) paraphrase: "Is it in virtue of knowing or being known that [divine thought] is good?" Aristotle does say that if divine thought had something else as its object, and so was a potentiality, its value would depend on that other object (1074b28–33); but since divine thought is *not* a potentiality, and so does *not* think a separate object, we cannot directly infer that the value of divine thought depends on the value of its object, viz., itself. In thinking about *Meta.* Λ.9, I have depended heavily on the interpretations of that difficult chapter offered in Brunschwig (2000) and Kosman (2000). Both, however, believe that the goodness of divine thought is due to itself *qua* act of thinking, not *qua* excellent object of thought (Brunschwig 2000, 292–293; Kosman 2000, 312–317).

power, they should be ostracized from the city. But what determines proportionality? It is the well-functioning or good of the whole. Thus, Aristotle says a city can be well-proportioned even if it has a king, provided that his extraordinary power works to the benefit of the community (*Pol.* 1284b13–15). Likewise, a ship that is two stades long is out of proportion (to its sail? the oars?) because it is too large to sail easily.[12] Symmetry, then, is very much like order. In both cases a thing possesses it when its parts are determined in a certain way with reference to the end of the whole. But while order is concerned with the arrangement of all the parts, symmetry is a matter of the properties of those parts taken singly. When each part of a thing is shaped and sized so that it can function in harmony with the other parts for their common good, then the thing as a whole has symmetry.

There is reason to think, too, that definiteness or boundedness (*hôrismenon*) is a property connected to the good. In *Parts of Animals* I.1 641b18–19 Aristotle argues that the presence of order and definiteness in celestial bodies betrays the fact that they do not exist by chance. But since for Aristotle a chance event is one that appears to be, but is in fact not, for a genuine *telos* (*Phys.* 196b17–24), we can infer that the order of the celestial bodies reveals that they have a final good. The idea seems to be that when things have a boundary or limit that is a true *horos*, they are limited at *just that point* for the sake of fulfilling their function. So, in *Politics* 1326a5 ff. (cited in part above), Aristotle is concerned not just that the city be properly ordered but that its magnitude not exceed a certain limit in either direction (i.e., is neither too large nor too small). If it is too large or too small, it will not be able to function in such a manner as to secure the citizens' happiness. Once again, this limit on magnitude is determined by the city's end or good.[13]

In general, then, something is beautiful when it displays—through the order of its parts, the proportion of those parts, and the limitedness of the whole—effective teleological organization. A beautiful or fine thing is one arranged and determined for the sake of its good. But there must be more to beauty or fineness than the mere presence of teleological order, for the presence of order would show only that the thing is natural or the product of craft. If we examine other of Aristotle's remarks about *to kalon*, we find that visibility or "showiness" is essential to Aristotle's conception. At *Poetics* 7 1450b34–36, Aristotle says that "to be beautiful (*to kalon echein*) an ani-

---

[12] Two stades = 1,200 feet, or approximately four football fields (Kraut 1997, not. ad 1326a5–b25). John Cooper has reminded me that many boats today, for example aircraft carriers, are more than two stades long. We need not think that Aristotle would find these ships out of proportion, however, for aircraft carriers have different technology and different purposes from those Aristotle knew. A very large size is in proportion to the technology and purpose of an aircraft carrier.

[13] Ross 1924, not. ad 1078a35: "The *megethos* which is mentioned in the *Poetics* [1450b36] and in *Pol.* 1326a33 as an element in beauty answers to *hôrismenon* here [*Meta* M.3]." I will discuss this passage from the *Poetics* in a moment.

mal and everything made up of parts must not only be ordered but must also be of a non-arbitrary size." It turns out that the proper size depends on what can be seen or in some analogous way comprehended.[14] If something is too large, its unity and wholeness (*to hen kai to holon*) will be lost on the people contemplating it; if it is minuscule, they will not be able to see it at all (*Poet.* 1450b38–1451a3). But even when the eye is literally capable of seeing an object, it may still be too small to be beautiful (*NE* IV.3 1123b7: small people cannot be beautiful). For it may be difficult to distinguish its different parts, and thus to discern their relationship to each other and to their common good.[15] It seems, then, that in order to be beautiful or fine, not only must a thing be ordered with reference to its good, but this arrangement must also be manifest or apparent.[16] The length of a plot, for instance, is finer "the longer it is consistently with its being comprehensible as a whole (*sundêlos*)" (1451a9–11). (Thus, the problem with small people is that their order, symmetry, and definiteness do not strike the senses immediately or as clearly as these properties do in larger [though not gargantuan] people.) Something is *kalon*, then, not simply when its arrangement is determined by its good. It is *kalon* when its orientation to the good is, in the relevant sense, visible. As we shall see, this aspect of the fine will be of particular importance to our understanding of why the morally virtuous agent values his fine actions for their own sakes.

2. *To Kalon* in Human Action

So far we have been talking about the fine as it appears in numbers and geometrical figures, in plants and animals, and in cities and stories. It is time now to examine what *to kalon* is in human action.[17] When we recall that Aristotle defines moral virtues as intermediate dispositions, poised between two vices (*NE* II.6), it is clear that they have the formal characteristics of the fine we discovered in other kinds of beauty. The virtuous person feels and

---

[14] The Greek word is *theôria*, which can mean 'looking at' or 'contemplation'. In the biological examples here, Aristotle seems literally to mean 'sight'. But he must be making a point about an extended sense of *theôria*, since he intends his remarks to apply to the magnitude of a plot. The right size for a plot is one whose unity can be easily grasped by memory (1451a3–6).

[15] Lucas 1968, not. ad 1450b38–39.

[16] This does raise the question of whether, for Aristotle, beauty and fineness are relative to us in such a way that beauty would be different for different kinds of perceivers/cognizers. However, if Aristotle thinks we are paradigm perceivers of the *kalon*, as he surely does, then beauty would not be radically relative, although it would still be a relational property.

[17] Aristotle discusses the fine in human action at length in *Eudemian Ethics* VIII.3, but what he says is obscure, particularly his claim that the fine person transforms ordinary goods into fine ones, and I cannot offer a satisfactory interpretation without presupposing the account of the fine I develop in this chapter. Since offering such an interpretation would not shed any independent light on what Aristotle's basic notion of the fine in action is, I will set it aside for now. For discussions of *to kalon* in *EE* VIII.3, see Broadie 1991, 373–388; and Whiting 1996.

acts proportionately to his condition. Just like a skilled artisan, he takes neither too much nor too little (1106b8–14). Thus, virtuous actions display symmetry; their parts are scaled to each other proportionately to the task at hand. When a magnificent person gives money, for example, he gives the right amount of money to fund the right project in a way that is appropriate. The beginning of *NE* VI is even more explicit in attributing the formal properties of beauty to the intermediate, virtuous states.[18] There, Aristotle says that he seeks the *horos*, or limit, of the intermediate virtuous states (1138b23–24). As it turns out, the standard of right reason—which, in the last chapter, I argued is wise contemplation—sets the boundaries of the virtues (1138b25, b34). Thus, there is a connection between a virtue's being an intermediate state and its displaying (or rather, the actions to which it gives rise displaying) the formal properties of symmetry and boundedness constitutive of the fine.

Of course, in order to be beautiful, it is not enough that an action be ordered, determined, and made symmetrical by the human good. This effective teleological order must also be visible. In *NE* II.6, where Aristotle explains the doctrine of the intermediate, he does not emphasize the showiness or quasi-aesthetic appeal of virtue. But even there I am not sure it is altogether absent from Aristotle's concerns. As we will see, the *kalon* produces a certain kind of pleasure. Now according to Aristotle we become virtuous by practicing, for example, eating neither too much nor too little, but just the right amount (1104a22–27). With sufficient practice, the child comes to take pleasure in the action itself, not merely in the expectation of reward for good behavior. It seems quite possible to me that the sort of pleasure the child learns to take is pleasure in the fineness of his action. Or consider Aristotle's discussion in *NE* II.9 of how difficult striking the intermediate is. Anyone can get angry when provoked or give money to someone who asks, but not just anyone can do these things well. "Nor is it easy; for which reason it is rare, praiseworthy, and fine (*kalon*)" (1109a29–30). The difficulty of intermediate, virtuous actions makes them notable; it brings them into public view. So although the doctrine of the intermediate makes particularly clear that morally virtuous actions exhibit the formal features of order, symmetry, and boundedness, there is evidence to suggest that, by being intermediate, they also have the visibility that all fine things possess.

We need to establish, though, that according to Aristotle these are the very features that make morally virtuous actions fine. That is, we need to show that the visible teleological order, symmetry, and boundedness of virtuous actions makes them beautiful. It is difficult to know how to identify these abstract features in actual virtuous actions, however. Where do we see the

---

[18] Although *NE* VI was probably composed separately from the rest of the *NE*, it is usually assumed that the first lines of the book are a new introduction to the material, composed specifically for the *NE* (Gauthier and Jolif 1970, not. ad VI.1).

boundedness, for example, in a courageous action?[19] It would be helpful, then, to find a more complete description of the fine as it pertains to human action in particular. Now, there is much less evidence for Aristotle's understanding of beauty in human actions than there is for his understanding of other kinds of beauty. But I believe what we do have shows that, as we would expect, for Aristotle actions are fine for the very same reasons that the rest of the world, both natural and unmoving, is. Namely, actions are fine when they display, in a noticeable way, orientation to and determination by their proper, human good.

In the remainder of this chapter I will support this general claim about what makes actions fine. I do not intend my remarks to prove the more specific claim that, according to Aristotle, actions are fine when they are oriented to the most excellent exercise of reason. That argument will come in the next chapter. However, I will sometimes *assume* that the human good is rational activity for the purposes of providing examples. Nevertheless, the general account of the fine I develop here is intended to stand independently of any specific account of *eudaimonia*.

One final remark: I claimed at the beginning of this chapter that the basis of the fineness of virtuous actions also explains their being worth choosing for their own sakes. Given the analysis of the fine I have now developed, this means virtuous actions are fine and worth choosing for themselves because they display their ordering, symmetry, and determination by the human good. In chapter 5, I argued that morally virtuous action is intrinsically valuable because its truthfulness approximates theoretical excellence. When we put these claims together, the conclusion is this: according to Aristotle, when morally virtuous (chosen) actions display their ordering, symmetry, and determination by the most excellent form of rational activity (i.e., by the human good), they grasp the practical truth and thereby approximate theoretical truth. In other words, the virtuous person grasps the practical truth and thereby approximates theoretical knowing when he acts in a way that shows his love of truth, the possession of which is the human good. The visibility of this commitment, as well as the commitment itself, is desirable and practically good. For in the press of practical life, where a person must feed himself, engage in business with other people, and fight battles, either verbal or physical, the virtuous agent will not have time to revel in the excellent reasoning he takes to be the source of his happiness. Indeed, his pursuit of food and other necessities might, in less competent hands, give the mistaken impression that he finds happiness in external goods. This is particularly true for the philosopher, who understands that the most excellent reasoning is theoretical and not practical at all. Since the demands of practical life literally keep him from contemplation, he has reason to act in a way that shows (if only to himself) how precious theoretical reasoning is to him. But the point

---

[19] See Cooper ([1996] 1999, 274–275) and Tuozzo (1995, 146–148) for further discussion.

holds also for those merely morally virtuous people who, when they think of the excellence of reason, think first of excellent practical reasoning. We use practical reason to get something done, and when the appropriate time arrives for action, the virtuous person must go ahead and act, and then go on to the next problem. There is no time (or at least there will not always be time) for him to dwell on the goodness of the reasoning by which he lives. He has reason, therefore, to choose morally virtuous actions for themselves. Since they are fine, they make clear that *this*—excellent reasoning, and not glory or power or whatever else political action may bring—is what makes life worth living. Morally virtuous action, because it is fine, is a way to celebrate the agent's conception of human flourishing amid the pressures of practical life. Thus, the visible order, symmetry, and boundedness of virtuous actions make them intrinsically, and not just derivatively, valuable.

3. The Account of Fine Action at *Rhetoric* I.9

The *Rhetoric* presents some of the clearest evidence we have for Aristotle's understanding of the fine in action. There, he gives us two ways of approaching the fine:

> Whatever is praiseworthy (praised?), being chosen (choiceworthy?) for its own sake, is *kalon*, or whatever, being good, is pleasant because it is good. (*Rhet.* I.9, 1366a33–34)[20]

Let us take the second clause first. A fine action is one that is pleasant (to whom?) *because* it is good.[21] Aristotle could mean one of two things. Either the goodness of a fine thing, X, causes it to be pleasant; or A takes pleasure in X because A thinks X is good. No doubt, Aristotle believes both. After all, the pleasant is the apparent good, and nothing is so persuasive as the truth. So if something is good, its goodness may well cause it to seem that way too. But I take it that what Aristotle wants to emphasize here, in the *Rhetoric*, is that fine actions are pleasant because they seem, to their agents and to those assessing them, to be good. We enjoy hearing about fine actions, or witnessing them firsthand precisely because they seem to us to be good.

---

[20] I am not certain whether the *epaineton* and *haireton* should be translated indicatively. (Roberts in Barnes 1984 translates both words normatively.) I am inclined to think that *epaineton* should be translated as 'praiseworthy' since otherwise the fineness of an action would be indeterminate until it is praised. Praise, however, is meant to be a *response* to the *kalon*. *Haireton* is a bit trickier, since Aristotle might mean that an action is *kalon* if it is praiseworthy, *provided that* the praiseworthy action has been chosen for its own sake. (Kennedy [1991] translates the passage this way, for example.) However, since Aristotle believes that actual choice ought to be guided by choiceworthiness, it is unlikely that he would commend an action's being *chosen* for its own sake if it were not also choice*worthy* for its own sake.

[21] Notice that Aristotle emphasizes that the pleasantness of fine things is grounded in their goodness by using two kinds of causal construction.

That is, Aristotle is defining the fine in terms of the peculiar kind of pleasure such items give rise to. The fine is what produces the pleasure we take in goodness.[22] It is pleasant, but pleasant for this particular reason, that it is good. The fine is, we might say, the morally pleasant.

I do not mean to suggest that the fine is morally pleasant in too narrow a sense. What we find to praise in fine acts will not be limited to applications of universal rules of morality or even particular benefit to others or to the common good. I mention this now to mark a contrast between my view and that of Terence Irwin (1985a). Relying in part on the passage we have been discussing from *Rhetoric* I.9 Irwin argues that virtuous actions are praiseworthy, and thus fine, because they aim at the good of the community. Since the definition of virtue that Aristotle gives in the *Rhetoric* is one that emphasizes its praiseworthy features, and "since the feature of virtue that is properly praised is its tendency to benefit others, this is also the feature that makes it fine" (Irwin 1985a, 127). Now Irwin is probably right that, in this passage of the *Rhetoric*, Aristotle describes virtue with an eye to those features that will strike the audience as fine. And I agree that the moral virtues do tend to promote the well-being of others.[23] The coincidence of individual flourishing and public happiness is, after all, no coincidence for political animals. And certainly in *Rhetoric* I.9 Aristotle describes virtue as a capacity to do well by others (1366b3–4). But it is not clear to me that the public utility of morally virtuous actions is what makes them fine and praiseworthy, even as Aristotle describes them in the *Rhetoric*. The fine person, according to Aristotle, benefits others and does not seek his own profit, but his motivation does not appear to be altruistic. Rather, the fine person, according to the *Rhetoric*, benefits others for the sake of fame and honor (1366b34–1367a17). It is this regard for fame and honor over vulgar profit that appears to draw the admiration of others, for it reveals the person's worthier, we might almost say aristocratic, character.[24] Consider also the following:

---

[22] The implication, for students of rhetoric, is that orators should describe those they want to praise as fine in terms that correspond to the audience's sense of the good.

[23] However, I think Irwin's translation of *NE* 1120a11–12 is misleading in the support it seems to give for his position. Aristotle says there that it is more characteristic of virtue to do well (*eu prattein*) by others than to be done well (*eu paschein*) by them. His point is that it is more characteristic of virtue to be active than to be passive (Gauthier and Jolif 1970, not. ad 1120a4–15). Rogers ([1993] 1999, 346–347) also notes that Aristotle implies here that being done well by is also appropriate to the virtuous person, just not as appropriate as doing well by others.

[24] Rogers ([1993] 1999) also denies that *Rhet*. I.9 supports Irwin's altruistic interpretation of the fine in action on the grounds that there are passages, such as the one I cite above, that do not fit Irwin's interpretation. However, she is more inclined than I am to read the *Rhetoric* as a hodgepodge of popular opinions about the fine, which Aristotle may or may not endorse. Although I believe there is a certain truth in this interpretation—I agree that Aristotle is not here trying to present a systematic and philosophically defensible account of the fine—I do think it is possible to tease out a common thread in his examples of fine actions which he would, with some qualifications, endorse as an analysis of the fine.

And profitless possessions are fine; for they are more free (*eleutheriôtera*). And the peculiar characteristics of a people are fine, and the signs of the things praised by them, for example wearing one's hair long in Sparta; for that's a sign of the free man, since it's not very easy for a person with long hair to do any menial (*thêtikon*) work. And it's fine not to do any mechanical (*banauson*) trade; for it's characteristic of the free man not to live for another (*pros allon*). (*Rhet*. I.9 1367a27–33)

This passage ought to make us reconsider Irwin's analysis of what is so noteworthy about the virtuous person's tendency to help others, according to Aristotle or, more correctly, according to Aristotle's assessment of popular opinion. If all fine choices have in common that they benefit other people, why is it fine to wear one's hair long? And why is there nothing in the least bit fine about menial labor? Making good horseshoes may not be as dramatic as leading a battle, but surely it does an awful lot of good. This suggests that, for Aristotle, the fineness of benefiting others is not just in the value of the benefit conferred, but in the freedom with which it is given. In giving, perhaps lavishly, the virtuous person demonstrates that he does not need to worry about providing himself with the necessities of life. Nor are his actions constrained by the *obligation* to further the interests of anyone else (as they are for a slave). But the generous person does not use his freedom to escape from society; rather, he uses his freedom to generate ties and create for himself a special place within society. The virtuous person is praised for his generosity not merely on account of its utility, then, but because it is a certain embodiment of freedom.[25] In other words, according to the *Rhetoric*, if doing good to others is fine, that is primarily because in doing good the agent rises above being a mere selfish animal and shows himself to be an excellent specimen of a *political* animal. But this, I will argue in the next chapter, is a feature actions

---

[25] The Greek word for generosity is *eleutheriotês*, or 'conduct befitting a free man, a man of good birth" (Joachim 1951, not. ad 1119b22–1122a17). The association of the *kalon* with freedom is one Aristotle would probably accept as (part of) his considered opinion about all the moral virtues. Aristotle frequently contrasts the *kalon* with the necessary (*anagkaion*). Aristotle calls behavior necessary when it is compelled by punishment or the threat of punishment (*NE* 1116b2–3, 1180a4–5). Behavior (and the pleasure that may attend it) is also necessary when it is instrumentally, as opposed to intrinsically, valuable (1120b1, 1147b24, 1155a28–29, 1171a24–26, 1176b3). Both kinds of necessity involve the idea that the agent is not directly pursuing his vision of the good, but is at most putting himself in the position to do so by gratifying his basic animal desires and providing himself with the social stability necessary for the happiness of any political animal (or, in the case of the liberal person, by supplying himself with the money necessary for virtuous giving; 1120b1). Slaves and the downtrodden live entirely under the yoke of necessity. People who are able to perform fine actions, on the other hand, act in a way that presupposes that they are free (enough) of the burden of meeting these needs. The contrast between the *kalon* and the necessary supports my claim that, according to Aristotle, actions are fine because they show the agent to be in a flourishing condition, and not primarily because they benefit others. See also chapter 7, section 1, below, for a discussion of freedom, courage, and *to kalon*.

could have even when they do not benefit others.²⁶ Thus, morally virtuous actions are not fine because they promote the common good. They are fine because they reflect the agent's understanding of his own *eudaimonia*.

When we read Aristotle's remarks in this light, we see that the account of the fine he offers in the *Rhetoric* is consistent with his account of the fine elsewhere. A person's action is fine when it expresses the agent's freedom as a political animal. When the virtuous person chooses for its own sake to act in just this way, doing neither too much nor too little, he shows his commitment to and value for his life as free. But in ancient Athens, this is tantamount to saying that fine actions are oriented in a visible way to the value of human flourishing or goodness. For according to the popular Athenian conception, the desirability of life in a democracy, particularly as compared with life under Persian rule, was closely tied to the citizens' freedom (*Pol.* VI.2). Thus, the description of fine action in *Rhetoric* I.9 supports the view that actions are fine when they are determined to be as they are by the human good.²⁷ It is this manifest orientation to the human good that elicits praise.²⁸

---

²⁶ Irwin's (1985a, 137) interpretation of the fine has difficulties in explaining why self-regarding virtues, such as temperance, also produce fine actions. He suggests that the generous person eats for the sake of health because he has an intermediate character formed by reflection on the fine. But how has reflection on the need to benefit the community established this disposition? Does the temperate person think that he needs to keep himself healthy so he won't be a burden on the community, or so he will have the strength to help others? I see nothing in the NE to suggest that the temperate person must hold a utilitarian view of his own health.

It also is not clear to me even in the case of generosity (as Aristotle discusses it in NE IV.1) that the fine is determined by what conduces to the common good. The generous person hits the mean by giving the right amount to the right people at the right time (1120a24–26). Wasteful people, on the other hand, give excessively, since "sometimes they make rich those who ought to be poor, and would give nothing to those with moderate characters, but a lot to flatterers or providers of some other pleasure" (1121b5–7). The criterion for true generosity seems to be that the recipient has a character that *deserves* help. Giving in this fashion may in fact benefit society at large, but that consideration does not seem to be moving Aristotle's generous person.

Finally, I do not believe Irwin's altruistic interpretation of the fine is supported by Aristotle's claim that the more people an action benefits, the finer it is (1094b9–10, 1121a27–30). Such actions may well be more beautiful because their teleological arrangement is more clearly visible.

The only place Irwin's interpretation of the fine as benefiting the common good is explicitly endorsed by Aristotle is in the *Politics*. The beautiful city is one that is arranged for the benefit of the citizens. But since the happiness of the citizens is the end and good of a city, this conception of its beauty should come as no surprise, and in no way undermines my interpretation of the *kalon* in action. See Rogers ([1993] 1999) for a point-by-point response to Irwin's position.

²⁷ We need not assume that Aristotle gives a specific account of the human good in the *Rhetoric* when he reports the popular sense that freedom is a mark of fine character. The discussion in the *Rhetoric* leaves it quite vague as to what this admired freedom is a freedom *for*. Popular imagination has it that the noble character lives as he chooses, but it does not specify *what* he chooses to do. Whatever use of this leisure is appropriate would, presumably, be happiness.

²⁸ Aquinas seems to hold the view about the fine in action that Irwin endorses. In his commentary on Aristotle's discussion of courage, he explains that the dangers relevant to courage (the dangers of war) are most fine because they allow the brave man to act for the sake of the common good (III.xiv.538). Aquinas seems to justify this view on the grounds that, in acting for the sake of the common good and being the cause of a greater good, a person is most like

When I said, then, that the fine is the good in its guise as pleasant, I do not mean to presuppose a specific, or a specifically moral, account of what this goodness is. Fine actions, just as all fine things, please us because they make apparent the appropriate good, in this case human flourishing.

Now I said that, elsewhere, Aristotle describes the pleasant as the apparent good. This might make Aristotle's definition of the fine seem utterly uninformative, for all it would be saying is that fine things are pleasant—that is, appear good—because, being fine, they appear to us to be good. But this is to work ourselves into an unnecessary muddle. When Aristotle says that the pleasant is the apparent good, he does not mean that we take pleasure in all and only those things that we judge, rationally, to be good. Rather, he means that pleasant things demand our attention. When something strikes us as pleasant, it presents itself to us as to be taken. The pleasant, like the good, is naturally attractive whether or not, from the point of view of reason, it is really worth taking at all. Thus, in describing the fine as what is pleasant because it is good, Aristotle means that the apparent goodness of fine things—rather than some other qualities they might have—has the quasi-sensory appeal of all pleasant things. It is the good in its guise as attractive.

What strikes us as *kalon* need not actually be good, however. We can be wrong about what really is *kalon* just as we can be wrong about what really is pleasant. This is the second point of Aristotle's definition of the fine as what is pleasant because it is good. In describing our reaction to the fine as a species of pleasure, Aristotle is saying that the appearance of goodness we react to is not, primarily, a matter of rational judgment.[29] Rather *to kalon* strikes us (in the gut, so to speak) as desirable because it is good. Thus, it would be more correct to say that the fine is what is pleasant because it *seems* good.

We can see that already Aristotle's description of the fine in human action corresponds to his definition of beauty in other contexts. In general, a thing is beautiful when it has an evident orientation to its good. Here, in the *Rhetoric*, fine actions are defined as those whose goodness strikes the sensibility of those who see them.

4. *To Kalon* and Spirited Desire

Aristotle also says in this passage of the *Rhetoric* that the fine is whatever is praiseworthy when it is chosen for its own sake. Praise, of course, is the

---

God, the ultimate source of all goodness (I.ii.30). This is an excellent argument for supporters of the political life to make against supporters of the philosophical life. But it is interesting that, in *NE* X, Aristotle never says that people are godlike insofar as they cause goodness. Any godlikeness virtuous people may display is due to their exercise of reason (see chapter 8, below). I suspect Aristotle and Aquinas agree in thinking that being godlike is paradigmatically fine, but they disagree on the nature of the divine. Aristotle's position reflects his belief that divine activity is essentially contemplative. Aquinas's God is creative.

[29] We will return in a moment to what part of the soul *to kalon* does appeal to.

appropriate response to something that is manifestly, plainly good.[30] It is the public recognition that certain behavior was worth choosing. This is why virtuous deeds done on a grand scale are so deserving of praise; they are not just good, they are good in a way that all can admire. (Of course, once a good action is brought to our attention, it will be visible as good. Thus all good actions are, at least potentially, praiseworthy.) The fine, in other words, is what is esteemed. This connection Aristotle draws in the *Rhetoric* between *to kalon* and praise should alert us to another source of information about the nature of the fine in action. For praise and blame are important methods of moral education, at least for a child who is on the road to virtue and is not utterly intractable (*NE* 1128b15–19).[31] Thus, praise and blame—the public acknowledgment that an action is or is not fine—are central to preparing a child to be virtuous. But moral education for Aristotle is a matter of shaping the child's soul. Thus, the examination of the role praise and blame play in moral education may teach us what part of the soul is naturally receptive to the fine. And this, in turn, may teach us something about the fine itself.

Following Plato's account in the *Republic*, Aristotle conceives of this education as a shaping through habituation of two kinds of desire—*epithumia* (appetite) and *thumos* (spirited desire)—to accept the eventual development and rule of reason.[32] (Platonic education in poetry is an education through habituation since Plato thinks that in some sense children practice the behavior of fictional characters in the poetry they learn [*Rep.* 394d–398b].) That is to say, early moral education shapes the desire for pleasure (*epithumia*) and, as I believe, the desire for *to kalon* (*thumos*).[33] Aristotle does not say

---

[30] Aristotle says praise is not the appropriate response to the best things, but only to those things in proper relation (*to pros ti pôs echein*) to the best things (*NE* I.12 1101b12–23). If the *kalon* in actions is synonymous with the praiseworthy, notice that this passage from *NE* I.12 confirms my earlier claim that a *kalon* action is effectively oriented toward the human good. Notice, also, Aristotle's implication that praised things are not most final (1102a1–4). We should remember this when, in *NE* X, Aristotle says that although virtuous activity is most fine (and thus most praiseworthy) it is not the highest good.

[31] Or, as Burnyeat (1980, 78) puts it, "[S]hame is the semivirtue of the learner."

[32] Notice how Aristotle mentions with approval Plato's claim that we ought to be trained from childhood to take pleasure in the right things (1104b11–13; cf. 1103b23–25). And though Aristotle does not mention in the *NE* the role poetry and music play in moral habituation, he does in *Pol.* VIII.5 1340a14 ff. See Burnyeat (1980, 79 ff.) for further discussion.

[33] There are two issues here: first, that Aristotle recognizes two species of nonrational desire, and second, that moral education shapes them both. As to the first, Cooper ([1996] 1999, 264–266) has argued persuasively that when Aristotle lists the three objects of choice at *NE* II.3 1104b30–34 as the fine, the beneficial, and the pleasant, he is referring to the three kinds of desire hypostatized by Plato in the *Republic*: thumoeidic, rational, and appetitive. If Cooper is right about this, as I think he is, then we should conclude that the fine is the object of thumoeidic desire as such. For in the same passage Aristotle says the vicious person makes mistakes about all three kinds of object. But with respect to the pleasant and the beneficial, the vicious person goes wrong by thinking that things are genuinely pleasant or beneficial when in fact they are not. Likewise, then, the vicious person should mistake *to kalon* in the same fashion; he desires

much more about spirited desire, but Plato had quite a bit to say.[34] According to Plato, the desire characteristic of *thumos* is competitive. It admires others and desires to be admired in turn. *Thumos*'s desire for the high regard of others develops into a desire for *self*-esteem as well.[35] As the proper object of *thumos*, the *kalon* must be the sort of thing to gratify those naturally competitive longings.

I have spoken just now as if it were obvious that for Plato, as for Aristotle, spirited desire aims at the fine. However, although Plato says *thumos* aims at things that are fine, such as honor and victory, he never says the fine is its object. I cannot give a full defense of my reading of the *Republic* here, but it is important to see that the Platonic account of moral education, adopted in its essential elements by Aristotle, depends on the connection between spirit and *to kalon*.[36]

---

something as *kalon* that is not, in fact, fine at all. Cf. Broadie (1991, 93) for the view that, according to Aristotle, there is an antecedent desire for the *kalon* that must be educated. Regarding the second issue, I have already suggested that moral education teaches delight in the fine when it teaches delight in the intermediate. Surely this pleasure can be nonrational, since we can imagine a young person delighting in good actions for themselves before having the understanding and experience necessary for practical wisdom. Below I will argue that this nonrational desire and pleasure is spirited (*thumoeidic*).

[34] In the *Republic* Plato says there are three parts of the soul corresponding to these three kinds of desire. Aristotle, on the other hand, attributes all these desires (or, rather, two of them) to a single part of the soul: the irrational part having a share in reason in a way. This is because, as we saw in NE VI.2, Aristotle thinks that all desire has the same function: to pursue the human good. The fact that different kinds of desire pursue the good under different descriptions is apparently irrelevant to the question of whether they are to be attributed to the same part of the soul. Consequently, whereas Plato attributes separate virtues to *epithumia*, *thumos*, and reason, Aristotle does not (Cooper [1996] 1999, 263). According to Aristotle, moral virtue (considered separately from *phronêsis*) is the virtue of the entire desiring part.

[35] Cooper [1984] 1999, 130–136.

[36] Cooper ([1996] 1999, 263) believes that Aristotle innovates when he says (or implies) that *thumos* aims at the fine. Plato, on the other hand, thinks that the proper objects of *thumos* are victory, honor, and so forth. Now clearly Plato does say that victory and honor are the objects of *thumos* (*Rep.* VIII–IX, passim). There are two things, though, that make me doubt that Aristotle is really innovating about the object of *thumos*. First, Aristotle presents the three objects of desire as a distinction with which his audience will be familiar. Since Plato's three kinds of desire would have been familiar to Aristotle's audience too, it would have been natural for them to link each object with its appropriate kind of desire, leaving *thumos* with *to kalon* (Cooper [1996] 1999, 265–266). Now if Aristotle thought he was contradicting Plato on this point, it would have been entirely typical of him to indicate that his thought was a new one. Furthermore, if the three objects of desire and the three kinds of desire were familiar distinctions in the Academy, it seems likely that someone before Aristotle would have thought to put them together. And if this mapping had been rejected by Plato, we could expect that Aristotle would feel the need to defend it. But he does not. Then, when we turn to the *Republic*, we see that the objects of *thumos* according to Plato—victory and honor—are typically associated with the *kalon*. Someone who is victorious is (apparently) outstandingly good, and that is why honor is his due. (See my discussion of greatness of soul in chapter 7, section 3, below.) Although Plato does not himself explicitly describe the object of *thumos* as *to kalon*, it seems to me that he would have had no objection to doing so.

There is no doubt that, in the *Republic*, the moral education of the guardians ends in their love of the fine and beautiful (403c6–7).[37] The training in poetic and musical appreciation leads the young men "unwittingly, from childhood on, to resemblance, friendship, and harmony with the beauty of reason (*tôi kalôi logôi*)" (401d1–3).

> Anyone who has been properly educated in music and poetry will sense it acutely when something has been omitted from a thing and when it hasn't been finely (*kalôs*) crafted or finely (*kalôs*) made by nature. And since he has the right distastes, he'll praise fine things (*kala*), be pleased by them, receive them into his soul, and, being nurtured by them, become fine (*kalos*) and good. (*Rep.* 401e1–402a1)[38]

The question is, does this education train the spirited part of the soul to love the fine, or does it teach it to love what really is fine, as opposed to a false image of the fine?[39] The significance for our investigation into the nature of the fine is this. If moral education teaches children to love a true versus a false image of the fine, that suggests that spirited desires as such aim at the fine. All by themselves, they are oriented toward fineness and only lack a connection to a true versus a false image of it. Thus, we could use the nature of this sort of desire in general as a way of understanding the fine itself. Now prima facie it looks as if the moral education of the guardians molds a sensitivity to or interest in *to kalon* that is already present in children. After all, this education is an aesthetic education, and such education normally seeks to influence the student's preexisting, or normally developing, sense of what is aesthetically pleasing or beautiful. No doubt aesthetic education does more than merely redirect a fully robust interest in the beautiful; it also strengthens this interest. But that is not to say that it creates an interest in beauty and the fine *ex nihilo*. If children did not already have some antecedent interest in the fine and beautiful, no amount of lambasting certain stories as shameful or praising others as fine would have any effect on their tendency to take pleasure in one sort of story rather than another. (This is why I say that Plato ought to have believed that there is a natural desire for the fine, even if he did not. His theory of moral education presupposes it.) Indeed, the fact that children take pleasure in stories at all suggests that a capacity for

---

[37] I thank Jonathan Beere and Zena Hitz for discussion of the following material on the *Republic*. I hope I have gone some way toward answering their objections to the general idea.

[38] This and all other translations from the *Republic* in this section are from Grube and Reeve (1992).

[39] Someone might object that the training in music and poetry does not train *thumos* since, at 410d–411e, Socrates suggests that this training affects the philosophical part of the soul, while the physical training affects *thumos*. We should not make too much of Socrates' use of *philosophos* here, however, since earlier he called dogs *philosophoi*, as well (376b). All of the poetic training occurs before the children develop reason of their own (402a). A properly trained soul will, at this stage, love reason, but he will love it for its beauty (401d). Also, this is training of soldiers, the part of the city that later turns out to correspond to *thumos* in the soul.

nonappetitive and quasi-rational pleasure is innate. (And the fact that children naturally take pleasure in *praise* suggests an innate interest in beauty, at least with respect to themselves.) But in addition to these general remarks on aesthetic-moral education, there is more specific evidence in the *Republic* that Plato's moral education shapes an antecedent interest in the fine.

In the first place, the poetic education of books II–IV is a response to Adeimantus's complaints about the quality of contemporary moral education. Whereas Glaucon's challenge emphasizes the apparent fact that injustice is good or beneficial (362b5), Adeimantus faults the counterarguments available in the culture (362e1–4):

> When fathers speak to their sons, they say that one must be just, as do all the others who have any charge of anyone. But they don't praise justice itself, only the high reputations it leads to and the consequences of being thought to be just, such as the public offices, marriages, and other things Glaucon listed. (*Rep.* 362e4–363a5)

This mode of praising justice is lent further authority by the poets, who claim that the reward of justice is in material luxury. "In their stories, they lead the just to Hades, seat them on couches, provide them with a symposium of pious people, crown them with wreaths, and make them spend all their time drinking—as if they thought drunkenness was the finest (*kalliston*) wage of virtue" (363c4–d2).[40] Adeimantus, like Aristotle, presumes that praise is of the fine. The problem, Adeimantus says, is that his culture does not find in justice anything fine and praiseworthy that cannot more readily and pleasantly be achieved by vice. People pay lip service to the fineness of justice and moderation, but in fact, Adeimantus says, people always praise those who are rich and powerful, regardless of whether or not they are virtuous (363e5–364b2). The implication is that justice in itself is really not so fine after all. And poetry is in large part responsible for this impression.[41]

Under these circumstances, it is not surprising that the first step of Socrates' educational reform is to excise from the repertoire all stories that have the effect Adeimantus complains of. Socrates says the criterion for choice among the stories is whether or not they are fine (377b11–c2). What soon emerges, however, is that Socrates rejects any stories that lionize a false image of the fine. So, for example, Socrates purges all stories that give a bad image of the gods (377e1–2). It cannot be that the traditional stories about the gods do not depict them as fine at all, for even though the gods are good, our first instinct is to think of them as glorious. Rather, it is in part because the traditional stories glorify the gods under a false conception of their nature that they must be censored. The gods almost by definition lead the most beautiful and noble lives. Thus, they are the ultimate standard for human

---

[40] We see that Plato is ready to admit that people are attracted to things based on a false conception of the fine.

[41] Contra Annas (1981, 65), what Adeimantus's challenge adds is not "relatively minor."

glory, pride, and, on the other hand, shame.[42] If children hear stories of these paragons of the fine cheating, lying, and otherwise behaving unjustly, they will come to find such behavior admirable (or at least not shameful), which is to say that they will come to think it is fine. Thus, Socrates says that the guardians may only hear and learn to delight in stories that depict the gods as acting in accordance with their goodness. Otherwise, the guardians will never come to find bad behavior shameful (378b1–e1). All of Socrates' rules for proper stories about the gods, then, are not meant to direct our feelings of esteem toward the *kalon* rather than some other object; rather, Socrates wants (or ought to want) to mold our perception of the *kalon*, which we naturally esteem, to fit the form of what is good. (Stories that do this will, in turn, be most beautiful [378e2].)

The same is true for stories about the heroes. The delight people take in listening to the Homeric legends is in part, at least, due to the pleasure of hearing about, admiring, and praising the glorious deeds of great men. But what Socrates reveals is that our admiration is not really justified by the virtuous behavior of the heroes. For example, Achilles' lamentation is an unsuitable model for children. (This is not, perhaps, the first example of disgraceful behavior in the *Iliad* we would think of!) Nevertheless the ancient Greeks apparently *did* praise and admire Achilles. If their praise was based on anything, it can only have been based on a false sense that Achilles is *kalon*. The work of Socratic moral education, then, is to teach children to take aesthetic pleasure in—to perceive as fine—images of what is truly good and only them.[43] Because they learn to perceive these images as fine, the images become role models with reference to which the children direct their competitive thumoeidic desires.

Now because the early molding of the future guardians' sense of the fine is a training of *thumos*, it reveals a few things about the fine. First of all, if *thumos* is the natural human desire to be outstanding, then the *kalon*, insofar as it is the proper object of *thumos*, must be able to satisfy that desire. This suggests that fine actions are a somewhat narrower set than good actions, or actions choiceworthy for their own sakes. For if fine actions are not superior to ordinary decent (i.e., not shameful) behavior, then they will not satisfy our competitive desire. This confirms what we learned by examining *Rhetoric* I.9. There we saw that fine actions are good in a way that is apparent

---

[42] Evidence that the gods are the standards of what is *kalon* is in the tendency to describe heroes, such as Achilles, with the epithet "god-like." (See also *Rep.* 390e–391e on Achilles.) And the heroes are, above all, *kalon*. Also, at *Rep.* 381c, Socrates says the gods are the most beautiful and best.

[43] The purification of images is not limited to the content of the poems. Socrates also asks Glaucon to choose musical modes and poetic meters that will imitate a moderate and ordered— i.e., a fine—life (*Rep.* 399c1–4, 399e8–400a7). See *Rep.* VIII 549c–550b, where the timocratic youth (the one ruled by his *thumos*) comes into being because his education in the praiseworthy and fine does not correspond to what really is good.

and appealing to our feelings. Related to this point, we saw in the *Rhetoric* that because the fine is the object of praise and blame, the fine is in some sense public. This too is implicit in the thought that *to kalon* is the proper object of *thumos*, for in Plato's account it is characteristic of *thumos* to feel shame when the agent is caught being associated with ugliness, in a broad sense. (This is true even when, as in the case of a fully developed sense of shame, the public is internalized.) Thus, if the fine is to be the particular concern of spirited desire, it must be showy.

Notice that a person pursues what he takes to be fine as a way to satisfy his desire really to be outstanding, then he must think that the fine object really is good. And as we have seen, Plato does think that the truly fine is in some way a manifestation of the human good. Children can grope for the fine on their own, without the benefit of reason. But their *thumos* is trained when a reason external to them, embodied in their parents and the laws, trains their sense of beauty to correspond to the human good. This, then, is the second thing the *Republic*'s discussion of the training of *thumos* can teach us about the fine: The truly fine either *is* a modality of the good, or it points to what is good.

Finally, we do not praise fine actions so much as we praise fine *people* for their fine actions, and this points to the third feature of the *kalon* revealed by Plato's *Republic*. According to Plato, spirited desires are connected to the agent's self-esteem. When *thumos* succeeds in achieving its goal—the possession of what it considers to be fine—the agent feels he is an admirable person, worthy to be praised. This aspect of spirited desire is what makes it so important to give children the proper moral education, for the sense of the fine they develop in childhood determines what kind of person they take to be flourishing and worth becoming. Becoming this spirited ideal is no idle fantasy, either. Since *thumos* is connected to self-esteem, a person will not feel entirely satisfied with himself unless he is seen to be (or can see himself being) fine. (And when his failure to be fine is apparent, he will be ashamed.) So when Aristotle says that morally virtuous agents act for the sake of the fine, if he believes that the fine is the object of Platonic spirited desire, it is likely that he thinks actions of morally virtuous agents reveal their own sense of worthiness.[44] When a person chooses to act in a certain way for the sake of the fine, he thinks of his actions as appropriate to the kind of person he is (or aspires to become). I will return to this point in a moment.

The argument I have just made about the *Republic*—that *thumos* as such desires the fine—will undoubtedly seem a stretch to some. It cannot be denied that Plato nowhere in the *Republic* says that *thumos* seeks the fine.[45] So

---

[44] Cf. Broadie (1991, 92–93, 127) for a discussion of the idea that, in the *NE*, acting for the sake of the fine is tied to the agent's sense of self-esteem.

[45] Indeed, as Hobbes (2000, 4) reminds us, the typical complaint of commentators is that there seems to be *no* coherent goal of *thumos* at all.

let me concede for the sake of argument—although I do not believe this is true—that Plato's *thumos* desires fine things only after it has been properly educated. Still, the three points I made about the fine as it appears in the *Republic* stand.[46] For even if *thumos* only finds satisfaction in what the agent takes to be fine once it has been trained to do so, the fact remains that there must be something about the fine that naturally satisfies the general human desire to be outstanding. So let me repeat what Plato's discussion of moral education can teach us about the fine. First, we can expect that the fine will in some way or other wear its desirability on its sleeve. For by possessing this quality, fine actions gratify the agent's natural spirited desire to be victorious in competition. Second, if the fine person can be *seen* to be in possession of the good, then it must also be true that he seems, in virtue of possessing the fine, to have the good. Thus, the fine must point to the superior value of what is good. Third, the fine in action must be such as to satisfy the desire for self-esteem. We can expect, then, that it will be genuinely revealing of the sort of life the agent considers to be worth living. The fine action will seem to the agent to be worthy of his ideal self. The upshot is that, if Aristotle accepts Plato's characterization of spirited desire and believes, as Plato does, that this desire is satisfied by the fine, then he must also think of the fine in human action as I have just described it. Fine actions are ones that are visibly appropriate to the agent's ideal sense of himself.

It is important to notice that for Aristotle, as for Plato, actions are praised as fine when they are seen to be appropriate to the agent as fulfilling a human ideal. Aristotle often associates fine actions with what is fitting or appropriate (*prepon, prosêkon, emmelês*).[47] And at *Topics* 135a13 Aristotle actually says that the fine *is* the fitting (cf. *Topics* 102a5–6). Now, Aristotle's description of virtuous actions as ones that are performed "at the right time, with the right things, to the right people, for the right end, and as one ought" (*NE* 1106b21–22) emphasizes that the virtuous person fits his actions to his circumstances. But we should not infer from this that the virtuous person slavishly molds himself to meet the contingencies. For an important part of what makes virtuous actions fitting is that they are appropriate to the agent himself. This is particularly apparent in Aristotle's discussion of the vices opposed to greatness of soul, the virtue concerned with the appropriate response to great honors (*NE* IV.3). We might expect that vain people, on the one hand, and the small-minded, on the other, go wrong in claiming too much or too little credit for themselves, respectively. But this is not the most important part of their error. The real problem with the small-minded person is that he does not attempt noble deeds because he does not think he is

---

[46] Nevertheless, I think my claim that we ought to try to understand *to kalon* as what satisfies spirited desire is stronger if this sort of desire as such aims at the fine.

[47] Rogers ([1993] 1999, 338) argues that when Aristotle says that the virtuous person acts "in accordance with worth (*kat' axian*)," he means that the action is fitting.

worthy of them (1125a19–27). The vain person, on the other hand, tries to perform actions that are more honored (*entimoi*) than his worth warrants. When he does, his actions are foolish; they are not fine (1125a27–29). This suggests that, in general, virtuous actions are fine because they are appropriate to the agent as well as to his circumstances. The virtuous agent is one who has the (or a) correct conception of human flourishing and achieves it. His actions are fine in part because, by being appropriate to him, they express his successful orientation to the human good.

Let us sum up what we have seen so far. All things are fine when they are visible as ordered, proportioned, and bounded by their good. We saw that morally virtuous actions have these formal features since they are, by definition, intermediate. Furthermore, since hitting the intermediate is such a hard thing to do, virtuous actions are praiseworthy. This link between the *kalon* and praise, reinforced by the *Rhetoric*, suggested that the agent's desire for the fine is, in part at least, *thumoeidic*, or spirited. Thus, we saw that fine actions must be appropriate to the agent's sense of his ideal self. But what is the conception of the human good to which the virtuous person aspires and that orders, proportions, and bounds morally virtuous action? The *Rhetoric* suggests that it is political independence that nevertheless affirms its ties to the community. The flourishing person is free within a community but does not make himself free of it. This is a part of the common conception of happiness which, I believe, Aristotle never rejects. But it is an incomplete conception. For what will the happy person do with his freedom in community? In this light, we ought not to forget Aristotle's considered view that happiness is excellent activity of reason, and that the practically wise person is a lover of truthfulness.

If my account of the fine and my interpretation of Aristotle's position on the human good are correct, the following ought to be true. When the morally virtuous person acts in a way that is appropriate to his sense of himself as a (successful) lover of truthfulness, his actions are determined to be just as they are by the human good, the most excellent activity of reason. And since the basis of their fineness is also the reason for their being choiceworthy for their own sakes, we can conclude that the intrinsic value of morally virtuous actions is in their orientation to a correct conception of the human good.

This point, though it should be obvious, bears repeating. In Aristotle's account, moral virtue depends on a conception of the human good that is sufficiently distinct from particular occasions of morally virtuous action to serve as their principle of order, symmetry, and boundedness. For virtuous activity, insofar as it is fine and choiceworthy for its own sake, is just action—including deliberation—in appropriate relationship to the human good. The *phronimos* grasps the truth on a particular occasion by ordering his action in the precise way that is appropriate to himself as flourishing. Thus, he must have some vision of human flourishing with reference to which he can determine what is appropriate. This is not to say that excellent practical rationality cannot constitute the morally virtuous agent's conception of happiness. (Indeed, Aristotle thinks some happy moral agents have just this conception [*NE* X.8].) But it does mean that he must have a way of thinking about practical excellence that is something more than or different from the appropriate acts themselves. He may, for example, think of practical excellence as a form of truthfulness and calibrate his particular acts against the standard of the practically truthful ideal.[48] To say that the human good is virtuous activity, then, although correct in its way, is not as informative as it might at first appear.[49] Of course, if we have been brought up well, we can use our intuition of which actions are virtuous as a way of discovering the truth about the human good. Indeed, this may be our only method of inquiry (*NE* I.4 1095b4–6: only those raised in fine habits should study the objects of *politikê*). But as Aristotle and Plato would say, that would be an inquiry *toward* first principles and not from them (1095a30–b8).

There is another consequence of Aristotle's thinking that actions are fine when they are determined to be as they are by the human good. However acutely we may be able to recognize it, we cannot fully understand the fineness of virtuous actions without a substantive account of *eudaimonia*. This may be why Aristotle does not say anything informative about *to kalon* in the *Nicomachean Ethics*. He is not fully in the position to do so until he concludes his investigation.[50] The account of happiness sketched in *NE* I.7 as "activity of the soul in accordance with virtue, and if there are many virtues, in accordance with the best and most final" is progressively developed—through the analysis of the moral virtues, the argument that theoretical wisdom is better than practical wisdom, and the discussion of our nature as social and political in the books on friendship—until finally he concludes in book X that contemplation is perfect happiness. This is not to say, however, that Aristotle wrote his chapters on the moral virtues in ignorance of his conclusion. I believe that a careful examination of those discussions will show (1) that Aristotle conceives of virtuous actions as pointing to the value of some good beyond themselves, that is, that they are ordered, made symmetrical, and bounded by some further good, and (2) that this good is activity in accordance with the highest form of rational excellence available to human beings. Since Aristotle believes that this is *theôria*, in the final analysis morally virtuous actions will be fine and worth choosing for their own sakes because they are appropriate to the philosopher, whether the virtuous agent understands this or not.

---

[48] The correct conception of *eudaimonia* would not provide us with a precise rule for action. At some level the *phronimos* must just *see* what is appropriate at the particular moment to the flourishing human being.

[49] Aristotle's definition of the human good in *NE* I.7 as "activity of soul in accordance with virtue" is somewhat more informative than this, since he has already made clear that the virtue in question is *rational* virtue.

[50] Of course, as I argued in the previous section, Aristotle thinks the *horos*, or limit, of the virtues is theoretical contemplation. Since fine things are bounded (*horismena*), *NE* VI implicitly contains an account of the fine in action.

CHAPTER SEVEN

Courage, Temperance, and Greatness of Soul

IN THE LAST CHAPTER I argued for a general account of the fine in action. Virtuous actions are fine when they are ordered, made proportionate, and bounded by the human good. This teleological arrangement must be visible and must gratify the agent's sense of self-esteem. Now the human good, according to Aristotle, is the most excellent use of reason. And as we have seen, though practical wisdom is an excellence of reason, theoretical wisdom is more perfect. Thus, there is a sense in which all virtuous actions, insofar as they are fine, ought to show that the agent is oriented to the precision and truthfulness best exemplified in theoretical contemplation. The agent need not be aware of the true theoretical nature of human happiness, however. So long as he gauges the appropriateness of his actions with reference to the ideal of truthfulness, he need not be aware that theoretical reasoning is that standard in order to act finely. At least this is a possibility we can and should leave open.

Of course, the theoretical standard of rationality will be implicit in morally virtuous activity even if it goes unrecognized by the agent himself. Thus, it ought to be possible to be led by reflection on the nature of moral virtue to an understanding that *theôria* is the highest human good. In this chapter, I will attempt just such a task of reflection in order to show that Aristotle's moral virtues are fine because they point to the superior value of the most perfect reasoning, which is contemplative.[1] I will examine three of the virtues Aristotle discusses—courage, temperance, and greatness of soul. I choose these virtues because their treatment in the NE is the most extensive, with the exception, of course, of justice. Also, at the end of his account, in NE X, Aristotle divides the virtues into the military and peacetime virtues (1177b6–7). Courage is the quintessential military virtue, and temperance, along with justice, is especially important in peacetime (*Pol.* VII.15 1334a22–28).[2] In covering these virtues, then, we cover both aspects of the life of action.

---

[1] Others have argued that the virtuous use of goods is the one that promotes contemplation, either directly or indirectly, by fostering a condition of the soul capable of prolonged philosophical study (Kraut 1989; Tuozzo 1995). My task in this chapter is different. I want to argue that virtuous actions are fine because they express the value of contemplation regardless of whether, on any particular occasion, they do promote contemplation.

[2] Actually, one of the most important peacetime virtues, according to the *Politics*, is *philosophia* (1334a23, a32). Whether this is a theoretical virtue or a practical attitude toward wisdom is unclear.

The lacuna in my discussion, obviously, is justice. Aristotle's account of justice is clearly concerned with proportionality. The just distribution of goods by the state is in proportion to the citizens' merit (1131a20–26). In rectificatory justice the judge looks to arithmetical proportion in assigning penalties (1132a1–2). So we might expect Aristotle's account of justice in *NE* V to be fertile ground for information about the fine in action. But in fact I have not found it to be useful for my purposes. Unlike his discussions of other moral virtues, Aristotle is more interested in mapping the structure of just actions themselves than in describing the psychology of the person who acts from justice. It is true that he contrasts the just person to the grasping, pleonectic person (1129b1 ff; 1136b21 ff.), putting one in mind of Plato's unjust tyrannical soul. Are we to imagine that for Aristotle, too, the just person is attracted to just actions precisely because they produce order and harmony in the city and soul? If so, we would want to know whether Aristotle's just person chooses just actions as one sort of order among many, or whether there is something about civic order in particular that appeals to him. Although I suspect we can develop an Aristotelian account of the just person's motivation, we would have to travel deep into Aristotle's political theory to do it. Thus, I will not pursue the possibility here.[3] What follows are three studies of the fineness of Aristotelian moral virtues.

1. Courage: *NE* III.6–9

I begin with courage which, more than any of the other moral virtues, is defined in relation to the fine. Courage proper is displayed by determining which dangers are most fine to withstand (III.6); the courageous person is described as acting for the sake of the fine (1115b12, b20–24, 1116a11, a15, b3, b31, 1117a17, b9, b14);[4] the state most like true courage, citizen's courage, is similar because it, too, is chosen for the sake of the fine (1116a27–29); while the other apparent forms of courage fail to meet the standard of virtue because they are not chosen for the sake of the fine (1116b2–3, b22,[5] 1117a7–8, a15–17). Aristotle emphasizes the beauty of courageous actions not simply because they are traditionally considered to be the most glorious. More important, the fineness of courage explains how brave actions meet his requirement that virtuous actions be chosen for their

---

[3] Kraut (2002, chap. 4) presents an interesting discussion of the psychology of the just person. Another way to approach the problem of the fineness of justice would be to examine the fineness of the related virtue of friendship.

[4] Aristotle's formulations vary. At different times Aristotle describes the courageous person as acting, enduring, choosing, and being brave for the sake of the fine. 'For the sake of' translates *toû kaloû heneka*, *dia to kalon*, and *hoti kalon*.

[5] Mercenaries fear death more than what is shameful, or *aischron*. The implication is that truly brave people are disposed to avoid the shameful more than death. *Aischron* is the opposite of *kalon*, and like *kalon* it blends ethical and aesthetic evaluation.

own sakes. The circumstances of courageous action are so painful—terror, wounds, and possibly even death—that unless we bear in mind that the end at which the courageous person aims is *kalon*, and thus pleasant, it will seem psychologically impossible for a person both to be rational and to perform brave actions wholeheartedly (1117a35–b2). Although the circumstances of courage are painful, courageous actions are pleasant insofar as they are choiceworthy for the sake of the fine. When Aristotle talks about the fine goal of courage, he cannot mean only the fine victory and honors that, no doubt, the brave person hopes his actions will achieve. If these were the only respects in which the brave person enjoyed his behavior, that would indicate that he valued his actions only as means to an end. Rather, when Aristotle says the courageous person takes pleasure in the *kalon* end of his action, he must also mean that, insofar as a courageous action itself touches (*ephaptetai*) *to kalon*, then in that particular way it will be pleasant to the courageous person.[6] The brave person is drawn to the beauty of his action, much as Plato's noble lovers in the *Symposium* fall in love with images of *to kalon* realized in the changeable world.[7]

But what exactly attracts the brave person as fine? It would be absurd to suggest that brave actions always attract the morally virtuous person because they seem appropriate to the philosopher, and Aristotle does not do so. Indeed, the brave person, acting as he does under the pressures of battle, seems hardly to have the time to think of much beyond the importance of victory. Thus, courage provides a particularly difficult case for my claim that morally virtuous activity is fine because it is oriented toward the value of contemplation. Nevertheless, I believe Aristotle's discussion in *NE* III.6–7 shows this much: that courageous actions are fine because, in being ordered, proportioned, and bounded just as they are, they make clear the agent's commitment to the human good, which he conceives as the excellent, rational use of a peaceful, political life. The appropriateness of his actions to a person committed to the excellent rational use of a leisurely citizen's life is what makes them fine. Once I have established this claim, I will explain how, from this point, we can see that the beauty of courageous actions depends on the value of contemplation.

---

[6] At 1117b15–16 Aristotle says courageous activity is pleasant insofar as it "touches" the *telos*. I assume that the *telos* is whatever the fine thing is for the sake of which the courageous person acts. (1) Aristotle says repeatedly that the brave person acts for the sake of the fine, and as we know from the previous chapter, the fine is pleasant. Thus the fine is an obvious candidate for the pleasant *telos* of courageous action. (2) At 1117b1–4 Aristotle says that brave people take pleasure in their end just as boxers take pleasure in honors. But honors, satisfying as they do our thumoeidic competitive desires, are pleasant because they are fine.

[7] Dirlmeier (1964, 347) notices that Aristotle describes the courageous person "being in touch" with the fine using the same verb (*ephaptetai*) as Plato uses to describe the fully educated lover "touching" the beautiful or fine itself (*Symp.* 212a). Notice that Diotima describes the *brave*, the temperate, and the just as lovers of the Beautiful (*Symp.* 208c1–d2, 209a1–8, 212a2–7).

Let me begin where Aristotle does, with the limitation of courage to the battlefield.[8] Aristotle's rationale is in part that the danger of death in battle is the greatest and most fine (1115a29–35). Thus, reflecting on the context of courage may illuminate what, in Aristotle's opinion, is the fineness peculiar to courage. I want to set aside one potentially appealing interpretation. We might guess that courage is a matter of being fearless in really scary situations. Aristotle's claim that the danger of death in battle is the proper sphere of courage might seem to support that assumption. After all, few things are likely to be more horrible than standing firm as you watch the enemy advance against you. Withstanding such horrors would be fine, in this account, because it reveals the superiority of the human spirit to the slings and arrows of fortune. Courage would be a sort of encounter with the sublime. But this will not do as an interpretation of the *Nicomachean Ethics*. The dreadfulness of death alone is insufficient to explain why war is the proper sphere for courage. After all, even though Aristotle says there is an attitude toward death at sea or from disease that is characteristic of the courageous person (viz., fearlessness and irritation at losing his life in this way), death in these circumstances is not fine (though neither is it shameful), and thus it is not, properly speaking, courageous (1115a28–29, a35–b6). I do not mean to suggest that the magnitude of the threat posed by imminent death is irrelevant to the beauty of courageous actions. As we saw in the previous chapter, the bigger things are, consistent with the visibility of their order, symmetry, and boundedness, the finer (*Poet.* 8 1451a10–11). My point is only that we cannot understand why courageous actions and their circumstances are fine solely by reference to the magnitude of the threat they tackle.[9]

In part, Aristotle's rather restrictive definition of courage is due to his insistence that courage is a matter of being fearless (*adeês*) in a technical sense (1115a33).[10] It is arguable that, in Aristotle's account, fear involves

---

[8] Aristotle's limitation of courage to battle is not only strange to our ears; it stands in contradiction to Socrates' assumption in the *Laches* (191c-e) that courage can be shown at sea, in illness, and in poverty.

[9] Gauthier and Jolif (1970, not. ad 1115a23) argue that Aristotle limits the scope of courage to the risk of death in battle because he thinks the most proper object of fear is death. Actually, Aristotle believes that fear is of *painful* death, or indeed of any very painful harm (*Rhet.* II.5). The scope of courage is limited to fear of death in battle not because this is most properly fear, but because this danger is the finest to endure.

[10] This can be confusing when compared with Aristotle's report at *NE* III.6 1115a9 that some define fear as the expectation of harm (*kakos*). The brave person *is* afraid in this sense of fear. He thinks death in battle is a serious misfortune and in no way seeks that danger (1117b7–8, 1116a7–9). However, he does not avoid danger either, if it would be fine to endure it. And that shows that the brave person does not meet Aristotle's considered definition of fear in *Rhet.* II.5 as the expectation of evil *plus* the desire to avoid it. (The fact that fear requires some hope of safety, however faint, indicates that it involves the desire to flee.) When Aristotle does call the brave person fearless (1115a33), we should assume he has the fuller *Rhetoric* definition in mind. Pears (1980, 174–175).

both a belief that harm is immanent and a desire to avoid it. Now the courageous person can (and should) believe it would be a grave misfortune to suffer the harm he faces (1117b9–13), and he can idly wish that he did not have to endure it. But he cannot have a motivating desire to avoid the field of battle where suffering harm is a real possibility so long as he thinks it would be fine, to endure it. Otherwise he would be torn between remaining with his comrades and fleeing to safety. By contrast, someone trapped in a boat in a terrible storm in no way chooses his situation and would appropriately do everything he could to get away.[11] Thus, it is appropriate to be afraid in the technical sense when faced with such a death. This idea—that courage cannot properly be shown in the face of evils we ought to try to avoid—fits well with Aristotle's claim that although disrepute, friendlessness, envy, and violence against one's family are bad, it is not, strictly speaking, courage to face them well (1115a10–23). Acting appropriately with respect to the risk of harm to one's family or with respect to the risk of disgrace *does* require trying to avoid those dangers. Thus Aristotle rules out the proper endurance of certain misfortunes as occasions for courage because it is not ignoble, and may even be fine, to fear them (1115a12–13, a22–23). On the other hand, the fearlessness of the soldier is fine because risking death in this context is in some sense worth choosing.

I suggest that enduring military dangers well is especially fine in part because they are not undertaken idly. The courageous person's fearlessness in this particular context suggests that he protects something he correctly considers to be valuable.[12] Aristotle does not think that just any willingness to die counts as courage. A person who kills himself on account of his poverty, or for love, or to avoid any sort of pain is not courageous but cowardly (1116a12–14). Poverty is not a good reason to give up life altogether. So one reason truly courageous actions occur in battle must be that warriors fight over something genuinely worthwhile. Presumably this will be the political dominance or the autonomy of their own community. At least, according to Aristotle, war is for the sake of peace and the political freedom that makes leisure possible (*Pol.* 1333a30–b3, 1334a14–16; *NE* X.7 1177b4–12). (Although Aristotle does not mention it, surely slavery is one of the more terrifying risks of war. See *Pol.* 1333b38–41.)

---

[11] Does not Aristotle say that the brave person will be fearless in the face of death at sea (1115a35–b2)? Yes, and insofar as he is hopeless, he will not try to flee. But my point is that the brave person does not choose death at sea as in any way good, whereas he does choose death in battle if necessary.

[12] As Pears (1980, 185) has argued, all courage, and certainly Aristotle's courage, requires an external goal. Pears thinks that the external goal is always related to one's own safety or survival. But unless we extend the external goals beyond these we face the problem Pears himself raises of explaining how Aristotle can think it possible to exhibit anything like courage in illness or hopeless situations.

Now I said before that an action will be fine in part because it is oriented to the human good. It is important to see that insofar as warlike actions aim to preserve political autonomy and peace, they do aim at the human good. For as we saw in our discussion of self-sufficiency, human beings are by nature political animals. Thus the human good, the end which by nature we seek, must be realized in the context of a political community. (Notice that when Aristotle says that human beings are political animals, he is not offering a definition of our specific essence, excellence in which would constitute happiness.[13] Rather, to say that we are political is to say that we as individuals seek our good in a communal way. "Political animals are ones which all have some one common function (*ergon*), and this property is not common to all gregarious animals" (*History of Animals* 488a7–9). Thus identifying our nature as political does not yet answer the question of our most final end. It does not, in other words, authorize the conclusion that excellent political activity is happiness. Instead, it reveals that whatever our highest good may be, we will realize it jointly with other members of our political community.)[14] In Aristotle's account, then, wars that are fought for the sake of peace and political freedom are legitimate and undertaken for the sake of some-

---

[13] At *History of Animals* 488a9–10 Aristotle says that bees, wasps, ants, and cranes are political too. At *Pol.* 1253a7–9 he says that human beings are more political than other animals, but I agree with Kullman (1991, 101) that our being more political is explained by our specific essence as animals having reason.

[14] Kraut (2002, 247–248) argues that by *political animal* Aristotle sometimes means only that human beings are naturally sociable as, for instance, at *Pol.* III.6 1278b17–21: "It has been said in our first discourses . . . that by nature human beings are political animals. That is why, even when they do not need assistance from each other, they have no less of a desire to live together." But here Aristotle seems to be inferring our sociability from our political nature. This would be a reasonable inference since, if we are by nature the sort of thing that achieves its good only in the context of political community, then we ought by nature to have a desire to live together.

Kraut also argues that unless *political animal* can mean simply 'sociable animal,' Aristotle will have no reason to call women and slaves (who cannot be citizens) "political" (2002, 249). I agree that this is a more complicated problem, but there seem to be at least two responses. First, women and slaves are by nature parts of the household, which is an association for the sake of a common good (*NE* VIII.12 1162a16–29, re women; *Pol.* 1252a34: masters and slaves have the same interest); thus women and slaves are at least as political as bees(!). Second, women and slaves are by nature part of the household, but the household is by nature fully realized only when it is a part of a *polis* (*Pol.* 1252b30–1253a1); thus whatever good women and slaves are capable of achieving, they achieve it most fully in the context of political community. (See also *Pol.* 1253a15–18 where the sense of good and bad, just and unjust qualifies human beings as members of the city *and* the household. And see *Pol.* 1269b14–19, where the status of women as part of the household makes them part of the city and a proper object of the statesman's craft.) Thus it seems to me that the phrase *political animal* as applied to human beings never means simply 'sociable animal' and always means 'animal which by nature achieves its highest good jointly with others in the context of political community.' But whatever the political status of women and slaves may be, when Aristotle calls free adult men "political animals," one thing he has in mind is that their happiness is achieved in a political community that seeks happiness as a common good.

thing genuinely worthwhile.[15] They are undertaken for peaceful political community in which alone human happiness is possible.

So brave actions are fine in part because they aim to protect the peace and autonomy necessary for the good life. Now, it may look from the way I have described it so far as if the fineness of courage is a function of its instrumental value. But this cannot be correct. The fineness of an act of courage is not tarnished by its failure to achieve its end. It is not only the victors who are brave. Furthermore, as I said in the previous chapter, what makes something fine is the same as what makes it worth choosing for its own sake. Thus I do not mean to say that brave actions are fine because they play a certain instrumental role. Rather, the point is that actions aiming at peace and freedom *at the risk of death* are the expression of a certain character. Let me explain how this is so. According to Aristotle, death is the greatest misfortune because life is the condition of the possibility of having anything good at all (1115a26–27). Thus, if a person is willing to give up his life, that must mean that the possibility for good that life affords is significantly less valuable to him without the presence of that good thing he seeks to protect. So a person who chooses (and is not compelled) to endure military dangers shows that a life of peaceful freedom is more valuable to him than mere life itself. In fact, we can go further and say that the courageous soldier shows that life is precious to him not simply because it is the necessary condition of having any old good thing or other, but because it contains *this* good—the freedom of his family or state—for which he risks his life. It is the value of this life that makes the risk of death worth choosing and fine, rather than rash and foolish. Thus, the beauty of brave actions is not owed chiefly to their *consequences*, but to the fact that the soldier *risks his life* to secure those consequences. In the extremity of the choice, the agent makes his (good) character visible.

This is why, even though there is a characteristic way a brave person will face the threat of financial ruin, for example, such actions are called brave only by extension (1115a17–22). For though such "brave" actions reveal that the agent values a certain kind of behavior more than money (and this is certainly a fine thing to show), they do not reveal what is true of the genuinely brave person, namely, that a certain way of living is the very condition of his cherishing his life *tout court*. This may seem an extreme way of stating Aristotle's conception of courage, but the point is made explicit in his discussion of the great-souled man's courage: "He does not expose himself to trifling dangers, nor is he a lover of danger . . ., but he will face great dangers,

---

[15] Unfortunately Aristotle also sometimes suggests that the enslavement of those naturally suited to servitude is also a legitimate purpose of war (*Pol.* 1255b37–39). For our interpretive interests, though, we should see that even here war is being justified by reference to the political life it makes possible. Since Aristotle thinks that slaves are a necessary part of the household (1253b4; 1256b23–26), he also thinks they are a necessary part of the city.

and when he is in danger he is unsparing of his life, because life is not worth living in any old way (*hôs ouk axion on pantôs zên*)" (*NE* IV.3 1124b6–9). The same thought is probably also behind Aristotle's claim that the happier a person is, the more distressed he is by the prospect of death in battle (1117b9–13). A happy person has more to lose but also, for the same reason, more to fight for. A willingness to risk death shows that for the sake of which the brave person thinks everything else is worth having.[16] Since military courage appears to protect a specifically political way of life, the human good as he understands it ought to be connected to political freedom.[17]

A brief examination of two derivative forms of courage substantiates what we have so far discovered about the fineness of bravery. The state of habit most similar to true courage is what Aristotle calls political courage, or citizen's courage (1116a15 ff.). Citizen's courage, like true courage, springs from a desire for the fine (1116a28–29). And like the person of true courage, the citizen fights to protect his city. Why, then, does Aristotle withhold the title of full courage to the citizen? The problem with the citizen seems to be that although he acts for the sake of *to kalon*, his understanding of *to kalon* is undeveloped.[18] He finds the *kalon* in the honors given by his community, and the shameful or *aischron* in their reproaches (1116a28–29). That is to say, he finds the *kalon* in what is honored, rather than in what is honorable. Thus the citizen fights for the sake of a fine goal that is entirely beyond the fighting itself. He wants the honor of his fellow citizens, but there is no need to think that he finds anything fine or pleasant in the standing firm itself.

---

[16] This is not to say that the courageous person would commit suicide if he is defeated. Aristotle seems to think that, in general, suicide is an act of cowardice (1116a12–15). Perhaps we should put Aristotle's point this way: The courageous person tries to protect the ideal conditions for his possession of the human good, but it may be possible for him to possess the good in less than ideal circumstances (indeed, this is quite likely since happiness is the exercise of rational virtue). Even when this is not possible, he may hope to possess the good again. The point remains that the courageous person risks his life in order to protect a life that is positively worth choosing.

[17] Aquinas (III.xv.544) notices that brave actions are appropriate to the agent in another way, which I think we should not overlook. According to Aristotle, we fear things that we believe are superior to us in strength. Thus, when a person is able to master his fear, and is right to do so, that means that the feared object is not beyond his power to resist. It follows, then, that a weakling cannot be brave, for it will never be right for him to be hopeful in the face of the enemy. If, indeed, Aristotle believes this, he will be in the Homeric tradition of thinking about courage not simply as an attitude of mind but also as a form of physical excellence. Courage, at least on a grand scale, would require gifts of fortune. This fact will be relevant to the sufficiency of moral virtue.

[18] It seems right to me to call the citizen's conception of the fine undeveloped rather than simply wrong because there are signs that the citizen's courage is the courage of one who is learning how to be fully brave. For instance, Aristotle says that such courage comes from virtue because it comes from a sense of shame (1116a27–28). Shame, as we saw in the previous chapter, is the "semivirtue of the learner" (Burnyeat 1980, 78). Furthermore, the sense of shame of the brave citizen, grounded as it is in the praise and blame of the citizenry, is characteristic of a less mature stage of development, before the source of judgment has been internalized.

(Think of the warriors of the *Iliad*, and particularly of Achilles, who seem not to gain any reward from their actions beyond the glory and honor they elicit from others.) Presumably, though, the truly courageous person would choose and take the appropriate pleasure in resisting the enemy even if he knew his heroism would go unrecognized. That is because resisting the enemy in just the way that the brave person does makes clear what kind of person he is.[19] This is why his action appeals to him as fine and worth choosing for its own sake. There is an immediacy to the brave person's choice that seems not to be a part of civic courage.

In its immediacy, true courage resembles another derivative form of courage, *thumos* courage. (*Thumos* understood now not as the source of all spirited desires, but as a sort of bestial, instinctive rage.) The person who fights from *thumos* is like an animal who attacks because it has been wounded (1116b25). In the *Rhetoric*, Aristotle says that anger (*orgê*) involves the desire to take revenge for a wrong (II.2 1378a30–32). Thus, the person (or animal) who charges the enemy from *thumos* does not look to some future reward as the source of his motivation. He attacks because he wants to make the enemy suffer for the wrong they threaten; thus his reward, that is, the pleasure at which he aims, is entirely in the blows and wounds he inflicts (1117a5–7). Now if the *thumos*-brave person *chose* his action as, all things considered, the right one and chose it *for the reason* the brave person acts, then he too would be fully courageous (1117a4–5). But *thumos* courage is not full courage because it does not issue in actions chosen for the sake of the fine (1116b30–31). In other words, although the *thumos*-brave person runs risks without looking to any ulterior reward, his risk taking does not reflect his understanding that there is some good—presumably a life of political freedom—which is so precious that it is worth defending with his life itself, if necessary. The courageous person, on the other hand, like the person who acts from citizen's courage, chooses his action because it does show what makes his life particularly precious.

Indeed, I would suggest that Aristotle considers actions from *thumos* to be inferior to true courage not only because they are not chosen for the sake of the fine but also because they could not possibly, in themselves, express the value of political life to the agent. This is so for two reasons: first because animal actions do not express self-*understanding* at all, but second because actions from *thumos* are also experienced by nonpolitical animals (1116b24–26).[20] Actions from *thumos* do not spring from a sense of the dignity of life in a free community; they are reactions to a kind of animal

---

[19] Of course, the brave person is not *only* interested in expressing his priorities. He cares about protecting his city! My point is only that he finds the actions *fine* because acting for this end at risk of this cost makes evident how clearly he understands the human good.

[20] Some animals other than human beings are political (see note 13, above), though human beings are the most political of all (*Pol.* 1253a7–9). But Aristotle's reference to wounded animals in the woods suggests that in our passage he has in mind wild boar and other game ani-

pain (1116b31–32). Aristotle believes this is true even for human acts of courage from *thumos*. When a person charges into battle from *thumos*, he is spurred only by the pain of fear, not by any sense that his action is noble (1116b30–35). In this respect, his action is not essentially any different from other actions from *thumos* performed in the service of sexual desires, hunger, and other appetites and pains we suffer in common with animals (1116b34–1117a2). According to Aristotle, a human action from *thumos* courage, however much we may be glad to see it on the battlefield, says nothing more about the agent's values than does a mule's stubborn refusal to move from the feed trough even when beaten, or than does a libertine's willingness to risk death for an affair (1116b35–1117a2). In Aristotle's account, all these agents act from pain, rather than from any positive conception of what makes life worth living. Or, perhaps more precisely, to the extent that *thumos* courage reveals anything about the agent's values, it is not the life of political freedom that is shown to be most important to him.

Actions from citizen's courage, on the other hand, although they are not chosen with the immediacy of genuinely courageous and *thumos*-courageous actions, do reflect the agent's partial grasp of the importance of life in a free community. He acts for the sake of fine honors, already implying that he cares about his place in his community. Furthermore, if such a person lives in a community that honors courageous actions—that is, endurance in battle—his sense of the *kalon* will be headed in the right direction. In particular, he will understand that physical safety is not valuable on just any terms whatsoever. For this reason, citizen's courage is superior to the courage of a mercenary. The mercenary's tendency to stand firm in the face of the enemy does not reveal anything about his values (except, perhaps, that he wants money). Rather, he acts as he does because he is skilled in fighting battles (1116b9–12). Consequently, when a mercenary realizes that he has lost the advantage over the enemy, he will flee; the citizen, on the other hand, will remain and die (1116b15–19). The reason for the citizen's action is that he, like the truly courageous person, prefers death to shameful safety (1116b19–23). In other words, life is valuable for him because it is lived under certain conditions. The importance of those conditions—in the citizen's case, being an honored member of his community—makes it worthwhile to risk life itself in order to protect them.[21]

---

mals, which he does not, in fact, think are political. I suppose he might be willing to say that bees attack from *thumos* . . . in which case their attacks would approximate civic courage.

[21] This characterization of a citizen's courage as revealing his ultimate values is to be found in Pericles' funeral oration (Thucydides, II.42): "[T]he present revolution of these men's [the dead Athenians] lives seem[s] unto me an argument of their virtues . . . there was none of these that preferring the further fruition of his wealth was thereby grown cowardly, or that for hope to overcome his poverty at length and to attain to riches did for that cause withdraw himself from danger. For their principal desire was not wealth but revenge on their enemies . . . choosing rather to fight and die than to shrink and be saved, they fled from shame, but with their bodies they stood out the battle."

Courageous actions are fine in part because they manifest the importance to the soldier of his political nature.[22] In a moment I will explain why this is only part of the story. (In brief, peace and freedom are valuable only to the extent they are used well. Thus, true courage must manifest commitment to the worthwhile use of political freedom in order to be fine.) Now, however, I want to point out that Aristotle's notion of the fineness of courage corresponds to our sense—both ours today and that of the ancient Greeks—of what makes courageous actions so admirable.

Pericles makes this explicit in his funeral oration. He praises the Athenian dead because the city they fought to protect was worth dying for.[23] Consider also the Spartans' heroic stand at Thermopylae, for example, where (according to Herodotus) four thousand Greeks defended a narrow mountain pass against three million Persians.[24] (Whether or not Aristotle approved of contemporary Sparta, the battle of Thermopylae was popularly considered a triumph of Spartan courage.) For three days Xerxes sent waves of fresh warriors from the various lands of the Persian empire to attack the Greeks. The Greeks managed to survive for a while by dividing into units based on nationality and taking turns defending the pass. In the end, however, the Greeks found themselves surrounded by the massive Persian army. Except for the Spartans and the Thespians, all the Greeks retreated or surrendered. In the final hours, fewer than three hundred men closed ranks against the Persians, first fighting with spears, then with swords, and finally "the Greeks defended themselves with knives, if they still had them, and otherwise with their hands and teeth, while the Persians buried them in a hail of missiles, some charging them head on and demolishing the wall, while the rest surrounded them on all sides" (Herodotus, VII.225). Every Greek was killed. This is, to me at any rate, a chilling but stirring scene, but only if we suppose that the Spartans were fighting for good reason. (Otherwise, Herodotus is describing the metamorphosis of proud men into cornered beasts.) The Spartans thought it was essential to protect the freedom of their city at all costs. Earlier, when asked by a Persian why they did not simply come to terms with Xerxes, the Spartans replied,

---

[22] Perhaps people have not always thought of courage as fine to the extent that it manifests the value of community to the agent. Homer's heroes, particularly in the final showdown between Hector and Achilles, seem to manifest the value of individual prowess. More important to me is the claim that we and Aristotle's contemporaries tend to think (though perhaps not exclusively) of courage as a particularly social virtue.

[23] "Such is the city for which these men, thinking it no reason to lose it, valiantly fighting have died." Pericles goes on to say that his encomium to Athens is in fact a praise of the dead (Thucydides, II.41–42).

[24] In fact, scholars now believe that the battle of Thermopylae pitted about 6,000–7,000 Greeks against a much smaller Persian army than Herodotus describes. (It is not clear how large Xerxes' army was, but it probably was not larger than 100,000 ([Hornblower and Spawforth 1996].) I will stick to Herodotus's story, however, because his telling of it gives a sense of what this story of courage meant to the Greeks. Information about the battle at Thermopylae and all translations of Herodotus are from Waterfield (1998).

158 • Chapter Seven

> This recommendation of yours, Hydarnes, is not based on a balanced assessment of the situation. You have only half the picture. Although you know what it's like to be a slave, you've never experienced freedom and you have no idea whether or not it's a pleasant state. If you had experienced it, you'd be advising us to wield not spears, but even battleaxes in defense. (Herodotus, VII.135)

The actions of the Greeks at Thermopylae seem fine and thus courageous because they express the fact that these men preferred defending the free life—which we must assume is really valuable—to life itself. Their deaths express this in two ways. First, the Spartans and Thespians died to protect the integrity of their cities and the freedom of other Greek states, with whom they had bonds of friendship. Thus the objective of their fighting was the protection of a way of life. But furthermore, the very manner in which the Spartans and Thespians defended Thermopylae, their discipline in the face of terrible odds, their closing ranks in a circle, expressed the supreme value for them of political freedom.[25] The Greeks at Thermopylae died as *political* men, and not simply as individuals. The memorial erected to the Spartans at Thermopylae after the Persians were finally repulsed shows that this is precisely what the Greeks found to admire in the Spartans' courage: "Go tell the Spartans, stranger passing by, that here obedient to their laws we lie."[26]

Finally, to take a last, more recent example, the firemen who trudged up the stairs of the burning World Trade Center as office workers were streaming out have become icons of courage. We honor the valor of people who refuse to leave the wounded and endangered behind. How are we to explain the basis for our admiration for such behavior? Perhaps we admire it as an example of altruism, that is, as an example of someone placing the interests of others over his own. But I think there is another and more subtle explanation: Such action reveals the agent as having linked his sense of self-respect to the well-being of the rest of us citizens. When a fireman enters a burning building or a soldier risks his life to save a comrade, he reveals his commitment to a conception of his life as valuable as political (in Aristotle's sense). He is the sort of person who has friends, who lives his life within the bonds of reciprocal goodwill, in a mutual pursuit of the good life. For him, it is better to die than to turn his back on his political nature and live as an individual. We admire these firemen, I believe, because in the face of the severest temptation, they kept their priorities in the right place.[27]

---

[25] Recall my interpretation of the beauty of courage as described in *Rhet.* I.9 (pp. 134–136). I argued there that, according to Aristotle, people admire and praise courage and all other dispositions to act for the sake of another because they are marks of freedom. Now we can say that courageous actions are fine because they express the agent's conception of himself as free and worthy to be free.

[26] Translation from Pressfield (1998).

[27] Let me be clear: I do not intend to imply that anyone who fled the World Trade Center had his priorities out of joint. Firemen occupy a special role that makes it appropriate for them to enter burning buildings and the rest of us (usually) to stay out of harm's way. Nor do I intend

So far I have argued that risk of death in battle is especially fine, according to Aristotle, because it is appropriate to one devoted to happiness realized in free and peaceful political community. But at the beginning of this discussion I claimed that the courageous person is committed to "the excellent rational use of a leisurely citizen's life" (p. 149). How do we get from the idea that the brave person is committed to the *polis* to the idea that he seeks happiness as *rational* activity?

I do not believe that anything in Aristotle's discussion of courage points explicitly to the claim that the highest good is contemplation. There are two things to notice, however. First, bravery will not be truly virtuous if it is not, in fact, the case that running the risk of death is preferable to living without a free life of this sort. Thus, the choiceworthiness of courage depends on the value of political freedom and peace. The person who admires courage, as Aristotle's students presumably do, can be led to ask why freedom is so extraordinarily valuable. What is freedom for? Today we might care about political freedom because it allows for the possibility of self-determination and self-expression. So for us, perhaps, political freedom is important as the condition of the possibility of the creative life. But this is not why Aristotle thinks political freedom is so important. War is for the sake of peace, he says, but the business of peace, once it has been achieved, is for the sake of leisure (*Pol.* 1334a14–16; *NE* 1177b4–6). But leisure is possible for us needy human beings only in the context of community. Indeed, in Aristotle's account the *polis* exists to satisfy a natural human desire for the satisfaction of more than our basic, physical needs (*Pol.* I.2 1252b15–30).[28] The purpose of political organization, over and above the family, is to make possible the pursuit of leisure activities (*Pol.* VII.14 1333a35–36; 1334a4–5; VII.15 1334a14–16). Thus, for Aristotle, political freedom and peace are worth the risk of death because they allow for leisure.[29]

But, of course, leisure is valuable only if it can be used well. ("If it is disgraceful in men not to be able to use the goods of life, it is particularly

---

to say that the firemen themselves who fled when they realized that the situation was hopeless acted against courage. In the account I am describing, it is central to courage that the brave person seek to protect his community. Thus, in a hopeless situation it is appropriate to seek to live to fight another day.

If I am right about the fineness of courage, then we do not admire courageous actions because they are altruistic, at least not if altruistic means "supportive of the well-being of others without thought to one's own." In the Aristotelian account I have been articulating, we admire courage because it is characteristic of one who understands his own well-being as essentially political, and so intertwined with the well-being of his community. This is clearly something Aristotle believes (*NE* VI.8 1142a9–10, IX.8 1169a6–11).

[28] Aristotle believes that people join family units to satisfy their basic needs and join cities for the sake of the good life (*Pol.* I. 2 1252b15–30).

[29] Thus, although the Spartans may appear brave, Aristotle thinks they are savage and brutal. Their lawmakers have misunderstood the value of peace and the proper use of leisure. This misunderstanding is reflected in their moral education, which seeks to inculcate only courage, but which has in fact given brutality the lead over the fine (*Pol.* 1333a41–1334a10, 1338b9–36).

disgraceful not to be able to use them in time of leisure—to show excellent qualities in action and war, and when they have peace and leisure to be no better than slaves" [*Pol.* VII.15 1334a36–40]). Now according to Aristotle, happiness is found in leisure (*NE* X.7 1177b4). Indeed, as we saw before, the reason well-functioning cities aim to create the condition of leisure is that cities by nature aim at happiness for the citizens (*Pol.* VII.14–15). So, since Aristotle believes that *eudaimonia* is excellent rational activity and, in particular, contemplation, we should not be surprised to learn that he thinks free citizens at leisure need philosophy (*Pol.* VII.15 1334a22–25, a31–34; *Meta.* A.1 981a22–25: philosophy requires leisure). Thus, in Aristotle's complete account, the possibility of the most excellent expression of reason is what makes leisure worth wanting and worth dying for. All truly brave people express their commitment to free and peaceful political life as the place where rational excellence can flourish. Since this most excellent activity is *theôria*, the possibility of contemplation is what makes courageous actions worth undertaking. My point here is not to argue that the philosopher has reason to value the political aspect of his nature. (That argument will come in the next chapter.) My point, rather, is that people who admire courage and its commitment to political life have reason to value the best use of leisure, and this, according to Aristotle, is philosophical.

Let me summarize where we have come so far. I began with the principle that since things are fine when they are ordered to their good, we ought to be able to discover what Aristotle thinks is the good of human action by reflecting on what makes courageous actions fine. It turns out that courage on the battlefield is particularly fine because it makes evident the agent's commitment to life in a peaceful and free political community. The brave person's attachment to this way of life is so profound that he is willing to risk the loss of life itself in order to protect it. But according to Aristotle, peaceful political life is valuable because it makes possible the conditions of leisure in which alone happiness is to be found. Thus, if the brave person's actions are to be genuinely fine (and not just apparently so), they must express his commitment to a political community that fosters the most excellent use of leisure. Aristotle has already argued in *NE* I.7 that excellent activity of reason is the good at which each individual and the whole *polis* should aim. But notice that if reflecting on the beauty of courage leads us to reflect on the value of a properly ordered political community, we will soon be led to ask: What are the excellent rational activities a community can support? Philosophical contemplation, Aristotle thinks, will emerge as the best. Thus, I conclude that courageous actions are fine because they show the agent's ultimate commitment to a way of life in which the most excellent activity of reason is possible.

This interpretation finds confirmation when we notice that the rationality of the brave person himself is integral to his nobility, as Aristotle describes it. I mentioned before that the description of *thumos* courage suggests that the brave person conceives of himself as a political animal. It also suggests, I think, that this political nature, which the truly brave person esteems and expresses in the risks he takes, is an essentially rational form of life. Aristotle says wild beasts on the attack are not brave "because being driven by pain and *thumos*, they rush to danger without foreseeing the dangers" (1116b34–35). The uncontrolled raging of an animal is the very opposite of the cool soldier who keeps his head. While the brave person can consider the consequences of various strategies, the soldier overtaken by *thumos*, as Aristotle describes him, cannot restrain himself from rash and pointless aggression. His inability to act on the basis of deliberation makes him no better than a senseless beast. So even if the courageous person, as Aristotle describes him, need not think of himself as a philosopher, he does need to take pride in himself as rational.[30]

It is sufficient for courage, then, that the brave person orient his behavior with reference to the value of leisure, political freedom, and rationality. Nevertheless, the value of contemplation still provides the ultimate foundation for the choiceworthiness and beauty of his actions, whether he knows it or not. The courageous person will act precisely as he does for the sake of leisure in his community; it is his consciousness of the value of leisure that makes him risk his life when he does and in the manner that he does. But since leisure is valuable for the sake of contemplation, it is correct to say that the courageous person acts for the sake of *theôria*, not necessarily as a conscious aspiration, but as the source of value for his actions. In the same way, Plato's lover in the *Symposium* loves *to kalon* itself when he loves a beautiful boy, even before he has completed the ascent to the form.

In conclusion, then, the exercise of courage approximates contemplation by being structurally similar to it, insofar as it is an exercise of practical reason and truthfulness. But when we examine what, on a particular occasion, the brave person takes to be truthful, we see that he chooses actions that—through their order, balance, symmetry, and ulterior goal—manifest his commitment to rational excellence in community as happiness. By acting

---

[30] It is interesting to notice that the expression of rationality forms part of our own notion of a noble death as well. To take but one recent example, a soldier in Vietnam wrote home:

> On the next day, our platoon was the lead. We had just started up the side of the mountain when we discovered that not everyone had left the camp. Someone in a bunker opened up on our point man, and all of us dropped to the ground. As we were crouching, our radio-telephone operator (the R.T.O.) happened to stroll down the path from the direction of the firing machine gun, stopping just above me. The R.T.O. dropped his radio and casually said to the lieutenant, "You'll have to find another R.T.O. I've been shot." He then continued strolling down the path. He must have been severely wounded, because he never returned. I was impressed by his casual approach, and hoped that I would act as well when I was wounded. (*New Yorker* 1999 & 2000, 97)

The appearance of sanity (although, no doubt, the soldier was in shock) raises this death above the merely pitiable.

just this way in the face of the dangers of war, the courageous person shows that he values the excellent use of leisure in community above mere life itself. And we have seen that this evident orientation of the courageous person to the value of leisure is what makes his actions fine. The value of leisure in a free community is the source of the actions' intrinsic value, that is, of their being choiceworthy for their own sakes. But since the value of leisure in a free community depends on the value of rational excellence, and of contemplation in particular, we can conclude, although Aristotle does not do so in his discussion in *NE* III.6–9, that the activity of courage is ultimately choiceworthy for the sake of contemplation. That is to say, paradigmatic courageous actions have the form they do because the excellently rational life of a citizen in a free city is the best one. And as Aristotle argues in *NE* X.7–8, this life is contemplative.

2. Temperance: *NE* III.10–12

Aristotle's discussion of temperance immediately follows his discussion of courage and is meant to be coordinate with it as the other "virtue of the irrational part" (1117b24). All the moral virtues are, in part, excellences of the part of the irrational soul having a share in reason. What Aristotle must mean is that temperance and courage are virtues concerned with feelings—pleasure and fear, respectively—that we experience in virtue of our animal, as opposed to our specifically human, nature. As we saw in the contrast between true courage and *thumos* courage, bravery is a matter of feeling fear *as a human being*—as a rational, political creature. In doing so, the brave person shows that he values his life as more than mere animal existence. As we shall see, the theme of experiencing animal passions *as a human being* becomes the focus of Aristotle's discussion of temperance.[31] "Intemperance" Aristotle says, "would seem to be justly a matter of reproach because it is present not insofar as we are human beings, but insofar as we are animals" (1118b2–3). Temperance concerns the pleasant pursuit of things that are necessary for our life insofar as we are animals. Insofar as we are animals, we need food, drink, and sexual intercourse. Indeed, we strongly desire them—so much so that, once we possess the luxury of relative leisure, we could easily give it over to their indulgence. It would be a shame to be willing to risk mere brute life in battle, for example, or to toil in business for the sake of a leisure lived for the sake of animal pleasures.[32] The temperate person is someone whose attitude to animal pleasures reveals that he thinks of and values himself as a *human* animal—that is, as a rational, and specifically as

---

[31] Gauthier and Jolif (1970, not. ad 1118b1–4) say that according to Aristotle, to be temperate is to be a man rather than a beast.

[32] This is one of Aristotle's criticisms of hedonism (*NE* X.6 1176b30–1177a1).

a *noninstrumentally* rational, animal.³³ In taking enough to eat but no more, in accepting a moderate amount of condiments when available and appropriate but in not missing them when they are absent, Aristotle's temperate person, I will argue, reveals that he loves the most excellent rational activity for its own sake as the highest human good. But of course Aristotle believes that the most excellent use of reason and one that is quintessentially noninstrumental is contemplative.³⁴ So although the temperate person himself may not be aware of this, temperate actions are fine and choiceworthy for their own sakes because they are determined—in their order, proportion, and shape—by contemplation.³⁵

As in the discussion of courage, Aristotle begins the discussion of temperance by determining its sphere: Which pleasures are the concern of temperance? (Not all pleasures are occasions for temperance, any more than all fears are occasions for courage.) After setting aside pleasures of the soul, such as the pleasures of learning and of gratified ambition, and what we might call cultural pleasures—listening to music, going to the theater—Aristotle says the scope of temperance is the pleasures we share with the beasts (1117b28–1118a1, 1118a23–25). This might lead us to believe that temperance is concerned with purely physical pleasures, but Aristotle explicitly denies this (1118a1–3). After all, there are many sensory pleasures in which a person may overindulge without being called intemperate. The delight we take in the smell of apples or of roses, for example, is not the concern of temperance, Aristotle says (1118a10–11). Rather, bestial pleasures are a subset of the physical pleasures experienced by human beings. So what is bestial pleasure, and what about it makes its right indulgence an occasion for virtue?

---

³³ By *noninstrumentally rational* I mean that the exercise of reason is an end in itself. Aristotle sometimes calls bees and other animals *phronimoi*—practically wise—but the most he probably means is that they "deliberate" as a means to an end not involving reason (see chapter 5, note 53, above). Broadie (Broadie and Rowe 2002, 27) take temperance to affirm the value of our *practical* rationality.

³⁴ Thus, while Gauthier and Jolif (1970, 238) argue that temperate actions are determined by the demands of reason, they are thinking of practical rather than theoretical reason.

³⁵ A reader turning from Aristotle's discussion of courage to his discussion of temperance may well notice that the insistence on the fineness of virtuous actions in the former is almost entirely absent in the latter. Only after nearly two chapters on temperance does Aristotle use the word *kalon*, and then he does so only to say that the temperate person avoids pleasures that are contrary to the fine (*para to kalon*), not to say that he acts for the sake of the fine (1119a18). This asymmetry is curious. Perhaps Aristotle emphasizes the fineness of courage because he is concerned to show that there is a respect in which the brave man's very painful actions bring pleasure to him. We should not suppose, however, that in Aristotle's account temperance does not positively aim at the fine. Aristotle concludes his discussion of temperance by saying that "the appetite (*to epithumêtikon*) of the temperate person harmonizes with his reason (*tôi logôi*); for the aim (*skopos*) of both is the fine (*to kalon*)" (1119b15–16).

Aristotle says that animals experience only those pleasures that supervene on the upkeep of their physical being (1118a18–23).[36] These are the appetitive pleasures.[37] Primary among these are the pleasures of eating—that is, the pleasure of feeling the food fill an empty belly—and of sex. Thus, Aristotle argues, animal pleasure is pleasure associated with touch (1118a24–27, b1). If animals delight in any of their senses, they do so only to the extent that those senses help them satisfy these basic nutritive desires (including here the sexual ones; see *DA*. II.4). So, for instance, dogs do not enjoy the smell of rabbits simply because of the way they smell, but because it puts them in mind of eating rabbits (1118a18–20).[38] And Aristotle claims that when lions take pleasure in the lowing of the ox, that is only because they are anticipating a tasty meal (1118a20–22). Indeed, it would be more correct to say that, although a lion may become excited by the sound of a lowing ox, it does not take pleasure in that sound per se. Rather, the lowing is the cause of the lion's anticipatory pleasure in devouring the ox. And this capacity of the lion's to take anticipatory pleasure is quite useful to it, since it helps it to find its way to its dinner. Indeed, we can imagine that the lion becomes more and more excited as it gets closer to the ox. And the ox, for its part, delights in the smell of the pasture only insofar as it promises sufficient cud to chew.[39] Animal pleasure, then, is the physical pleasure that supervenes on nutritive and generative activities or on their anticipation.

Now, human beings can feel these physical pleasures as well. After all, we too have a share in nutritive soul. But unlike animals, we can take pleasure in the activity of our senses for its own sake. That is to say, we do not enjoy sights and sounds associated with eating and sex only because through them we anticipate these nutritive and generative pleasures. As Aristotle says at the beginning of the *Metaphysics*, "even apart from the usefulness of our senses, they are loved for themselves; and above all others the sense of sight" (980a22–24). The reason is that perception, and particularly seeing, is a matter of making distinctions and noticing differences and similarities. More important, in Aristotle's theory, perception is a matter of receiving the form of the perceived object. Thus, perception is quasi knowledge and, according

---

[36] Aquinas, III.xix.611.

[37] Notice that when Aristotle says that temperance is not concerned with the psychic pleasures of *philotimia* (love of honor) and *philomatheia* (love of learning) (1117b28–29), he in effect rules out the pleasures of *thumos* and of reason, respectively.

[38] Stewart (1892, 308) and other British commentators have taken the part of dogs against Aristotle. "I agree with Grant in thinking that this view according to which 'brutes have no pleasure of hearing or smell or sight except accidental ones, namely when sounds indicate to them their prey or food' is questionable. Some animals seem to derive pleasure from music. A dog will sit for an hour at a time at a window looking with evident pleasure and interest at people and vehicles passing in the street.... That a dog experiences *psychikai hēdonai*, such as those of friendship, performance of duty, and vanity, is pretty obvious."

[39] This unphilosophical view of cattle is given the lie in *The Story of Ferdinand*, by Munro Leaf.

to Aristotle, we delight in it as such (*DA* III.3). Because we human beings are theoretically rational creatures, who desire knowledge simply for its own sake, we can delight in the activity of our senses not only insofar as it helps us to sustain our physical being but also insofar as it is the actualization of our rational nature. That is, we can delight in the lowing of the ox not only because we know it will make good eating but also because we recognize it as the sound that it is. We can take pleasure in this sound, in part, insofar as we say to ourselves, "There is the lowing of the ox."[40] Indeed, according to Aristotle this is precisely the delight we take in watching drama. Even when tragedy terrifies us, we take pleasure in seeing that "this is a that" (*Poet.* 4 1448b10–19).[41]

Aristotle limits the sphere of temperance to the pleasures of nutrition and generation, then, because they alone provide the opportunity for showing that the agent conceives of himself and the life worth leading as more than animal. Other physical pleasures, like the pleasure of watching tragedy, already presuppose our rational nature regardless of whether we indulge in them correctly. Likewise, Aristotle must exclude the pleasure of smelling apples and roses because these pleasures are not (or are not necessarily) connected to appetite. Even the pleasure of getting a back rub, which we today might consider the paradigm of sensual indulgence, is outside the sphere of temperance for Aristotle (1118b4–8). Back rubs, occurring for the Greeks in the context of the *gymnasium*, are the activity of someone who already has accepted a place in the *polis*. Thus, for Aristotle, back rubs, whether experienced rightly or not, are cultural pleasures, characteristic of a free person. The fact that these pleasures are not the concern of temperance does not mean that we cannot abuse them. Aristotle thinks people can either enjoy the specifically human pleasures as they ought or indulge in them excessively or insufficiently (1118a5–6). In other words, there are virtues and vices with respect to the human pleasures. But they are not fine (or *aischron*) in quite

---

[40] This idea of Aristotle's may seem odd. Surely we delight in certain sounds and sights as beautiful whether or not we recognize their source. (See *Poet.* 1448b17–19, where Aristotle himself allows this.) As we saw in the last chapter, however, things are beautiful when they strike us as effectively organized for the sake of their good. Thus Aristotle ought to think that, even when we do not know what a beautiful object is, it seems beautiful because it seems to have effective teleological order (and symmetry, etc.). Furthermore, Aristotle seems to think that it is, in principle, possible to find *all* successful natural objects beautiful (*PA* 645a21–26). Their order, symmetry, and boundedness is visible for all who have eyes to see. To take a craft example, we may be greatly irritated by the sound of a power mower on a peaceful Sunday afternoon. But the same sound can be pleasant if we think of it as the sound of neighbors engaged in industrious, homey activity.

[41] This is the pleasure we take in all mimetic art. When looking at a painting, we take pleasure in seeing that this set of lines and colors is a man. In poetry, presumably, we take pleasure in seeing that this is the sort of thing that kind of person would do in these circumstances (*Poet.* 9 1451a36–b7). However, see Halliwell (1986, 70–81, and chaps. 5–7) who argues that we learn far more complicated lessons from tragedy in Aristotle's view.

the same way, for the abuse of the human pleasures can never be utterly brutish, and so can never show that a person imagines happiness to be found in a life fit only for animals.[42]

The virtue of temperance, then, is a matter of feeling physical pleasures connected to nutrition and generation in the right *human* way. Aristotle does not mean that we should not take pleasure in the raw physical sensation of getting full when we are hungry, or of quenching our thirst. After all, human beings are animals and therefore, Aristotle thinks, it is virtually inconceivable that any person could avoid these pleasures (1119a5–7). A flourishing *human* life cannot do without the animal pleasures (1119a9–10). But nor can a *human* being flourish unless he typically experiences those pleasures in a manner appropriate to his *human* nature.

In NE IV.11 Aristotle criticizes the intemperate person for eating too much. But it would be a mistake to think that the intemperate person goes wrong only or even primarily in the quantity of his sensual indulgence and not in his attitude toward those pleasures. Though both will take pleasure in food, Aristotle says the temperate person does not take pleasure in the same things the intemperate person enjoys (1119a12). Aristotle may have in mind that while, for example, the intemperate person gorges himself on foie gras, the temperate person will prefer a snack of, say, hummus. But this alone does not do justice to Aristotle's memorable description of the gourmand as one who prays to god to extend his neck so that he can enjoy the sensation of ingesting food for longer (1118a32–33). The intemperate person does not simply eat more than a temperate person would. He attends to and delights in the most bestial aspect of eating: the way it feels (1118a29–32). The object of the intemperate person's desire is the brutish pleasure of touch (1118b1–4). Of course, he will take some delight in senses other than touch. But just like an animal, he will delight only in those sensations, such as the smell of food or of perfumes, that promise the satisfaction of his sensual appetites (1118a12–13). His mistaken evaluation of the pleasures of touch—he loves them above all others, Aristotle says—causes him to seek them out more than he ought.[43]

---

[42] Perhaps Plato's cicadas in *Phaedrus* (Ferrari 1987, 27–28) or his lovers of sights and sounds (*Rep.* 475d) are people who abuse human pleasures.

[43] Thus, in my reading, *over*indulgence is just one way of expressing a misconception of the human good common to all forms of intemperance. One might think, however, that Aristotle's doctrine of the mean requires us to put the emphasis on the excessive *amount* of physical pleasure the intemperate person pursues. Hursthouse ([1980] 1999, 109–117) has argued that Aristotle illegitimately combines two ways of being intemperate: One may eat too much for health, and one may indulge, perhaps infrequently, in odious pleasures. While I agree with her that Aristotle presents his doctrine of the mean as being more self-evident than it is, I disagree that Aristotle has confused two kinds of interpretation. According to Aristotle, overeating, just as eating the wrong things, is a way of indulging in animal pleasure *more* than is *kalon*. Though the intermediate standard of the *kalon* is often health, the ultimate standard is contemplation. See Tuozzo (1995, 146–148) for a different way that temperance might be fine insofar as it is

This description of the intemperate person suggests that the temperate person will distinguish himself not only in *how much* he eats but in what he attends to while he is eating. He will feel no particularly strong attachment to the mere physical pleasures, for he will be able to see them as supervening on activities instrumental to something beyond themselves. We can imagine that if indulging his senses is what he is after, he would listen to music or look at paintings. Of course, the temperate person will recognize that he must eat for his health. When he does so, however, the manner of his eating will reflect his sense of what is fine, or at least not contradict it (1119a18). Unlike the self-indulgent person, he will discriminate among the various tastes and textures and make a judgment of their quality (1118a27–29). Of course, it would be wrong to imagine the temperate person differing only in what aspect of nutritive sensory pleasure he enjoys. Someone who doggedly pursued eating and sex so that he could experience their sights and tastes and sounds would perhaps be as misguided as the more ordinarily intemperate person. The temperate person recognizes these physical pleasures as ones that essentially supervene on the activity of what Aristotle calls the nutritive soul. Thus, it is rational to pursue them only to the extent of physical need and only insofar as they promote (or at least do not interfere with) health (1118b16–17, 1119a16–18). However, insofar as the temperate person naturally desires the bestial pleasures for their own sakes at all, he will value them as an occasion to use his senses as an expression of his rational nature.[44] When he pursues them well, he transforms a bestial activity into something fine, that is, oriented to the human good. Eating in just the way he does is appropriate to someone who finds happiness is excellent rational activity chosen for itself.

The temperate person manages to satisfy his animal nature, and thereby experience appetitive pleasures, in a way that expresses his human, rational nature. This is a difficult business. The physical pleasures are powerful seducers, tempting us to lead our lives for their sakes. When the temperate person finds it choiceworthy and fine to act in *just this way* in the presence of food and sex, he shows not only that he *is* more than an animal but that he conceives of himself and his life as more than animal. In particular, he shows that *rational* pleasure rather than sybaritic indulgence is the best use of leisure. (Temperance, remember, is one of the principal moral virtues of peacetime and leisure.) Now, the temperate person need not think of metaphysical spec-

---

determined by the value of contemplation. Temperance, according to Tuozzo, is that disposition of the appetites that gives the soul "psychic leisure" for contemplation, while the associated vices disrupt and distract the soul. Whereas this general account of the fineness of virtue has some plausibility in the case of temperance (although his account of the vice of insensibility is a bit of a stretch), I find his application of it to courage and liberality to be ultimately unconvincing, but fascinating.

[44] He will enjoy the *pleasure* of eating for this reason. The eating itself he will value as necessary to his health.

ulation when he thinks of the appropriate use of leisure. He may well think that leisure is best spent watching a play, talking with friends after dinner, or worshiping the gods. But, as a matter of fact, all these activities are expressions of our theoretical nature.[45] Thus, if this is the vision of the good the temperate person's actions express, he shows that he thinks of himself as theoretical, although this is perhaps not the word he himself would use. But even if a person has a specifically practical conception of the best use of reason, he may still be temperate. So long as he thinks happiness is the most excellent rational activity and responds to animal pleasures in a way appropriate to his rational nature, his actions will be fine and worth choosing for their own sakes. That is because, in being oriented to the best rational activity, they *are* oriented to contemplation, whether the temperate person understands this or not.

3. Greatness of Soul: NE IV.3

I will conclude my examination of the morally fine with a virtue that might seem an odd and uncharitable choice: *megalopsychia*, or greatness of soul.[46] Aristotle's description of the great-souled person has been considered by many otherwise sympathetic readers of the *Nicomachean Ethics* as utterly repellent.[47] He seems to think he is a prize specimen of humanity and is, as a consequence, haughty in the extreme. I suspect that many admirers of Aristotle would like to pass over these pages of the *Nicomachean Ethics* in silence. But Aristotle thinks of the great-souled man as a paragon of spiritual beauty (1123b6–8). Thus, if we want a more detailed account of what makes virtuous actions fine in Aristotle's view, we cannot ignore this virtue. In the course of my discussion I hope to show that greatness of soul as Aristotle describes it is after all an admirable trait of character. But my purpose is not to defend *megalopsychia*. Rather, I will argue that, once again, morally

---

[45] I have already explained how aesthetic enjoyment is an expression of theoretical reason. Conversation with friends will be a use of theoretical reason to the extent that it aims not at action but at understanding. Also, the happiest friends will spend their time in philosophical inquiry (1177a32–34), and all virtue friendships are good because they provide some sort of intellectual satisfaction (*NE* IX.9). Religious worship is perhaps more of a stretch, although it is not clear that Aristotle saw it as such, for in Greek *theōria* can refer to religious observance. The first definition for *theōria* in Liddell, Scott, and Jones (1968; hereafter LSJ) is "sending of *theōroi* or state ambassadors to the oracles or games"; the second definition is "being a spectator at the theatre or games." Dramatic productions and games had religious overtones. Think, for example, of Socrates coming from the races at the beginning of the *Republic*. See also *EE* 1249b17, where the happy life aims at the *theōria* of god.

[46] The name of this virtue is sometimes translated (by Ross, for instance) as 'pride'. For reasons that will become apparent at the end of this section, I think this is a misleading translation. I agree with White (1992, 250 n. 4) that 'dignity' is an appropriate translation, but I will use 'greatness of soul' as the more common one.

[47] For example, Hardie 1978; MacIntyre [1966] 1998, 78–80.

virtuous actions are fine because they are ordered, made symmetrical, and bounded by a specifically rational use of leisure as the highest good. In fact, the discussion of greatness of soul indicates more directly than do the discussions of courage and temperance that this highest form of rational activity is philosophical contemplation.

Greatness of soul is the disposition to want the right external goods in the right way as a reward for one's excellence. But whereas the unnamed virtue with respect to honor discussed by Aristotle in the following chapter seems to be concerned with the regulation of the natural desire for honor per se, greatness of soul is focused more on one's understanding of oneself as already worthy of honor. The vices of vanity and small-mindedness are opposed to the virtue because they incline the agent to think himself more or less worthy than he really is. It would be more accurate to say, then, that greatness of soul is the disposition to want the greatest honors as one ought to want them when one is, in fact, deserving of them. Or, as Aristotle puts it, "the great-souled person seems to be the one who, being worthy of great things, thinks himself worthy of great things" (1123b1–2). It is a prerequisite of this virtue, then, that one already possess and "be great in" each of the other moral virtues (1123b30).[48] This is so not simply because one must in fact be good in order to deserve the honors of the good. In addition, the great-souled person, when he reflects on his condition of moral goodness, correctly concludes that it entitles him to the greatest of external goods—honor. It is understandable, then, that Aristotle says, "greatness of soul seems to be a kind of ornament (*kosmos tis*) of the virtues; for it makes them greater, and does not come to be without them" (1124a1–3). *Megalopsychia* ornaments the other moral virtues because it is the virtue concerned with honoring and calling attention to the excellence of courage, temperance, generosity, and the like.[49]

In this sense, then, greatness of soul takes its cue from and is dependent on the value of outstanding morally virtuous action. But it is interesting to notice that the great-souled person seems to be concerned above all with the *truthfulness* of his claims. The great-souled person is justifiable in his disdain for others because he forms his opinions truthfully (1124b5–6). He makes his loves and hates evident because he cares more for the truth than for the opinion of others (1124b26–28). And he speaks and acts openly (*phanerôs*) not only because he disdains others but because he is by character inclined to truthfulness (*alêtheutikos*; 1124b29–30). Since the actions of both the small-minded and the vain reveal their ignorance of themselves (1125a19–22, a27–28), we can assume that the great-souled person knows himself, as well. That is to say, he knows that he is, in truth, great (cf. 1123b29 and 1124a3, where

---

[48] Aristotle says here that the great-souled person is great in all of the other virtues, but the context suggests that he has in mind the practical, and not the theoretical, virtues. Or at least there is no reason at this time to think he includes theoretical virtue.

[49] Broadie in Broadie and Rowe 2002, 30.

Aristotle emphasizes that the great-souled are "in truth" great-souled). Thus, although greatness of soul is a virtue that honors the value of the other moral virtues, it is fair to say that the agent with this virtue cares in particular for the truthfulness exhibited by his peculiar virtue and the activity of those other virtues. The great-souled person is, then, a lover of truth.

But just how good does the great-souled person think his morally virtuous actions are? Consider Aristotle's description: He shrinks from action unless the deed is great and noteworthy (1124b25–26). He is idle (*argon*); the uncharitable might call him lazy (1124b24). In fact, his whole style is evocative of leisure; his way of walking, for instance, is slow and unhurried (1125a14–16). Worthy of honor though the great-souled person considers his grand and good actions to be, it is hard not to get the impression that these statesmanlike actions are not at the center of his life.[50] As W.R.F. Hardie has remarked, Aristotle's portrait of the great-souled person is mainly negative: "[T]he character of the *megalopsychos* is such that he does *not* seek danger, has *few* needs, is *rarely* moved to action, is *not* given to praise or admiration or the pursuit of grudges, *eschews* gossip or personal talk. Why tell us only what he does *not* talk about?" (1978, 66). What *does* the great-souled person do all day?

Gauthier has argued that he is a philosopher (1951, 104–117; Gauthier and Jolif 1970, 286–298).[51] The great-souled person is leisurely (and Aristotle's remarks in NE X.6 suggest that this leisure will not be passed in pleasant amusements), self-sufficient, remote from the world. The magnanimous person looks lazy, and *Politics* VII.3 suggests that this is how the philosopher looks to the politician.[52] And in NE X.7–8 the contemplative life is said to embody these characteristics while the political life devoted to moral virtue does not. But in addition, according to Gauthier, Aristotle's discussion of the great-souled man evokes Socrates. Both are indifferent to good and bad fortune, but both are willing to accept what honors can be given, as, for instance, when Socrates assesses his penalty at free meals in the Prytaneum at public expense (*Apology* 36b–e). Neither Socrates nor Aristotle's great-souled man thinks life is worth saving at any cost, consequently both are conspicuously brave. Both always speak the truth. And if all this were not enough, Aristotle actually says that the great-souled person is ironic (1124b30)! The upshot, if

---

[50] I grant Curzer's (1991, 139) argument that the great-souled person's engagement only in great virtuous actions is compatible with his spending most of his time on those actions. Arranging a public festival, for instance, though a single act of magnificent generosity (*megaloprepeia*) might well be time-consuming. However, this would not explain the impression Aristotle says people have that the magnanimous person is idle. Hardie (1978, 73) admits that the aloofness and (apparent) inactivity of the great-souled person is a difficulty for any interpretation that sees him as primarily involved in political affairs.

[51] Stewart (1892, 335–336) also interprets the great-souled person as being devoted to *theôria*, although unlike Gauthier he does not see a portrait of Socrates here.

[52] Gauthier does not note this connection to the *Politics*, but see Gauthier and Jolif (1970, not. ad 1124b24) for a detailed discussion of how the adjective *argos* was often associated in Athens with the philosophical life.

Gauthier is correct, is that the philosopher living for the sake of theoretical contemplation is also the most glorious in his practical wisdom.

However tempting this interpretation may be, it is overinterpretation to say at this point in the *Nicomachean Ethics* that this paragon of moral virtue is a philosopher. Aristotle never mentions *theôria* in this chapter on greatness of soul.[53] Instead, we should draw the more modest conclusion that the great-souled person lives his life for what he can achieve at leisure, whatever that may be.[54] We need not assume, nor should we yet, that this activity is definitely philosophical. However, Gauthier is surely right that Aristotle's evocation of Socrates here is important, particularly when coupled with the great-souled person's interest in the truthfulness of his actions. However the great-souled person spends his time, one possibility we are certainly being invited to consider is that this hero of moral greatness passes his time in philosophical conversation with his fellow citizens at leisure.[55]

Although the great-souled person is at leisure and may be engaged in philosophy, his greatness of soul is expressed in his pursuit of honors and in his assessment of his *practical* performance.[56] So it is in Aristotle's description of how he seeks honor for moral virtue that we will discover the fineness of this particular virtue. Roughly the first third of the chapter describes the great-souled person's relationship to honor in very general terms: He measures his worth by his actual worth, and what he's worthy of is honor. But

---

[53] Rees (1971, 242) and Hardie (1978), who reject Gauthier's interpretation. Gauthier (1951, 105–106) admits the point but discounts it on the grounds that Aristotle often only hints at the superiority of contemplation.

[54] That is to say, he spends his days in the citizens' *agora* of Aristotle's ideal city. This is the part of the city from which all nonleisurely activities, including political activities such as the law courts and civic administration, are excluded (*Pol.* VII.12). Though Aristotle does suggest that the highest magistrates will conduct their activities here (1331a35), the only activity proper to the citizens' *agora* described at any length is gymnastic exercises for the old men who are beyond the age of active political rule.

[55] Hardie (1978, 77 n. 10) argues that even though Aristotle cites Socrates, among others, as an example of greatness of soul in *Post. An.* 97b15–25, this does not support the case that the great-souled person in *NE* IV.3 is a philosopher, since "Socrates was known for his courage in military and political action and not only as a philosopher." I agree that *Posterior Analytics* does not support Gauthier's case. (Aristotle is simply using Socrates and others as examples of magnanimity his audience will be inclined to accept.) However, it is a mistake to divorce Socrates' military exploits from his being a philosopher. Socrates' temperance and courage are the effects of his silencing the demands of his body so that his soul may be unencumbered in its search for truth. The intuition that Socrates and the magnanimous person are not philosophers insofar as they honor moral virtue depends on a sense that the philosopher as such cannot care for excellence in practical life. But Plato's Socrates suggests a different story. And I will argue in the next chapter that Aristotle believes commitment to practical excellence to be an integral part of the philosophical life.

[56] Contra Gauthier (1951, 113), who believes that philosophical contemplation is the *only* thing worthy of great honors. Aristotle says at 1123b29–32 that since the great-souled person is worthy of the greatest honors, he must be good and indeed great in each of the virtues. He then lists courage and justice as examples.

in 1124a5 Aristotle becomes more specific: "He will be moderately pleased by great honors given by upstanding people (*spoudaioi*) . . . but he will completely disdain honor from chance people and for small things" (1124a5–11). It is in the second half of this sentence that the great-souled person begins to seem unbearably haughty. In fact, as we read on, it emerges that in accepting the honors due him, the great-souled person wants to assert his superiority over others. In itself, honor is not particularly important (1124a16–20), but it is the mark of a superior. The great-souled person is ready to play the benefactor and delights in remembering the benefits he has conferred, since such behavior is characteristic of superiors. On the other hand, he is ashamed when he has to ask for help and doesn't like to remember the help others have given him once the debt has been repaid, since this is the behavior of inferiors (1124b9–15).[57] What of beauty does Aristotle find here?

First, we should not imagine that the great-souled person flaunts his superiority everywhere. His attitude to people in the middle of the social scale is moderate and he would consider it boorish to assert his superiority over the humble and lowly (1124b19–22). Instead, he makes a point of being honored only by the upstanding (*spoudaioi*), people of distinguished rank (*tous en axiômati*), and the well-off (*tous en eutuchiais*) (1124a6, b18–19). In other words, the great-souled person asserts his superiority over those who are, or are generally considered to be, successful. Now since the magnanimous person is correct in his claims, his superiority is no doubt a considerable accomplishment (1124b20).[58] But furthermore, he wants to be recognized *by* the lesser great. Presumably, his life will be distinguished from theirs—will be visible—as superior only if those who generally take themselves to be superior recognize that he is better. So in developing an account of what makes greatness of soul fine, we must take into account that he is only animated to seek distinction when in the company of the truly or conventionally great.

Second, we should notice that though the great-souled person demands to be honored by the great, he does not seek the sort of honors such people usually pursue. In the line immediately following the ones I just discussed above, Aristotle says, "He does not seek things held in honor (*entima*), or that in which others excel" (1124b23–24). If Aristotle had stopped with the first clause, we would interpret him to mean that the great-souled person's actions are not motivated by honor. But the second clause suggests that inso-

---

[57] I agree with Curzer (1991, 138) that there is no need to suppose that the great-souled person is slow to repay his debts. Rather, he doesn't like to dwell on past circumstances of material inferiority. Thus I agree with Hanley (2002, 17–18) that there is little reason to paint the magnanimous person as altruistic.

[58] Aristotle says that his accomplishment is difficult. As I argued in the last chapter (p. 131), the difficulty associated with hitting the mean is a mark of the fine.

far as he is motivated to pursue honor, what he holds in honor is *different* from what others pursue.

If we put these two passages together, it begins to seem as if the great-souled man wants to distinguish himself from and assert his superiority over those who lead a political or statesman's life, at least as that is conventionally understood. It is those of distinguished rank and the wealthy who have particular clout in the city. And it is marks of civic importance—sponsorship of civic events, political power, wealth, important family liaisons—that are generally held in honor and in which the distinguished and wealthy excel. But, as we saw, it is the things typically honored and in which others excel that do *not* attract the great-souled person's attention. Thus, it might at first be thought that the great-souled person is superior to the rich and distinguished in virtue of having more of what they themselves possess. Just as it is appropriate for the strongest person to make a display of his strength against those who are themselves strong, so also the great-souled would display his greater power and good fortune against the powerful and fortunate civic movers and shakers. But if the great-souled person does not even join the competition where the rich and distinguished claim success, he cannot be superior to them on their own terms, so to speak.

If this is the situation, we can see some point to the great-souled man's being great. One does not need to be a student of Plato's to think that the rich and powerful are always likely to think that they alone are happy. (Think, for example, of the story of Solon and Croesus.) If the great-souled man's life is not a conventionally political one—and his apparent laziness indicates that it is not—then these people are likely not to recognize him as their equal in happiness, much less their superior. Thus, we ought not to imagine the great-souled man as swaggering when he is in the company of the rich and powerful. Rather, his being great is a matter of refusing to defer to or to be condescended to by those who have, at best, a secondary claim on happiness. And the great-souled man acts this way from the knowledge that his life is in fact the best. Aristotle's depicts the great-souled man's haughtiness as like that of a person devoted to the life of the mind or, to take an un-Aristotelian example, an artist, insisting on his dignity in the company of Bill Gates and Bill Clinton. So one reason greatness of soul is fine is that it shows the keenness of the agent's understanding of the human good as exemplified by himself.

The point is not so much that the great-souled person succeeds in being honored by these pretenders to the best life. After all, even honor is a small thing to him (1124a19). Rather, Aristotle's worry is that if the best person is not alive to his superiority over the conventionally successful, then he may neglect the fine responsibilities that typically fall to the best people in society. Aristotle's claim that undue humility (*mikropsychia*) is more opposed to greatness of soul than is vanity (1125a32-33) bears this out. The problem with the overly humble person is not that he is slow to toot his own horn; his fault lies in giving up respect to those whose claim to happiness is less than his own. He lacks an appropriate sense of self-respect. The result is that he does not undertake to do the noble and good things that it is appropriate for him to do.[59] (We can imagine a politically informed citizen who, in a time of national crisis, avoids taking a political stand on the grounds that his opinions on political matters are not important.)[60]

This suggests another reason Aristotle might have considered greatness of soul fine. So far I have left open the possibility that the great-souled person devotes himself to moral virtue as his highest good, though granted not in any conventional sense. He does not rush to battle or the law courts or other places he might display his superior moral virtue, but lives for what he can accomplish at leisure. Now, greatness of soul, understood as the virtue that honors other moral virtues, is an important virtue for anyone who spends his time in leisure. Such a person may seem to have no regard for the business, the laboring over necessities, that makes up much of the life of the *polis*. In acting with greatness of soul, he shows his high regard for those great actions which themselves honor his political nature.[61] But at this point it would be willful not to notice the similarities between the portrait of the great-souled man and Socrates. For although anyone who spends his time in leisure needs greatness of soul, it is particularly important for the philosopher, since the philosopher's preferred use of leisure is entirely unconcerned with human beings and human affairs. But though the philosopher does not live for political involvement as a statesman, his idleness is not the result of alienation from or rejection of the city (or so I shall argue in the next chapter). Thus he above all needs to show that his remoteness from the world in which moral virtue is most gloriously exercised is not a disdain for moral virtue itself. Excellent action is also truthful. So greatness of soul is fine in part because it shows that the agent looks beyond conventional busyness to a happiness found in leisure. The echoes of Socrates in this chapter suggest that this leisure is spent in philosophical conversation. But as embodied by the philosopher, greatness of soul is fine also because it displays his understanding that something of the truthfulness he loves is to be found and cherished in practical excellence.

---

[59] Aquinas (IV.xi.786) emphasizes this connection between lack of self-knowledge and failure to do good works in his discussion of *mikropsychia* (translated by Litzinger as 'small-mindedness') but attributes the ignorance to laziness.

[60] The vice opposed to greatness of soul should not really be called humility, then, when that is conceived in terms of the Christian virtue. Someone who has Christian humility is not marked by a sense of inferiority to others; he is conscious of his dependence for his worldly success on the grace of God. His humility is primarily before God, not his fellow men.

[61] Hanley (2002, 17) argues for a similar conclusion from a rather different angle. According to him, Aristotle's considered view is that greatness of soul is expressed not so much in heroism as in "the context of peaceful civic life." I agree that greatness of soul does have this civic face. But I would point out that this is compatible with the philosopher's being great-souled, since Socrates, too, was loyal to his city. (It is not, however, compatible with Hanley's explanation of why magnanimity comes to be expressed in harmony with civic life.)

CHAPTER EIGHT

Two Happy Lives and Their Most Final Ends

COURAGE AND TEMPERANCE—the virtues of war and the virtues of peace—and greatness of soul are fine and choiceworthy for their own sakes because they reveal the agent's commitment to the supreme value of some use of leisure that displays his rational and political nature. When a person protects a wounded comrade or eats at a dinner party or accepts honors with dignity in a moderate way, he shows that in his view the rational use of leisure makes life worth living. As we know, Aristotle thinks that the best use of leisure is in philosophical contemplation. *Theôria*, after all, is the paradigmatic way of grasping the truth that all other rational activity, and in particular morally virtuous activity, approximates. Thus, when the *phronimos* acts for the sake of the fine in action, he shows that his understanding of practical truthfulness is determined by the best use of leisure, which is in fact theoretical. And since excellence in practical truthfulness is an approximation of theoretical truthfulness, the agent's morally virtuous action is simultaneously worth choosing for the sake of contemplation.

When we turn to NE X.6–8, we see Aristotle draw these observations to their logical conclusion. Morally virtuous action, choiceworthy as it is for itself, is choiceworthy for the sake of a distinct *eudaimonia* (1177b2–15). Contemplation, on the other hand, is choiceworthy for itself alone (1177b1–2). Thus contemplation is our most final end, the human good, and perfect or most final (*teleia*) *eudaimonia* (1177b24–25). The philosopher who devotes everything he does to contemplation leads the happiest human life (1178a6–8). In the first section of this chapter I will trace Aristotle's presentation of this argument.

Now, as in the first book of the *Nicomachean Ethics*, in NE X.6–8 Aristotle takes the finality of a good to be a particularly important mark of its being *eudaimonia*.[1] Thus, he is concerned to show that contemplation has

---

[1] Aristotle also uses other criteria from NE I.7 for determining the eudaimonic good, in particular self-sufficiency. As I argued in chapter 3, self-sufficiency in NE I.7 refers to the sufficiency of *eudaimonia* to be an end of human striving. It is likely that the meaning of self-sufficiency changes somewhat when we get to the discussion of NE X.6–8, but even so, I believe it still refers to the sufficiency of an activity as an end. This is particularly clear in NE X.6 1176b3–7: "[I]t is clear that we must consider happiness to be one of the ends choiceworthy for its own sake and not one choiceworthy on account of some other thing; for happiness lacks nothing but is self-sufficient. And [activities] are choiceworthy for themselves from which nothing beyond the activity is sought." Activities that have their ends entirely in themselves are, by this formulation of the criterion, self-sufficient. Although it is beyond my task here to make

this feature. But he also considers a new worry: If, as we learn now for the first time in the *Nicomachean Ethics*, contemplation is the divine activity, is it right to think of it as the end of a genuinely *human* life? If not, then it is not clear that a human being ought to pursue it as happiness (1177b26–31). Aristotle argues in NE X.7 that the philosophical life is both divine and the life of our truest self (1177b31–1178a7). However, the argument leads him to make two modifications in NE X.8 of the rather triumphant intellectualism of his previous chapter. First, Aristotle concedes that the political life lived "in accordance with the other virtue" is also happy, although in a secondary way (1178a9–10).[2] He is not very forthcoming about his reasons for this concession, but I will argue in the second section of this chapter that they are twofold: (a) the political life also aims at the excellent activity of our human self, and (b) this morally virtuous activity is itself divine in a way. Second, Aristotle insists that the philosophical life must be lived in the awareness of the philosopher's human context (1178b5–7, 1178b33–1179a9). The philosopher is not a god but a human being who is as godlike as it is possible for a political animal to be.

Properly understood, Aristotle's discussion in NE X.8 of these two qualifications to the praise of the philosophical life in NE X.7 can help us solve a problem that does not seem to have bothered Aristotle very much, but has been frustrating to his modern interpreters. Aristotle believes that the philosophical life includes moral virtue (1178b5–6). But as we have seen in the two previous chapters, and in particular in the discussion of courage, morally virtuous activity celebrates a distinctively *political* vision of the leisurely life. Why should the philosopher have any interest in that? His political nature is unavoidable, of course, but the external goods that human beings acquire in community are a hindrance to his theoretical activity (1178b3–5). So what reason does the lover of contemplation have to choose virtuous actions that celebrate this aspect of his nature? In fact, it is not hard to imagine reasons for the philosopher to reject moral virtue, for the demands of virtue may be an additional impediment to contemplation. Why, for example, should a philosopher want to be courageous, given that courage may require him to give up his life? So, even if morally virtuous action is choiceworthy for the sake of contemplation, it is not clear that it is the *best* choice for that end.

---

this argument, I believe that the self-sufficiency of an activity to be an end is also what Aristotle has in mind at NE X.7 1177a27–b1.

[2] Broadie (1991, 438 n. 72) argues that the reference of *deuterôs* (secondary way) is *eudaimonestatos* (happiest) in the previous line, and not *eudaimôn* (happy), so that Aristotle is saying that the life lived in accordance with the other virtue is *happiest* in a secondary way. I do not see how this issue can be decided on the basis of the text (or grammar) alone, since it seems equally natural to me to read this as saying that while the theoretical life is happiest, the life in accordance with the other virtue is happy in a secondary way. But whatever we take *deuterôs* to qualify, the result will be that the life in accordance with the other virtue comes in second place.

Aristotle does not provide an explicit solution to this problem. He seems to think that the mere fact of the contemplator's necessary engagement in practical affairs is sufficient to guarantee that he will act virtuously. "Insofar as he [the philosopher] is a human being and lives with many people, he chooses to act in accordance with [practical] virtue" (1178b5–6).[3] Nevertheless, I believe his answer is implicit in his discussion in NE X.7–8 of the happiness of the philosophical and political lives. In brief, Aristotle's position is this: The lover of contemplation will want to possess contemplation to the extent that his nature allows. Now, in fortunate circumstances, our nature allows us to exercise our theoretical reason. But even in the best of circumstances, the time we spend engaging our theoretical reason will necessarily be extremely short in comparison with the time we must spend using our practical reason. Our animal and political nature requires that we figure out how to acquire all kinds of goods for ourselves, including the time to spend contemplating. So the lover of contemplation, if he wants to participate in contemplation as much as he can, must find a way to extend the possession of contemplation into his practical life. This he can do by exercising *phronêsis*. For as we have seen, morally virtuous action not only reveals the philosopher's commitment to contemplation, it approximates contemplation. Since human life is so overwhelmingly practical, morally virtuous action provides a way to possess contemplation that the philosopher cannot ignore. If he were to act against moral virtue for the sake of what could only be a relatively short period of contemplation, he would deprive himself of a kind of possession of his highest good for most of his life.

In the third section of this chapter I will argue for this solution to the problem of the place of moral virtue in the happy life. But before I discuss this and the other issues I have raised, I should defend two assumptions I am making that may seem controversial.

1. THE COMPETITION BETWEEN THE PHILOSOPHICAL AND POLITICAL LIVES

I assume that the theoretical life and the "life in accordance with the other virtue" (1178a6–9) are competing alternatives, and not two aspects of the same life.[4] By this point in Aristotelian scholarship, my assumption is proba-

---

[3] Cooper ([1975] 1986, 164) reads Aristotle as saying that the philosopher acts in conformity with, but not from, moral virtue. (Cooper retracted this general view of the philosopher's connection to moral virtue in Cooper [1987] 1999.) However, Aristotle normally uses the phrase "activity in accordance with virtue" to mean activity that *is* fully virtuous. There is nothing sinister in his use of *prattein* (to act) here instead of *energein* (to be active) since he has just been stressing that moral virtue is expressed in *praxeis* (actions).

[4] Keyt (1983; 1989) argues that they are two aspects of the same life. So also, in slightly different ways, do Gauthier and Jolif (1970, 860–864) and Stewart (1892, 443–444).

bly not particularly controversial. Still, it is important enough that it ought to be defended. I do not believe that the question can be decided by the meaning of *bios* alone,[5] although Aristotle seems usually to refer to something like a biographical life (or to a "complete" portion of such a life) when he writes *bios*. However, Aristotle's use of *bios* in NE I.5 can guide us in the interpretation of this word in NE X. That is because in NE X.6–8 he settles the question he first raised in NE I.5 of which of the three traditional happy lives—the voluptuary's, the politician's, or the philosopher's—is the best.[6] (In fact, at NE I.5 1096a4–5 Aristotle promises to describe the theoretical life later; NE X.7–8 is the place he does it.) Now David Keyt (1989) has argued that *bios* means 'occupation or career' and so that one may lead two *bioi* simultaneously in different areas of one's life. We may think, perhaps, of Thomas Jefferson, who was a farmer and an architect. Now in the first place, Keyt's conclusion strikes me as rather anachronistic. One has to divorce one's occupation from one's overall social position in order for it to be psychologically possible to have two independent careers at once; Jefferson, after all, did not lead a farming life and an architectural life; he led the life of a gentleman farmer. But also, Keyt's interpretation is clearly not what Aristotle has in mind in NE I.5, for there the three lives in competition for the title of happiest are conceived as mutually exclusive alternatives. Each life is distinguished by what it takes to be the most valuable human good. The political life is one in which honor or virtue or something else (morally virtuous activity, as it turns out) is taken to be the ultimate concern of a life worth living. The voluptuary, on the other hand, values pleasure above all else. It is hard to imagine how a person could value two goods as independently (and not jointly) most valuable without suffering some kind of schizophrenia, or at least conflict (and so unhappiness). And in fact, Aristotle describes the three allegedly happy lives of NE I.5 as being embodied by separate people, implying that in the ideal case, at least, these lives are not led by the same people. There is no indication that one of the "refined men of action," such as a Callicles, for example, sometimes leads a theoretical *bios* just because he dabbles in philosophy.[7] Of course, a person may vacillate in his opinion about what makes a life worth living. A person may, when he is sick, think that happiness is health, and then when he is well, decide it is in fact wealth (NE I.4 1095a23–25). If a person lives with first the one opin-

---

[5] Cooper [1975] 1986, 159–160; Cooper [1987] 1999, 229 n.14.

[6] Keyt, the primary defender of the two-aspects view, sees a continuity in Aristotle's discussion of lives in NE I.5 and X.6–8. Broadie (1991, 372; Broadie and Rowe 2002, 439), Kraut (1989, 17–19), and Roche (1988b, 112–113), all of whom reject Keyt's interpretation of *bios*, agree that the lives discussed in NE X.6–8 are the same in kind (though not necessarily exactly the same) as those discussed in NE I.5.

[7] I take the point about the significance of Aristotle's embodying the three lives in distinct characters from Roche (1988b, 112–113). Joly (1956, 15) argues that, traditionally, "lives" were seen as incompatible.

ion and then the other for long enough, perhaps Aristotle would say that he has lived two lives.[8] But Aristotle appears to consider this an unfortunate situation, and in any case it does not prove that a *bios* is only an aspect of life. A *bios* is a life with a point (which may, in theory at least, be an inclusive end), and a person can only steer his life toward one point at a time.

Of course, the possibility of literally leading a new life does show that *bios* does not strictly refer to the entire span of one's time alive. According to Aristotle, not everyone who is alive has a *bios*. At least, it is not clear to him that slaves have *bioi* at all (1177a8–9). Perhaps, then, we should say that a *bios* is a sufficiently lengthy period of time in which one acts for the sake of a goal of one's own choosing, a goal that seems to the agent to make his life as divinely happy as it could be.[9] A *bios* not only has a point, it has a point in light of which the agent more or less consciously makes his choices. This definition of *bios* has the advantage of explaining why, according to Aristotle, human beings and gods can both lead the theoretical life. So long as both make contemplation the goal of their lives (a *telos* that is continuously realized, in the case of the gods), both gods and men will lead the same sort of life. Any differences in the particularities of how they achieve that goal will (contra Keyt [1989, 17]) be irrelevant to the question of what life they lead.

The other assumption I have made is that the life lived "in accordance with the other virtue" (1178a9) is the political life, the life of a statesman or prominent citizen. Sarah Broadie, for example, has argued that this life is "the modest life of practical virtue without significant leisure" for contemplation (1991, 429–430).[10] It is true, of course, that Aristotle does not explicitly mention nobility, with which we might expect the *politikos* to be particularly concerned (NE I.5 1095b22–30), until well into the passage describing this secondarily happy life (1178b3, b13). Furthermore, he does not call this life the political life. He does, of course, call the person who aims at the activity of moral virtue the *politikos* (1177b12, 1178a27). It may be, though, that the *politikos* is just one of the people who leads the life in accordance with moral

---

[8] However, Aristotle does not use the word *bios* in NE I.4, where he mentions that people may change the teleological focus of their lives. Note that the possibility of changing lives that I am considering here is not the same as Keyt's (1983, 373) suggestion that a person might lead the military life in the summer and the agricultural life for the rest of the year, since a person who cycles through occupations every year knows and intends while he is engaged in one activity to participate in the other later. In my interpretation, these various activities are all part of the same *bios*, as Aristotle uses that term in NE I.5 and X.6–8. See Cooper [1987] 1999, 229 n.14.

[9] See chapter 2, section 3 for my argument that a *bios* is characterized by its most final end.

[10] Although she seems to have changed her view in Broadie and Rowe 2002; at least there she calls the secondarily happy life the political life. Cooper ([1975] 1986, 166–167) argues that the life "in accordance with the other virtue" is the mixed life of moral and intellectual excellence. I believe my first argument discussed next against Broadie's interpretation rules out Cooper's interpretation as well, provided that by "mixed life" we mean a life that aims at an inclusive end.

virtue. Still, there are two reasons I think we ought to interpret the secondarily happy life, the life in accordance with the other virtue, as the political life. First, as I said before, Aristotle seems in *NE* X.6–8 to want to decide the contest between the three lives described in *NE* I.5. It would be odd for him to consider and reject the life of pleasure (*NE* X.6) and award the honor to the theoretical life (*NE* X.7–8), but to ignore the political life altogether and instead discuss some new life as if we already knew what it was. (This would be particularly surprising to Aristotle's audience of future statesmen who, we can imagine, arrived at his lectures assuming that the political life is the best.) Furthermore, in *NE* I.5 Aristotle is coy about what the end of the political life really is (1095b30–1096a2). If we take the life in accordance with the other virtue to be the political life, he will be solving this problem. The political life aims not at virtue but at actions in accordance with moral virtue.

The dependence of the secondarily happy life on external goods provides a second reason to interpret it as the political life. For the amount of external goods Aristotle claims are necessary for this life would be necessary only for someone who has devoted himself to performing virtuous actions on a grand scale. To take one example, Aristotle says the temperate person needs abundant means and power (*exousia*) in order to perform temperate actions (1178a33).[11] But surely this is just false if Aristotle is talking about a modest virtuous life. After all, a little later he says that the happy person will not need many great external goods in order to do fine things (1179a1–5). Aristotle's explanation for the temperate person's need of *exousia* is revealing. Without it, "how will he or any of the other virtuous people be manifest (*dêlos*)?" (1178a33–34). (Notice that Aristotle does not say that a person needs *exousia* in order to act temperately in the first place. He needs it for his temperance to be clear.)[12] The implication seems to be that the person leading the life "in accordance with the other virtue" needs a prominent financial and social position in order to perform particularly prominent virtuous actions. Indeed, Aristotle says that the greater and more fine the actions are at which a person aims, the more he will need by way of external goods (1178b1–3). But surely the person who aims at morally virtuous actions in this grand way is the *politikos*.

In my interpretation, then, Aristotle equates the political life with the life lived in accordance with practical virtue. We should see that this is a reasonable identification for him to make. The *phronimos* chooses his morally virtuous actions because they express the importance to him of rational leisure.

---

[11] Irwin (trans. 1985, not. ad 1178a32) interprets *exousia* as being any amount of means by which a person can find something to desire and display temperance with respect to. But Gauthier and Jolif (1970, not. ad 1178a33) interpret Aristotle as saying here that temperance requires *a lot* of money and power. LSJ defines *exousia* thus: "I. power or authority (to do a thing); II. office, magistracy; III. *abundance of means*."

[12] Gauthier and Jolif (1970, not. ad 1178a33) say that Plato (*Rep*. II), Isocrates, and the Stoics all shared this idea that temperance is manifested most of all in *exousia*.

It is for this reason that his actions are fine and choiceworthy for their own sakes. Now if a person cares about the fine in action, he has reason to choose fine actions that are grand. For, as we saw in chapter 6, above, something in general is fine when it makes manifest its orientation to the good, and the bigger it is, the finer it is by reason of its magnitude (*Poet.* 8 1451a10–11). Thus, the bigger a virtuous action is, the more beautifully it shows the agent's conception of what makes life worth living, and the better it is as an action of that sort. I am suggesting, then, that grand virtuous actions are paradigmatic of moral virtue, and they are so because of all human actions they are the most fine. Aristotle's description of the great-souled man supports this suggestion. (Indeed, Aristotle says that "greatness of soul is in greatness [*megethei*] just as beauty is in a great body" [1123b6–7].) The great-souled man deserves the greatest honors because he performs the best actions (1123b17–21, b26–27). But the great-souled man's actions, few though they may be, are all *big* (1124b6–8, b24–26). Now the philosopher can count himself lucky when the opportunity for great actions arises without feeling the need to seek such occasions out. (As I suggested in the previous chapter, the great-souled man may well be a philosopher, not a statesman.) But the person who values morally virtuous action above all else will rationally seek fulfillment in paradigmatically virtuous actions. Since these are grand and require a more than modest amount of external goods (1178b2–3), the person who lives for the sake of morally virtuous activity will not only prefer grand acts, he will guide his life into venues where such acts are possible. But the person who makes a business of virtuous action on a grand scale is surely the *politikos*. At least, Aristotle says that "of morally virtuous actions, the political and military ones are outstanding for their beauty and size" (1177b16–17). A person of modest means and position can live for the sake of morally virtuous activity, of course, and he will have nothing to *reproach* himself for from the point of view of moral virtue. But neither will his life be the paradigm of the life lived for the sake of "the other virtue." That life is the statesman's. As we shall see, Aristotle exploits this idea that the politician is the paradigm of moral virtue in his argument that morally virtuous activity is subordinate to contemplation.

2. The Superior Finality of Contemplation

I turn now to Aristotle's argument in *NE* X.7 that theoretical activity is the most final end of human life. Aristotle begins with the following claim: "If happiness is activity in accordance with virtue, it is reasonable that it be in accordance with the best [virtue]; and this would be [the virtue] of the best part" (1177a12–13). It is no surprise, after Aristotle's argument in *NE* VI that *sophia* is the highest form of *theoretical* reason, that the activity of the best part of the soul should turn out to be theoretical and not practical activity (1177a17–18).¹³ As Aristotle told us, theoretical wisdom contemplates the most divine things, while practical reason examines the same kind of objects that concern the beasts (VI.7 1141a25–28). Aristotle uses this point in a more general form as his first argument in favor of the superiority of theoretical activity (1177a19–21).

However, Aristotle's claim that it would be reasonable for happiness to be the activity of the best (*kratistê*) virtue, given that it must be activity of some virtue or other, is reminiscent of the conclusion of the function argument in *NE* I.7.¹⁴ There Aristotle concludes from considerations of the human function that "the human good is activity of the soul in accordance with virtue, and if there are many virtues, in accordance with the best (*aristên*) and most final (*teleiotatên*)" (1098a16–18). As I argued in chapter 2, Aristotle is interested in the idea of function in *NE* I.7 because the excellent performance of a thing's function is the same as its end. (Notice that he introduces the function argument as a fuller specification of *eudaimonia* as the best good and final end [1097b20–25].) Since the function of a flautist is to play the flute, everything he does (insofar as he is a flautist) is directed toward fulfilling this goal well. Thus, by recalling the function argument in *NE* X.7, Aristotle reminds us of the special status of the finality of the human good: The human good is a final activity that expresses our human nature. As we will see in the next section, this is an important fact.

If I am right that the beginning of *NE* X.7 recalls the function argument and thus Aristotle's claim that the human good is the most final end, then it reminds us that Aristotle must do more than show that contemplation is merely an end. He must also show that it is a most final end, choiceworthy

---

¹³ I take it that the reference at *NE* X.7 1177a18–19 to a prior discussion refers to *NE* VI.7. Broadie (Broadie and Rowe 2002, not. ad 1177a17–18) also thinks that the reference is to *NE* VI.7 if anywhere. Stewart (1892) takes the reference to be to *NE* I.5, since *NE* VI was originally part of the *Eudemian Ethics*. But if that work was written earlier, Aristotle could have composed this sentence of *NE* X in the knowledge that he would incorporate the material on the intellectual virtues from the *EE* into this new work. Gauthier and Jolif (1970, not. ad 1177a19) take Aristotle's point to be that contemplation fits the criteria for the human good agreed upon in *NE* I, but take 1177a18 itself to refer to the *Protrepticus* (not. ad 1177a17–18). Broadie (Broadie and Rowe 2002) suggests that if *NE* X was written independently of *NE* VI and its division between theoretical and practical reason, we need not take *theôrêtikê* in 1177a18 to be contrasted with practical reason. There are two reasons I think we should understand Aristotle to be implying a contrast, however. First *NE* X.6–8 continues the discussion of *NE* I.5, and in I.5 the theoretical life is taken to aim at a conception of happiness that, whatever it is, is something other than the moral virtue (or, as we learn, morally virtuous activity) at which the political life aims. So Aristotle's audience would have heard *theôrêtikê* at 1177a18 as an answer to the question of which of the lives of practical and theoretical accomplishment was better. Second, even in the *Protrepticus*, where Aristotle does not distinguish sharply between theoretical and practical reason, theoretical activity is contrasted with practical rational activity, at least insofar as that is productive. So the important contrast between these two uses of reason would not be a surprise to those who were not familiar with the more radical claims of *NE* VI.

¹⁴ Agreement on this point appears to be universal.

for its own sake alone and never for the sake of anything else.[15] He begins this project in the passage from 1177b1–4: "And this [activity, i.e. theoretical activity] alone would seem to be loved on account of itself; for nothing comes from it beyond the contemplating, but from practical affairs we obtain more or less beyond the action." The tripartite division of ends found in NE I.7 has been collapsed into two tiers (as found in NE I.2): ends loved only for themselves and ends loved for the sake of something beyond themselves. (Literally, Aristotle claims that contemplation is the only end loved for itself, not that it is the only end loved *only* for itself, but in the interests of keeping this consistent with his repeated claims that morally virtuous actions are loved for themselves, I think we should interpret him as having the weaker claim in mind.)[16] It is appropriate for Aristotle to ignore the special case of middle level ends, however, since his project is to find the most final end. Whether an end is loved for itself or not, so long as it is loved for something else as well, it will not meet the finality criterion for the highest good.[17] In this argument, Aristotle is not concerned with whether morally virtuous activity is loved for its own sake. The question is whether it is also choiceworthy for the sake of something further.

Now the uselessness of contemplation is a familiar point (NE VI.7 1141a34–b8, VI.12 1143b19–20) and so, too, is the idea that all morally virtuous actions, choiceworthy as they are for their own sakes, also seek to bring about some result or other, whether it be victory, health, or a proportionate distribution of goods. But the fact that contemplation is pure activity (*energeia*) while morally virtuous activity is activity in process (*kinêsis*) is not really enough for Aristotle's argument that contemplation is more final than morally virtuous action. For in bringing about victory, health, and just distributions of goods, the morally virtuous person is perpetuating conditions amenable to the exercise of practical virtue. In other words, it is not clear simply from the fact that actions are activities in *kinêseis* that morally virtuous action aims at an end that is genuinely distinct from and beyond itself. Thus, as he must, Aristotle adds a further argument.

---

[15] Lawrence (1993, 14) has argued that that Aristotle's interest in NE X.7–8 "is not primarily one of 'devotion' but one of 'constitution.' " The life of perfect happiness is the ideal life under ideal circumstances, while the secondarily happy life is the ideal "however circumstanced," i.e., also in conditions that are less than ideal. Stimulating as his argument is, I do not agree for two reasons. First, Aristotle's evocation of the function argument and his subsequent argument that contemplation is more final than morally virtuous action suggest that he is still thinking of *eudaimonia* as a most final end and, therefore, as an object of devotion, not constitution. Second, the secondarily happy life is a life of grand moral action and so requires good fortune. Thus, it too seems to be an "ideally circumstanced, or utopian, ideal" (though perhaps less ideally circumstanced than the best philosophical life) and not a "however circumstanced ideal."

[16] So also Cooper [1975] 1986, 156 n. 12. Irwin (trans. 1985, not. ad 1177b1) actually translates it as, "study seems to be liked because of itself alone" because it is a *possible* reading of the Greek and is more suited to the context.

[17] Kraut (1989, 191) agrees.

As I suggested in section 1, fine actions on a grand scale such as those the statesman is inclined to perform are paradigmatically virtuous actions. What Aristotle wants to argue in the passage from 1177b4–25, I suggest, is that these paradigmatically virtuous actions at which the political life aims necessarily lead beyond themselves to circumstances in which such actions are no longer called for. In other words, I take Aristotle's argument not to be that all morally virtuous actions are choiceworthy for independent results beyond themselves (although this may be true), but that paradigmatic virtuous actions characteristic of the statesman's life aim at circumstances in which such grand actions are uncalled for.

> And happiness seems to be in leisure; for we are unleisurely in order that we may be at leisure, and we wage war in order that we may live in peace. Now the activity of the practical virtues is either in political life or in war, and actions in these circumstances seem to be unleisurely. Wartime actions are altogether unleisurely (for no one chooses to wage war or provoke war for the sake of waging war; for if someone made enemies of his friends in order to bring about battles and slaughter, he would seem to be altogether bloodthirsty). But the activity of the statesman is also unleisurely and, beyond the political activity itself, obtains power and honors or at any rate happiness for the [statesman] himself and for the citizens, a happiness which is other than the political activity and which, it is clear, we seek as being other. Then if, of the actions in accordance with virtue, the political and military ones stand out in beauty and size, but are unleisurely and aim at some end and are not chosen for their own sakes, while on the other hand, the activity of *noûs* seems, because it is theoretical, to be exceedingly serious and not to aim at any end beyond itself . . . this would be perfect [or most final, reading *teleia* in light of *haplôs teleion* at 1097a33] happiness of man.

There are two important assumptions in this argument. The first is that all outstandingly fine actions are unleisurely; the second is that all unleisurely activities are choiceworthy for the sake of leisure activities. Let's consider the second assumption first.

Aristotle assumes that unleisurely actions are worth undertaking for the sake of leisure. Thus, to use the terminology of *NE* I.7, leisure is more final than unleisureliness and is its end. Aristotle does not mean, of course, that everyone always does go about their unleisurely business with an eye to being at leisure. (We all know people who toil only to create more work for themselves.) Instead, his point must be that there is something failed about unleisurely actions that do not lead toward leisure, for leisure is their end. Now this may seem surprising after Aristotle's rejection of pleasure as the human good. For in the argument at 1176b27–1177a1 he seems to say that leisurely relaxation is not the most final end and, for that reason, is not happiness:

> For it would be strange for the end to be amusement (*paidian*), and to engage in business and go to trouble one's whole life for the sake of amusing oneself. For we

choose everything so to speak for the sake of something else except for happiness; for this is an end. But to exert oneself and toil for the sake of amusements would seem silly and utterly childish. On the other hand, to amuse oneself in order to exert oneself, as Anacharsis says, seems to be correct; for amusement is like a break, and being unable to toil continuously, people need a break. But a break is not an end.

But Aristotle is not denying here the claim of leisurely activity to be the end. He is criticizing a particular use of leisure. The problem with the voluptuary is that he spends his leisure in amusements that are properly enjoyed as only a break from work. He is not mistaken insofar as he takes leisurely activity to be the human end. (Indeed, the fact that amusing oneself is a way of spending one's leisure time is one of the few arguments in favor of thinking of pleasure as the human good [1176b16–17].) Leisure (*scholê*) in Aristotle's sense is not a time of relaxation (though it may be used that way); it is the condition of being free from the demands posed by our natural desire for the necessities of life. A leisurely life is one that is not driven by the need to satisfy necessary desires.[18]

From this point of view Aristotle's assumption that unleisurely activity is choiceworthy for the sake of leisure is quite plausible. For if unleisureliness is the business of toiling to satisfy necessary animal desires and social obligations, this can be worth choosing only on the assumption that it is worthwhile to live in circumstances in which those demands are met and no longer press upon us. My point is not that people would no longer eat or sleep or have sex if leisure were not possible. Animals take care of their bodily needs, after all, and we are animals. Rather, I am suggesting that unleisureliness is *chosen*, in Aristotle's sense, as something good because it leads to leisure. A sign of this is that human unleisureliness is guided by leisure as a *telos*. Unlike animals, most people do not work only to satisfy the desire of a moment. They try to provide for future appetitive desires so that when those arise they may free themselves of them without toil. (Some people's work never gets them ahead. This is felt as oppressive in part because the point of labor ultimately is to be free from labor.) So unleisureliness is choiceworthy for the sake of leisure time. But since leisure is worth having only if there is some valuable activity with which to occupy it, we can say that unleisurely activities are properly choiceworthy for the sake of some valuable leisure activity. This activity that makes leisure worth having, of course, will be *eudaimonia* (1177b4).

The crux of Aristotle's argument for the imperfect finality of morally virtuous action comes in the next step. According to Aristotle, all morally virtuous action is found either in battle or in political affairs (1177b6–8). Since both these contexts are unleisurely, morally virtuous action must be choiceworthy for the sake of some independent use of leisure. Aristotle's division of morally

---

[18] Leisure is the condition of a gentleman, as opposed to a slave or a laborer (Stewart 1892, not. ad 1177b4).

virtuous action into military and political actions is not exhaustive, and this may seem to vitiate his argument. Since Aristotle treats political activity as the activity of the statesman, he seems to have overlooked the moral virtue of the private citizen. Could not private moral activity be the use of leisure for the sake of which unleisureliness is worth choosing? I do not think Aristotle has simply made a mistake here, however, for at 1177b16–17 he explicitly says that the military and political activities he has shown to be unleisurely are only some of the morally virtuous actions. So Aristotle is aware that his typology of moral action is only partial. But he also says here that these virtuous military and political actions are outstanding in their size and beauty. As I argued in the previous section, this means that military and political actions, when performed well, are paradigms of virtue. Thus, in charity to Aristotle, I think we should read his argument as directed in the first instance toward showing that the exemplars of moral virtue are imperfectly final ends. I will say in a moment how we might extend his conclusions to the rest of moral virtue.

We can readily admit that wartime actions, and a fortiori excellent wartime actions, are unleisurely. As Aristotle says, only a bloodthirsty brute would choose war for its own sake (1177b9–10). But political actions aim at something beyond themselves as well. Aristotle probably has in mind an idea such as this: The politician, the one who exercises the political art, is a craftsman (1094a26–b7). As such, the good at which he aims is conceptually distinct from his own happiness. (See 1094b7–10, where the statesman's goal of happiness for the city is distinguished from the goal of personal happiness.) Thus, attractive as it may seem in itself to exercise political influence, that exercise is always (or at least ought to be) shaped by the further and separate good the statesman hopes to achieve by it.[19] The typical political leader may be guided by the hope of glory, but ideally, political action aims at happiness for oneself and fellow citizens, a happiness that is sought as being something independent of the political action itself (1177b13–15).[20] (Of course, even the honor-loving statesman seeks honor as happiness [*NE* I.5 1095b22–23].) The good statesman not only tries to produce peace, he seeks to provide occasions in which that peace can be enjoyed. In other words, he arranges for the good use of leisure (*Pol.* VII.14 1334a2–6). Where he directs his energies will depend on his own understanding of human flourishing. Perhaps he will arrange

---

[19] If Aristotle's argument deploys the finality criterion as he developed it in *NE* I, it is not sufficient for him to show that political actions are often *chosen* for the sake of an independent end. He must convince us that they are choice*worthy* for the sake of an independent end. Of course, as usual, Aristotle takes typical patterns of choice to be evidence for genuine *telē*. See Broadie (1991, 422–424) for a different interpretation.

[20] I take the force of the *ge* (at any rate) at 1177b14 to be that whatever else may come from political action, such action is certainly pursued (or at least ought to be pursued) under the assumption that it produces happiness. This is a truism of Platonic and Aristotelian political theory. The statesman's job is to produce happiness or advantage for the citizens ruled (e.g., *Rep.* 347d4–6; *NE* I.2 1094a27–b7).

for athletic games, or the building of temples or libraries.[21] But whatever form these grand political gestures take, they are guided by a conception of happiness that is other than the production of such gestures themselves. For the provision of the good use of leisure is business.[22] So all morally virtuous action, at least in its most exemplary forms, is unleisurely and choiceworthy for the sake of something beyond itself.[23]

Perhaps we can put Aristotle's point this way. The most fine uses of our practical reason occur in circumstances where there is a challenge to overcome. By facing hardship in an orderly way, the virtuous person shows there is something above his mere animal nature that makes his life worth living. But the very fact that practical reason judges the challenges of war and political business worth moving beyond suggests that such circumstances and the sort of virtuous activities that only they make appropriate are not the ultimate human value. The upshot is that paradigmatically virtuous actions, that is, political and military virtuous actions, however intrinsically valuable they may be given the circumstances, necessarily look to an independent end beyond themselves. And since the peacetime moral actions of an ordinary citizen are more modest examples of the same type of activity, they too ought to look beyond themselves.

It may not be immediately obvious that modest moral virtue has an aspect of unleisureliness as well. Of course, temperance is displayed in the unleisurely course of gratifying animal desire. But wit is also a virtue and can be used when there is no business at hand. (Of course, the famous wit of the Spartans was often produced under pressure. And Samuel Johnson's wit rises from mere pleasantness to virtue against the backdrop of the suffering of his life.) In any case, if Aristotle does not allow a dinner party to be a use of leisure, he not only flouts without explanation the cultural meaning of the symposium, but he rigs the definition of leisure in favor of *theôria*'s being the only possible (and not just the best) use of leisure time. Now Aristotle does think that moral virtues are expressed in leisure (*Pol.* VII.15 1334a14), and it is possible that he slightly overstates his case against the finality of morally virtuous action in *NE* X.7. But perhaps he thinks that moral virtue is used with respect to the unleisurely aspects of leisure. In other words, moral virtue is unleisurely because it regulates leisure insofar as it is affected by animal desires and not by the leisure itself, that is, the condition of not being *driven* by such desires. Aristotle seems to have something like this in mind at *Politics* VII.15 1334a24–34 when he explains how particularly

---

[21] Cf. *Pol.* VII.14 1333b5–26, where Aristotle criticizes contemporary Greek legislators for arranging affairs with respect to a pleonectic vision of happiness.

[22] Cf. *Theaetetus* 172c8–e5, 175d7–176a1, on the unleisureliness of the *politikos*.

[23] Aristotle offers another reason for thinking that the statesman's use of moral virtue is unleisurely at *Pol.* VII.13 1332a7–15. The statesman often finds himself using practical virtue to make the best of a bad situation. For instance, the good judge's meting out of punishment is just, but it would be better if he never had to punish in the first place.

important it is for citizens at leisure to be trained in justice and temperance. We need these virtues especially in leisure because the abundance of leisure makes people prone to hubris. Clearly Aristotle's thought here is that these moral virtues are valuable in leisure because they keep us from destroying leisure and allow us to use it for some other activity (in the *Politics*, presumably philosophy or the enjoyment of music and poetry).[24] Of course, this solution does not tell us what to make of virtues such as wit. However, we should not underestimate the significance of showing that the *most* paradigmatic virtuous actions are less final than contemplation, for it is these paradigmatic actions that are under consideration as the highest good. Aristotle shows that they cannot be the highest human good. Instead, they are choiceworthy for the sake of that most lovable of the uses of leisure: philosophical contemplation.

Of course, human nature being animal and political as it is, we can never fully move beyond the circumstances that make political activity, not to mention modest moral activity, appropriate. It would be deeply unrealistic to count practical activity as failed simply because it never succeeds in producing stable and uninterrupted leisure for the agent and others. Human nature cannot avoid business and toil. But Aristotle does not think such actions are failed. On the contrary, given the circumstances, which we shall see are inalienable to our nature, Aristotle thinks that all practically virtuous actions are choiceworthy for their own sakes.[25] What I have tried to argue in the last two chapters, however, is that morally virtuous action is fine and choiceworthy for its own sake because it expresses the agent's orientation to the good, which now Aristotle explicitly says is in leisure. Thus, although morally virtuous actions aim to be and often are productive of leisure and happiness, this is only an aspect of the more general way in which they are choiceworthy for the sake of contemplation. They are choiceworthy for their own sakes and for the sake of contemplation because in their instrumentality and in their manner they express the agent's commitment to the supreme value of leisure whose best use is in theoretically virtuous activity.

3. Human Approximation of Divine Life: Part One

Immediately after Aristotle draws the conclusion that contemplation is more final than morally virtuous action and is, therefore, happiness, he elaborates on his position in a way that raises a problem:

---

[24] I have in mind Aristotle's claims that the virtue of *philosophia* is important for times of leisure (1334a23), and that musical education trains children for the proper use of free time (1341b40–41).

[25] At 1177b8 Aristotle says that military actions are altogether unleisurely. Perhaps Aristotle thinks that war, unlike peacetime political life, is not essential to human life, and so we can, consistently with our nature, hope to leave military circumstances behind altogether. Cf. *Pol.* VII.2 1324b41–1325a10.

But a life of this sort [i.e. the theoretical life] would be higher [*kreittôn*] than a human life; for a person will live this way not insofar as he is a human being, but insofar as there is something divine in him; and the activity of this part is as much superior to activity in accordance with the other virtue as this part is superior to the compound.[26] So if *noûs* is divine compared to the human being, the life in accordance with this [i.e. *noûs*] is also divine as compared to the human life. (1177b26–31)

The project of the *NE* is to discover the *human* good and the activity that is the *human* function. If theoretical activity is divine, is it correct to think of it as our human end at all?

Aristotle's comment in the next line suggests that in some respects, at least, the terms of this objection are not accurate. It may well be that *noûs* is divine, but

[w]e must not heed those who advise us to think human things since we are human and to think mortal things since we are mortal, but we must be like immortals insofar as possible [*eph' hoson endechetai athanatizein*] and do everything toward [*pros*] living in accordance with the best thing in us. (1177b31–34)

Aristotle's advice here harkens back to passages we discussed in chapter 4. If contemplation is divine, that is no reason to turn the focus of our lives elsewhere. All living things seek to immortalize themselves by imitating god. Indeed, if god's activity is noetic, as *Metaphysics* Λ.7 and *NE* X.8 tell us it is, human contemplation will be among the most successful of activities displaying this natural tendency. Now, this argument is a meta-ethical and indeed a meta-physical argument. It provides support for the philosophical life from the standpoint of the cosmos, so to speak. But Aristotle must also address this worry about the divinity of contemplation from the standpoint of his ethical theory. If contemplation is divine, can it be the human good? Is there any way that contemplation can express our human nature, or must we think of philosophers as possessed by god and in some sense not really human at all?[27]

Aristotle claims that human beings are most of all (*malista*) their faculty of contemplation (1178a7). By this he must mean that human beings are, in the strictest sense, contemplative creatures.[28] But what does it mean to

---

[26] Aristotle refers either to the compound of practical reason and the body (which implies the passions as well), or the compound of practical reason and the nonrational part of the soul that shares in reason in a way (i.e., passions and appetite) (Broadie and Rowe 2002, not. ad 1177b28). Both interpretations are supported by Aristotle's discussion of the compound later at 1178a10–21. It does not matter, for my argument at least, which of these interpretations is correct.

[27] As Whiting (1986, 88–89) rightly points out, if Aristotle is claiming in 1177b27–28 that the contemplative life is possible in virtue of a capacity that is *not* human, but divine, then he is abandoning the project of *NE* I to discover the *human* good.

[28] Scott 1999, 232.

say that we are, strictly speaking, *noûs*? Presumably, if we are *noûs* in the strictest sense, then in another respect or way we are something else, in our case the compound of practical reason and the nonrational soul (1177b28–29). Aristotle's discussion in NE X.8 of the philosopher's behavior insofar as he is human (*hêi anthropos*) does suggest that the human essence is to be identified in some sense with the compound of body, passions, and practical reason.[29] But what relation do these two ways of being human have to each other?[30]

I think it is important to remember that at the end of NE X.7 Aristotle is trying to show that *noûs* is human because he must resolve a worry that the divinity of contemplative activity might seem to pose to his theory of happiness; he is not concerned to explain the sense in which our compound nature also is human or how we can be human in two distinct ways. Thus we should not take Aristotle's silence on the status of our compound nature to be indicative of his answer to these questions. Still, I believe that his argument for the identity of *noûs* and human nature reveals that he has in mind a teleological model for the relationship between these sides of ourselves:

> For even if [*noûs*] is small in bulk, in power and worth it excels everything else by much more. And each person would seem to be this [i.e. *noûs*], if in fact it is authoritative [*kurion*] and better. So it would be strange if someone should choose not the life of himself but of something else. And what is said now agrees with what was said before; for what is proper to each nature is best and most pleasant for it; and the life in accordance with *noûs* is best and most pleasant for human beings, if in fact this [i.e., *noûs*] is especially [*malista*] human being. (1177b34–1178a7)

Aristotle's assumption seems to be that each person is to be identified with the most authoritative element of his nature. It is not clear here why he thinks that *noûs* is the most authoritative element. Perhaps its similarity to the divine nature is meant to establish that. Consider, however, another possibility, available to us from the standpoint of ethics. If our theoretical reason is authoritative, it must be authoritative over the other aspects of our soul and the activities they produce. But authority, as we have encountered it in the NE at least, is often a matter of finality.[31] As we saw in NE I.1–2, one craft

---

[29] See Whiting (1986, 88–90) for a defense of this interpretation on the basis of keeping NE X consistent with NE I.

[30] Two influential possibilities that have been discussed in the scholarly literature: (1) *noûs* might be separated and entirely alien from the compound of practical reason and the nonrational soul (Cooper ([1975] 1986, 168–180); (2) *noûs* might be a particularly important part or aspect of a composite nature that includes *noûs* and *to suntheton* (Cooper [1987] 1999; Keyt 1983; and Whiting 1986).

[31] *Protrepticus* B60–61 also suggests a teleological account of the parts of the human being (reason, part of the soul that follows reason, and body), and there too the one for the sake of whose end the other parts are arranged is said to be the most authoritative. It is not clear to

has authority over another when the activity of the lower craft is choiceworthy for the sake of the activity of the authoritative craft. Indeed, the political art is considered the most authoritative of all because the ends of all other crafts are choiceworthy for the sake of its architectonic end (1094a26–27).[32] And in NE VI.13 we saw that full-fledged moral virtue combined with *phronêsis* is authoritative over the natural virtue with which we are born because perfected moral virtue is a more mature realization of natural virtue and the state toward which it normally develops (1144b4, b17). So an authoritative capacity or craft is one that directly gives rise to an activity or product for the sake of which the subordinate activities are worth choosing. (A general has authority over his troops because they must act for his end.) It seems possible, then, that Aristotle thinks that *noûs* is authoritative because its activity is the most final human end toward which all our other actions ought, by nature, to aim. (Notice how at 1177b33–34 he says that we should do everything toward living in accordance with the best part of our soul—*panta poiein pros to zên*—suggesting that the natural consequence of a part's being best is that its end is most final.) Now if this is what he has in mind by saying that *noûs* is authoritative, then he will have provided the proof of the authority of *noûs* in the argument immediately preceding the objection (1177b4–25, quoted in the previous section). The activity of *noûs* is choiceworthy for its own sake alone, while the activity of practical virtue (certainly, at least, in paradigmatic cases) is subordinate to it. The former, then, ought to be authoritative over the latter. Aristotle hinted as much at the end of book VI when he assured us that theoretical wisdom would not take orders from *phronêsis*.[33]

---

me, however, whether in the *Protrepticus* reason is most authoritative *because* its end is most final or because it gives orders to the other parts of the human being (though obviously these facts are related). *Protrepticus* B65–69 argues that contemplative knowledge, as opposed to productive knowledge, is the most desirable excellence of reason. When we combine this with the connection drawn between being better/more desirable and the authoritative part of the soul, this may suggest that reason is authoritative because its end is most final. However, as Cooper ([1975] 1986, 169 n. 22) points out, Aristotle does not draw a sharp distinction between theoretical and practical reason in the *Protrepticus*, and in any case, when he does explain the authority of reason, he appeals to its giving orders to the rest of the soul (B61).

[32] See also 1168b30, where the good man is said to assign the noblest goods to the most authoritative element of himself. There is some question whether this passage is consistent with Aristotle's claims in NE X.7 (Cooper [1975] 1886, 172–173), but since in my interpretation moral actions do honor theoretical *noûs*, it does not seem to me impossible to read them as consistent. In choosing noble deeds, the true self-lover would act for the sake of his *noûs*.

Kurios does not always refer in the *NE* to the most final end, or to what is productive of the most final end. In the discussion of the voluntary, something is *kurios* when it is an efficient cause (1110a3, a6, 1114a3, a32, b32). In the discussion of courage, military commanders are called *kurioi*. This could mean that their goals are those for the sake of which soldiers must act, but it probably means that the commanders have the power to cause them harm. Cf. 1129b16, 1139a18, 1147a26, b10.

[33] See also *EE* 1249b9–21.

If I am right to associate the authority of *noûs* with its being productive of the most final end of which human action is capable, then it is evident why we ought to think of this part of the soul as being especially what we are. For the most final human end is the human function, and our function defines our essence. When Aristotle says that we are *malista noûs*, he is not restricting this as a description of our essence. Rather, he means to say that the activity of *noûs*, divine as it may be, is also the fullest expression of our *human* nature, where this is to be understood as the most final end toward which human nature as a whole strives.[34] The relationship between human nature as noetic and human nature as merely anthropic, then, is that between more and less final goals of human striving. We are now in a position to understand the sense in which Aristotle intends those potentially troubling lines at 1177b27–28: "for he will live this way [viz. theoretically] not insofar as he is a human being, but insofar as there is something divine in him." The part of ourselves by which we contemplate, and in virtue of which contemplation can be our goal, is in some way or other divine and not merely human. But though *noûs* is not *merely* human, it is *most truly* human; it is not alien to our nature.[35] So Aristotle's advice to make ourselves as immortal as possible is defensible even within the framework of the *Nicomachean Ethics*, according to which an end ought to be pursued as most final when it is our distinctively human good.

The simultaneous humanity and divinity of contemplation is an important point. As we have seen, the gods are paradigms of happiness. Indeed, Aristotle says things are happy only to the extent that their lives resemble the contemplative existence of the gods.

> And of human activities, the one most akin to this [contemplative activity of the gods] is most of the character of happiness [*eudaimonikôtatê*]. And a sign of this is also that the rest of the animals do not have a share of happiness since they are entirely deprived of this sort of activity. For the whole life of the gods is blessed,

---

[34] At *DA* 416b23–25 Aristotle says we ought to call each soul after the capacity for the sake of which the other capacities are organized. (Since plant souls nourish themselves for the sake of reproduction, it is right to call them reproductive souls.) So, presumably, our souls are called noetic because our other soul capacities are organized for the sake of *noûs*. If this is what Aristotle means by calling us *malista noûs* in the NE, he does not mean that we are, strictly speaking, *noûs* alone; he means that all the capacities of our souls—nutrition, reproduction, perception, locomotion, etc.—are nested (see *DA* 414b30 ff.) and teleologically ordered for the sake of noetic capacity. (I thank David Charles for bringing this to my attention. See also Menn 2002, 121–122.)

[35] Aristotle says at 1178a22 that the activity of *noûs* is separated from the passions (taking the contrast to be with 1178a19–20), but I agree with Whiting (1986, 85) that Aristotle means that the activity of *noûs* is not directly engaged with the passions, not that human *noûs* could exist without the body. Aristotle may well think this, of course, but it is not his point here. Here Aristotle is setting up an argument that theoretical activity is more independent of the goods of fortune and thus more of the character of happiness. So 1178a22 is not evidence against my claim that, according to Aristotle, *noûs* is properly human nature.

but for human beings [life is blessed] to the extent that there is some similarity (*homoiôma ti*) to this sort of activity; and none of the other animals is happy, since they in no way participate in *theôria*. (1178b22–28)

The only reason that *we* human beings can be happy is that *we* (and not some alien part of us) are capable of activity that is truly godlike and happy. Thus, in defending the philosophical life as happy, it is important for Aristotle to show that *noûs* is both genuinely human and divine (1178b8–22, immediately preceding the passage cited above). Human contemplation is not nearly as perfect as divine thought, of course. It is interrupted by hunger and fatigue and sheer mortality (1178b33–35; *Meta*. Λ.7 1072b24–25). It can grasp only a finite number of truths at a time, while presumably the gods can grasp them all at once. Nevertheless, when we contemplate in our human fashion, we acts as immortals in a way and simultaneously realize our human nature to the fullest extent possible. That is the reason why the philosophical life is the happiest.

4. Human Approximation of Divine Life: Part Two

But once Aristotle explicitly makes the connection between happiness and godlikeness, we must realize that excellent theoretical activity is not the only way in which we human beings resemble the gods. For as I have argued, the excellent use of practical reason resembles wise human theoretical reasoning. Since this latter is an imperfect version of divine contemplation, morally virtuous action should be godlike too, though in a more removed way.[36] If so, the life lived for the sake of activity in accordance with moral virtue ought to be happy, although in a secondary way. That is to say, contemplation will be most final (*teleia*) happiness, the eudaimonic good that never is chosen for the sake of anything else. But there will be another good—morally virtuous activity—that, although less final than contemplation, can nevertheless function as the most final end of a happy (in a secondary way) human life. This secondarily happy and godlike life will be the political life.

Now Aristotle does argue in *NE* X.8 1178a9–22 that the life in accordance with the other virtue (i.e., practical virtue) is happy in a secondary way (*deuterôs*).[37] But the argument in this passage does not say anything about the resemblance between moral and divine activity. In fact, Aristotle does not say much in defense of the happiness of the political life at all. He first says that the activities in accordance with moral virtue are human (1178a9–10),[38]

---

[36] Kraut 1989, 62–64. Aristotle's point in denying morally virtuous action to the gods depends on the alleged absurdity of thinking of gods as political creatures. I say more on this at p. 195, below.

[37] See note 2, above, on the reference of *deuterôs*.

[38] As Broadie (Broadie and Rowe, 2002, not. ad 1178a9–10) points out, Aristotle may not intend this to be a justification of the political life's *happiness* at all. He may intend it to justify

and then launches into an explanation of how morally virtuous action is inextricably linked to our animal and political condition. Morally virtuous actions are performed with respect to other people; they concern the passions and the body (1178a10–16). Excellence of character is connected to the passions in many ways, and practical wisdom cannot be disengaged from excellence of character (1178a16–20). By the time we reach the end of this passage it is hard not to feel that Aristotle is more intent on showing that practical virtue is tied to our animal condition than he is on showing that the actions arising from such virtue are excellent and happy. Furthermore, his argument that divine activity is contemplative may seem to rule out the possibility that there is anything divine about morally virtuous action. For Aristotle's argument is that it is absurd to think of the gods engaging in practical activity of any kind since anything to do with practical action is unworthy of the gods (1178b10–18).

As I said, Aristotle does not say much by way of justifying the happiness of the political life. Presumably, he did not think it needed much defense. Nevertheless, I believe he commits himself to the claim that practically virtuous activity is godlike and happy in a secondary way, for unless he accepts it, his own principles require him to deny that the political life is happy. At 1178b28–32 Aristotle says:

> So far as contemplation extends, happiness does as well. And those to whom contemplation is more present are also happier, not by chance, but on account of the contemplation; for this is more prized on account of itself. So that happiness would be contemplation of a sort (*theôria tis*).

This passage comes immediately after the one cited above in which Aristotle ties the happiness of a life to its godlikeness. Clearly, he means to say that happiness extends as far as contemplation does because contemplation is the divine activity. Now, scholars sometimes read this passage as suggesting that a life is happy only to the extent that it includes time spent pondering metaphysical truths. But this cannot (or at least should not) be what Aristotle means, for this passage comes *after* his claim that the political life is happy, yet there is no suggestion that the *politikos* does philosophy in his spare time. Furthermore, according to Aristotle, a life is happy in virtue of aiming (successfully) at *eudaimonia*, and the political life aims at the activity of moral virtue. So literal contemplation cannot be what makes this life worth choosing, even if the statesman does spend time exercising his theoretical reason. How could the political life be happy if happiness depends on literal contemplation?

---

the political life's being *in second place*. The tenor of the rest of this passage is in harmony with the latter interpretation, but then that would leave Aristotle with no explicit justification for the happiness of the political life at all.

One might suggest that we read Aristotle as saying here that contemplation is responsible for the happiness of only the philosophical life.[39] But this cannot be correct either. The utter failure of the beasts to participate in contemplation in any way is supposed to explain why they cannot be happy. If the presence of contemplation is just one way to grasp happiness, his claim that the beasts do not participate in contemplation would be insufficient to rule out the possibility of their happiness.

But let us think about Aristotle's argument about the beasts (1178b22–28) a moment more. He says that animals do not *participate* in contemplation in any way (1178b24: *to mê metechein*; 1178b28: *oudamêi koinônei*). By contrast, human beings are happy insofar as there is some similarity (*homoiôma ti*) between their activity and contemplation. What if we read the vocabulary here in a Platonic spirit? If we do, Aristotle is saying that beasts cannot be happy because their activity does not participate in, that is, approximate the contemplative activity of the gods.[40] By implication, then, any human life that is happy will be happy in virtue of its approximation to divine contemplative life. A fortiori, the happy political life must be happy in virtue of its godlikeness. Now Aristotle thinks it is absurd to imagine the gods as possessing moral virtue (1178b10–21), but not because there is anything per se undignified about exercising practical reason when in political circumstances. What is unworthy of the gods is the thought of their being tied to (much less finding their leisure in) political circumstances in the first place. For as Aristotle tells us at the beginning of the *Politics*, the *polis* arises to meet the insufficiency of the individual (I.2 1252a26–27). If the gods were political, that would imply that they were dependent (and perhaps even mortal) creatures. *This* is what makes it outlandish, from Aristotle's point of view, to think of the gods' activity as morally virtuous action. But these considerations do not rule out the possibility that morally virtuous action is godlike enough to count as happiness for *us*.[41] The actualization of *phronêsis* is not theoretical contemplation, but it is, according to my interpretation, *theôria . . . tis*.[42] That is to say, the activity of practical wisdom is contemplation . . . of a sort. But *theôria tis* is what Aristotle concludes happiness must be at the end of this stretch of argument (1178b32).[43] He makes this qualifi-

---

[39] Kraut (1989, 63) might be read as making this argument, though elsewhere (58, 64) he makes an argument that is similar to my interpretation of this passage.

[40] *DA* II.4 and *GA* II.1 claim that animals imitate divine activity through reproduction. Aristotle could be inconsistent on this point. Or, more likely, he could think that reproduction does not capture the specifically rational aspect of divine contemplative activity, and so it does not qualify as a kind of happiness.

[41] Contra Sedley 1999, 324.

[42] In fact, outside the debate about happy lives, *theôrein* often refers to *practical* contemplation. See *NE* 1139a6–8, 1140a10–14, 1141a25–26 for unambiguous examples.

[43] *Theôria tis* could also be translated as 'a kind of contemplation,' i.e., a species of contemplation. But for reasons I have just mentioned, such a translation would confuse this stretch of argument. *Theôria* in distinction to morally virtuous action has been established as the goal of

cation, I suggest, to account for the happy influence of excellent practical reasoning in the political life. In this interpretation we can understand what justification Aristotle has for counting the political life as happy in a secondary way. Courageous, temperate, and just actions are not only expressions of virtue, they are godlike.[44] But since we are happy to the extent that we engage in godlike contemplation (1178b28–30), where this refers both to the proportion of time spent in *theôria* and to the varieties of *theôria* possible for a human being,[45] the political life aimed at excellent practical reasoning is happy. The divine activity extends into human life not only through human contemplation but also through morally virtuous activity.

5. Choosing Moral Virtue for the Sake of Contemplation

As I mentioned at the beginning of this chapter, it is not clear that morally virtuous action is always the most choiceworthy practical option from the point of view of the love of contemplation. Does the philosopher, living his life for the sake of contemplation, have reason to be morally virtuous in Aristotle's account? There are two parts to this problem. First, virtuous action, and in particular courage, reveals the importance to the agent of a distinctly political use of leisure. But Aristotle makes a point of saying that the philosopher could contemplate on his own (1177a32–34). Furthermore, the external goods with which moral virtue is concerned are an impediment to the philosopher (1178b4–5). Why, then, should the philosopher *embrace* his political nature as moral virtue, in my interpretation, requires him to do? The second aspect of the problem is that, even if the philosopher has reason to embrace his political context, why should he want to be a morally virtuous citizen? He may, of course, want to *appear* to be virtuous sometimes, to ease relations with his neighbors. But why should he choose the unshakable moral character that may sometimes prevent him from maximizing his time in contemplation?

There are two ways of addressing these problems that are consistent with my interpretation of how morally virtuous action is choiceworthy for the sake of contemplation, but that I find unsatisfactory.[46] The first strategy takes

---

the philosophical life, so *theôria* cannot include the activity of practical wisdom as a species. But the life aimed at practical wisdom has already been deemed happy in a way; thus it must include *theôria tis*.

[44] See *NE* I.2 1094b10, where the statesman's activities are called more godlike than the actions of a private citizen.

[45] Broadie (Broadie and Rowe 2002, not. ad 1178b29–30) for these two possible interpretations.

[46] These strategies are similar to ways of solving the problem that scholars who do not share my view of the teleological relation between morally virtuous action and contemplation tend to propose. The first "two natures" solution is natural to philosophers who interpret *eudaimonia* as an inclusive end, e.g., Cooper ([1987] 1999) and Whiting (1986); see also Lawrence

its cue from Aristotle's suggestion at NE X.7–8 that human beings have two natures (or two aspects of the same nature), that is, a noetic nature and an anthropic nature found in the compound of practical reason and desire. I will call this the "two-natures strategy" for explaining the place of moral virtue in the philosophical life. The idea is this: Morally virtuous activity is choiceworthy for the sake of contemplation because it approximates contemplation; but it is a good we *must* choose and indeed embrace because it is the excellent exercise of our anthropic nature. If we were not morally virtuous, there would be a part of our nature that was frustrated, and that condition could not be a happy one. Now the two-natures strategy is on the right track insofar as it gives the philosopher a positive reason to embrace the rational virtues of his political and animal nature. The happy life, according to this interpretation, is one in which the virtues of *all* parts of the soul (or at least all parts of the rational soul) are exercised. But in its effort to find a place for *practical* virtue in the happiest life, this solution neglects the fact that, according to Aristotle, a life can be happy, albeit in a secondary way, without the possession of *theoretical* virtue. (At least, I assume from his silence on this question that *theôria* is not a necessary constituent of the political life.) If Aristotle really thought that a life must gratify all aspects of our rational nature in order to be happy, then he ought not to call the political life happy. It is of no use to appeal to the fact that the political life is happy only in a secondary way. If a life without excellent theoretically rational activity can be happy in any way at all, then by the logic of the two-natures strategy, a philosophical life without excellent practically rational activity should be happy in some way or other as well.

But there is a deeper problem with the two-natures strategy for explaining the place of moral virtue in the philosophical life. Although this strategy allows the philosopher to think of moral virtue as valuable from the point of view of contemplation (it is an approximation of contemplation and reveals his love for contemplation), the philosopher is not compelled to be virtuous for reasons that have anything to do with his philosophical goal. What moves him is the value of fulfilling his anthropic nature. From the point of view of philosophy, it might still be better to be morally mediocre. But if that is so, then in this interpretation, the philosopher, in choosing morally virtuous action, would not do everything for the sake of happiness. I take it for granted, however, that in Aristotle's account *eudaimonia* is the focus of *all* the happy person's choices (see chapter 2, section 3c, above).

The second possible interpretation of the place of moral virtue in the contemplative life is to argue that morally virtuous action is always the most effective route to maximizing contemplation. Let us call this the "instrumen-

---

(1993). The second "instrumentalist" strategy is adopted by Kraut (1989) and Tuozzo (1995), although Kraut thinks we may sometimes have reason to choose virtuous actions independently of their connection to happiness.

talist strategy." Now, this strategy has the merit of justifying the philosopher's choice of morally virtuous actions from the point of view of his love of contemplation. But it, too, is unsatisfactory. Aristotle does think that morally virtuous action tends to produce conditions suitable for contemplation; this instrumental connection to leisure is one of the ways in which virtuous actions may be fine. Nevertheless, it is implausible to think that each and every virtuous action maximizes the agent's time for philosophy, as the case of courage shows.[47] A glorious death does not maximize the agent's contemplation, even in the long run. We can make the instrumentalist strategy more sophisticated, however. For even if particular morally virtuous actions do not always maximize contemplation, Aristotle might think that a virtuous state of character is a necessary condition for contemplation.[48] According to this more sophisticated version of the instrumentalist strategy, Aristotle would be saying that the happy person spends as much time as possible in philosophy, but since his human nature, with its appetites and emotions, tends to deflect him from this task, he ought to cultivate the moral virtues that regulate these tendencies.

Now I find it quite plausible to think that many of the Aristotelian moral virtues tend to support contemplation by freeing the soul of distracting emotions. Of course, it is not clear that *all* of them do. For instance, Aristotle says that under certain conditions, say when someone insults a member of your family, it would be wrong not to get angry (*NE* IV.5 1126a6–8). But anger is a distraction, and from the point of view of contemplation we might be better off without it altogether. And while generosity and wit may not positively disrupt philosophy, I cannot see what benefit they do it, either. But let us suppose for the moment that moral virtue in general is beneficial to contemplation. Now if the moral virtues are worth the philosopher's while because they *control* his anthropic desires, we might wonder if a state of continence would not serve the philosopher just as well. And if continence would do just as well, it might actually be preferable since—not being a steady state of character—it might allow the philosopher to act against

---

[47] It is more plausible to think that each virtuous action maximizes the community's chances for contemplation, although even this is not certain. Might not the Trojans have had more time for philosophy if they had struck a deal with Agamemnon to return Helen and be spared? But even if we do suppose that all virtuous actions maximize the contemplation of the community, we would need to explain how acting for the sake of the communal happiness at the expense of one's own could make one happy. (I assume that, according to Aristotle, an action must aim ultimately at the agent's being happy in order to be rational. Kraut [1989] disagrees. See Irwin [1991] for a response to Kraut.)

[48] Tuozzo (1995) makes this sort of argument. Plato appears to have something like this in mind when he requires in the *Republic* that future philosophers be trained in moral virtues. They will need courage to face the challenges of the ascent from the Cave and temperance to resist the temptations of distracting pleasures (*Rep.* 502d ff., 514a–520a). Of course, since Plato does not distinguish our practical and theoretical rational faculties, it is not surprising that he thinks the excellent reasoner must have all the virtues of reason.

moral virtue when that would maximize his opportunities for contemplation. I am not arguing here that continence would, in the end, be just as effective as full moral virtue at producing contemplation. I am only suggesting that it might, in order to put into relief the kind of strategy the instrumentalist is proposing. For in order to defend himself against the view that continence is preferable, the instrumentalist must insist that moral virtue is indispensable for the happiest life because it is more efficient than any other character trait at producing contemplation. In other words, the more the instrumentalist defends his view, the more irrelevant the intrinsic value of moral virtue for the happy life comes to seem. Of course, the instrumentalist strategy allows the philosopher to recognize the intrinsic value of morally virtuous action, but that understanding plays no role in his decision that he will not live without it. A final demerit of this account is that it does not explain why the philosopher should want to celebrate the political aspect of the leisure in which he contemplates.[49]

So let us turn to the first half of the problem first: Why should Aristotle's philosopher choose actions that valorize a specifically political use of leisure? Aristotle makes it clear that the human philosopher must make allowances for the nonnoetic aspects of his nature if he is to live well. Because we are human beings, our nature needs external goods so that we may eat and be healthy (1178b33–35). And because the philosopher is a human being, he will live in community with other people (1178b5–7). Presumably he will need other people to supply him the necessities of life and perhaps even a little relaxation. So even though the philosopher lives for theoretical wisdom, he cannot avoid dealing with circumstances in which moral virtue could be exercised. So far, though, we see no reason for the lover of contemplation to regard political and animal life as anything more than a necessary burden.

But though Aristotle tends to minimize the philosopher's connection to community in order to exalt the theoretical life, he does say at one point that it would be better for the philosopher to have fellow workers (*sunergoi*;

---

[49] Because, according to my interpretation, paradigmatic moral actions are unleisurely and thus choiceworthy for the sake of an independent *eudaimonia*, I cannot avail myself of Broadie's (1991, 410–419) interpretation of the relationship between practical and theoretical virtuous activity in the happiest life. She argues that theoretical activity "celebrates" a well-lived practical life. Though it is true that celebration is not an instrumental relationship (Broadie 1991, 413), it is nevertheless teleological as I understand it. For if X celebrates Y, X must be in some way or other appropriate to the value of Y, and X will be valuable as a celebration because Y is valuable. Indeed, we even say that we engage in celebration for the sake of the thing celebrated. Since I read Aristotle as saying that contemplation is more final than morally virtuous action, where this means that morally virtuous action is choiceworthy for the sake of contemplation, I do not think he can mean that contemplation celebrates (i.e., is choiceworthy for the sake of) practical virtuous activity. Nevertheless, I do think that celebration provides a model of noninstrumental teleology that ought to be explored. Perhaps we could say that the fineness of morally virtuous actions celebrates contemplation.

1177a34). Why does Aristotle think this is so? One is reminded of Aristotle's argument at *NE* IX.9 1170a4–11 that the happy person will need friends (*philoi*) because they enable him to be more continuously active. If Aristotle is making the same point here, then the philosopher has reason not just to tolerate political life but to embrace it in its most intimate forms. After all, friends pursue their conception of the good together (*NE* IX.12 1172a1–6, where he mentions philosophical friends in particular). Since the friend is another self in whose mirror we come to know ourselves and the worth of our joint activities, contemplation with a friend will keep the philosopher directly aware of the value of contemplation when he might otherwise become bored. Philosophical conversations with friends and fellow workers will be less prone to interruption than solitary pondering. Furthermore, the philosopher will to some extent participate in the contemplative activity of his friends even when he cannot be with them. (Plato, for instance, had in some extended sense a share of the philosophical discussions among his students even when he was not with them.) So the political or social expression of human contemplation will be more continuous for this reason as well, and so will be more like the continuous contemplation of the gods which the happy person imitates.[50] Communal contemplation is also more powerful and far-reaching than the thinking of a solitary person. Even if a person does not literally do philosophy with friends, he takes part in a scholarly project that extends back through the centuries. (This was true even for Aristotle, who often begins his speculation with a review of the theories of his predecessors.) This scholarly tradition, which depends on our political nature, allows the philosopher to proceed more quickly to the contemplation of truths without having to do so much of the hard work of taking wrong turns in his speculation. It is in the interest of someone who loves knowing more than discovering, then, to join an intellectual community. For a human being, contemplation in this context will be more perfect than it would be by himself.

So Aristotle's philosopher ought to cherish a specifically political use of leisure. Thus there will be no contradiction in his choosing morally virtuous actions that are fine and choiceworthy for their own sakes precisely because they reveal the agent's commitment to such an end. But even if the philosopher has reason to live with other people, why should he want to treat them virtuously, particularly when the acquisition of moral virtue prevents him from acting viciously when that might be more conducive to contemplation?

As we have seen, although the philosopher longs to use his theoretical reason, it is not possible for him to ignore his practical life. As a human being, he just finds himself as a child, a citizen, a spouse, and a parent.

---

[50] Both these suggestions for how communal contemplation might be more continuous than solitary contemplation are special applications of more general points made by Cooper ([1977a] 1999, 345–351) concerning the importance to happiness of shared activities.

(Though in some sense, of course, we choose the latter two roles, Aristotle believes that they are entirely natural.) And this communal life brings with it, whether we like it or not, situations that must be confronted. Someone insults his family, and the philosopher will react; the Persians have swept through Thermopylae, and he will either defend his allies or not. Or, to bring things closer to the philosophical life as we know it, we find ourselves as members of university departments and must take a stand, if only a neutral one, on hiring decisions, the awarding of grades, and where to take visitors for dinner. Since these decisions cannot be avoided, the philosopher *must* decide how to make them. Indeed, it will be a consequence of his time spent in contemplation that he realizes this. The philosopher contemplates the order of the cosmos, but he cannot have succeeded in understanding this order if he does not understand his place in it as practical and political.[51] So the peculiarly human problem, for the philosopher as well as for everyone else, is to figure out how to gratify our divine nature in this embodied, communal human life. Aristotle tells us we should aim at happiness as a target in all that we do.

It is very hard for us to shake the intuition that within a eudaimonistic system of practical reasoning there is no reason *not* to maximize happiness. When Aristotle says that contemplation, as happiness, is the most final end, it is natural for us to think he is advising us to amass as many minutes of contemplation as possible. I hope to have shown by now that there are more ways to act for the sake of an independent end than purely instrumental ones. To make contemplation a most final end, then, does not automatically commit the philosopher to maximizing it, come what may. After all, when a carpenter makes a house his final end *qua* carpenter, he does not set about building as many houses as possible. Rather, he makes the completed house the target of his actions. Happiness, or the human good, as Aristotle conceives it in the *Nicomachean Ethics*, makes a life happy and worth choosing *by being its most final end*. In other words, it is because the happy person is successful in making his choices for the sake of *theôria* that he is happy. That is Aristotle's point in defining the human good as an end from the beginning of the *Nicomachean Ethics*. Thus a life is not made more valuable by containing more instances of the eudaimonic good. It might be preferable to choose two hours of contemplation over one hour. (This is, after all, one way to act for the sake of contemplation.) But the life as a whole will not be more valuable simply in virtue of its having an hour more contemplation than it might otherwise have had. Aristotelian happiness does not make a life good by being present in it in any old way. Happiness—contemplation—makes a life good by being present as a *skopos*, or target, of excellent practical reasoning. Thus, it absolutely does not follow from the claim that happiness is contemplation that a person would be better off by maximizing it.

---

[51] I thank John Cooper for this point.

Aristotle makes this point clear in his criticism of one of Eudoxus's arguments for hedonism (*NE* X.2). Eudoxus argues that pleasure is the good because, when added to other things, it makes them better (1172b23–25). But according to Aristotle, this argument shows only that pleasure is *one of* the good things, since any good whatsoever is made more choiceworthy by the addition of another good (1172b26–28).[52] So it is not a mark of *the* good that it can improve other good things; any good can do that. What is a mark of the good, Aristotle says, is that it cannot *be* improved. *The* good (as opposed to *a* good) cannot be made more choiceworthy by the addition of any other good thing (1172b32–34). This point is important for our interpretation of how, according to Aristotle, moral virtue figures in the happiest philosophical life. Since the human good cannot be improved, it is a mistake to think that, according to Aristotle, the philosopher will *necessarily* improve his condition (will move to a higher level of happiness) by adding more moments of contemplation to his life. That is not the sort of good happiness is. (See chapter 3, section 5, above.)

Now Aristotle's argument in *NE* X.2 is sometimes misunderstood in a way that seems to do damage to my approach to the *Nicomachean Ethics*. Readers of this passage often think that, since the good (*eudaimonia*) cannot be improved, an instance of the eudaimonic good, whatever it is, cannot be made more desirable by the addition of any other good thing. And this train of thought leads scholars to conclude that, according to Aristotle in this passage at least, *eudaimonia* must be an inclusive end.[53] For what good other than the set of all good things would not be improved by the addition of something desirable? This inference is unwarranted, however. Inclusivist interpreters see Aristotle's argument against Eudoxus as licensing the following *reductio*: If contemplation is the human good, then a single instance of contemplation could not be made more choiceworthy by anything else; thus, an instance of contemplation could not be improved by even another instance of contemplation; but two instances of contemplation *are* better than one; therefore, contemplation alone is not the human good. But Aristotle's remarks in *NE* X.2 do not commit him to this argument. In addition to being *the* good, contemplation is also *a* good thing. And, as Aristotle says, *everything* (*pan*) is more choiceworthy with the addition of another good thing (1172b27–28; cf. I.7 1097b18–20). So, just because contemplation is something desirable, an hour of it will improve any other good thing, including an earlier hour of contemplation. Indeed, as I argued in chapter 3, it is highly unlikely that Aristotle, as a reader of the *Philebus*, would think that

---

[52] The flaw in Eudoxus's argument is evident, Aristotle says, when we recall Plato's argument in the *Philebus* that pleasure itself is not the good since *it* can be improved by the addition of *noûs* (*Philebus* 21a ff.). The consideration Eudoxus tries to use in favor of hedonism can actually be turned against it (1172b28–31).

[53] Crisp 1994 is a good example of this approach.

instances of contemplation cannot be improved. For immediately after Socrates makes the argument about the improvability of pleasure that Aristotle cites against Eudoxus in NE X.2, Socrates argues that *noûs* cannot be the good for the same reason that pleasure cannot: Contemplative activity can be improved by the addition of another good, in this case pleasure (*Philebus* 21d ff.). The premise that contemplation plus pleasure or any other good is better than contemplation alone is so commonsensical that it is impossible to believe that Aristotle could read the *Philebus* and nevertheless believe that an instance of contemplation could not be made more choiceworthy by the addition of anything else. So what does Aristotle mean by saying, as does Plato, that *the* good cannot be improved by the addition of any other good thing if he also believes that the good is contemplation?

The first thing we should notice is that, although Aristotle agrees with Plato that *the* good cannot be improved, his reason for citing the *Philebus*'s argument against hedonism is *not* that he thinks it proves that pleasure is not the good. That is, the fact that moments of pleasure can be improved does not, according to Aristotle, show that hedonism is false, as Plato thought it did. (In fact, the overall tenor of NE X.2 is that no one before Aristotle himself has managed to explain why pleasure is not the good.) Rather, Aristotle's point in citing the *Philebus* is simply to show that the kind of argument Eudoxus makes in favor of hedonism can also be used against it. So the fact that Aristotle cites the *Philebus* does not show that he thinks *instances* of the eudaimonic good are unimprovable.

Aristotle's point in saying that the good cannot be improved must be that when we consider something as *the* good, it does not become better—more good in the way that the good itself is good—by adding other good things to it. Now, as I have argued in chapter 2, according to Aristotle in the *Nicomachean Ethics*, the good is good in the sense of being the most final end of action, that for the sake of which we do everything else. So when Aristotle says the good cannot be improved even though all particular good things can be made more choiceworthy, he means that the eudaimonic good plus anything else does not take on more of the character of the most final end than the eudaimonic good on its own possesses. Contemplation plus anything else is not more the most final end than contemplation itself is. That is because, since contemplation is that for the sake of which *everything* else is worth choosing, anything else we could add to contemplation would actually be choiceworthy for the sake of contemplation. Adding goods to contemplation, then, does not yield an end that is more final than contemplation—*eudaimonia*—on its own. And this remains true even when the good we are adding is more moments of contemplation.

Thus, to return to the problem of whether the happy person should maximize contemplation, once a person has experienced the contemplation of the universe and organizes his life for its sake, contemplation, as happiness, is a permanent part of his life. There is nothing he needs to do to improve his condition as happy. Ceteris paribus, having three more years of contemplation would be preferable to only one more year, of course. No doubt the philosopher would like to contemplate as much as he can. But this is *not* because that is just what it means for *theôria* to be the good and his most final end. To consider a good most final does not *mean* it is the good we try to maximize.[54] The philosopher wants to have as much contemplation as he can because contemplation is especially valuable among other good things from the point of view of valuing contemplation as a most final end. But the philosopher faces a practical problem when he decides between contemplating a while longer and doing something else. That practical problem of how best on this occasion to act for the sake of happiness is not *automatically* resolved in favor of the former simply because contemplation is his highest goal.

So, to return to our problem, why does Aristotle think that the happy philosopher will be morally virtuous? Perhaps we can find a clue—though admittedly an inconclusive one—in Aristotle's explanation for why the philosopher will most of all be loved by the gods:

> And the person who is active in accordance with *noûs* and takes care of this [part of his soul] seems to be in the best state and to be most loved by the gods. For if the gods have some care for human affairs, as it seems they do, it would be reasonable for them to take pleasure in the best thing and the one most akin to them (and this would be *noûs*) and to do well by those who love this most of all and honor it since they take care of things dear to them [i.e. the gods] and act correctly and finely [*orthôs te kai kalôs prattontas*]. (1179a22–29)[55]

The philosopher loves and honors *noûs*, and in this the gods take pleasure. But the gods also judge that the actions through which the philosopher shows his love of *noûs* are fine and correct. It is possible, perhaps, that the gods have different standards for beauty in action than human beings do. But a far more likely interpretation is that philosophers express their love of *noûs* through the fine actions of moral virtue. For as we have seen (chapter 6), morally virtuous actions are just those actions through which a person makes clear his love of the human good. This passage seems to say, then, that the gods love human beings who realize their divine nature *and* who act

---

[54] So *pace* Lawrence 1993, if Aristotle is saying in NE X.7–8 that contemplation is the highest good for the sake of which the happy person makes all his choices, he is not committed to the absurd thought that the happy person should value only contemplation and maximize it at all costs.

[55] Stewart (1892, not. ad 1179a22) doubts the authenticity of this passage. True, what Aristotle says here does not fit well with his description of the unmoved mover in *Meta.* Λ (though see Bodéüs [2000] for the argument that the unmoved mover is not a god). However, the idea that the gods care for human affairs fits perfectly well with what Aristotle has said about the gods in NE X.8. We cannot think of gods as acting virtuously, but that is no reason they cannot love and reward people.

in a way that honors this divine aspect of themselves. Morally virtuous actions are the actions that honor the divine in us.

Why would the gods care whether human beings honor *noûs*? Why wouldn't it be enough for the philosopher to secure their love by maximizing contemplation, perhaps at the expense of moral virtue? One plausible explanation might be this: Human beings are not gods, and so they cannot contemplate continuously, or even most of the time. It is important, then, from the point of view of currying divine favor, that human beings find a way, even when they are not doing philosophy, to show that contemplation—the divine activity—is what makes their lives worth living. For by showing their love of contemplation, they affirm their sense of identity with the divine part of their souls. It is understandable, then, why the gods love human beings who not only spend time exercising their theoretical reason but who also in their excellent practical reasoning reveal their understanding of the superior value of the contemplative life.[56]

So, to return to the point of view of the philosopher deciding whether or not to be morally virtuous: Since the philosopher thinks that contemplation is the supreme value and wants to be happy, Aristotle says he has reason to try to extend *theôria* and happiness as far as possible into his life. He wants to make his human life—both insofar as it is noetic and insofar as it is emotional and political—as much informed by the value of contemplation as possible. Given that the human contemplator cannot engage continuously in the activity he values above all others, he must find some other way to approximate it (so as to extend a kind of contemplation and godlikeness into his practical life) and a way to show in his practical life where his heart is. This he does by acting in accordance with the most perfect practical truthfulness of morally virtuous activity. The glorious thing about morally virtuous actions, in Aristotle's theory, is that they tend to maximize *eudaimonia*, or contemplation, while themselves both approximating it and celebrating it. Given that by far the majority of our lives is taken up with practical concerns, I suspect Aristotle would wonder what possible reason a human lover of contemplation could have to deny himself *this theôria tis*.

We may be disappointed that Aristotle does not give us an algorithm for determining when the happiness of our lives will be best promoted by choosing to contemplate and when it would be better to engage in particularly human affairs. But his silence should not come as a surprise. Aristotle offers only an outline of happiness. And though he ultimately tells us that contemplation is the ultimate goal upon which practical reason must keep its eye,

---

[56] Broadie (Broadie and Rowe 2002, not. ad 1179a22–32) suggests that in this passage Aristotle reinterprets the virtue of piety to refer to contemplative activity. His claim at *NE* I.6 1096a16–17 that piety requires us to prefer truth supports her interpretation. I would add that Aristotle intends *all* virtuous activity to be expressions of piety, for in all these ways human beings make themselves similar to and loved by the gods.

it is not clear what love of contemplation will tell us to do in conflicts between having time for contemplation and attending to the needs of others. On the one hand, love of contemplation leads us to want more moments of contemplation. On the other hand, love of contemplation leads us to cherish practical truthfulness as one of the most valuable of all human goods, and it is the truth of our practical situation that happiness is achieved only in lives that are distinctively animal and political. The person who singlemindedly acquires goods for himself at the expense of his family and fellow citizens fails to understand who he is. But how exactly to strike the balance requires an eye for the fine. Practical wisdom must work out the details in action. I suspect that Aristotle would think that individual decisions about when to pursue contemplation directly will be influenced by the person's particular social position.[57] If his community is at peace and there is no pressing need among his family and friends he can meet, then most likely it will be appropriate for him to theorize. If there is a major political decision that must be made, however, or if it is his turn to make provisions for the leisure of his fellow citizens, then moral virtue requires that he turn aside from his study and act.

But however the philosopher chooses to act, he will be guided by a practical virtue that is not radically different from the fine moral habits in which he was trained. In other words, choosing moral virtue for the sake of contemplation does not yield a systematic revision of moral requirements. For instance, if a philosopher is at a party, he will not leave early in a way that might offend his hosts and make him seem a spoilsport to the other guests. He cannot, in his practical life, approximate perfect theoretical truthfulness unless he recognizes the truth of himself as not only rational, but also political and animal. Though his love of contemplation will lead him to avoid making friends with people who disdain philosophy and try to keep him from it, his love of truth will also lead him to recognize that as a political animal it is good for him to have friends. Furthermore, he will understand that when he is at a party with friends, he is part of a community. Since every community is organized for the sake of a common good (*Pol.* I.1 1252a1–2; *NE* VIII.9), the philosopher will see that as a member of the community it is good for him to care for that common good, in this case the relaxation that comes with companionship and laughter. Thus, respect for practical truthfulness will cause the philosopher to attend to the needs of his community in a way that we ordinarily associate with moral virtue. But this is something the person who does everything for the sake of contemplation will want to do. The more he acts in accordance with moral virtue, the more deeply divine activity extends into his life and the more he becomes a mortal god, happy insofar as it is possible for a human being to be.

---

[57] See Lawrence (1993) for an interesting discussion.

We began by wondering how a life devoted entirely to the monistic good of contemplation could be recognizable as a happy life in Aristotle's sense, a life worth choosing and admiring, a fully flourishing life lacking nothing. What place would such a life have for proper moral concern? Aristotle's answer is this: When we protect those we love courageously, dine with them temperately, give to them generously, and accept their honors with greatness of soul, we grasp the practical truth—we are embodied, political animals who find our rational happiness only in common with others. Grasping this practical truth approximates contemplation and is worth choosing for its sake. So nothing prevents the philosopher from valuing morally virtuous action. Indeed, the way in which such activity is worth choosing for the sake of contemplation makes it worth choosing for its own sake. As an approximation of the highest good, it embodies the intrinsically valuable character of wise contemplation and can, in its own right, extend *theôria tis* into that practical part of our lives where theoretical contemplation cannot reach. Thus morally virtuous action finds a place in the happiest philosophical life because it is worth choosing for the sake of contemplation *and* because it is worth choosing for its own sake. This is how the lover of wisdom, like a skilled archer, keeps his target clearly in view.

APPENDIX

Acting for Love in the *Symposium*

1. Possessing the Object of Love

In chapter 4 I claim that to love the divine or anything else in a Platonic sense is to try to imitate its nature insofar as that is possible, and I argue that this is the sort of love Aristotle refers to when he says the Prime Mover moves as an object of love. However, there are questions that might arise for this story with respect to the interpretation, not so much of Aristotle as of Plato's *Symposium*. There is a sense in which this interpretation of the *Symposium* is obviously correct. At the very beginning of Socrates' encomium to love, Diotima argues that love is the desire for happiness, and that happiness—the possession of the good and beautiful forever—is the divine condition (*Symp.* 204d3–e7). Thus love is one form of the universal desire to be like a god. However, it might be thought that for Plato it is not the gods, but the beautiful that is the object of love. In the *Symposium*, assimilation to the divine is a welcome but unintended consequence of loving the beautiful— which activity is not an imitation of the beautiful. So treating something as an object of love in the Platonic sense is not a matter of approximating it. If this is correct, then my claim that the *Symposium* supports a traditional reading of *Metaphysics* Λ, according to which the first heaven expresses its love for the Prime Mover by approximating it, is false. Platonic love does not imitate its object. Thus, if Aristotle is referring to Platonic love in *Metaphysics* Λ.7, he is not referring to a relation of approximation (or so the objection would go).

Of course, Aristotle's Prime Mover is also divine. So we might reply to this objection by saying that, as a matter of fact, Diotima ultimately denies that *to kalon* is the object of love. At 206e2–3 she tells Socrates that "love is not of the beautiful, as you think." Instead, love is "of generation and giving birth in the beautiful." Since generation turns out to be the mortal approximation to immortality, why not conclude that the object of love is the divine insofar as it is immortal? In this account, the effect of love would be to imitate its object—in this case the immortal and divine.

The question at issue is what, according to Diotima, love wants. Does it want immortality and divinity, which it achieves by approximation? Or does it want something beautiful and ultimately the Beautiful itself? Despite Diotima's claim at 206e2–3, it is not at all clear that she ever truly abandons the idea that love is of the beautiful. For even after the discussion of reproduction and immortality, she describes the lover at different stages of the ascent as a lover of various beautiful things: Explicitly, he is said to be a lover of beautiful bodies (*Symp.* 210a7, 210b4–5), and if we follow the pattern established in these passages, he becomes a lover of beautiful souls, customs, knowledge, "a great sea of beauty," and finally of the Beautiful itself. Furthermore, Diotima says that seeing or knowing the Form of the Beautiful is the ultimate goal, or *telos*, of love (210e2–6, 211c1–2). Thus, the beautiful is always, in some sense, the object at which love aims.

Furthermore, when Diotima tells Socrates that love aims at giving birth in the beautiful, I do not think she can mean that beauty is only contingently related (as a necessary breeding ground) to the lover's ultimate object of giving birth. Beauty is the appropriate breeding ground for love because love's offspring is beautiful. For instance, the *logoi*, which the lover releases through his contact with the beautiful, are themselves described as beautiful (*Symp.* 210a8, 210d4–5). Of course, they are also described as virtuous, and at the apex of the ascent Diotima says that the lover stops producing images of virtue and gives birth to the true thing. This suggests that those *logoi* that the lover begat lower on the ladder of love and that Diotima described as beautiful are in some way or other images of virtue (or at least that some of them are). But this only supports my suggestion that giving birth *in* beauty is a matter of giving birth *to* beauty. Virtue, after all, in addition to being good, is also beautiful. What Diotima seems to want to forestall, then, when she says at 206e2–3 that "love is not of the beautiful *as you think*" (my emphasis) is a *simple-minded* equation of the lover's goal with beauty, such as Aristophanes and Agathon had made in their earlier speeches. Love is, of course, attracted to the beautiful person. But love is also, and more truly, of the beautiful words and deeds the lover produces under the influence of love, and through which he has a share of immortality. But in claiming that love aims in a direction other than we might have thought, Diotima is not denying that love's ultimate object is essentially beautiful.

The upshot, then, is that I cannot straightforwardly make the following argument about the *Symposium*: The object of love is immortality; lovers, with the aid of the beautiful, try to come as close to immortality as possible; therefore acting for the sake of the object of love, according to Diotima, is approximating that object as closely as possible. For, as I argued above, Platonic love is also of the beautiful and of the good. Indeed, it is hard to understand why anyone would desire immortality at all unless he was thinking of it as divine immortality, that is, immortal possession of the good and the beautiful. It is not immediately obvious, then, that the Platonic lover's relationship to his end is one of approximation.

So let us turn to the *Symposium* and Socrates' and Diotima's discussion of the nature of love. There are two things I hope to show. First, that even when Plato (via Aristophanes and Diotima) conceives of love as aiming at possession of the beautiful, he is conceiving of human beings as always achieving that end by approximating a more perfect possession: divine possession. To aim at the beautiful, in love, is to try to become like a god. Thus, love always acts for the sake of its end by imitating the divine. Second, I want to suggest that imitating the divine is, itself, a way of approximating the Forms of the Good and the Beautiful. Or, in other words, the gods possess these Forms by becoming like them. Thus, when we imitate the gods' possession of the Good and the Beautiful, we imitate their approximation to the Good and the Beautiful.

Two preliminary points that Socrates discusses with Agathon before his speech proper are worth our attention. First of all, Socrates argues, in opposition to the earlier encomiasts who described love as divine and beautiful, that love is a state of insufficiency. This conclusion is meant to follow from the claims that love takes an object—in Socrates' words, love is always *of* something—and that this object is an object of desire (*Symp.* 199e6–7). Since we do not desire what we already have, it must follow that we do not have in the appropriate way whatever it is that we love.[1] Either we do not have it at all, or we do have it but do not hold it as securely as we would like.[2]

Love, then, is a state of insufficiency. But from this we should not infer that it is a state of mere deprivation. Instead, love is somehow intermediate between privation and fulfillment. This is the point of Diotima's own myth about the origins of love (*Symp.* 203b2–e5). Love, she says, is the child of Poverty, scrounging around the gates of a party, and Resourcefulness, one of the guests, sated to drunkenness. Thus, it is the heritage of Love both to lack the beautiful and good and also to be endowed with the cunning necessary for attaining it. Diotima seems to want to make two points with this myth. First of all, she wants to say that although love is a condition of lacking the beautiful, it is a state of felt deprivation. It does not possess its good, but it is not ignorant of this fact either. Thus, it is an intermediate state. Second, and related, unlike a state of mere deprivation, love is a positive, hopeful orientation toward what will satisfy the lover's lack. In both these senses, love is analogous to right opinion: neither missing the truth entirely nor having an account of the truth that would render its grip on truth secure (*Symp.* 201e10–202b5).[3] (Another point of analogy: Just as true opinion can mistake itself

---

[1] If I am right that *Meta.* Λ.7 alludes to the *Symposium*, then this is another point of similarity between Platonic love and the relation between the heaven and the Prime Mover. So long as the heaven is a lover of the Prime Mover, it can approximate it, but it can never achieve its form fully.

[2] Socrates argues that when it looks as if someone desires something he already has, what's really happening is that he desires to *keep* what he already has (200d3–7). The connection between love and a desire for permanent possession of its object will become a centerpiece of Diotima's account of love.

[3] The analogy goes like this: Ignorance has no grasp of the truth (mortal condition without love has no grasp of happiness); knowledge holds it firmly (divine condition holds happiness firmly); and opinion has it, but only insecurely (the lover's condition is an approximation of divine happiness). Of course, in the *Republic* Plato says that knowledge and opinion, because they are separate powers, must have different objects. This might seem to cast doubt on my

for knowledge, so too a lover can mistake his condition for divine happiness.)[4] Thus, Diotima says that love stands between the divine and the merely mortal, between ignorance and wisdom. Love is not a god—he is not happy and in possession of the good and the beautiful—but his seeking is directed toward what will satisfy his insufficiency. Or, to put the personification in human terms, being in love is not itself the possession of happiness; it is the condition of pursuing what (one thinks) will fill the want and thereby bring happiness.[5]

The idea that love is a state of insufficiency aiming at fulfillment is one we have already encountered in the *Symposium* in Aristophanes' speech. According to Aristophanes, lovers long for their "other half" from whom divine justice has permanently separated them (*Symp.* 190b5–191a6; 193a1–3). Lovers cannot ever be reunited with their other halves in a completely satisfactory way—i.e., a way that would once again put them in a position to rival the happiness of the gods. (Preventing this was precisely the reason Zeus chopped them in half to begin with.) Nevertheless, Aristophanes says that in love (and in particular, sexual love) we can come as close to that perfect union as is possible for us (*Symp.* 191c8–d3, 192e5–193a1). So Aristophanes and Diotima agree that love is desire, and thus deprivation, seeking its natural object.

Aristophanes and Diotima disagree in one respect, however, relevant to our Aristotelian purposes. According to Aristophanes, the object of love is to approximate as closely as possible our antecloven state. Lovers want to approach as closely as they can the state of being one entity, physically and metaphysically (*Symp.* 192d3–e4). This desire is not an odd and brute desire, according to Aristophanes' story, since lovers' desire for reunion is a desire to return to a position that rivaled the gods. The rather pathetic couplings of the split lovers are attempts to achieve a semblance of that godlike happiness they used to have when they were whole.[6] Now, Diotima agrees that

---

claim that knowledge and opinion grasp truth to varying degrees. However, because the objects of truth and opinion are related (viz., the latter is a shadowy reflection of the former, just as the object of love is an image of the divine condition), opinion has an insecure grasp on the truth *in virtue of* having an image of truth as its object.

[4] Contra Price 1989, 20.

[5] Is Diotima's account mistaken here? She seems to be correct when she suggests that love opens the floodgates of desire for a condition in one's own life that no mortal object of love could ever realistically provide. Spending time with a person we love allows us to imagine how happiness might be possible, but it is not (at least not normally) the entire content of that happy vision. Think of a stereotypical lover's daydream: "And we can get married, and have a beautiful, old house that we'll fix up, and have a garden where we'll have parties for our interesting friends, and we'll take regular, adventurous vacations...." As this daydream suggests, however, Diotima does seem to go wrong—or at least not to do justice to our ordinary understanding of love and happiness—when she suggests that the ladder of love can be kicked away once happiness is achieved. Lovers want more than the beloved can provide, but the beloved's presence seems to be a necessary element in the lover's vision of happiness.

[6] My student, Steven Simon, has pointed out that the circular shape and movements of the antecloven lovers mirror the circular shape and movements of their heavenly parents (*Symp.* 190b).

ordinary love is an approximation to something else. Furthermore, she agrees that this other state is the condition of divine happiness (*Symp.* 202b10–d11). But in Diotima's account, Aristophanes has misidentified the nature of the divine happiness lovers approximate. For Aristophanes, the lover seeks a reunion with *this* beautiful person. Sex is an approximation of a union with *this* beloved. The implication is clearly that perfect union with a particular beautiful person is divine, or at least as divine as we aspire to. Diotima, on the other hand, suggests that the sense of insufficiency that drives a lover toward a particular beautiful thing cannot be completely satisfied by the possession of that beautiful thing. For the true object of love, in her account, transcends any particular person with whom we might happen to fall in love. Love is a desire for divine happiness, all right, but life spent with a single good or beautiful thing could not satisfy this desire. Instead, as Diotima says later, divine happiness comes through the possession of the Good and the Beautiful themselves; all other beloveds are merely approximations to these true objects of love (*Symp.* 211b2–3, 212a2–5).[7] Thus, contra Aristophanes, love is not, strictly speaking, a desire for the particular sensible beloved. Love of a particular beautiful thing can only be an inadequate approximation of the complete possession of the Beautiful or the Good itself, achieved most perfectly (for human beings, at least) by knowing the Form.

This is why, I believe, Diotima describes love as a desire for generation and immortality (*Symp.* 206e2–207a4). These desires are not separate from the desire for the good or beautiful. Rather, they are desires for possessing the good and beautiful in a particular, that is to say, permanent way (or something as close to that as possible for a mortal creature).[8] What the philo-

---

[7] I will leave to one side the question of how the Good and the Beautiful are related in the *Symposium*.

[8] Thus, lovers desire immortality not as a *precondition* for permanent possession of the good but as a *mode* of possessing the good. Or, to put it another way, lovers desire to have immortality "mixed in" with their possession of the good. (What Diotima literally says is that lovers "desire immortality with [the] good . . . if in fact love wants to possess the good always" [*Symp.* 207a1–3].)

In this reading, Diotima's argument is (contra Rowe 1998, 248–249) quite plausible and to the point. If what we want is literally to possess the good and the beautiful forever, and if this is impossible, it makes a certain sense to approximate immortal possession of the good by generation. Procreation, after all, is not just a second-best immortality; it is a second-best way to possess forever the good as those pregnant in body conceive it. (These are the ones who typically express love through sex, according to Diotima [*Symp* 208e1–5].) For surely those pregnant in body believe happiness to be a mode of sensible existence. Thus, in procreation they replicate themselves in the only form through which they think it is possible to possess the good. (Thus I disagree with Rowe [1998] that reproduction is evidence only of a desire to live forever; it expresses a desire to live with the good forever.) Notice how two other of Diotima's examples of reproduction replicate that aspect of a lover's self to which his conception of happiness attaches. Achilles is mentioned as one of those who produce glorious deeds under the influence of love (*Symp.* 208c1–e1); but Achilles and the other lovers of honor surely identify their selves with their reputations and happiness with good reputation. Thus fame for them is not just an imitation of immortality; it is an imitation of immortal happiness. Finally, the psy-

sophical (as opposed to the Aristophanic) lover learns at the end of his ascent is that the enduring, sufficient possession of the good and beautiful for which he longs can be achieved only by the godlike contemplation of the Form (*Symp.* 212a2–7). All those other beautiful things that are ordinarily taken to be the proper objects of love are, in fact, only images of the truly beautiful (*Symp.* 211b2–3, 212a4). It is impossible, therefore, for a lover's grasp of them to be anything more than an image of the true grasp he desires. Sex and conversations with the beloved aim at the birth of children and the production of *logoi* and noble deeds. But the significance of these productions can only be understood when we see them as imperfect attempts at a more perfect, eternal possession of the more perfectly good and beautiful.

I hope all this is enough to show that, according to the *Symposium*, the behavior ordinarily associated with love (and with all the lower rungs of the ladder of love) is in fact an approximation to possession of the more ultimate object of love understood as divine happiness. In other words, whenever someone falls in love, whether he realizes it or not, he creates, to the extent possible for him at that time, an approximation of the divine condition.[9]

The account of love Socrates develops in his second speech in the *Phaedrus* makes it clearer that love aims at imitating, insofar as possible, the divine condition.[10] According to Socrates' myth, all human souls have followed in the chorus of one of the Olympian gods (*Phaedrus* 248a1–4, 249e4–250a1). When they become embodied and fall in love, not only do they take their beloved to be an image of a god, the beloved actually is an image of the god that lover followed (*Phaedrus* 251a1–7, 252e1–2, 253b1–4).[11] Thus, unlike the particular lover in the *Symposium*, which is described only as beautiful, the beloved in the *Phaedrus* is not only beautiful but quasi-divine. The Phaedran lover expresses his love by trying to make himself like the god he sees reflected in his beloved. The lovers "are well equipped to track down their god's true nature with their own resources because of their driving need to gaze at the god [i.e., at the boy who is the image of the god],[12] and as

---

chic lovers who are initiates in the erotic mysteries are clearly philosophers (or at least they end up that way; *Symp.* 210d6) who identify their selves with their reason and assure its perpetual association with the philosophical good by producing good and beautiful *logoi*.

[9] It is interesting to notice that Aristophanes' lovers also need divine revelation to understand what their erotic desire is really for (*Symp.* 192d5).

[10] I do not mean to treat the accounts of love in the *Symposium* and *Phaedrus* as entirely continuous; there are differences as well. In particular, since the *Phaedrus* espouses a belief in the immortality of all souls, it is not immortality in particular that Phaedran lovers imitate. However, with respect to what I am taking to be the core of Platonic love—that the lover acts for the sake of his beloved by imitating it—I believe the *Phaedrus* and *Symposium* are in agreement.

[11] I agree with Ferrari (1987, 183) that the lover does not impose his vision of the god on the boy but develops the boy's latent godlikeness.

[12] Nehamas and Woodruff 1995, 42 n. 107. All translations of the *Phaedrus* are from Nehamas and Woodruff 1995.

they are in touch with the god by memory they are inspired by him and adopt his customs and practices, so far as a human being can share a god's life (*kath' hoson dunaton theou anthrôpôi metaschein*)" (*Phaedrus* 253a1–5; cf. *Phaedrus* 252c3–d: the lover imitates [*mimoumenos eis to dunaton*] the god he followed; and 248a: the soul, while in heaven, is said to "make itself most like" [*eikasmenê*] the god it follows). But at the same time that love is a desire for divinity, it is also a desire to "feast on" the Beautiful itself, for the shock of love is caused not so much by seeing the god in the beloved as by seeing the Beautiful in him (*Phaedrus* 215a3: the boy imitates [*memimêmenon*] beauty well). It is the sight of an image of the Beautiful that causes the lover's wings to sprout and thereby initiates the 3,000-year (if he's lucky) journey back to the Beautiful itself (*Phaedrus* 251c5–8). (In fact, the Beautiful is not the only Form the soul will see when it returns to the god's chorus, but notice that all the Forms mentioned are either the Beautiful or forms of virtues that are, presumably, beautiful themselves; *Phaedrus* 247d5–7, 254b5–6.) Thus, the *Phaedrus* agrees with the *Symposium* that love is a desire to possess the Good and the Beautiful by approximating divine happiness.

But how do the gods possess the Good and the Beautiful? This brings me to the second point concerning Platonic love that I want to discuss. In my interpretation of the *Metaphysics*, I appealed to the idea that Platonic love is an imitation of its *telos*. But as I have described the accounts in the *Symposium* and *Phaedrus* so far, it looks as if Platonic love as experienced in human life seeks, in an imperfect way, to possess one of its ends—the Beautiful—and, in so doing, imitates the other—the divine. In other words, it is not yet clear that love seeks to approximate its object.

Here again the *Phaedrus* can help us. It is true, in both the *Phaedrus* and *Symposium* that souls possess the Good and the Beautiful by contemplating the Forms. How this works is, I confess, obscure to me. But one thing is perfectly clear: The gods and all divine things are beautiful and good (*Phaedrus* 246d8–e1). (Recall that in the *Phaedrus* the human beloved reminds his lover of both his god and the Beautiful; surely one reason the beloved is an image of the god is that he is beautiful.) That is to say, the gods possess the Good and the Beautiful in the typical Platonic way: They participate in those Forms. Their possession is perfect precisely because they necessarily are beautiful and good (*Symp.* 202c). But since participation is approximation, that means that the divine condition is the most perfect approximation of the Forms of the Good and the Beautiful. Their condition is only an approximation, however. In whatever way it is that Plato imagines souls become good and beautiful by contemplating these realities, it is significant that the gods in the *Phaedrus* must make periodic *journeys* to the field of Forms (they do not live with the Forms continually) and that they must *feed* on the Forms (*Phaedrus* 247a8–c2, d1–5). The gods are not good and beautiful in the way that the Forms themselves are; rather, the gods participate in the perfect being of the Beautiful as parts of the world of becoming. Thus, in the *Phaedrus*, lovers become like the Good and the Beautiful by imitating the gods they follow. The same holds, I suggest, for the *Symposium*. Sensible beautiful things, divine happiness, reproduction in the beautiful, the Beautiful itself are not mutually exclusive answers to "What is the object of love?" All love objects are, or are approximations of, the Beautiful, and all lovers become like the thing they love as much as possible.

Why, then, does Plato need to conceive the lover's activity as an approximation of the divine at all? Why not just skip the divine altogether? Although I have argued that love is ultimately a desire to become like the Beautiful, we cannot avoid the fact that Plato is no less committed to thinking of love as an imitation of the divine. This is my suggestion. The problem with the Forms as objects of imitation for us is that we must imitate them in a life. How are we to imagine exemplifying the unchanging reality of the Forms? The natural way to do so is to imagine the life of a perfect living being, the life of a god.[13] (Notice how in the *Phaedrus* human souls do not journey to the Forms on their own but seem to be able to get there only by following in the chorus of one of the gods, each of whom has his own way of life.) The gods by definition are most perfect approximations of the Good and the Beautiful, though what that similarity amounts to is hard, if not impossible, to say. (For one thing, they are always the cause of good [*Rep*. 379c] and cannot appear ugly [*Rep*. 381c].) Thus, in Plato's account, our own loving approximation of beauty and goodness is best understood as an imitation of divinity. What is it to be like the unchanging Forms, perfectly in the realm of being and not of becoming? It is to be an immortal; and that is a condition we imitate by giving birth in beauty. But we should see that our imitation of the divine in this respect is itself a way of becoming as much like the Form as it is possible for us to be. Now from this point of view one might wonder, in Aristotelian fashion, what good the Forms of the Good and the Beautiful are doing in this story at all, since it is the gods who are the paradigms of living beauty. If I am correct that Aristotle invokes Platonic love in *Metaphysics* Λ.7, it is significant that the beautiful object of the first heaven's love is the divine itself. It reflects Aristotle's general conviction that the transcendent Forms are a useless level of explanation. However, I hope I have shown that despite that difference, Aristotle can and does appeal to the form of teleology described in the *Symposium*.

2. The Intrinsic Value of Intermediate Objects of Love

We saw in the section above that to love something, in the Platonic sense, is to join oneself to it by approximating it, insofar as that is possible. But reading the *Symposium* also reveals that this description of teleological approxi-

---

[13] As Sedley (1999, 312) notes, "the standard for justice is not the Form of justice. It is god."

mation is seriously incomplete. Perhaps the most memorable aspect of Diotima's account of love is that it is a story of the lover's ascent from a lower to a higher way of living (*Symp.* 210a1 ff.). True, erotic love of all different kinds of beautiful things is ultimately a desire for the Beautiful and Good. But more important, provided that the lover is the right sort of person and is led correctly and in order, love is a developmental process from images of the object of love to the genuine article (*Symp.* 210e2–5, 211b7–d1). Beginning with the love of beautiful bodies, the lover, in virtue of his experience, falls in love with a succession of more perfectly beautiful objects, from beautiful souls to beautiful customs and practices, to the sciences, then to a "vast sea of beauty," until at last he loves directly the Form of the Beautiful, which was what he truly desired all along.[14] It is evident, then, that in Diotima's account the lower experiences of love do not simply approximate the perfect experience. They provide an opening through which the lover may ultimately be led to feel the attractions of the Good his experiences approximate.[15] It is precisely because the lower rungs are similar to their *telos* that they are able to serve this educational purpose. Indeed, part of what is beautiful about the lower objects of love and the products to which the lover gives birth in their presence is not just their similarity to *to kalon* itself but their ability to direct the noble lover to the Good. Or, to switch dialogues to the *Phaedrus*, the experience of falling in love is not simply one of seeing the god reflected in the beloved but one of sprouting wings to return to his service.

The educational aspect of Plato's account of erotic love might raise doubts as to its suitability as a model for the way in which Aristotle's happy philosopher chooses morally virtuous actions for the sake of contemplation. My idea was that the Platonic model of love describes agents acting *noninstrumentally* in a broad sense for the sake of an ulterior end. Their pursuing an intermediate object of love is for the sake of possessing the ultimate object, not by producing it, but by approximating it. Since the intermediate object is an imitation of something intrinsically valuable, it too will be worth choosing for its own sake. Furthermore, the Platonic model was supposed to show how agents need not be aware that their intrinsically valuable action (the middle-level end) has an end beyond the immediate one. They can understand the subordinate end as a most final end, choiceworthy for its own sake alone. But if Plato's account of love in the *Symposium* is essentially an account of moral education, we may wonder whether his objects of love are not merely instrumentally valuable after all.

It is, in fact, a well-known criticism of Plato's *Symposium* that Diotima does not, in the end, leave room for the lover to recognize any intrinsic value

---

[14] I do not want to venture here an opinion about how this process works. I will say, though, that it seems likely to me that it is not just the lover's contemplation of the beautiful thing that leads him to the next level but also the experience of giving birth to *logoi* in its presence.

[15] I thank Jonathan Lear for bringing this to my attention.

in the particular boy he began by loving.[16] Instead, Diotima's lover steps on the intermediate objects of love and leaves them behind as he climbs ever closer to the Form of the Beautiful. Worse still, as the lover climbs from love of a particular body to love of bodies in general and then on to love of a particular soul and from there to love of souls in general, Diotima claims that the lover despises the love he has just left behind (*Symp.* 210b5–6, c5–6, c7–d3). This disparaging attitude toward the intermediate objects of love is thought to be an inevitable part of this theory precisely because Plato conceives of them as images of and stages toward the ultimate object of erotic concern. Socrates began his instruction with Diotima assuming that love was of particular beautiful things (*Symp.* 204d5–6), but Diotima soon corrects him. It is hard not to read the passage at 206e2–5, where Diotima says that love is "not of the beautiful as you think" but is "of reproduction and birth in beauty," as claiming that the lover does not really want the particular beloved but *instead* wants to be joined to the Beautiful itself through generation. The beloved himself is a mere necessary condition for the human ascent to the Forms.

Now although it is certainly true, in the *Symposium*, that the lover stops feeling erotic love for the initial beloved as he climbs the ladder, I believe it is a mistake to think that, when he does, the lover considers his former beloved as a mere instrument. True, there is a shift in attitude, but what changes is that the lover no longer sees the beloved as the ultimate object of his mad desire and longing—there are other things, arising from his reproduction with the beloved, that captivate him more. There is no reason to think, though, that the lover does not continue to see the beloved as beautiful and continue to want to spend time with him. This fact is clearer in the *Phaedrus*, where Socrates says that after philosophical lovers enslave their sexual appetites, they turn their attention jointly to the lifelong pursuit of understanding (256a7–c1). But although the *Symposium* focuses more on the individual ascent of the lover, there is reason to think that even there the lover continues to cherish his first beloved. Diotima says once the lover pregnant in soul gives birth in his beautiful beloved, he "in common with the beloved nurtures the newborn; such people, therefore, have much more to share [lit. have much more of a *koinônia*, a community or fellowship] than do the parents of human children, and have a firmer bond of friendship" (*Symp.* 209c4–6).[17] How are we to understand this friendship? Diotima explicitly invites us to compare the relationship between the philosophical lover and his beloved before and after the "birth" to the relationship between physical lovers. Let us see how Diotima describes that transition:

---

[16] Most famously Vlastos [1969] 1981, 10, 20 ff. See also Adams (1999, 152 ff.) for a more detailed discussion of a similar criticism.

[17] This and the next quotation from the *Symposium* are translated by Nehamas and Woodruff (1989).

Footed and winged animals alike, all are plagued by the disease of Love. First they are sick for intercourse with each other, then for nurturing their young—for their sake the weakest animals stand ready to do battle against the strongest and even to die for them . . . they would do anything for their sake. (*Symp.* 207a7–b6)

It is clear that the physical lover, after he has given birth, turns his erotic attentions to his offspring. But his love for his offspring is now something he shares with his mate. In fact, their mutual love for the beautiful or divine happiness embodied in their offspring is the basis of the parents' friendship. The same ought to be true of the lovers who give birth to *logoi*, then. The lover's love of this particular beautiful person causes him to give birth to *logoi*. Once he does, he and the beloved both turn their love toward the speeches and arguments the lover has produced. Erotic love gives way to philosophical friendship. What the lover comes to despise, then, is not the beloved but his belief that he could most of all approximate divine happiness through possessing this person. As he progresses through the erotic mysteries, the lover comes to believe that happiness lies in each new level of rational understanding. But presumably, precisely because the more perfect vision of happiness was first reflected in this particular beautiful person, the lover chooses to be with his erstwhile beloved for his own sake, but now as a friend. (We can imagine that members of Aristotle's audience experience a similar change in attitude toward their object of love. They begin by thinking that morally virtuous action is the key to a life worth living. But as the lectures progress, they come to see it as an approximation of contemplation. They continue to cherish morally virtuous action, not as the most important thing in life, but now as a reflection of their true love: theoretical wisdom.)

Thus I see no reason to read Diotima's account of love as advocating an exploitative attitude toward the intermediate objects of love.[18] Once the lover comes to see that his first love is a pale image of something better, he will, of course, no longer pursue him as the most ultimate object of his striving. But insofar as the first beloved continues to be an image of this ultimate object, he will continue to be as intrinsically valuable as anything in the natural world, in the Platonic account, can be.

---

[18] Nothing I have said is meant to defend Plato from the other, related charge that the Platonic lover does not care for the individuality and particularity of the beloved, and thus does not truly love him (Vlastos [1969] 1981). See Ferrari (1987, 182–184) for a persuasive response to an aspect of Vlastos's criticism. Still, his response leaves untouched the worries about particularity that Adams (1999, 156) raises. Love, he argues, ought to lead us to care about *this particular* person in a manner that's different from our concern for other instantiations of the lovable kind. I will not discuss this problem here, however. Outside the context of interpersonal relations, we do not make it a requirement of desiring X for its own sake that we have the sort of concern for X's particularity that Adams describes. This suggests that the problem of particularity is a problem for Plato's account of love but not for using that account as a model for understanding Aristotle's middle-level ends.

Works Cited

Ackrill, J. [1974] 1980. "Aristotle on *Eudaimonia*." In *Essays on Aristotle's Ethics*, ed. A. O. Rorty, 15–33. Berkeley: University of California Press. (Originally in *Proceedings of the British Academy* 60.)

Adams, R. 1993. "Truth and Subjectivity." In *Reasoned Faith: Essays in Philosophical Theology in Honor of Norman Kretzmann*, ed. E. Stump, 15–41. Ithaca, N.Y.: Cornell University Press.

———. 1999. *Finite and Infinite Goods: A Framework for Ethics*. New York: Oxford University Press.

Allan, D. J. 1936. *Aristotelis, De Caelo*. Oxford: Oxford University Press.

———. 1971. "The Fine and the Good in the *Eudemian Ethics*." In *Untersuchungen zur "Eudemischen Ethik,"* ed. P. Moraux and D. Harlfinger, 63–71. Berlin: De Gruyter.

Annas, J. 1981. *An Introduction to Plato's Republic*. Oxford: Clarendon Press.

Aquinas, T. Trans. C. I. Litzinger 1964. *Commentary on Aristotle's* Nicomachean Ethics. Notre Dame, Ind.: Dumb Ox Books.

Barnes, J., ed. 1984. *The Complete Works of Aristotle*. Princeton, N.J.: Princeton University Press.

———, trans. and comm. 1994. *Aristotle: Posterior Analytics*, 2nd ed. Oxford: Clarendon Press.

Barney, R. 1999. "Comments on Irwin, 'The Monism of Practical Reason.' " Unpublished manuscript.

Berti, E. 2000. "*Metaphysics* Λ. 6." In *Aristotle's* Metaphysics *Lambda*, ed. M. Frede and D. Charles, 181–206. Oxford: Oxford University Press.

Bodéüs, R. 1993. *The Political Dimensions of Aristotle's* Ethics, trans. J. Garrett. Albany: State University of New York Press.

———. 2000. *Aristotle and the Theology of the Living Immortals*, trans. J. Garrett. Albany: State University of New York Press.

Broadie, S. 1990. "Nature and Craft in Aristotelian Teleology." In *Biologie, Logique et Metaphysique chez Aristote*, ed. P. Pellegrin and D. Devereux, 389–403. Paris: Editions du Centre National de la Recherche.

———. 1991. *Ethics with Aristotle*. Oxford: Oxford University Press.

———. 1993. "Que fait le premier moteur d'Aristote? (Sur la théologie du livre Lambda de la *Metaphysique*)." *Revue philosophique de la France at de l'Étranger* 183: 375–411.

———. *See also* S. Waterlow.

Broadie, S., and C. Rowe, trans. and comm. 2002. *Aristotle: Nicomachean Ethics*. Oxford: Oxford University Press.

Brunschwig, J. 2000. "*Metaphysics* Λ.9: A Short-Lived Thought-Experiment?" In *Aristotle's* Metaphysics *Lambda*, ed. M. Frede and D. Charles, 275–306. Oxford: Oxford University Press.

Burnet, J. 1900. *The Ethics of Aristotle*. London: Methuen.

———. 1901. *Platonis Opera*, vol. 2. Oxford: Oxford University Press.

Burnet, J. 1902. *Platonis Opera*, vol. 4. Oxford: Oxford University Press.
Burnyeat, M. F. 1980. "Aristotle on Learning to Be Good." In *Essays on Aristotle's Ethics*, ed. A. O. Rorty, 69–92. Berkeley: University of California Press.
Bywater, I. [1894]; 1988. *Aristotelis: Ethica Nicomachea*, reprint. Oxford: Clarendon Press.
Caston, V. 1999. "Aristotle's Two Intellects: A Modest Proposal." *Phronesis* 44: 199–227.
Charles, D. 1986. "Aristotle: Ontology and Moral Reasoning." *Oxford Studies in Ancient Philosophy* 4: 119–144.
———. 1999. "Aristotle on Well-Being and Intellectual Contemplation." *Proceedings of the Aristotelian Society* vol. 73 supp: 205–223.
Charlton, W., trans. and comm. 1970. *Aristotle: Physics, Books I and II*, 2nd ed. Oxford: Clarendon Press.
Cooper, J. [1973] 1999. "The *Magna Moralia* and Aristotle's Moral Philosophy." In *Reason and Emotion*, 195–211. Princeton, N.J.: Princeton University Press. (Originally in *American Journal of Philology* 94.)
———. [1975] 1986. *Reason and Human Good in Aristotle*. Indianapolis: Hackett Publishing (Originally Harvard University Press.)
———. [1977a] 1999. "Friendship and the Good in Aristotle." In *Reason and Emotion*, 336–355. Princeton, N.J.: Princeton University Press. (Originally in *Philosophical Review* 86.)
———. [1977b] 1999. "Plato's Theory of Human Good in the *Philebus*." In *Reason and Emotion*, 150–164. Princeton, N.J.: Princeton University Press. (Originally in *Journal of Philosophy* 74.)
———. 1981. "Review of Anthony Kenny, *The Aristotelian Ethics*." *Nous* 15, 366–385.
———. 1982. "Aristotle on Natural Teleology." In *Language and Logos*, ed. M. Schofield and M. Nussbaum, 197–222. Cambridge: Cambridge University Press.
———. [1984] 1999. "Plato's Theory of Human Motivation." In *Reason and Emotion*, 118–137. Princeton, N.J.: Princeton University Press. (Originally in *History of Philosophy Quarterly* 1.)
———. [1987] 1999. "Contemplation and Happiness: A Reconsideration." In *Reason and Emotion*, 212–236. Princeton, N.J.: Princeton University Press. (Originally in *Synthese* 72.)
———. [1996] 1999. "Reason, Moral Virtue, and Moral Value." In *Reason and Emotion*, 253–280. Princeton, N.J.: Princeton University Press. (Originally in *Rationality in Greek Thought*, ed. M. Frede and G. Striker.)
Crisp, R. 1994. "Aristotle's Inclusivism." *Oxford Studies in Ancient Philosophy* 12: 111–136.
———, trans. 2000. *Aristotle: Nicomachean Ethics*. Cambridge: Cambridge University Press.
Curzer, H. 1991. "Aristotle's Much Maligned *Megalopsychos*." *Australasian Journal of Philosophy* 69: 131–151.
Dirlmeier, F, trans. and comm. 1964. *Aristoteles, Nikomachische Ethik*. Berlin: Akademie-Verlag.
Devereux, D. 1981. "Aristotle on the Essence of Happiness." In *Studies in Aristotle*, ed. D. O'Meara, 247–260. Washington D.C.: Catholic University of America Press.

Elders, L. 1972. *Aristotle's Theology: A Commentary on Book Λ of the Metaphysics*. Assen: Koninklikjke Van Gorcum.
Ferrari, G. 1987. *Listening to the Cicadas: A Study of Plato's* Phaedrus. Cambridge: Cambridge University Press.
Fortenbaugh, W. 1975. "Aristotle's Analysis of Friendship: Function and Analogy, Resemblance and Focal Meaning." *Phronesis* 20: 51–62.
Frankfurt, H. [1992] 1999. "The Usefulness of Final Ends." In *Necessity, Volition, and Love*, 82–94. New York: Cambridge University Press. Originally in *Iyyun* 41.)
Frede, D., trans. 1993. *Plato: Philebus*, Indianapolis: Hackett Publishing.
Frede, M. 1996. "Aristotle's Rationalism." In *Rationality in Greek Thought*, ed. M. Frede and G. Striker, 157–173. Oxford: Oxford University Press.
Furley, D. 1996. "What Kind of Cause Is Aristotle's Final Cause?" In *Rationality in Greek Thought*, ed. M. Frede and G. Striker, 59–79. Oxford: Oxford University Press.
Gauthier, R.-A. 1951. *Magnanimité: L'idéal de la grandeur dans la philosophie païnne et dans la théologie chrétienne*. Paris: Librairie Philosophique J. Vrin.
Gauthier, R.-A., and J. Y. Jolif, trans. and comm. 1970. *L'Éthique à Nicomaque*. Louvain: Publications Universitaires.
Gosling, J.C.B., trans. and comm. 1975. *Plato: Philebus*. Oxford: Oxford University Press.
Greenwood, L.H.G., comm. 1909. *Aristotle: Nicomachean Ethics Book Six*. Reprint, New York: Arno Press.
Grube, G.M.A., trans. 1992. *Plato: Republic*, rev. C.D.C. Reeve. Indianapolis: Hackett Publishing.
Hackforth, R. 1958. *Plato's Examination of Pleasure: A Translation of the Philebus with Introduction and Commentary*. Cambridge: Cambridge University Press.
Halliwell, S. 1986. *Aristotle's Poetics*. Chapel Hill: University of North Carolina Press.
Hanley, R. P. 2002. "Aristotle on the Greatness of Greatness of Soul." *History of Political Thought* 23: 1–20.
Hardie, W. [1965] 1967. "The Final Good in Aristotle's *Ethics*." In *Aristotle: A Collection of Critical Essays*, ed. J. Moravcsik, 297–322. Notre Dame, Ind.: University of Notre Dame Press. (Originally in *Philosophy* 40.)
———. 1978. " 'Magnanimity' in Aristotle's Ethics." *Phronesis* 28: 63–79.
Heinaman, R. 1988. "Eudaimonia and Self-Sufficiency in the *Nicomachean Ethics*." *Phronesis* 33: 31–53.
Hicks, R. D. 1907. *Aristotle, De Anima*. Cambridge: Cambridge University Press.
Hobbes, A. 2000. *Plato and the Hero: Courage, Manliness and the Impersonal Good*. Cambridge: Cambridge University Press.
Hobbes, T. [1628] 1989. *Thucydides: The Peloponnesian War*, intro. D. Grene. Chicago: University of Chicago Press. (N.p.)
Hornblower, S., and A. Spawforth. 1996. *The Oxford Classical Dictionary*. Oxford: Oxford University Press.
Hursthouse, R. [1980] 1999. "A False Doctrine of the Mean." In *Aristotle's* Ethics: *Critical Essays*, ed. N. Sherman, 105–119. New York: Rowman and Littlefield. Originally in *Proceedings of the Aristotelian Society*.)
Irwin, T. 1981. "Aristotle's Method of Ethics." In *Studies in Aristotle*, ed. D. O'Meara, 193–223. Washington, D.C.: Catholic University of America Press.

Irwin, T. 1985a. "Aristotle's Conception of Morality." *Proceedings of the Boston Area Colloquium in Ancient Philosophy* 1: 115–143.

———. 1985b. "Permanent Happiness: Aristotle and Solon." *Oxford Studies in Ancient Philosophy* 3: 89–124.

———. 1991. "The Structure of Aristotelian Happiness." *Ethics* 101: 382–391.

———. 1995. *Plato's Ethics*. Oxford: Oxford University Press.

———. 1999. "*Republic* 2: Questions about Justice." In *Plato 2: Ethics, Politics, Religion, and the Soul*, ed. G. Fine, 164–185. Oxford: Oxford University Press.

———, trans. 1985. *Aristotle: Nicomachean Ethics*. Indianapolis: Hackett Publishing.

Joachim, H., comm. 1951. *Aristotle: The Nicomachean Ethics*. Oxford: Clarendon Press.

Joly, R. 1956. "Le thème philosophique des genres de vie dans l'antiquité classique." *Mémoires d'Académie Royale de Belgique* 51, tome 29.

Judson, L. 1994. "Heavenly Motion and the Unmoved Mover." In *Self-Motion: From Aristotle to Newton*, ed. M. L. Gill and J. Lennox, 155–171. Princeton, N.J.: Princeton University Press.

Kant, I. [1785] 1997. *Groundwork of the Metaphysics of Morals*, trans. M. Gregor. Cambridge: Cambridge University Press. (N.p.)

Kennedy, G., trans. 1991. *Aristotle, On Rhetoric: A Theory of Civic Discourse*. Oxford: Oxford University Press.

Kenny, A. 1992. *Aristotle on the Perfect Life*. Oxford: Oxford University Press.

Keyt, D. 1983. "Intellectualism in Aristotle." In *Essays in Ancient Greek Philosophy*, vol. 2, ed. J. P. Anton and A. Preus, 364–387. Albany: State University of New York Press.

———. 1989. "The Meaning of ΒΙΟΣ in Aristotle's *Ethics* and *Politics*." *Ancient Philosophy* 9: 15–21.

Kirk, G., J. Raven and M. Schofield. 1983. *The Presocratic Philosophers*, 2nd ed. Cambridge: Cambridge University Press.

Korsgaard, C. 1996a. "Aristotle and Kant on the Source of Value." In *Creating the Kingdom of Ends*, 225–248. Cambridge: Cambridge University Press.

———. 1996b. "Two Distinctions in Goodness." In *Creating the Kingdom of Ends*, 249–274. Cambridge: Cambridge University Press.

Kosman, A. 1994. "Aristotle's Prime Mover." In *Self-Motion: From Aristotle to Newton*, ed. M. L. Gill and J. Lennox, 135–153. Princeton, N.J.: Princeton University Press.

———. 2000. "Metaphysics Λ 9: Divine Thought." In *Aristotle's* Metaphysics Lamda. ed. M. Frede and D. Charles, 307–326. Oxford: Oxford University Press.

Kraut, R. 1989. *Aristotle on the Human Good*. Princeton, N.J.: Princeton University Press.

———. 2002. *Aristotle: Political Philosophy*. Oxford: Oxford University Press.

———, trans. and comm. 1997. *Aristotle: Politics, Books VII and VIII*. Oxford: Clarendon Press.

Kullman, W. 1985. "Different Concepts of the Final Cause in Aristotle." In *Aristotle on Nature and Living Things: Philosophical and Historical Studies*, ed. A. Gotthelf, 169–175. Pittsburgh: Mathesis Publications.

———. 1991. "Man as a Political Animal in Aristotle." In *A Companion to Aristotle's Politics*, ed. Keyt and Millers, 94–117. Oxford: Blackwell Publishers.

Laks, A. 2000. "*Metaphysics* Λ.7." In *Aristotle's* Metaphysics *Lambda*, ed. M. Frede and D. Charles, 207–243. Oxford: Oxford University Press.
Lawrence, G. 1993. "Aristotle and the Ideal Life." *Philosophical Review* 102: 1–34.
———. 1997. "Nonaggregatability, Inclusiveness, and the Theory of Focal Value: *Nicomachean Ethics* I.7.1097b16–20." *Phronesis* 42, 32–76.
———. 2001. "The Function of the Function Argument." *Ancient Philosophy* 21, 445–475.
Liddell, H., R. Scott, and H. Jones (LSJ). 1968. *A Greek-English Lexicon*. Oxford: Clarendon Press.
Lucas, D. W., comm. 1968. *Aristotle: Poetics*. Oxford: Clarendon Press.
MacIntyre, A. [1966] 1998. *A Short History of Ethics: A History of Moral Philosophy from the Homeric Age to the Twentieth Century*, 2nd. ed. Notre Dame, Ind.: University of Notre Dame Press.
McDowell, J. 1998. "Some Issues in Aristotle's Moral Psychology." In *Mind, Value, and Reality*, 23–49. Cambridge: Harvard University Press.
Mele, A. [1985] 1999. "Aristotle on *Akrasia, Eudaimonia*, and the Psychology of Action." In *Aristotle's Ethics: Critical Essays*, ed. N. Sherman, 183–204. New York: Rowman and Littlefield. (Originally in *History of Philosophy Quarterly* 2.)
Menn, S. 1992. "Aristotle and Plato on God as Nous and as the Good." *Review of Metaphysics* 45: 543–573.
———. 2002. "Aristotle's Definition of Soul and the Programme of De Anima." *Oxford Studies in Ancient Philosophy*, 22: 83–139.
Nagel, T. [1974] 1979. "What Is It Like to Be a Bat?" In *Mortal Questions*. Cambridge: Cambridge University Press. (Originally in *Philosophical Review* 83.)
Nehamas, A., and P. Woodruff, trans. 1989. *Plato: Symposium*, Indianapolis: Hackett Publishing.
———. trans. 1995. *Plato: Phaedrus*. Indianapolis: Hackett Publishing.
New Yorker. 1999 & 2000. "Annals of History: American Soldiers Write Home." Dec. 27 & Jan. 3: 88–99.
Nussbaum, M., trans. and comm. 1978. *Aristotle's* De Motu Animalium. Princeton, N.J.: Princeton University Press.
———. 1986. *The Fragility of Goodness: Luck and Ethics in Greek Tragedy and Philosophy*. Cambridge: Cambridge University Press.
Otto, R. [1917] 1923. *The Idea of the Holy*, trans. J. W. Harvey. Oxford: Oxford University Press.
Owen, G. [1960] 1979. "Logic and Metaphysics in Some Earlier Works of Aristotle." In *Articles on Aristotle*. Vol. 3., *Metaphysics*, ed. J. Barnes, M. Schofield, and R. Sorabji, 13–32. London: Duckworth Publishing. (Originally in *Aristotle and Plato in the Mid-Fourth Century*, ed. I. Düring and G. Owen.)
Pangle, L. 2003. *Aristotle and the Philosophy of Friendship*. Cambridge: Cambridge University Press.
Pears, D. 1980. "Courage as a Mean." In *Essays on Aristotle's Ethics*, ed. A. O. Rorty, 171–187. Berkeley: University of California Press.
Pressfield, S. 1998. *Gates of Fire: An Epic Novel of the Battle of Thermopylae*. New York: Doubleday.
Price, A. 1989. *Love and Friendship in Plato and Aristotle*. Oxford: Oxford University Press.

Purinton, J. 1998. "Aristotle's Definition of Happiness (*NE* 1.7, 1098a16–18)." *Oxford Studies in Ancient Philosophy* 16, 259–297.
Rees, D. 1971. " 'Magnanimity' in the Eudemian and Nicomachean Ethics." In *Untersuchungen zur Eudemischen Ethik*, ed. P. Moraux and D. Harlfinger, 231–243. Berlin: De Gruyter.
Reeve, C.D.C. 1995. *Practices of Reason: Aristotle's* Nicomachean Ethics. Oxford: Clarendon Press.
Richardson, H. 1992. "Degrees of Finality and the Highest Good in Aristotle." *Journal of the History of Philosophy* 30: 327–351.
Roche, T. 1988a. "*Ergon* and *Eudaimonia* in *Nicomachean Ethics* I: Reconsidering the Intellectualist Interpretation." *Journal of the History of Philosophy* 26: 175–194.
———. 1988b. "The Perfect Happiness." *Southern Journal of Philosophy* 27 supp., *Aristotle's Ethics*, 103–125.
Rogers, K. [1993] 1999. "Aristotle's Conception of Το καλον" In *Aristotle: Critical Assessments*, ed. L. Gerson, 337–355. London: Routledge. (Originally in *Ancient Philosophy* 13.)
Rose, V. [1886] 1966. *Aristoteles Fragmenta*. Stuttgart: Teubner.
Ross, W. D., comm. 1924. *Aristotle, Metaphysics*. Oxford: Clarendon Press.
Ross, W. D. 1950. *Aristotelis, Physica*. Oxford: Oxford University Press.
———. 1957. *Aristotelis, Politica*. Oxford: Oxford University Press.
———. 1958. *Aristotelis, Topica et Sophistici Elenchi*. Oxford: Oxford University Press.
———. 1959. *Aristotelis, Ars Rhetorica*. Oxford: Oxford University Press.
Rowe, C. 1975. "A Reply to John Cooper on the *Magna Moralia*." *American Journal of Philology* 96: 160–172.
———. 1998. "Socrates and Diotima: Eros, Immortality, and Creativity." *Boston Area Colloquium in Ancient Philosophy* 13: 239–259.
Scott, D. 1999. "Primary and Secondary *Eudaimonia*." *Proceedings of the Aristotelian Society* 73 supp: 225–242.
Sedley, D. 1999. "The Ideal of Godlikeness." In *Plato 2: Ethics, Politics, Religion, and the Soul*, ed. G. Fine, 309–328. Oxford: Oxford University Press.
Stewart, J. A. 1892. *Notes on the Nicomachean Ethics*. Oxford: Clarendon Press.
Tuozzo, T. 1995. "Contemplation, the Noble, and the Mean: The Standard of Moral Virtue in Aristotle's *Ethics*." In *Aristotle, Virtue and the Mean*, ed. R. Bosley, R. Shiner, and J. Sisson, 129–154. Edmonton: Academic Printing and Publishing.
Vlastos, G. [1969] 1981. "The Individual as an Object of Love in Plato." In *Platonic Studies*, 3–42. Princeton, N.J.: Princeton University Press. (N.p.)
Waterfield, R., trans. 1998. *Herodotus: The Histories*. Oxford: Oxford University Press.
Waterlow, S. 1982. *Nature, Change, and Agency in Aristotle's* Physics. Oxford: Oxford University Press.
———. See also S. Broadie.
Weller, C. 2001. "Intrinsic Ends and Practical Reason." *Ancient Philosophy* 21: 87–112.
White, S. 1990. "Is Aristotelian Happiness a Good Life or the Best Life?" *Oxford Studies in Ancient Philosophy* 8: 103–143.

———. 1992. *Sovereign Virtue: Aristotle on the Relation between Happiness and Prosperity.* Stanford, Calif.: Stanford University Press.

Whiting, J. 1986. "Human Nature and Intellectualism in Aristotle." *Archiv für Geschichte der Philosophie* 68: 70–95.

———. 1996. "Self-Love and Authoritative Virtue: Prolegomenon to a Kantian Reading of *EE* viii.3." In *Aristotle, Kant, and the Stoics*, ed. S. Engstrom and J. Whiting, 162–199. New York: Cambridge University Press.

Wilkes, K. [1978] 1980. "The Good Man and the Good for Man in Aristotle's Ethics." In *Essays on Aristotle's Ethics*, ed. A. O. Rorty, 341–357. Berkeley: University of California Press. (Originally in *Mind* 87.)

Index Locorum

Aristotle
 Categories
  1a1–6, 89n.35
 De Caelo (DC)
  II.12
   292b3–10, 28n41; 292b15–25, 77–78
 De Anima (DA)
  II.2, 414a14–28, 86
  II.3, 414b30 ff., 192n.34
  II.4
   415a25-b7, 77, 81; 415a25–28, 86; 415b1–2, 86; 415b2–3, 75n.9; 415b5, 82; 415b9–17, 105; 415b20–21, 75n.9; 416b23–25, 192n.34
  III.10 433b13–16, 74n.7
 Eudemian Ethics (EE)
  I.2
   1214b10–11, 34; 1219a35–39, 42n.68
  II.1, 1220a3–4, 27n.39
  VIII.3
   1249b9–21, 191n.33; 1249b13–16, 76; 1249b15, 75n.9; 1249b16–19, 38n.62, 120n.60; 1249b17, 168n.45
 Generation and Corruption (GC)
  II.6, 333b12 ff., 78n.16
  II.10
   336b32–34, 82; 337a1–7, 80n.23, 82, 87
 Generation of Animals (GA)
  II.1
   731b22 ff., 77; 731b24–732a1, 80n.23
  III.2, 753a7–17, 114n.52
  IV.10, 778a4–9, 110
 History of Animals (HA)
  I.1
   488a7–9, 152; 488a9–10, 152n.13
  IX.5, 611a15–16, 114n.52
  IX.7, 612b18–31, 114n.52
  IX.39, 623a7–8, 114n.52
  IX.46, 630b18–21, 114n.52
 De Motu Animalium (MA)
  6, 700b28–29, 35
 Magna Moralia (MM)
  I.2, 1184a14–25, 66
 Metaphysics (Meta.)
  A.1
   980a22–24, 164; 980a27ff, 114; 980b21–24, 114n.52; 981b5–6, 110–111n.46; 981a22–25, 160; 981b27–29, 111; 981b27–982a1, 112
  A.2
   982a19–82b10, 105; 982b4–10, 112n.48
  A.9, 1074b23–34, 106n.35
  A.10, 1075a11 ff., 126
  α.2
   994b13–14, 19; 994b14–16, 19–20
  B.2, 996b12, 13
  Δ.16, 1021b23–25, 13
  E.1, 1025b18–24, 97n.11
  Θ.6, 1048b22–25, 12
  Θ.8, 1050b28–29, 80n.23, 82, 87
  K.1, 1059a35–38, 127
  Λ.1, 1069b1–2, 74
  Λ.4, 1070b34–35, 74
  Λ.6
   1071b5–11, 73; 1071b7, 73n.4; 1071b8–9, 73n.4; 1071b10, 73n.4; 1071b12–19, 75; 1071b20, 75; 1072a4–6, 78n.16
  Λ.7
   1072a24–26, 74; 1072a24–27, 74n.7; 1072a26–27, 74; 1072a26–29, 78; 1072a27–28, 74; 1072a28, 79; 1072a34, 79; 1072b1–2, 76; 1072b1–3, 76; 1072b2, 75n.9, 79n.20; 1072b3, 78; 1072b7–8, 76; 1072b9, 79n.21; 1072b11, 79; 1072b14–15, 91n.38; 1072b14–26, 91; 1072b15, 76; 1072b24–25, 193; 1073a3–5, 74, 78; 1073a5–11, 128

Metaphysics (Meta.) (cont.)
  Λ.8, 1074a38–1074b14, 74n.5
  Λ.9
    1074b23–34, 105–106n.35;
    1074b25–26, 128; 1074b28–33,
    128n.11; 1074b33–35, 128;
    1074b36–38, 128n.11; 1075a7–10,
    76
  Λ.10
    1075a11 ff., 126; 1075b24–28, 78
  M.3
    1078a21–8, 128; 1078a30-b6,
    105n.35; 1078a31, 127; 1078a33–
    35, 105n.3; 1078a35, 129n.13;
    1078a36–78b1, 126
Nicomachean Ethics (NE)
  I.1
    1094a1–3, 1, 15; 1094a2–3, 21;
    1094a4–6, 16; 1094a5–6, 39;
    1094a9, 26n.37; 1094a9–16, 17;
    1094a15–16, 36
  I.2
    1094a19, 20n.26; 1094a19–20, 19;
    1094a20–21, 19; 1094a22–24, 1, 8,
    121; 1094a24, 8n.2; 1094a26-b7,
    186; 1094a26–27, 191; 1094a27-
    b7, 186n.20; 1094a28-b2, 21;
    1094b2–3, 21; 1094b5–6, 21;
    1094b6, 21; 1094b6–7, 21;
    1094b7–10, 186; 1094b9–10,
    136n.26; 1094b10, 196n.44
  I.3
    1094b11–27, 110n.45; 1094b19–27,
    104; 1094b23–27, 98n.13; 1094b35–
    195a3, 17n.17; 1095a5–6, 100
  I.4
    1095a14–17, 28; 1095a14–22, 22,
    30n.44; 1095a16–17, 27; 1095a20–
    25, 34n.56; 1095a22–23, 25n.34;
    1095a23–25, 22, 178; 1095a30-b8,
    146; 1095b4–6, 146
  I.5
    1095b22–30, 62, 179; 1095b22–23,
    24, 186; 1095b26–28, 24;
    1095b28–29, 24n.32; 1095b29–30,
    24; 1095b30–1096a21, 180;
    1095b32, 24; 1096a4–5, 24, 178;
    1096a6–7, 24; 1096a7–9, 24
  I.6
    1096a16–17, 205n.56; 1096b31–
    35, 50; 1096b2–4, 3; 1096b16–19,
    52–53n.9; 1096b26–31, 104n.33;
    1096b27–28, 88; 1096b30–31, 88;
    1097a1, 27n.40; 1097a8–11, 59
  I.7
    1097a15–25, 26; 1097a20, 26n.37;
    1097a22–24, 26n.38, 27, 28;
    1097a25-b6, 42n.68; 1097a28–30,
    45; 1097a28–34, 1, 8; 1097a29–30,
    29n.42; 1097a30, 29; 1097a30–34,
    30, 44; 1097a33, 184; 1097a34-b5,
    8; 1097a34-b6, 30; 1097b2–3, 9–
    10; 1097b2–4, 3, 31; 1097b2–5, 25;
    1097b3–4, 9, 40n.65; 1097b6–16,
    48; 1097b7–8, 52; 1097b8–11, 62;
    1097b14–15, 51; 1097b14–16, 47;
    1097b15, 58n.18; 1097b16–20, 63,
    64; 1097b17–20, 67; 1097b18–20,
    202; 1097b20, 47, 63n.25;
    1097b20–21, 52; 1097b20–25, 182;
    1097b25, 22; 1097b25–27, 43;
    1097b30, 22; 1097b34–1098a5, 44;
    1098a8–15, 95; 1098a16–17, 44;
    1098a16–18, 1, 44, 123, 182;
    1098a17–18, 42n.68; 1098a18,
    30n.43, 61n.22
  I.8
    1098b12–16, 32n.50
    1098b20–22, 121; 1099a29–31, 45;
    1099a29–32, 65; 1099a29–33, 48;
    1099b2–3, 60; 1099b2–4, 49
  I.9
    1100a2–9, 61n.22; 1100a4 ff.,
    49n.4
  I.10
    1100b12–13, 49n.4; 1100b25–26,
    61; 1100b34–1101a3, 61n.22;
    1101a8–11, 49n.4
  I.11, 1101a22-b9, 49
  I.12
    1101b12–23, 138n.30; 1102a1–4,
    138n.30; 1102a2–3, 21; 1102a2–4,
    15n.15
  I.13, 1102a23–26, 104n.33
  II.1, 1103b23–25, 138n.32
  II.2
    1103b34–1104a10, 104; 1104a22–
    27, 131
  II.3
    1104b11–13, 138n.32; 1104b30–
    34, 138n.33
  II.4
    1105a26-b2, 100n.20; 1105a28,
    100n.20 ;1105a29, 100n.20;

Index Locorum • 231

1105a31–32, 43; 1105a32, 2, 123; 1105b2–3, 100n.20; 1105b5–9, 117
II.5, 1095b22–30, 62
II.6
  1106b8–14, 131; 1106b14, 104; 1106b21–22, 144; 1106b27–28, 123
II.9
  1109a26–29, 124; 1109a29–30, 131
III.1
  1110a3, 191n.32; 1110a6, 191n.32
III.2
  1111b5–6, 101n.20; 1111b8–9, 102n.23; 1112a15, 100n.20
III.3
  1112a28–31, 100; 1112b16–17, 101; 1113a2–5, 100n.20; 1113a9–12, 101n.20
III.5
  1114a3, 191n.32; 1114b32, 191n.32
III.6
  1115a9, 150n.10; 1115a10–23, 151; 1115a12–13, 151; 1115a17–22, 153; 1115a22–23, 151; 1115a26–27, 153; 1115a28–29, 150; 1115a29–35, 150; 1115a33, 150; 1115a35-b2, 151n.11; 1115a35-b6, 150
III.7
  1115b12, 148; 1115b20–24, 148; 1116a7–9, 150n.10; 1116a11, 148; 1116a12–14, 151; 1116a12–15, 154n.16; 1116a15, 148; 1116a15 ff., 154
III.8
  1116a27–28, 154n.18; 1116a27–29, 148; 1116a28–29, 154; 1116b2–3, 135n.25, 148; 1116b3, 148; 1116b9–12, 156; 1116b11–32, 156; 1116b15–19, 156; 1116b19–23, 156; 1116b22, 148; 1116b23–1117a9, 117; 1116b24–26, 155; 1116b25, 155; 1116b30–31, 155; 1116b30–35, 156; 1116b31, 148; 1116b31–32, 156; 1116b34–35, 161; 1116b34–1117a2, 156; 1116b35–1117a2, 156; 1117a, 148; 1117a4–5, 155; 1117a5–7, 155; 1117a7–8, 148; 1117a15-b2, 149; 1117a15–17, 148; 1117a17, 148

III.9
  1117b1–4, 149n.6; 1117b7–8, 150n.10; 1117b9, 148; 1117b9–13, 151, 154; 1117b14, 148; 1117b15–16, 149n.6
III.10
  1117b24, 162; 1117b28–29, 164n.37; 1117b28–1118a1, 163; 1118a1–3, 163; 1118a5–6, 165; 1118a10–11, 163; 1118a12–13, 166; 1118a18–20, 164; 1118a18–23, 164; 1118a20–22, 164; 1118a23–25, 163; 1118a24–27, 164; 1118a27–29, 167; 1118a29–32, 166; 1118a32–33, 166; 1118b1, 164; 1118b1–4, 166; 1118b2–3, 162; 1118b4–8, 165
III.11
  1118b16–17, 167; 1119a5–7, 166; 1119a9–10, 166; 1119a12, 166; 1119a16–18, 167; 1119a18, 163n.35, 167
III.12, 1119b15–16, 163n.35
IV.1
  1120a11–12, 134n.23; 1120a24–26, 136n.26; 1120b1, 135n.25; 1121a27–30, 136n.26; 1121b5–7, 136n.26
IV.3
  1122a34–35, 124; 1123b1–2, 169; 1123b6–7, 181; 1123b6–8, 168; 1123b7, 130; 1123b17–21, 181; 1123b26–27, 181; 1123b29, 169; 1123b29–32, 171n.56; 1123b30, 169; 1124a1–3, 169; 1124a3, 169; 1124a5–11, 172; 1124a6, 172; 1124a16–20, 172; 1124a19, 173; 1124b5–6, 169; 1124b6–8, 181; 1124b6–9, 154; 1124b9–15, 172; 1124b18–19, 172; 1124b19–22, 172; 1124b20, 172; 1124b23–24, 172; 1124b24, 170; 1124b24–26, 181; 1124b25–26, 170; 1124b26–28, 169; 1124b29–30, 169; 1124b30, 170; 1125a14–16, 170; 1125a19–22, 169; 1125a19–27, 145; 1125a27–28, 169; 1125a27–29, 145; 1125a32–33, 173
IV.5, 1126a6–8, 198
IV.7, 1127a24, 99n.16
IV.8, 1128b15–19, 138
V.1
  1129b1 ff., 148; 1129b16, 191n.32

Nicomachean Ethics (NE) (*cont'd*)
V.3, 1131a20–26, 148
V.4, 1132a1–2, 148
V.9, 1136b21 ff., 148
V.10, 1137b14–19, 113n.51
VI.1
  1138b22–25, 120; 1138b23–24, 131; 1138b23–25, 120n.59; 1138b25, 131; 1138b25–32, 120; 1138b32–34, 120; 1138b34, 120n.59, 131; 1139a3–5, 94; 1139a5–8, 95; 1139a6–8, 95, 195n.42; 1139a8–11, 95; 1139a15-b13, 100n.20; 1139a15–17, 95
VI.2
  1139a18, 191n.32; 1139a21–22, 107; 1139a22, 101n.20; 1139a22–24, 100n.20; 1139a23, 102; 1139a23–26, 102; 1139a25–26, 121; 1139a27–31, 99; 1139a29–31, 107n.38; 1139a35–36, 100n.19; 1139b1–4, 121; 1139b4–5, 101n.20, 102; 1139b12, 95; 1139b12–13, 99n.16, 104
VI.3
  1139b18, 191n.32; 1139b32–33, 99n.16
VI.4
  1140a1–5, 96; 1140a10–14, 195n.42
VI.5
  1140a25–28, 101n.20, 109; 1140a25–30, 105; 1140b4–6, 119, 105; 1140b6–7, 118; 1140b7, 121; 1140b21–25, 101n.20; 1140b24–30, 108; 1140b25–30, 95n.6
VI.7
  1141a9–10, 104, 109; 1141a9–11, 109; 1141a12–14, 109, 113; 1141a14-b8, 112; 1141a16, 104; 1141a16–17, 109; 1141a16–20, 112n.48; 1141a17–19, 111; 1141a18–20, 105, 109; 1141a20–22, 109; 1141a20–28, 112; 1141a21–22, 112; 1141a22–28, 112; 1141a25–26, 195n.42; 1141a25–28, 114, 115, 182; 1141a28–1141b8, 112; 1141a29–33, 112; 1141a33–1141b8, 112; 1141a34-b8, 112, 183; 1141b2–3, 105; 1141b8–14, 115; 1141b9–14, 27n.40; 1141b16–18, 115; 1141b18–21, 115; 1141b21, 115
VI.8
  1141b23–24, 96; 1142a9–10, 159n.27
VI.10, 1143a9–10, 102n.25
VI.12
  1143b18–20, 115; 1143b19–20, 183; 1143b20–33, 115; 1143b33–34, 93n.2, 108; 1143b33–35, 115; 1144a3, 116n.55; 1144a3–6, 116; 1144a13–20, 117; 1144a20–28, 117; 1144a23–29, 117
VI.13
  1144b1, 117; 1144b4, 191; 1144b4–9, 117; 1144b7–8, 118; 1144b13–14, 119; 1144b14–17, 119; 1144b17, 191; 1144b24–28, 119; 1144b26–27, 118; 1145a6–11, 93n.2, 108; 1145a8–9, 120
VII.3
  1146b31–1347a24, 99n.18; 1147a26, 191n.32; 1147b10, 191n.32
VII.4, 1147b24, 135n.25
VII.6, 1149b12–13, 104
VII.13, 1153b29–32, 92n.41
VIII.1, 1155a28–29, 135n.25
VIII.3
  1156b7–8, 72n.1; 1156b9–10, 90
VIII.12, 1162a16–29, 152n.14
IX.8
  1168b30, 191n.32; 1169a6–11, 159n.27
IX.9
  1170a4–11, 200; 1170a8–10, 125; 1170b6–7, 72n.1
IX.11, 1171a24–26, 135n.25
IX.12
  1172a1–6, 200; 1172a11–14, 72n.1
X.2
  1172b23, 68n.35; 1172b23–25, 202; 1172b23–34, 50n.6; 1172b24, 90n.36; 1172b26–27, 68n.35; 1172b26–28, 66, 202; 1172b27–28, 68n.35, 202; 1172b28–31, 202n.52; 1172b28–34, 68n.35; 1172b31–32, 68n.35; 1172b31–34, 68n.35; 1172b32–34, 68n.35, 202; 1172b34–35, 68n.35

X.6
1176b3, 135n.25; 1176b3–7, 175n.1; 1176b16–17, 185; 1176b27–1177a1, 184; 1176b30–1177a1, 162n.32; 1176b32–1177a1, 36; 1176b33–77a1, 57; 1177a8–9, 179

X.7
1177a12–13, 181; 1177a17, 46; 1177a17–18, 182; 1177a18–19, 182n.13; 1177a19–21, 182; 1177a27–b1, 49n.5, 176n.1; 1177a32–34, 168n.45, 196; 1177a34, 200; 1177b1–2, 175; 1177b1–4, 183; 1177b2–15, 175; 1177b4, 160, 185; 1177b4–6, 159; 1177b4–12, 151; 1177b4–25, 184, 191; 1177b6–7, 147; 1177b6–8, 185; 1177b8, 188n.25; 1177b9–10, 186; 1177b12, 179; 1177b13–15, 186; 1177b14, 186n.20; 1177b16–17, 181, 186; 1177b24, 46, 89n.33, 90n.36; 1177b24–25, 175; 1177b26–31, 176, 189; 1177b27–28, 189n.27, 192; 1177b28–29, 190; 1177b31–34, 189; 1177b31–1178a7, 176; 1177b33, 91, 92; 1177b33–34, 2, 21, 46, 191; 1177b34–1178a7, 190; 1178a2–7, 86; 1178a6–8, 74n.5, 175; 1178a6–9, 177; 1178a7, 90, 189

X.8
1178a9, 90n.36, 179; 1178a9–10, 176, 193; 1178a9–22, 2, 193; 1178a10–16, 194; 1178a16–20, 194; 1178a19–20, 192n.35; 1178a10–21, 189n.26; 1178a22, 192n.35; 1178a27, 179; 1178a33, 180; 1178a33–34, 180; 1178b1–3, 180; 1178b2–3, 181; 1178b3, 179; 1178b3–5, 176; 1178b4–5, 196; 1178b5–6, 2, 46, 91, 176, 177; 1178b5–7, 176, 199; 1178b8–22, 114, 193; 1178b10–18, 194; 1178b10–21, 195; 1178b13, 179; 1178b22–28, 192–193, 195; 1178b24, 92, 195; 1178b27, 92; 1178b28, 92, 195; 1178b28–30, 196; 1178b28–32, 91, 194; 1178b29–30, 196.45; 1178b32, 195; 1178b33–35, 193, 199; 1178b33–1179a9, 176; 1179a1–5, 180; 1179a22–29, 204; 1179a22–30, 91

X.9
1179a22–32, 205n.56; 1179a35–b2, 100; 1179b22–30, 91; 1180a4–5, 135n.25

Parts of Animals (PA)
I.1, 641b18–19, 129
I.5, 645a21–26, 127, 165n.40

Physics (Phys.)
II.1, 193b12–18, 14
II.2
194a12 ff., 97n.10; 194a27–b15, 14; 194a29–30, 11; 194a35–36, 75n.9; 194a36–94b7, 17; 194b5–7, 18
II.3
194b30–33, 12; 194b32–35, 12; 194b35–195a3, 16–17n.17; 195a23–25, 13
II.5
196b10–13, 96; 196b17–24, 129
II.6, 197b22–28, 12n.7
II.7
198a25 ff., 14; 198a25–26, 14; 198b1–4, 14, 74n.7, 77
II.8
199a20 ff., 33; 199a30–32, 14
II.9, 200a14–15, 14

Poetics
4
1448b10–19, 165; 1448b17–19, 165n.40
7
1450b34–36, 129–130; 1450b36, 129n.13; 1450b38–1451a3, 130; 1451a3–6, 130n.14; 1451a9–11, 130
8, 1451a10–11, 150, 181
9, 1451a36–b7, 165n.41

Politics (Pol.)
I.1, 1252a1–2, 206
I.2
1252a26–27, 195; 1252a34, 152n.14; 1252b15–30, 159; 1252b30–1253a1, 152n.14; 1253a7–9, 152n.13, 155n.20; 1253a15–18, 152n.14
I.3, 1253b4, 153n.15
I.7, 1255b37–39, 153n.15
I.8
1256b15–22, 38n.62; 1256b23–26, 153n.15

234 • Index Locorum

Politics (Pol.) (cont'd)
II.9, 1269b14–19, 152n.14
III.6, 1278b17–21, 152n.14
III.8, 1279b11–15, 104n.33
III.13
    1284b8–22, 128; 1284b13–15, 129
VII.2, 1324b41–1325a10, 188n.24
VII.4
    1326a5-b25, 129n.12; 1326a5 ff., 129; 1326a33, 127, 129n.13
VII.12, 1331a35, 171n.54
VII.13, 1332a7–15, 187n.23
VII.14
    1333a30-b3, 151; 1333a35–36, 159; 1333b5–26, 187n.21; 1334a2–6, 186; 1334a4–5, 159; 1333a41–1334a10, 159n.29; 1333b38–41, 151
VII.15
    1334a14, 187; 1334a14–16, 151, 159; 1334a22–25, 160; 1334a22–28, 147; 1334a23, 147n.2, 188n.24; 1334a24–34, 187; 1334a31–34, 160; 1334a32, 147n.2; 1334a36–40, 159–160
VII.16, 1334b40–43, 188n.24
VIII.4, 1338b9–36, 159n.29
VIII.5, 1340a14 ff., 138n.32
Posterior Analytics
I.27
    87a31–33, 111; 87a33–34, 110; 87a34–35, 109
II.13, 97b15–25, 171n.55
II.16, 98b5–6, 110n.46
Protrepticus
    B60–61, 190n.31
    B65–69, 191n.31
Rhetoric
I.5, 1361b7–14, 127n.6
I.7, 1363b18–21, 65
I.9
    1366a33–34, 133; 1367a27–33, 135; 1366b3–4, 134; 1366b34–1367a17, 134
II.1, 1378a19–22, 102
II.2, 1378a30–32, 155
II.16, 1391a5, 78n.16
Topics
I.5, 102a5–6, 144
III.2, 117a18–21, 67n.33
V.5
    135a13, 144; 135a13–14, 124

Plato
Apology 36b-e, 170
Cratylus 388a-390d, 17n.19
Euthyphro 13b-e, 75n.9, 76
Gorgias
    485a-e, 84; 492d5–494a5, 70n.37; 492e7–493d3, 32n.52
Laches 191c-e, 150n.8
Phaedo 79c-d, 110n.44
Phaedrus (Phaed.)
    215a3, 215; 246d8-c1, 215; 247a8-c2, 215; 247d1–5, 215; 247d5–7, 215; 248a, 215; 248a1–4, 214; 249e4–250a1, 214; 251a1–7, 214; 251c5–8, 215; 252c3-d, 215; 252e1–2, 214; 253a1–5, 215; 253a4–5, 91n.37; 253b1–4, 214; 254b5–6, 215; 256a7-c1, 218
Philebus (Phil.)
    10e6–7, 57; 11b4–5, 55n.15; 12a6-b4, 32n.52; 20b ff., 52; 20d1–10, 50n.6; 20d4, 59; 20e4–22a2, 54; 20e5–6, 50n.6; 21a ff., 202n.52; 21a11, 50n.6; 21a14-b1, 50n.6; 21b2, 54; 21b3–4, 54n.14; 21b3–9, 55; 21dff., 203; 21d4–5, 54; 21d9-e2, 56; 22a9-b2, 53–54n.11, 59; 22b3–6, 59; 22c5–6, 57; 22d1–2, 57; 26e6–9, 58n.18; 27b1, 58; 27c-31b, 58; 30d10-e1, 58; 30e6–7, 57; 33b2–11, 56; 35e2–5, 57; 54c6-d2, 32n.52; 60c11-d1, 54n.11; 63c5-e7, 59; 63d5, 58; 63e3–4, 58n.19
Republic (Rep.)
    347d4–6, 186n.20; 357b-c, 31–32; 358a, 32; 362b5, 141; 362e1–4, 141; 362e4–363a5, 141; 363c4-d2, 141; 363e5–364b2, 141; 376b, 140n.39; 377b11-c2, 141; 377e1–2, 141; 378b1-c1, 142; 378e2, 142; 379c, 216; 381c, 142n.42, 216; 390e-391e, 142n.42; 394d-398b, 138; 399c1–4, 142n.43; 399e8–400a7, 142n.43; 401e1–402a1, 140; 401d, 140n.39; 401d1–3, 140; 402a, 140n.39; 403c6–7, 140; 410d-411e, 140n.39; 475d, 166n.42; 477c ff., 95n.6; 502d ff., 198n.48; 514a-520a, 198n.48; 549c-550b, 142n.43; 583e9–10, 32n.52; 598b1–5, 87

Index Locorum • 235

Symposium (Symp.)
190b, 212n.6; 190b5–191a6, 212; 191c8-d3, 212; 192d3-e4, 212; 192d5, 214n.9; 192e5–193a1, 212; 193a1–3, 212; 199c6–7, 212; 200d3–7, 211n.2; 201e10–202b5, 212; 202b10-d11, 213; 202c, 81, 215; 203b2-e5, 212; 204d3-e7, 210; 204d5–6, 218; 204e-205a, 81; 205a1–3, 32n.49; 206e2–3, 210, 211; 206e2–5, 218; 206e2–207a4, 72, 213; 207a7-b6, 219; 207c9–208b6, 81; 207e1–3, 213n.8; 208c1-d2, 149n.7; 208c1-e1, 213n.8; 208e1–5, 213n.8; 209a1–8, 149n.7; 209c4–6, 218; 210a1 ff., 217; 210a7, 211; 210a8, 211; 210b4–5, 211; 210b5–6, 218; 210c2–6, 211; 210c5–6, 218; 210c7-d3, 218; 210d4–5, 211; 210d6, 214n.8; 210e2–5, 217; 211b2–3, 213, 214; 211b7-d1, 217; 211c1–2, 211; 212a, 149n.7; 212a1–7, 149n.7; 212a2–5, 213; 212a2–7, 149n.7, 214; 212a4, 214

Theaetetus
172c8–35, 187n.22; 175d7–176a1, 187n.22; 176b1, 91

Other Ancient Sources
Epictetus, *Encheiridion* 2, 70n.37
Epicurus, *Letter to Menoeceus* 130–131, 70n.37
Herodotus, *The Histories* VII.135, 158
Isocrates
  Antidosis 266–269, 112n.50
  Panegyricus 48, 112n.50
Thucydides, *History of the Peloponnesian War*
  II.41–42, 157n.23
  II.42, 156n.21

General Index

Ackrill, John, 16n.17, 40–43
activity versus process, 11–12, 183
activity versus result, 16
actualization versus disposition, 9–10
aggregation of goods, 63–69
akribeia (precision), 103–105, 109–115
altruism, 134–136, 158
animals, 33n.54, 102n.23, 114–115, 155–156, 163–164, 195
approximation, teleological, 60, 72–73, 78–92, 189–196
Aquinas, 22n.28, 136–137n.28, 154n.17

bios. See life, kinds of
Broadie, S., 60n.21, 74–75n.7, 100n.20, 176n.2, 179, 199n.49

Charles, D., 88n.32, 89n.33
choice, 100–103, 117–119
complete life, 61n.22
contemplation, 5–7, 91, 125, 168n45, 176–177, 181–193
Cooper, J., 20n.26, 99n.18, 138n.33, 139n.36, 177n.3, 179n.10
courage, 4, 125, 148–162
craft, 18n.21, 35–36, 100n.20, 104n.32, 109, 110–111

desire: and practical reason, 98–103, 106–107, 117–119; spirited (*thumos*), 137–146; and teleology, 13–14, 19–20, 33–37. *See also* love
disposition versus actualization, 10
divinity, 76–78, 108n.40, 112–113, 189–193, 204n.55; activity of, 91, 128, 195; as object of approximation, 80–85, 86, 91–92, 193–196, 204–205; as object of love, 77–78, 86, 210–216

education, moral, 138–145, 154n.18
end(s), 1, 8–23, 83–84, 216–219; and desire, 13–14, 19–20, 33–34, 34–37; and form, 14, 17, 22–23, 37–38, 77–78; versus result, 11, 17; ways of acting for the sake of, 17n.18, 59–60, 79–83. *See also* finality criterion

eudaimonia, 1–2, 8, 21–25, 69–71, 185; as determining the *kalon*, 136, 146; love as desire for, 210–216; misfortune, effect of, 49n.4, 61n.22; monistic versus inclusive good, 1–3, 25–26, 40–46, 48–51; morally virtuous activity and, 43–46, 193–196; unimprovability of, 201–204; versus happy life, 1, 51. *See also* good, the human
Eudemian Ethics, 5, 130n.17
external goods, need for, 180, 199

finality criterion, 25–31, 39–40, 181–188, 201
forms, 5, 14, 77–78, 83, 89, 213–216
Frede, M., 98n.15
freedom, 135–136, 145
function, 22–23, 95, 103
function argument, 43–45, 182–183

Gauthier, R.-A., 170–171
generosity, 135, 136n.36, 198
god. *See* divinity
good, the human: unimprovability of, 68n.35, 201–204; uniqueness of, 22, 29n.42; versus goods, 17–20, 65–69. *See also eudaimonia*
greatness of soul, 125, 144–145, 153–154, 168–174, 181

happiness. *See eudaimonia*
Hardie, W.R.F., 170
hedonism, 23–24, 54–59, 68n.35, 178, 184–185
hierarchies of ends, 15–19, 33, 45
honor, 1, 24, 30, 62, 154, 169, 171–173
human nature: as noetic, 90, 189, 191–193, 197, 206; as political, 62–63, 135–136, 152, 157n.22, 188, 197, 200, 206
Hursthouse, R., 166n.43

imitation. *See* approximation, teleological
immortality, 80–83, 84–85, 91–92, 212–214
inclusivist interpretations, 1–3, 25–28, 40–43, 47–51, 63–69, 202–203

238 • General Index

intermediate ends. *See* middle-level ends
Irwin, T., 42–43, 134–136

justice, 122, 148

Keyt, David, 178
Korsgaard, C., 41n.66
Kraut, R., 6–7, 16n.17, 17 nn. 18 and 20, 41n.67, 73n.3, 152n.14

Lawrence, G., 183n.15
leisure, 125, 159–162, 170–171, 174, 184–188, 199–200, 205–206
life, kinds of, 22, 23–25, 178–180
love, 72–73, 78–82, 209–219

Magna Moralia, 66n.32
megalopsychia. *See* greatness of soul
middle-level ends, 9–11, 25, 30–34, 37–43, 72–73, 85–88, 216–219
moral education, 138–145, 154n.18
moral virtue, as intermediate state, 123–125, 166n.43

Pears, D., 151n.12
phronêsis, 99–102, 105, 108–120, 195
Plato, 5, 50–51, 53, 87, 91–92, 138 nn. 32 and 33, 139n.36, 149n.7
pleasure 23–24, 54–59, 92n.41, 133–134, 137, 163–167
political craft, 8n.2, 21, 180–181, 186n.20

precision (*akribeia*), 103–105, 109–115
Prime Mover, 73–80, 85, 111, 128, 204n.55, 210, 211n.1
process versus activity, 11–12, 183
pros hen predication, 89n.34–35

Richardson, H., 15n.14
Rowe, C., 213n8

Saint Thomas Aquinas. *See* Aquinas
Scott, Dominic, 90
self-sufficiency of happiness, 47–63, 69–71, 175–176n.1
slavery, 135n.25, 152n.14, 153n.15
Socrates, 170–171, 174
sophia. *See* wisdom
Spartans, 157–158, 159n.29, 187

telos. *See* end(s)
temperance, 125, 162–168, 180
"that for the sake of which," 11n.4, 75–76. *See also* end(s)
Thermopylae, battle of, 157–158, 201
thumos, 137–146, 155–156, 160–161, 162
truth, 4, 95, 99–103, 106–107, 118–121, 132
Tuozzo, T., 124–125n.3, 166–167n.43

Weller, C., 40n.63
wisdom, 108–114, 119

GPSR Authorized Representative: Easy Access System Europe - Mustamäe tee
50, 10621 Tallinn, Estonia, gpsr.requests@easproject.com